WITHDRAWN

WITHDRAWN

KLINCK MEMORIAL LIBRARY
Concordia College
River Forest, IL 60305

Macroeconomics

KLINCK MEMORIAL LIBRARY
Concordia College
River Forest, IL 60305

KLINCK MEMORIAL LIBRARY
Concordia College
River Forest, IL 60305

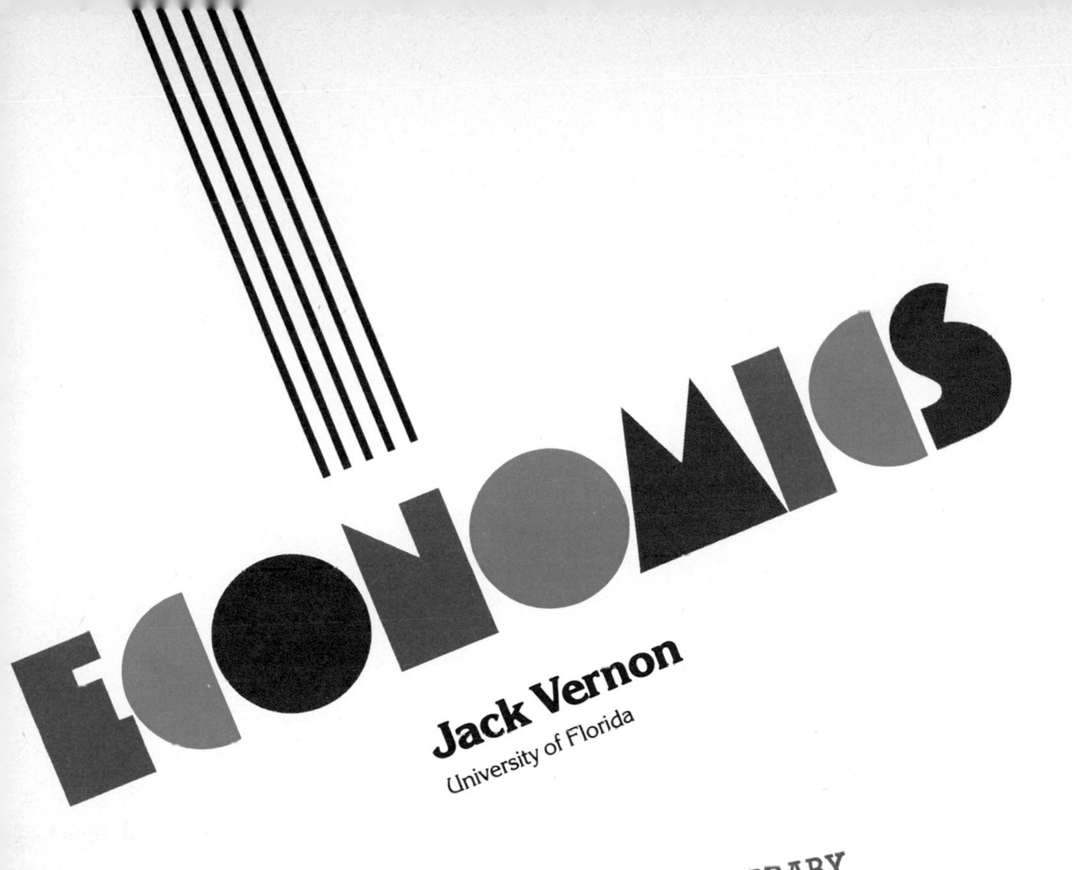

Jack Vernon
University of Florida

KLINCK MEMORIAL LIBRARY
Concordia College
River Forest, IL 60305

The Dryden Press
Hinsdale, Illinois

Copyright © 1980 by The Dryden Press
A division of Holt, Rinehart and Winston, Publishers
All rights reserved
Library of Congress Catalog Card Number: 79-51105
ISBN: 0-03-042336-8
Printed in the United States of America
0 987654321

Text and cover design by Harry Voigt
Copy edited by Beverly Peavler
Indexing by Ann Congdon

134617
G

To Margaret, Scott, and John

Preface

This book is intended as a textbook for intermediate level courses in macroeconomics. The emphasis is on problems of unemployment and inflation and the government's role as problem solver, but all of the topics ordinarily treated in macroeconomics courses are covered. My intention has been to set the coverage so that the book will be helpful and interesting both to economics majors and to students who are majoring in one of the business administration specialties or in other areas.

The book is organized in the manner which has become traditional for macroeconomics courses. Following an introductory section of three chapters, very simple macroeconomic models are presented. These models illustrate important concepts but neglect money market effects. The book then adds a money market and elaborates on the supply sector. Later chapters explore specialized topics such as monetarist and neo-Keynesian differences, classical economics, and economic growth. Chapter 19 adds a foreign sector. Chapter 20, the final chapter, summarizes and extends the discussion of macroeconomic policy which threads its way through the book.

Despite the traditional organization, the book possesses several distinctive features. One such feature is that Chapters 1 and 2, while introductory, are an integral part of the book. Chapter 1, in a section entitled "causes and cures," presents a verbal overview of the explanation macroeconomics offers for unemployment and inflation problems and the debate which exists concerning stabilization policy. Chapter 2 introduces the natural rate of unemployment concept, providing an early distinction between natural unemployment and unemployment which results from a shortfall of aggregate demand.

A second feature of the book is that it treats unemployment and inflation concurrently throughout. Inflation is examined even in the initial highly simplified models. This is important for maintaining student interest. Inflation is much in the news and much in the minds of students as a macroeconomic problem.

A third feature of the book is that it introduces both consumption and investment expenditures as sensitive to the interest rate in the initial IS-LM model presentation. Treating consumption expenditures as sensitive to the interest rate in the analytical chapters is important because the modern theoretical and empirical view is that such a relationship exists.

Is the book neo-Keynesian or monetarist in orientation? My hope is that it is neither—that it is, rather, modern. Nevertheless, neo-Keynesian and monetarist differences are fully treated, and both, as modern macroeconomics, are contrasted to the early Keynesian position. These matters are treated verbally in Chapter 1, extensively in Chapter 14 ("Keynesians, Neo-Keynesians, and the Monetarist Propositions"), and again in Chapter 20, the concluding chapter. Chapter 15 explores the origins of monetarism in classical economics.

As a pedagogical feature, there are a number of aids to the student: a chapter summary, key concepts for identification (tied to the glossary at the end of the book), questions and problems for review, and a list of references for further study.

I am indebted to Burton Abrams, Michael Connolly, John J. Klein, Michael Salemi, and several anonymous readers for their careful examination of the manuscript at various stages and their helpful comments. The book has benefited greatly from their suggestions. Also, I would like to thank my colleague, Norman Keig, for his advice and assistance regarding certain portions of the manuscript, particularly Chapter 2. And lastly I would like to thank Beverly Peavler, who has done a fine job in copy editing my manuscript, as well as Glenn Turner, Alan Wendt, Bernice Gordon, and Nedah Abbott at Dryden Press, who have given me much valuable assistance. Needless to say, the responsibility for the final product is my own.

Jack Vernon
University of Florida
November 1, 1979

Contents

Part 1 Introduction

Part 2 The Money Market Ignored

Part 3 Adding the Money Market

Part 4 Unemployment, Inflation, and Stabilization Policy

Part 6 Extensions and a Policy Summary

Part 1

Introduction

1

Macroeconomics: An Overview

The study of economics has two main branches, **microeconomics** *and* **macroeconomics**. *This book deals with macroeconomics, which is primarily concerned with the economy as a whole rather than with its individual units. U.S. economic history from 1929 to 1979 reveals that unemployment and inflation have been recurrent macroeconomic problems during recent decades.*

Macroeconomics is the branch of economics which deals with the performance of the economy as a whole. Its province is divided roughly into three parts.

First, it seeks to explain how the major economic aggregates which describe the economy's overall performance are determined. These include aggregate output, real income, and employment; the general levels of prices, wages, and interest rates; and the rates of unemployment, inflation, and per capita output growth. The division of aggregate output between consumption and investment goods and services and the level and balance of the government budget also are of interest.

Second, macroeconomics seeks to explain why problems relating to the economy's overall performance occur. Unemployment and inflation receive the most attention, but problems relating to economic growth and the balance of international payments are important.

Third, macroeconomics explores the government's role as problem solver. Monetary and fiscal policies are government's most important problem-solving instruments. General monetary policies are operations on aggregate supplies of bank reserves, bank credit, and money. (*Money,* in this book, is defined as cash, commercial bank checking and savings deposits, and checking deposits in other financial institutions.) General fiscal policies involve adjustments in government expenditures and tax programs. Price and wage controls, specific fiscal policies such as tax incentives to investment, and specific monetary policies such as consumer credit controls are other macroeconomic policy instruments.

Macroeconomics and Microeconomics

Macroeconomics is distinguished from microeconomics, the other main branch of economics, by its focus on aggregative performance. Microeconomics concentrates on the behavior of individual economic units. It inquires into the behavior of the individual household in allocating income and wealth among various consumption possibilities and assets for storing wealth. It also examines the process by which individual firms decide upon output levels and the resource combinations to produce them.

Obviously, macroeconomics also deals with the behavior of individual economic units in the sense that aggregate performance is the summation of individual performances. But macroeconomics focuses on the aggregate behavior. What determines output for an economy as a whole? What determines aggregate employment and unemployment? Why do prices rise rapidly during some years but rise only slightly or even decline during other years? Why has the proportion of the labor force unemployed exceeded 20 percent on occasion in the United States but fallen below 2 percent on other occasions? How should the government respond to problems of unemployment, inflation, inadequate per capita output growth over time, and balance of payment difficulties? These are the questions macroeconomics explores.

The Record

Before proceeding to the answers macroeconomics offers for these questions, it is useful to review briefly the record of performance of the U.S. economy relating to unemployment and inflation. These are the most important macroeconomic problems and the ones here considered first and at greatest length. Figure 1–1 presents the percent of the labor force unemployed and the percent change in consumer prices for the U.S. economy for the period 1929 through 1978. The most striking features of the period are the Great Depression of the 1930s and the rapid economic expansion and severe inflation associated with World War II and its aftermath. Even though 1929 is now a half century past, it presents a meaningful beginning point. Current attitudes toward macroeconomic problems and policies and the present legal and institutional framework in which macroeconomic behavior occurs bear important imprints from the severe economic disruptions of the 1930s.

The extremes for percent unemployment and percent change in prices occurred during the Great Depression and the disruptions associated with World War II. The depression yielded the highest unemployment rate (24.9 percent for 1933) and the greatest deflation rate (10.5 percent for 1932). Indeed, the unemployment rate remained above 20 percent for the four consecutive years 1932 through 1935 and above 14 percent for the ten consecutive years 1931 through 1940. It is no wonder that in 1946 the U.S. Congress passed an act charging the federal government with responsibility for maintaining maximum employment levels. It is important to recall that the U.S. economy has demonstrated itself to be capable of an unemployment rate of 24.9 percent.

World War II and its aftermath yielded the lowest unemployment rate and the highest inflation rate. The lowest unemployment rate is the 1.2 percent of 1944; the highest inflation rate is the 14.5 percent of 1947. The unemployment rate remained below 2 percent for the three consecutive years 1943 through 1945 in the wartime economy. Consumer prices rose by 71.6 percent from 1940 through 1948.

The most severe unemployment and inflation problems since the Great Depression and the aftermath of World War II have occurred relatively recently. The highest unemployment rate of the recent period, the 8.5 percent for 1975, does not approach the levels experienced during the early 1930s, but it is above the level most U.S. residents regard as acceptable. The highest inflation rate, the 11 percent for 1974, does approach the 14.5 percent for 1947, and the three-year consumer price increase of 28.7 percent from 1972 through 1975 is not far below the 33.7 percent increase recorded for 1945 through 1948.

An important feature of the 1970s differentiating them from the earlier experience is that unemployment and inflation have been problems at the same time, by the criteria of earlier years. During eight of the nine years 1970 through 1978, both the unemployment rate and the inflation rate

Figure 1–1 **U.S. Unemployment and Inflation Rates, 1929–1978**

The highest unemployment rates for the period 1929–1978 were recorded during the 1930s, the lowest during World War II. The highest inflation rate is the 14.5 percent of 1947, in the aftermath of World War II. The experience of the 1970s departs from the earlier experience in that unemployment and inflation have been problems at the same time, judged by earlier standards.

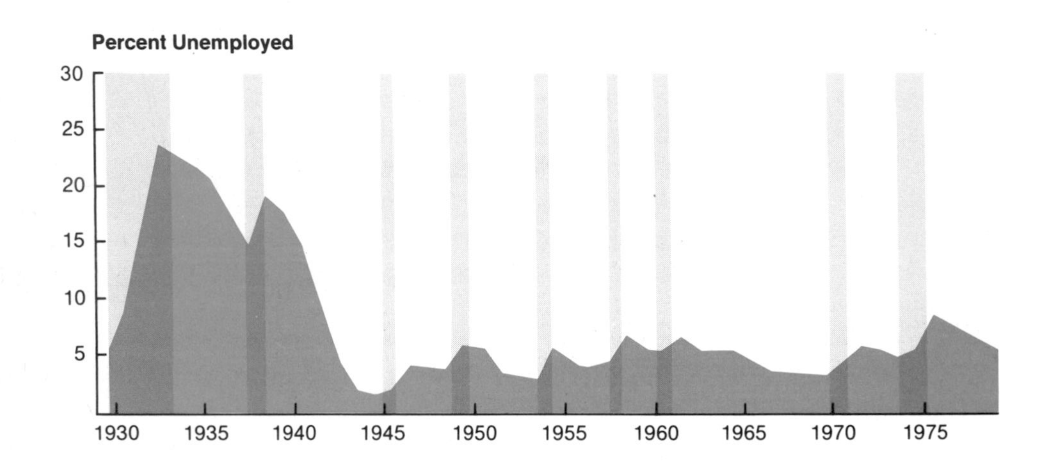

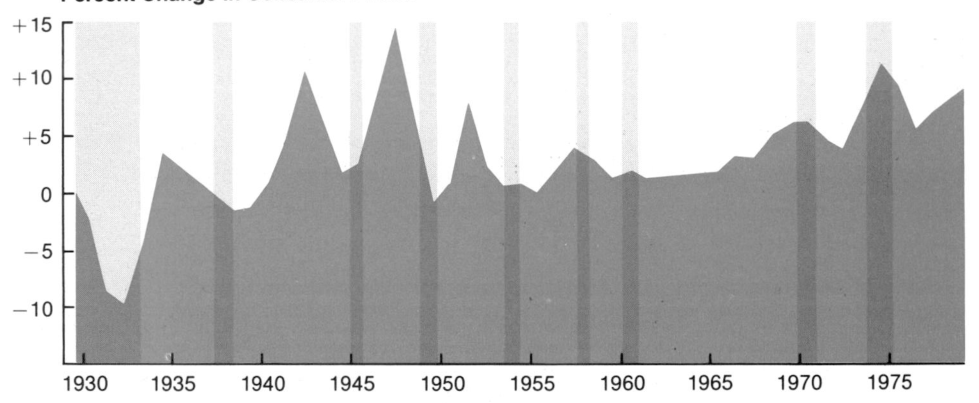

Shaded areas represent business recessions, covering peak to trough, using National Bureau of Economic Research reference dates.

Sources: President's Council of Economic Advisers, *Economic Report of the President* (Washington, D.C.: Government Printing Office, 1958), pp. 134, 160; *Economic Report of the President* (1979), pp. 214, 239; U.S. Department of Commerce, Bureau of Economic Analysis, *Business Conditions Digest,* January 1979, p. 10.

have exceeded 4 percent. The single exception is 1972, a year of mandatory price and wage controls, when the inflation rate was 3.3 percent. The greater than 4 percent unemployment and greater than 4 percent inflation combination does not appear in any of the earlier post–World War II years. It appears in only two years after 1929. The years are 1941 and 1942, and the relatively high unemployment rates of these years have been regarded as successes rather than problems, since they followed ten straight years of unemployment rates exceeding 14 percent.

The cyclical nature of movements in unemployment rates and percent changes in prices is apparent in Figure 1–1. National Bureau of Economic Research reference dates for general business peaks and troughs mark the business cycle in the figure. As a general rule, the percent increase in prices rises and the unemployment rate falls following general business cycle troughs. Following business peaks, the percent increase in prices diminishes, even becoming negative on occasion, while the unemployment rate rises. Exceptions include 1945 and 1974, when the percent increase in prices rose beyond the business peak. Both of these years followed the removal of price and wage controls.

Causes and Cures

What explanation does macroeconomics offer for unemployment and inflation? The first systematic explanation for both problems appeared in 1936, in John Maynard Keynes's pathbreaking book, *The General Theory of Employment, Interest, and Money.*[1] Writing in the midst of the Great Depression, Keynes was concerned chiefly with the unemployment problem, but the framework he provided is capable of handling full employment and inflation situations as well.

Keynes's View

To Keynes, the key factor was the strength of aggregate demand for output. If aggregate demand was insufficient to purchase the output of a fully employed economy, output would adjust to a lower level and involuntary unemployment would prevail. On the other hand, if excess demand was present, inflation would occur. The extra demand would bid prices upward.

[1] John Maynard Keynes, *The General Theory of Employment, Interest, and Money* (New York: Harcourt, Brace, 1936).

This Keynesian explanation seems simple enough in retrospect. Too little demand meant unemployment. Too much demand meant inflation. In fact, the explanation for unemployment was a significant innovation. The established economic doctrine of the time, labeled *classical economics* by Keynes, held that the economy always tends toward full employment. Price and wage reductions would restore full employment in the weak demand case. Workers who were unemployed or facing unemployment would agree to accept less than the prevailing money wage. With wages falling, competition among producers for sales would dictate that prices also fall, and the lower prices would stimulate demand.

Confronted by the Great Depression, Keynes quarreled with this theory. He doubted whether reductions in prices and money wages could restore full employment promptly, even if they were forthcoming. But, more important, he believed that worker resistance to money wage cuts would interrupt the process. Money wages, and therefore prices, were relatively inflexible downward in the short term. Whatever the merit of the classical view that price and wage reductions would restore full employment in the long term, the short-term response to insufficient demand, according to Keynes, was that output and employment would be fixed at less than full employment. Since this short-term response could extend for a year or more, the unemployment it involved was a serious burden and an important macroeconomic problem.

Keynes and the early Keynesians speculated that unemployment would be a chronic problem for the industrialized free-enterprise nations of the world in the absence of government action. Left to its own devices, aggregate demand might at times rise above the level necessary for full employment, causing inflation; but mostly it would fluctuate within the unemployment range. Unemployment was the general case, full employment the special case.

Modern Views

Today's macroeconomists for the most part accept the Keynesian view that aggregate demand for output relative to full-employment output is the key factor in unemployment and inflation problems, but they differ from Keynes and the early Keynesians in important respects. For example, Keynes emphasized fluctuations in business investment expenditures for plant, equipment, and inventories as the principal source of fluctuations in total demand. The flow of such expenditures depended on the state of business confidence, which was fluid and subject to change. A stock market crash, a failure of a large bank, or an international crisis could drastically affect business estimates of the future profitability of investment opportunities and occasion large fluctuations in the flow of investment expenditures. The fluctuation in total demand would greatly exceed the fluctuation in investment expenditures, since it would be aggravated by induced effects on consumer expenditures occurring as output, employment, and incomes began to change; but the fluctuations in investment expenditures would be the originating disturbance. (Keynes illustrated the aggravating influence of the consumer expenditure and income relationship with his famous multiplier effect, which will be discussed later in this book.)

Modern economists regard Keynes's emphasis on investment expenditures as exaggerated. They view fluctuations in government purchases, especially those associated with wars and their aftermaths, and fluctuations in consumer expenditures associated with tax changes as important disturbance items. Many see aggregate supply disturbances, such as the 1973–74 tripling of oil prices administered by the newly effective international oil cartel, as occasionally important. Almost all present-day economists see variations in the rate of money supply growth as an important historical source of aggregate demand fluctuations. Money supply disturbances work mainly by affecting interest rates and thereby interest-sensitive expenditures.

Indeed, Milton Friedman and other monetarists see money supply disturbances as the chief source of fluctuations in aggregate demand, including the very sharp reduction in demand responsible for the Great Depression of the 1930s.[2] In the monetarist view, the money supply is a problem if allowed to fluctuate but becomes a powerful automatic stabilizer for the economy if held steady, largely cancelling out the effects of Keynesian-style expenditure fluctuations. For example, as output, income, and expenditures begin to decline in response to a collapse in investment expenditures, the need for money balances declines, so that interest rates fall as wealth is shifted from money to securities. The lower interest rates on securities produce an offsetting increase in interest-sensitive expenditures, which moves aggregate demand and output back toward their initial levels. Keynes largely ignored these offsetting monetary effects, regarding them as weak.

[2] See Milton Friedman and Anna J. Schwartz, *A Monetary History of the United States, 1867–1960* (Princeton, N.J.: Princeton University Press, 1963), especially chap. 7. Milton Friedman, winner of the 1976 Nobel Memorial Prize in Economics, is a professor of economics at the University of Chicago and a senior research fellow at the Hoover Institute of Stanford University.

Keynesian and Modern Views on Macroeconomic Policy

Today's macroeconomics also differs significantly from that of Keynes and the early Keynesians in the area of macroeconomic policy. Since Keynes felt that investment expenditures, and hence total demand, are quite volatile, it followed that a program of discretionary stabilization policies by government is essential if nations such as the United States are to enjoy acceptable results with respect to price and employment goals. Governments should stimulate aggregate demand when it is too weak and diminish it when it is too strong. To use the modern phrase, governments should engage in demand management policies.

Further, in Keynes's view, the emphasis should be on fiscal policies. Monetary policies would not be very useful, especially in coping with the unemployment problem. They could reduce interest rates very little, if at all, in severe recessions, and whatever effects could be achieved on interest rates would have only small effects on aggregate demand, since expenditures were generally interest insensitive.

Specifically, Keynes recommended that governments affect the level of aggregate demand directly by adjusting the level of their own purchases of final goods and services. This could mean variations in government purchases of roads, public buildings, and other products of the private sector, including specially designed public works projects. It could mean variations in public service employment, that is, in workers employed directly by the government. Keynes himself did not emphasize the use of tax policies, as later economists have, probably because the income tax, which is the tax best suited to large-scale countercyclical variations, was not a substantial item during the 1930s.

Present-day macroeconomists depart from these Keynesian policy recommendations in varying degrees. Many, probably a majority, retain the Keynesian view that governments should conduct discretionary stabilization policies on a more or less continuous basis. However, almost all of these new Keynesians, who will be called *neo-Keynesians* here, would use monetary as well as fiscal policies, and many would rely chiefly on monetary policies.

Milton Friedman, the monetarist, has gone further. Friedman has recommended that governments employ discretionary stabilization policies only in extraordinary circumstances, such as those associated with wars and their aftermaths, when the need for them is clear. Otherwise, governments should confine themselves to stabilizing money supply growth, with the rate of growth attuned to long-term growth trends in full-employment output and money demand. Stabilizing the rate of money supply growth eliminates the money supply disturbances Friedman sees as the principal source of severe unemployment and inflation problems. Consequently, in ordinary circumstances, it produces an acceptable employment and price result. In the extraordinary circumstances in which discretionary stabilization policies should be used, Friedman and other monetarists would rely exclusively on monetary policies, except possibly in extremely serious depressions. Fiscal policies are too weak to be helpful, in the monetarist view. They provoke interest rate changes which produce largely offsetting effects on private investment expenditures and other interest-sensitive expenditures, leaving aggregate demand largely unaffected and interfering with the rate of growth of the capital stock.

In recommending stable money supply growth for ordinary circumstances, Friedman is not arguing that such a policy would provide a perfect employment and price result. His point is that it would produce an acceptable result, one which is superior to what likely would be achieved with discretionary monetary or fiscal policies. The difficulty with using discretionary monetary policies is that their impacts are uncertain and delayed. Moreover, the forecasting of the need for action is imperfect. As a result, Friedman argues, the monetary authority most often moves both too late and too strongly when it seeks to fine-tune the econony with variations in the rate of money supply growth, so that it destabilizes the economy instead of stabilizing it.

Monetarists argue that if discretionary monetary policies are to be used, whether on a continuous basis or only in extraordinary circumstances, it is at least essential to avoid the large swings in the money supply which have occurred in the past. To this end, they insist that the rate of increase in the money supply, rather than the interest rate or some similar variable, be employed as the monetary policy target and that the variations in the rate of increase be confined within a narrow range.

The Plan of the Book

The chapters which follow develop and illustrate the ideas introduced in this chapter and extend the discussion to other topics important to macroeconomics. For the most part, formal macroeconomic models are used as vehicles for the discussion. Macroeconomic models are simplifications from reality; they omit detail in order to highlight key relationships.

Part 2 begins with very simple models—exaggerated Keynesian models in the sense that they neglect money market effects entirely. Obviously, these models are incomplete, but they illustrate important macroeconomic ideas in readily understandable first approximations. They form the basis of preliminary discussions of how equilibrium output, income, and employment are determined, of how unemployment occurs when aggregate demand falls short of full-employment output, and of how inflation occurs when excess demand is present. In addition, they illustrate the important Keynesian investment multiplier concept and demonstrate principles of discretionary and built-in fiscal policies.

Part 3 adds a money market to the model and illustrates macroeconomic equilibrium with monetary influences present. Chapters 11 through 13 consider aggregate demand and supply disturbances as sources of unemployment and inflation problems and the mechanics of monetary and fiscal policies in the expanded model. The remaining chapters examine such matters as monetarism, classical economics, real balance effects, long-term growth, and complications arising in the international sector.

Summary

1. Macroeconomics deals with the performance of the economy as a whole. It seeks to explain how the economic aggregates which describe the economy's overall performance are determined, why problems regarding this performance occur, and what the government should do to alleviate the problems. Unemployment and inflation are the most important macroeconomic problems. General monetary and fiscal policies are the most important government problem-solving instruments.

2. For the United States, the most severe unemployment and inflation problems of the past half century occurred during the Great Depression of the 1930s and during World War II and its aftermath. The most severe problems since these events have occurred during the 1970s.

3. Modern macroeconomists for the most part accept the Keynesian view that aggregate demand for output relative to full-employment output is the key factor in unemployment and inflation. They differ with Keynes and among themselves as to the chief source of fluctuations in aggregate demand, the extent to which discretionary policies should be used, and whether monetary or fiscal policies should be emphasized.

Concepts for Identification

money
unemployment rate
inflation rate
business cycle
aggregate demand for output
multiplier effect
monetary policies
fiscal policies
public service employment

Questions and Problems for Review

1. What is the subject matter of macroeconomics? Identify the three basic parts of the province of macroeconomics and describe each part.

2. Distinguish between macroeconomics and microeconomics. Give examples of the types of questions with which the two branches of economics are concerned.

3. In what way does the experience of the 1970s as to unemployment and inflation differ from the experience of the preceding four decades?

4. Modern economists tend to agree with J. M. Keynes that aggregate demand for output relative to full-employment output is the key factor in unemployment and inflation problems. Explain its role.

5. What did Keynes emphasize as the originating disturbance in unemployment and inflation problems? How do modern economists differ on this point?

6. Why did Keynes feel that a program of discretionary stabilization policies by government was essential to acceptable price and employment results? What is the role of the multiplier concept in his position? Why did he recommend using fiscal rather than monetary policies in severe recessions?

7. What is Milton Friedman's position on the use of discretionary stabilization policies by government? Would Friedman emphasize monetary or fiscal policies if discretionary policies were used? Do neo-Keynesians agree with Friedman on these points?

References

Friedman, Milton. "The Role of Monetary Policy." *American Economic Review* 58 (March 1968): 1–17.

Friedman, Milton, and Heller, Walter W. *Monetary vs. Fiscal Policy.* New York: W. W. Norton, 1969.

Friedman, Milton, and Schwartz, Anna J. *A Monetary History of the United States, 1867–1960.* Princeton, N.J.: Princeton University Press, 1963, especially chap. 7 and 13.

Hansen, Alvin H. *A Guide to Keynes.* New York: McGraw-Hill, 1953.

Hansen, Alvin H. *Economic Policy and Full Employment.* New York: McGraw-Hill, 1947.

Keynes, John Maynard. *The General Theory of Employment, Interest and Money.* New York: Harcourt, Brace, 1936.

Klein, L. R. *The Keynesian Revolution.* New York: Macmillan, 1947.

Modigliani, Franco. "The Monetarist Controversy or, Should We Forsake Stabilization Policies." *American Economic Review* 67 (March 1977): 1–19.

2

Macroeconomic Problems and Macroeconomic Goals

Unemployment and inflation are considered the most prominent macroeconomic problems. Unemployment imposes a hardship on the unemployed individual and on the community as a whole; inflation redistributes wealth, producing losses for many members of the community, but gains for others. Economic growth, while traditionally considered less important as a macroeconomic issue in developed nations than unemployment or inflation, may become a more important issue in the future.

As indicated in Chapter 1, macroeconomics concerns itself chiefly with three basic questions. It asks how the major economic aggregates are determined, why problems relating to the economy's performance arise, and what the government should do about such problems. Chapter 1 has given a preview of the answers macroeconomics offers for these questions. Subsequent chapters will treat these answers in depth.

But before discussion of the answers proceeds, it is useful to consider for a moment the burdens imposed by unemployment and inflation. Most of us would agree that they are serious problems and that their prominence as such in the public mind is justified. But what are the burdens involved? Why are full employment and price stability important macroeconomic goals?

This chapter examines these questions; it also defines the full-employment unemployment rate, often called the natural rate of unemployment. A closing section looks briefly at economic growth as a macroeconomic goal.

The Unemployment Problem

Unemployment is a hardship for the individual or household directly affected and for the community at large. The hardship for the community at large is in part the sympathy employed workers feel for persons involuntarily unemployed, but it extends much beyond that. Unemployed workers do not produce goods and services, but they continue to consume them. At least some of this consumption is financed by taxes on employed workers. Moreover, severe unemployment may increase crime rates. It may also induce political changes, perhaps for the better, but possibly for the worse.

For the unemployed, the hardship is loss of income and status. Of course, the degree of hardship varies with the circumstances. If the unemployed worker is the single breadwinner of a household and the income loss is not replaced by another household member entering the workforce, unemployment ordinarily is a serious matter. If both husband and wife work, and one becomes unemployed, it is less serious. If the job-seeker is a teenager who has not yet established a separate household, unemployment is still less serious, unless the teenager's income would be a major portion of total family income.

The degree of hardship depends also on the length of the period of unemployment. In many cases, this period is only a few weeks. The average duration of unemployment for officially unemployed workers in the United States has been only about 5.5 weeks during recent years, being somewhat longer during recession years and somewhat shorter during business expansions.

Short-term unemployment usually does not provoke sharp reductions in living standards. Affected households often are able to draw on savings or borrow to cover temporary shortages. Moreover, most workers in the United States are eligible to receive unemployment benefits for periods of twenty-six weeks or more. During the 1974–75 recession, the period of eligibility was extended to fifty-two weeks.

In some cases, unions have bargained supplements to government unemployment benefits. A fund bargained by the United Auto Workers supplemented income for unemployed members with three or more years of experience during the 1974-75 recession, maintaining their income at approximately 95 percent of the pre-layoff level while reserves lasted. The food stamp program and other welfare programs provide additional income to persons whose income is low enough.

Types of Unemployment

Unemployment sometimes is classified as frictional, seasonal, shortfall, or structural. *Frictional unemployment* occurs as workers move between jobs in the normal course of job separation and job search. *Seasonal unemployment* occurs mainly in industries such as construction, recreation, and agriculture, where climate is a factor and where the workforce is accustomed to the seasonal nature of the job. *Shortfall unemployment,* often called cyclical unemployment, results from a shortfall of aggregate demand. It occurs during business recessions. Most frictional, seasonal, and shortfall unemployment in the United States is of the short-term variety. Shortfall unemployment can last for a year or more; however, post–World War II recessions have been relatively brief, falling short of a year in all cases except the 1974–75 recession, which lasted seventeen months.

Most of the long-term unemployment experienced by workers in the United States since the 1930s has been structural rather than shortfall. *Structural unemployment* occurs even when jobs are generally available because qualifications and requirements of job-seekers do not match requirements of jobs to be filled. It may result from technological advances which leave certain categories of job skills obsolete and overabundant. It may result from the decline over time in the demand for the product of specific industries. It may result from discrimination based on age, sex, race, or national origin.[1] It may result simply from inexperience or poor educational preparation, which are important underlying factors in unemployment among inner-city teenagers and young adults. Minimum-wage laws complicate this problem by requiring wage payments which often exceed the value of the services inexperienced job-seekers can offer employers.

Data for structural unemployment are not available as such, but during 1977 about 2 percent of the total United States labor force had been

[1] For middle-aged and older workers, what begins as cyclical unemployment may become structural unemployment unless union seniority provisions or employer policies offer protection. Once dislodged from a job, these workers may not be recalled, even after aggregate demand has recovered, if younger workers are available at lower wages. Age may prove to be a substantial disadvantage in securing other employment.

unemployed for fifteen weeks or more. Of course, this figure may be deceptively low, since many unemployed workers may simply stop actively seeking jobs after several months of unemployment and as a result may be dropped from the official unemployment and labor force statistics.

The Natural Rate of Unemployment

Does full employment mean zero unemployment? Obviously not. Most economists place the full-employment unemployment rate between 5 and 7 percent in terms of the U.S. economy of the 1970s. They speak of this as the *natural rate of unemployment,* defining it pragmatically as the unemployment rate at which increases in aggregate demand for output begin to spill mostly into price and wage increases instead of increases in output and employment. The unemployment which remains at this point includes structural unemployment as well as a normal amount of frictional and seasonal unemployment. It excludes shortfall unemployment, which results from a shortfall of overall demand for output.

The President's Council of Economic Advisers has estimated that an increase in the percentage of the labor force accounted for by teenagers raised the natural rate of unemployment for the U.S. economy from 4 percent in 1955 to 4.9 percent in the mid-1970s and speculated that other factors may have placed it closer to 5.5 percent.[2] Teenagers historically have had above-average unemployment rates. The other factors include an increased proportion of married women working, increased savings accumulations, and expanded income maintenance programs, which have made unemployment less burdensome and permitted workers to spend more time between jobs. Unemployment compensation programs have been liberalized during the 1970s, and the food stamp program has been greatly expanded. Herbert Stein, chairman of the President's Council of Economic Advisers during the administrations of Presidents Nixon and Ford, has suggested that the natural rate of unemployment may have increased to 7 percent during the mid-1970s.[3]

Most economists see the increase in the natural rate of unemployment as an important factor in the higher inflation rate and unemployment rate combinations of the 1970s, though the cost-push inflation associated with increased prices of oil and other imports also has been a factor. The

[2] President's Council of Economic Advisers, *Economic Report of the President* (Washington, D.C.: Government Printing Office, 1977), p. 51.

[3] Herbert Stein, "Full Employment at Last?" *Wall Street Journal,* September 14, 1977, p. 22.

increased natural rate of unemployment means that excess-demand inflationary pressures occur at higher unemployment rates than before.

Including structural unemployment in natural unemployment does not imply insensitivity to the very real hardship structural unemployment involves. It reflects instead the view that structural unemployment is best attacked through job training or public service employment programs, such as those provided for under the Comprehensive Employment and Training Act (CETA) since 1974. Curing structural unemployment with monetary and fiscal policies which simply affect the amount of overall demand with no attention to its composition is inefficient and expensive in terms of the inflation rate provoked.

Of course, since job training programs and public service employment transform unemployed workers into employed workers, they reduce natural unemployment and lower the full-employment unemployment rate. For example, if the full-employment unemployment rate is 6.5 percent, including 2 percent structural unemployment, removing half the structural unemployment through job training and public service employment programs reduces the full-employment target rate to 5.5 percent unemployment. Removing structural unemployment lowers the unemployment rate that general monetary and fiscal policies can be expected to achieve.

This means that legislative proposals which target unemployment rates below the natural rate may not be inflationary after all if they include specific measures to reduce structural unemployment. Of course, such proposals can be opposed on other grounds. Opponents argue that most specific measures to reduce structural unemployment are expensive, difficult to confine to persons who are truly structurally unemployed, and lacking in permanent effects. Public service employment has the additional disadvantage that it may tend to freeze persons who might eventually secure productive employment and valuable training in the private sector into relatively unproductive make-work government jobs.

The Inflation Problem

Inflation and Purchasing Power

Inflation shares prominence with unemployment as a macroeconomic problem because it creates substantial purchasing power losses for many members of the community. There are other aspects to the inflation problem, but that is the major one.

If prices rise and income fails to rise proportionately, income purchases fewer goods and services than before. Real income, that is, income adjusted for changes in purchasing power, declines. Moreover, households that have placed wealth in bonds, loans, or other ordinary debt securities suffer purchasing power losses in wealth as well as income, since the maturity values as well as the interest earnings on such securities are fixed in dollar terms. An ordinary bond which pays $500 per year plus $10,000 at the end of ten years continues to pay those amounts whether prices of goods and services remain constant or double. If prices do double, the $10,000 buys only half what it would have if prices had remained constant. Inflation also produces purchasing power losses in wealth placed in cash, demand deposits, and savings deposits.

It is largely a redistribution of real income and wealth that is involved here. In most periods of significant inflation, the economy remains near full employment, so that aggregate output, and the aggregate real income generated in producing it, grow slightly (1974 and 1975 were exceptions). Indeed, inflation probably enhances aggregate output and real income in the sense that employment and output are higher with inflation than they would have been had a vigorous anti-inflationary policy been pursued. Since someone must receive the real income, what some households lose in real income from inflation, others must gain. Similarly, what creditors lose from inflation, debtors gain. The holder of a mortgage loan loses purchasing power when prices increase because the mortgage repayment received is fixed in dollar terms. But the mortgage borrower realizes an exactly offsetting purchasing power gain. With prices higher, the borrower sacrifices less in goods and services forgone to make the fixed mortgage payment.[4]

Indexing. During recent years, *indexing* has attracted a good deal of attention as a means of limiting the redistribution of income and wealth resulting from inflation. Under indexing, debt contracts, pension contracts, and perhaps even wages, prices, and tax schedules are equipped with cost-of-living escalator clauses. For example, on a loan of $100 for one year, a borrower may be required to repay $105 if prices remain unchanged, but $115.50 if prices increase by 10 percent during the year. The real goods and services purchasable by the repayment thus are independent of the inflation rate, since $115.50 is 110 percent of $105.

[4] During periods of severe deflation, such as the early 1930s, borrowers lose and creditors gain, of course. An important part of the problem of the farmer in the early 1930s was that mortgage repayment costs remained fixed through farm incomes, reflecting food prices, declined.

With pension, wage, and price contracts, adjustments equal to the inflation rate are added.

In the United States, indexing has not spread much beyond pension plans, where it often is partial, although social security benefits and federal employee pensions are now fully cost-of-living indexed. As a general rule, debt contracts are not indexed for inflation in the United States. Suggestions that the federal debt be indexed often are heard but have not been followed. An informal indexing of debt contracts occurs, of course, in that the interest rates agreed upon in the market adjust upward to reflect lender and borrower expectations of inflation. But this practice has the desired effect only to the extent that the market correctly anticipates the rate of inflation. If the market expects prices to rise by 10 percent and adds 10 percent to debt contracts, creditors still lose and debtors still gain if prices in fact rise by 15 percent. On the other hand, if prices rise by only 5 percent, debtors lose and creditors gain.

Two major criticisms of indexing are generally made. First, when the government requires or encourages indexing, it is interfering with the freedom of individuals to arrange their economic contracts as they choose. Second, indexing prices and wages may incur some of the same economic inefficiency produced by mandatory price and wage controls. It can interfere with the ability of the price system to guide resources into the production of the goods and services desired by the community, unless care is taken to permit prices and wages to change to reflect market forces as well as inflation. This is relatively easy to arrange for debt contracts, but more difficult for prices and wages.

Who have been the gainers and losers from inflation in the United States? One study, covering the period 1955 through 1970, concluded that, looking at debtor and creditor effects alone, the very rich and the very poor had lost from inflation and the middle income group had gained.[5] Middle income households tended to be net borrowers—borrowing to finance homes, automobiles, and the like—and had gained from inflation, as did debtors in general. Market interest rates did not rise by enough during the period to fully compensate creditors for the purchasing power effects of inflation. The very rich had lost because they had little direct debt outstanding on which to make gains and had suffered substantial purchasing power losses on their extensive holdings of government securities and other debt securities. The poor price performance of the stock market

[5] G. L. Bach and J. B. Stephenson, "Inflation and the Redistribution of Wealth," *Review of Economics and Statistics* 61 (February 1974): 1–13.

after early 1966 complicated their problem. The very poor had lost from inflation when only debtor and creditor effects were considered, because they had little debt, being unable to borrow, and had placed the bulk of their small asset holdings in cash, demand deposits, and savings deposits.

The very poor have gained from inflation on balance, however, through participation in expanded federal welfare programs, an expansion financed in part by the federal government's gains from inflation. The federal government has gained from inflation in three ways:

1. It has gained as have debtors in general—interest payments per dollar of federal debt have not increased in proportion to the price level.

2. Individual federal income taxes have increased more than in proportion to prices, since both general tax exemptions and tax brackets have been specified in fixed dollar terms. For example, a family of four which earned $20,000 during 1978 paid about 18.5 percent of income in federal income taxes under the tax schedules then in effect. If inflation doubles the family's income, with the same tax schedule in effect, their federal income tax bill rises to just over 23 percent of income.

3. The final gain from inflation for the federal government arises in printing and spending (through the banking system) the larger supply of cash and coin needed to service the higher level of transactions in the economy.

Of course, it is not only the very poor who benefit from the federal government's gain from inflation. The gain or loss of each individual household from this source depends on its exact circumstance as a beneficiary of federal spending on the one hand and as a taxpayer and government creditor on the other.

Inflation and Foreign Transactions

A second aspect of the inflation problem concerns the difficulties inflation poses for a nation's position in international markets. If U.S. prices rise more rapidly than prices abroad and the dollar price of foreign currencies in foreign exchange markets is not permitted to rise proportionately, goods and services produced in the United States become more expensive relative to foreign-produced goods and services, both to U.S. residents and to foreigners. As a result, U.S. exports of goods and services tend to decline while imports tend to increase. This worsens the nation's balance of international payments. In addition, it creates hard times for

U.S. export industries and U.S. industries whose products compete with imports.

Of course, these effects can be prevented by letting the dollar price of foreign currencies rise in foreign exchange markets. However, there have been many instances historically in which nations, in the face of relative inflation, have tried to maintain the values of their currencies relative to foreign currencies (or their trading partners, to stimulate their own exports, have attempted to do it for them). In such instances, domestic exports have declined and imports increased.

Other Burdens from Inflation

A third problem with inflation is that it may induce resources, particularly skilled managers, into speculative rather than productive pursuits. This is probably a serious problem only when inflation rates are 50 percent per year or more. Such inflation presents profit opportunities in land and real estate speculation and inventory accumulation which divert efforts from the production and distribution of ordinary goods and services. Hence, the amount of ordinary output available on a per capita basis is diminished.

Economists sometimes make much of a fourth aspect of the inflation problem. When prices rise, the purchasing power of a dollar left in demand deposits and cash diminishes, as noted earlier. To counter this loss, households, firms, and governmental units may reduce their holdings of these assets in relation to their money expenditures. With demand deposits and cash reduced relative to expenditures, more time must be devoted to effecting transactions, since demand deposits and cash are held in part for this purpose. As a result, less time is available for producing goods and services, and total output is less. It seems unlikely that these losses are very great, however, or that such considerations are an important aspect of the inflation problem in the public mind.

Economic Growth as a Macroeconomic Goal

Economic growth has been less important than unemployment or inflation as a macroeconomic issue for the United States and the other industrialized nations of the West. On the whole, per capita real income growth has been satisfactory for these nations, while unemployment and inflation have been recurrent problems. The industrial revolution, which began in England during the eighteenth century, has provided each succeeding generation in the industrialized nations with a higher standard of living. Where individual households have not participated in this growth, the problem has been individual circumstances or temporary interruptions caused by war or cyclical recession rather than inadequate national per capita real income growth over time. As a result, growth has surfaced only occasionally as an important issue in the West. One such occasion was the Great Depression of the 1930s, when many feared that the severe unemployment and reduced real incomes of the period would prove to be chronic. A second occasion was the U.S. presidential election campaign of 1960, when economic growth emerged as a national security issue, raised to that status by high reported growth rates for the Russian economy and the early Russian technological successes in space ventures.

The recent focus of attention on the problem of population growth in the face of limited natural resources suggests that economic growth may become a more important issue in the future. We are reminded that land resources are finite and fossil fuel and other mineral resources exhaustible. If the growth trend becomes negative in the future, growth surely will increase in importance as an issue in the West. Whether the economic growth trend actually does become negative depends on the population growth rates which actually occur and on whether technological advances in energy sources, land usage, and production processes in general can offset the influence of limited natural resources. Prospects probably are not so dismal as the more gloomy forecasts suggest. While the problem obviously is a matter for concern, we are reminded of the much earlier, still-unfulfilled arguments of Thomas Malthus (1766–1834), who suggested that the pressure of population growth would permanently tend per capita real income toward the subsistence level.[6]

Summary

1. Unemployment is a problem for the unemployed and for the community as a whole. The major hardship for the unemployed is the loss of income and status. The extent of the hardship depends on the circumstances of the unemployed and the duration of the unemployment.

2. The full-employment unemployment rate, or natural rate of unemployment, is the rate of unemployment at which increases in aggregate demand for output begin to spill mostly into price and wage increases instead of increases in output and employment. It prevails

[6] Thomas Malthus, *An Essay on the Principle of Population,* 1st ed. 1798; rev. ed. 1803.

when shortfall unemployment has been eliminated. It includes normal amounts of frictional and seasonal unemployment, plus structural unemployment.

3. Inflation redistributes real income and wealth, producing losses for many members of the community. Debtors have gained and creditors have lost during recent U.S. inflations, since interest rates on debt securities have not risen by enough to compensate creditors for purchasing power losses. Redistribution of real income and wealth also has proceeded through the federal government's position as a gainer from inflation. Whether individual households gain or lose from this depends on their circumstance as beneficiaries of government spending on the one hand and as taxpayers and government creditors on the other.

4. The recent focus of attention on the problem of continued population growth in the face of limited natural resources suggests that economic growth may be a more important issue in developed nations in the future than it has been in the past.

Concepts for Identification

frictional unemployment
seasonal unemployment
structural unemployment
shortfall unemployment
natural rate of unemployment
real income
debtor
creditor
indexing

Questions and Problems for Review

1. What is the burden of unemployment for the unemployed? Identify the factors which determine the severity of the burden.

2. Which type of unemployment is most sensitive to general monetary and fiscal policies? Explain your answer.

3. Do inflation rates of from 10 to 20 percent per year impose a burden if aggregate output is unaffected? Explain your answer. Describe carefully any burden you perceive.

4. Assume that a person lends $100 for one year and receives $110 back at the end of the year, with prices of goods and services unchanged. Explain why the lender would have had to receive back $121 to be just as well off in purchasing power terms if prices, instead of remaining the same, had risen by 10 percent during that year.

5. If prices rise more rapidly in the United States than elsewhere and the U.S. government does not allow the dollar to depreciate in foreign exchange markets, the nation's balance of international payments tends to worsen. Explain this effect.

References

Bach, G. L., and Stephenson, J. B. "Inflation and the Redistribution of Wealth." *Review of Economics and Statistics* 61 (February 1974): 1–13.

Budd, E. C., and Seiders, D. F. "The Impact of Inflation on the Distribution of Income and Wealth." *American Economic Review* 61 (May 1971): 128–149.

President's Council of Economic Advisers. *Economic Report of the President.* Washington, D.C.: Government Printing Office, 1975, pp. 86–117.

President's Council of Economic Advisers. *Economic Report of the President.* Washington, D.C.: Government Printing Office, 1977, pp. 45–88.

Stein, Herbert. "Full Employment at Last?" *Wall Street Journal,* September 14, 1977, p. 22.

134617

3

Measuring the Economic Aggregates

The U.S. Department of Commerce constructs statistical measurements for aggregate output, output prices, expenditures, and income and for the major expenditure and income subaggregates. The Bureau of Labor Statistics of the Department of Labor produces statistics on the labor force, employment, and unemployment and also maintains the consumer price index.

This chapter looks at the definitions of the economic aggregates, at the sources of data for them, and at some of the procedures involved in their measurement. For the United States, many of the aggregates appear in the national income accounts maintained by the Department of Commerce. These accounts provide the figures for aggregate output, real income, expenditures, and prices and for the income and expenditure subaggregates. Quarterly and annual figures are published in the regular monthly issues of the *Survey of Current Business.*

Data for aggregate employment, unemployment, and the percent of the labor force unemployed are published each month by the Department of Labor in the *Monthly Labor Review.* The Department of Labor also maintains the consumer price index, which is a useful supplement to the implicit price deflators of the national income accounts as an indicator of price movements.

The *Economic Report of the President,* prepared by the President's

Council of Economic Advisers and published annually, is a handy single reference source for annual figures for all of these statistical series. Recent issues of the report present annual data beginning with 1939 for most series. Back issues extend the data through 1929.

Aggregate Output and Prices

Gross national product, or GNP, is the term the Department of Commerce employs for aggregate U.S. output. The department defines it as the dollar value at market prices of all final goods and services produced by the U.S. economy within a specified period.

This definition is worth careful attention. It reveals many of the procedures and problems involved in measuring aggregate output. For example, notice that the problem of representing an aggregate comprised of a host of diverse physical items with a single figure is solved by using the dollar as a common denominator. This is the same procedure individuals follow in representing net worth—which resides in cash, bank deposits, other financial assets, real estate, automobiles, and numerous other items of personal property—with a single figure.

The definition also indicates that market price is employed as the measure of value. Whether or not market price is in fact the best arbitrator of value in some aesthetic sense, employing it obviously is the appropriate and sensible course for macroeconomic analysis. It may be true that the services of the U.S. president are worth more than those of a star baseball player, despite the market's indication to the contrary, but the alternative to using market price as the measure of value is a Pandora's box. Whose preference system is to be used in assigning value, if not the market's? Moreover, it is market value which determines the prices and incomes which guide resources into production.

The definition indicates further that only final goods and services are included in the aggregate output measure; intermediate product is excluded. GNP does not include the value of the grain sold to the miller, plus the value of the flour sold to the baker, plus the value of the bread sold to the retailer, plus the value of the bread sold to the consumer. To do so would multiply the productive activity actually taking place by several times. GNP must include only the value of the final good, that is, the value of the bread when sold to the consumer, or, what amounts to the same thing, the value added at each stage of production.

Notice also in this part of the definition that aggregate output includes production of services as well as of goods. It includes the services provided by physicians, lawyers, sales personnel, and the like, as well as goods such as milk and automobiles. Services usually account for about one-quarter of GNP.

The GNP figure is further defined as measuring the product of the U.S. economy—the national product; it excludes the product of foreign economies. More specifically, it counts only the product of factors of production owned by U.S. residents. For example, in incorporating the value of a domestically produced automobile, the portion of the purchase price which covers the imported components of the automobile must be excluded. If the engine, or a portion of it, was produced in Canada and imported, that portion belongs to Canadian national product and must be excluded from U.S. product. Similarly, if the rubber for the tires was imported, that must be excluded. Moreover, if the U.S. automobile producer pays interest and dividend income to foreign residents who own stock or bonds issued by the U.S. producer, those values must be excluded, since they represent the contribution of production factors owned by foreigners.

Finally, notice that the GNP figure relates to production occurring within a specified period of time, ordinarily a quarter year or a full year. It is a flow of production, not a stock of wealth. Usually, when quarterly figures are reported in the press, they are reported at seasonally adjusted annual rates; that is, they are seasonally adjusted and multiplied by four. Thus the rate of production for the quarter in question can be compared directly to production rates for the preceding year or quarter, showing at a glance whether production is rising or falling. The quarterly figure, reported as a seasonally adjusted annual rate, indicates what annual production would be if production continued for a full year at the rate achieved during the quarter in question.

Current Dollars, Constant Dollars, and the Implicit Price Deflator

The national income accounts present GNP in both current and constant dollars, and they provide the implicit price deflator which associates the two. GNP in *current dollars* is aggregate output in money, or non–price deflated terms. GNP in *constant dollars* reflects real output. The *implicit price deflator* for GNP is the price index for aggregate output.

The current dollar figure is obtained by summing the dollar values of final products at the market prices which actually prevailed in each year. This means that changes in it reflect both price changes and changes in real output, without distinguishing between the two. The constant dollar figure, by contrast, is the sum of the dollar values of the various final products with each item valued at the market price which prevailed in a specified base year. In effect, it is the sum of current-period quantities multiplied by base-year prices. As a result, changes in the constant dollar figures reflect changes in real output only.

The price index for GNP is obtained by dividing the current dollar figures by the constant dollar figures and multiplying by 100. That is, for any year, the GNP price index figure, P, is:

$$P = \left(\frac{\text{GNP in current dollars}}{\text{GNP in constant dollars}}\right) \times 100. \tag{3-1}$$

The current and constant dollar GNP figures are always the same for the base year of the price index, of course; therefore, the price index figure for the base year is always 100.

Table 3–1 presents U.S. GNP in current and constant (1972) dollars for 1966 through 1978 and also shows the implicit price deflator, which relates to the two GNP series as indicated by Equation 3–1. Alternatively, the constant dollar figures can be thought of as the price-deflated values

Table 3–1

GNP in Current and Constant Dollars and the Implicit Price Deflator for GNP (Billions of Dollars)

	GNP in Current Dollars	GNP in Constant (1972) Dollars	Implicit Price Deflator for GNP
1966	$ 753.0	$ 981.0	$ 76.76
1967	796.3	1,007.7	79.02
1968	868.5	1,051.8	82.57
1969	935.5	1,078.8	86.72
1970	982.4	1,075.3	91.36
1971	1,063.4	1,107.5	96.02
1972	1,171.1	1,171.1	100.00
1973	1,306.6	1,235.0	105.80
1974	1,412.9	1,217.8	116.02
1975	1,528.8	1,202.3	127.15
1976	1,700.1	1,271.0	133.76
1977	1,887.2	1,332.7	141.61
1978	2,106.6	1,385.1	152.09

Source: President's Council of Economic Advisers, *Economic Report of the President* (Washington, D.C.: Government Printing Office, 1979), pp. 183–184, 186.

of the current dollar figures. In that case, Equation 3–1 is, in effect, rewritten as:

$$\text{GNP in constant dollars} = \frac{\text{GNP in current dollars}}{P} \times 100. \qquad 3\text{–}2$$

Table 3–1 illustrates that the approximate doubling of current dollar GNP from 1971 through 1978 resulted from a 25.1 percent increase in real output—($1,385.1 – $1,107.5)/$1,107.5—and an approximately 58.4 percent increase in prices—(152.06 – 96.02)/96.02.

Aggregate Expenditures and Aggregate Income

The national income accounts also present data for aggregate expenditures and aggregate income. Indeed, these data emerge in the process of measuring aggregate output, since aggregate output is estimated as the sum of the expenditures for it and as the sum of the incomes generated in producing it. To cite a simple example, when a bellhop who works only for tips shows a hotel guest to a room and receives a one dollar tip for the service, the national income accounts estimate the bellhop's product and build it into the GNP estimate both as a one dollar expenditure by the guest and as one dollar of income to the bellhop.

On the expenditures side, the GNP figure is built up chiefly from sales data for final products. On the income side, it consists mainly of income data provided by the Internal Revenue Service. Since each dollar of expenditures for final product becomes an income payment to a factor, if only as residual item profits (the difference between producer receipts and producer payments to others), the national income account figures for aggregate expenditures, output, and income always are equal.

Of course, not all product involves actual market expenditures and income payments. Where it does not, expenditures and income payments must be imputed using the prices the product would have commanded in market transactions. For example, when waiters and waitresses receive part of their compensation in meals, both an expenditure and an income payment must be imputed at the price the meals would have brought if sold to paying customers. Similar imputations are needed to record the product of live-in domestics, military personnel, university presidents, and others who receive room or board or both as a portion of their compensation. Imputations also must be made for the food farmers raise and consume themselves. (As a general rule, however, the national income accounts do not impute product for the work people perform for themselves in and around the home.) On the expenditures side, an imputation is made for the product of government workers, since most of this product does not involve a market expenditure. The income payments to government workers are used as both the expenditures and the income estimates.

Just as not all product involves an actual expenditure, not all money expenditures reflect final product. In fact, most do not, and these must be excluded when the aggregate output estimate is built up from the expenditures side. Aggregate expenditures for output, as well as aggregate output, refer to final product only. This means, as indicated earlier, that expenditures for intermediate product must be excluded. Similarly, money payments which are income payments rather than expenditures for final product must not be included when the product estimate is calculated from the expenditures side. Another large category of expenditures which must be omitted is that for financial assets; only the portion of these expenditures which reflects broker and dealer fees is incorporated into the GNP estimate. Similarly, expenditures for existing real assets such as houses, automobiles, paintings, and diamonds are excluded, except for the broker and dealer fees involved. Only expenditures for newly produced houses, automobiles, and so on are included, since only these reflect production occurring during the period.

The Expenditure Components

The national income accounts break down aggregate U.S. expenditures into four major components and then subdivide each of the components. These breakdowns are shown in Table 3–2, which presents U.S. aggregate expenditures for output in 1978. The major expenditure categories are *personal consumption expenditures, gross private domestic investment, government purchases of goods and services,* and *net exports of goods and services.*

Personal Consumption Expenditures

Personal consumption expenditures include expenditures for consumer durable goods such as personal automobiles, TV sets, and the like; expenditures for nondurable goods such as food; and expenditures for

U.S. Aggregate Expenditure and its Components, 1978, in 1972 Dollars (Billions of Dollars)

Table 3-2

Gross national product	$1,385.1
Personal consumption expenditures	891.2
Durable goods	144.7
Nondurable goods	339.1
Services	407.4
Gross private domestic investment	210.1
Fixed investment	199.6
Nonresidential	139.9
Structures	44.3
Producers' durable equipment	95.5
Residential	59.7
Change in business inventories	10.4
Net exports of goods and services	8.6
Exports	107.3
Imports	98.7
Government purchases of goods and services	275.2
Federal	100.5
State and local	174.7

Source: President's Council of Economic Advisers, *Economic Report of the President* (Washington, D.C.: Government Printing Office, 1979), pp. 184–185.

services. In general, consumer durable goods are goods having useful lives of more than one year. Nondurable goods ordinarily are used up within a year. Services expire as they are delivered.

Gross Private Domestic Investment

Gross private domestic investment breaks down into expenditures for producer structures and durable equipment (plant and equipment expenditures), residential construction expenditures (housing expenditures), and the change in business inventories. Including the change in business inventories is in a sense a qualification of the earlier statement that intermediate goods are excluded from the GNP estimate, since an increase in inventories means that an increase in intermediate goods is raising the GNP estimate. It is a necessary qualification, however, if the GNP estimate is to be a product rather than a sales estimate. For example, an automobile which was produced in late 1977 but ended the year in a dealer inventory rather than with a final purchaser should be counted in the aggregate output for 1977, since that is the year in which it was produced and contributed to incomes and employment. Including the change in business inventories in the aggregate expenditures figure accomplishes this.[1]

Government Purchases of Goods and Services

Government purchases of goods and services include federal, state, and local government components. While most of the discussion of government purchases in this book will concern the federal component, since federal fiscal policies to stabilize the economy are a major interest, state and local governments now account for well over half of total government purchases in the United States. Another important point is that government purchases of goods and services do not include government transfer payments. Transfer payments, such as social security benefits, unemployment compensation payments, and various welfare benefits, are excluded because they do not reflect productive activity in the period in which they occur. They are merely transfers of income from the government, ultimately from taxpayers, to transfer payment recipients. On the other hand, government wage payments under public service employment programs are treated as government purchases of goods and services, since these payments are regarded as reflecting the product of the government employees involved.

Net Exports

Net exports, the final major component of aggregate expenditures, are exports less imports of goods and services. Rather than separating out the imported element in each final good or service sold by U.S. producers individually, the national income accounts simply subtract imports as a lump sum from exports to get the net exports component. While this is a convenient way of getting the aggregate product and aggregate expenditures figures, and probably the only practical way, it has the disadvantage that the figures for consumption expenditures, gross private domestic

[1] It could be argued that all investment expenditures should be considered intermediate goods and excluded from the GNP estimate, since they are used to produce other goods rather than consumed for themselves. To do so would give a consumption rather than an output estimate, however.

investment expenditures, government purchases of goods and services, and exports include imported product. They do not reflect domestic production only.

An additional complication is that the exports item includes net exports of factor services. For example, it includes dividend and interest receipts of U.S. residents on holdings of foreign securities less dividend and interest payments by U.S. producers to foreign holders of their securities. This is a necessary adjustment to get the domestic U.S. product, since the domestic product is that produced by factors owned by U.S. residents.

Constant Dollars and Price Deflators for the Expenditures Components

The expenditures components are available in both current and constant dollars, and an implicit price deflator is available for each. These price deflators, or price indexes, behave differently from each other, of course, since the prices of the various types of goods and services change by different percentages in the actual world. They are obtained in the same way as the implicit price deflator for GNP as a whole. Constant dollar values are assembled for each component by summing the base-year dollar values for the items it includes. The implicit price deflator for each component then is obtained by dividing its current dollar value by its constant dollar value and multiplying by 100.

The Income Subaggregates

The national income accounts also provide subaggregates on the income side of the product measure. Table 3–3 summarizes the income subaggregates, indicating how they are related to gross national product (that is, to gross national income) and to each other. Data are presented for 1978.

Gross national product less capital consumption allowances is *net national product.* This is the income available to the community after allowance is made for replacing the capital goods used up in producing the gross product.

National income is essentially the income received by the private sector for sales of factor services in production, again excluding capital consumption allowances. National income therefore is roughly composed of net national product less indirect business taxes, though two minor items—business transfer payments (which are subtracted) and

Table 3-3

Relation of Gross National Product, Net National Product, National Income, Personal Income, Disposable Personal Income, and Personal Saving, 1978, Current Dollars (Billions of Dollars)

	Gross National Product	$2,106.6
Less:	Capital consumption allowances[a]	216.9
Equals:	**Net National Product**	1,889.7
Less:	Indirect business taxes and nontax liability	178.2
	Business transfer payments	10.7
	Statistical discrepancy	0.9
Plus:	Subsidies less current surplus of government enterprises	3.7
Equals:	**National Income**	1,703.6
Less:	Corporate profits[b]	160.0
	Net interest	106.1
	Contributions for social insurance	164.3
	Wage accruals less disbursements	0.0
Plus:	Government transfer payments to persons	215.2
	Personal interest income	158.9
	Dividends	49.3
	Business transfer payments	10.7
Equals:	**Personal Income**	1,707.3
Less:	Personal tax and nontax payments	256.2
Equals:	**Disposable Personal Income**	1,451.2[c]
Less:	Personal consumption expenditures	1,339.7
	Interest paid by consumers to business	33.8
	Personal transfer payments to foreigners	1.0
Equals:	**Personal Saving**	76.7

[a] Capital consumption adjustment is included.
[b] Inventory valuation and capital consumption adjustments are included.
[c] Subtotals may not add to totals because of rounding.
Source: President's Council of Economic Advisers, *Economic Report of the President,* Washington, D.C.: Government Printing Office, (1979), pp. 202–203, 208.

subsidies less current surplus of government enterprises (which is added)—also are involved. *Indirect business taxes* are items such as sales taxes and excise taxes, which accrue directly to the government when the product is sold and hence never become income to the private sector. *Business transfer payments* cover such things as fellowships granted to persons by businesses. They are excluded from national income because they are not payments made to factors for services rendered in production.

Table 3–4 breaks down national income according to the factors receiving it. Compensation of employees is essentially labor income. It includes wages and salaries plus supplements to wages and salaries such as employer contributions for social security, workmen's compensation, health insurance, and private retirement programs. The other national income components are property incomes, which include proprietors' income, corporate profit, rental income of persons, and net interest. *Proprietors' income* is the profit item for unincorporated businesses.

Table 3–4

U.S. National Income by Type of Income, 1978, in Current Dollars (Billions of Dollars)

Compensation of employees		$1,301.2
Wages and salaries	$1,100.7	
Supplements to wages and salaries	200.5	
Proprietors' income (unincorporated businesses)		112.9
Corporate profits[a]		160.0
Rental income of persons[b]		23.4
Net interest		106.1
National income		$1,703.6

[a] Inventory valuation and capital consumption adjustments are included.
[b] Capital consumption adjustment is included.

Source: President's Council of Economic Advisers, *Economic Report of the President* (Washington, D.C.: Government Printing Office, 1979), pp. 204–205.

Personal income is the income of the personal sector before personal tax and nontax payments. It drops those national income items which end up with business as retained earnings or with government, excepting personal tax and nontax payments, and adds government transfer payments to persons.

Disposable personal income, then, is personal income less the personal tax and nontax payments. Table 3–3 also includes the personal saving item from the national income accounts, although, strictly speaking, personal saving is not an income subaggregate. *Personal saving* equals disposable personal income less personal consumption expenditures and two minor items, personal transfer payments to foreigners and interest paid by consumers to businesses. This accords roughly with the national income accounts definition of saving as income not consumed.

Several of the income subaggregates have not proved very useful for general macroeconomic analysis and will not often be encountered in this book. For example, gross national product rather than net national product will be used as the measure for aggregate output. The gross figure relates more closely to price and employment behavior, since the demand for and the production of replacement capital goods are involved in employment and inflation results.

Disposable personal income—or, alternatively, disposable *private* income (which includes the retained earnings of corporations)—will be used as the determinant of personal consumption expenditures, since it is better suited to that purpose than national income or personal income. The national income measure and its breakdown by factor is useful chiefly when questions concerning factor shares in aggregate income arise, and that is not the major subject area of macroeconomics. The personal income measure, since it is available monthly rather than quarterly, is valuable to economists who are analyzing current business conditions and forecasting future trends.

Employment, Unemployment, and the Unemployment Rate

Statistics for employment and unemployment levels and for the percent of the labor force unemployed are provided each month by the Bureau of Labor Statistics of the Department of Labor. The basic data are collected for them by the Bureau of the Census as part of the current population survey by means of personal interviews with a scientifically selected sample of U.S. households. Approximately 50,000 households, scattered throughout the United States, are interviewed each month. Interviewers identify each household member as *employed, unemployed,* or *not in the labor force,* and the results are projected to provide estimates for the U.S. population as a whole.

Table 3–5 presents the estimates for 1978. The labor force equals employment plus unemployment, while the unemployment rate is unemployment divided by the labor force. Labor force, employment, and unemployment figures relate only to people who are civilians sixteen years old or older.[2]

[2] For a description of the monthly household survey and the concepts involved in the employment-related series constructed from it, see U.S. Department of Labor, Bureau of Labor Statistics, *Employment and Earnings* (Washington, D.C.: Government Printing Office, March 1978), pp. 139—148.

U.S. Labor Force, Employment, Unemployment, and Unemployment Rate, 1978 (Persons 16 Years of Age and Older)

Table 3–5

	Thousands of Persons
Total civilian labor force (excludes armed forces)	100,420
Employed	94,373
Unemployed	6,047
Unemployment rate (percent of the civilian labor force unemployed)	6.0

Source: President's Council of Economic Advisers, *Economic Report of the President* (Washington, D.C.: Government Printing Office, 1979), p. 214.

The employment category includes all persons who worked at all during the survey week, either as paid workers or in their own businesses, and also unpaid workers who worked fifteen hours or more in a business owned by another family member. It includes workers who were temporarily absent from work because of illness, strikes, or the like. It excludes persons whose only employment is work around the home or volunteer work. Each employed person is counted only once, in the principal employment.

Unemployment includes persons who did not work at all during the survey week but were available for work and had engaged in job-seeking efforts (answering a want ad, applying for a job) during the four preceding weeks. Also considered as unemployed are persons waiting to be called back to a job from which they have been laid off or waiting to report to a new job within thirty days. Unemployment also includes persons seeking only part-time work, providing that they are sixteen or over.

Unemployment Subaggregates

Tables 3–6 and 3–7 present some of the subaggregative data which are available for unemployment rates and unemployment, giving annual figures for 1978. These data, like the totals, are constructed from information provided by the monthly household survey and are available on a monthly basis. Subaggregates for the unemployment rate include breakdowns by race, sex, age, and other characteristics (Table 3–6). Subaggregates for unemployment indicate duration of and reason for unemployment (Table 3–7). Workers who lose or leave jobs differ from reentrants in that reentrants remain out of the labor force for a time before seeking new positions.

Table 3–6

U.S. Unemployment Rate Subaggregates, 1978 (Persons 16 Years of Age and Older)

	Unemployment Rate (Percent)
Total civilian labor force	6.0
White	5.2
Males	4.5
16–19 years	13.5
20 years and over	3.7
Females	6.2
16–19 years	14.4
20 years and over	5.2
Black and other	11.9
Males	10.9
16–19 years	34.4
20 years and over	8.6
Females	13.1
16–19 years	38.4
20 years and over	10.6
Selected groups	
Experienced wage and salary workers	5.6
Married men living with their wives	2.8
Women who head families	8.5
Full-time workers	5.5
Blue-collar workers	6.9

Source: President's Council of Economic Advisers, *Economic Report of the President* (Washington, D.C.: Government Printing Office, 1979), pp. 217–218.

Such breakdowns are useful in assessing the nature and significance of changes in the totals. For example, a sharp rise in the totals for unemployment and unemployment rate, if concentrated among teenagers and new entrants to the labor force, may reflect a rise in the natural rate of unemployment based on demographic factors rather than a movement toward cyclical recession.

The Consumer Price Index

The *consumer price index* reflects prices of goods and services purchased by urban consumers and relates to a "market basket" of about 400

Table 3-7

U.S. Unemployment Subaggregates, 1978 (Persons 16 Years of Age and Older)

	Thousands of Persons	Percent of Unemployed
Total civilian unemployment	6,047	100.0
Duration (average duration in weeks = 11.9)		
Less than 5 weeks	2,793	46.2
5–14 weeks	1,875	31.0
15–26 weeks	746	12.3
27 weeks and over	633	10.5
Reason		
Lost job	2,514	41.6
Left job	851	14.1
Reentering workforce	1,814	30.0
Entering workforce for first time	867	14.3

Subtotals may not add to totals because of rounding.
Source: President's Council of Economic Advisers, *Economic Report of the President* (Washington, D.C.: Government Printing Office, 1979), pp. 219–220.

items selected to represent the purchases of these consumers. It is an explicit rather than an implicit price index, being a weighted average of the prices charged for these items, with the weights selected from a base period in the past. The basic data for the index are collected from more than 50,000 reporters located in eighty-five urban centers across the United States. Food and fuel prices are collected monthly in all cities, while most other items are collected monthly in the five largest cities and bi-monthly elsewhere. The reporters include food stores, other retail stores, rental units, and homeowners. The Bureau of Labor Statistics of the Department of Labor maintains the index.

Until 1978, the consumer price index pertained to prices paid by urban wage earners and clerical workers only. Beginning in January 1978, it has presented a revised version of that series plus a broader series reflecting prices paid by urban consumers as a whole. The broader series adds salaried workers, self-employed workers, retirees, and unemployed persons.

The consumer price index is more widely known than the GNP implicit price deflator, and more widely reported. One reason for this is that it relates more closely to the cost of living facing consumers. It reflects prices of consumer goods and services only, and it includes prices of imports. Of course, the implicit price deflator for personal consumption expenditures from the national income accounts could provide that information; the major advantage of the consumer price index is that it is available monthly rather than quarterly. Also, it provides subaggregate price indexes for food, housing, apparel, transportation, medical care, and entertainment, whereas the implicit price deflator for personal consumption expenditures breaks down its data only into subtotals for consumer durable goods, consumer nondurable goods, and consumer services. Separate consumer price indexes are available for the large urban centers.

The consumer price index has recorded a higher inflation rate than the implicit price deflator for consumption expenditures during recent years. The consumer price index rose 44.9 percent from 1972 to 1977, while the implicit price deflator for consumption expenditures rose by 40.7 percent over the same five-year period. Most of this discrepancy reflects differences in items covered and differences in definitions of items covered.[3] As an example of a difference in items covered, the implicit price deflator for consumption expenditures includes prices on purchases by private nonprofit institutions, whereas the consumer price index does not. An example of a difference in the definition of an item covered is that the consumer price index treats prices on purchases of new automobiles as net of trade-in value, whereas the implicit price deflator uses the full retail value.

In part, however, the higher inflation rate for the consumer price index reflects the fact that it draws its quantity weights from past years when it weights items as to importance, while the implicit price deflator for consumption expenditures uses current-period quantity weights. If purchasers are shifting away from the items on which prices have increased the most, on balance, an index which employs back-year weights will record a higher inflation rate, even if coverage and definitions are the same. This is the *index number problem.* It occurs because the index using back-year weights will weight the items on which prices have increased the most more heavily than will the index using current-period weights.

Both the consumer price index and the implicit price deflator for consumption expenditures face the problem of adjusting for quality improvements. For example, prices for clothing have increased greatly since 1950, but many clothing items now include a permanent press feature not generally available in 1950. How much of the increase in clothing prices is

---

[3] U.S. Department of Commerce, Bureau of Economic Analysis, "Reconciliation of Quarterly Changes in Measures of Prices Paid by Consumers," *Survey of Current Business* 58 (March 1978): 6–9.

a pure price increase and how much reflects payment for a quality change which is a considerable advantage in terms of time and trouble? Similarly, how much of the increase in the price of an airplane fare from New York to Los Angeles since 1950 reflects inflation and how much reflects the quality improvement of halving the time spent in the air? Price indexes that include items on which quality has improved but that underadjust for the quality improvement overstate the inflation rate.

Does the consumer price index overstate the inflation rate significantly? Some observers believe that it does, noting the higher inflation rate it displays as compared to the implicit price deflator for consumption expenditures and the possibility that it underadjusts for quality improvements. Any serious overstatement of the inflation rate by the consumer price index is a matter for concern. The index is one of the targets for stabilization policies and the guideline for cost-of-living increments in social security benefits and other contracts. An overstating of the inflation rate by the index could result in overly restrictive stabilization policies in the first role and in a built-in inflation aggravator in the second.

Summary

1. The U.S. national income accounts are the basic source of statistical measurements of aggregate U.S. output, prices, expenditures, and income and for the major expenditure and income subaggregates. The measurements are available on a quarterly and an annual basis. Historical data begin with 1929. The Bureau of Economic Analysis of the Department of Commerce prepares and publishes the data.

2. The Bureau of Labor Statistics of the Department of Labor provides monthly statistics concerning the U.S. labor force, employment and unemployment levels, and the unemployment rate. Subaggregates for the unemployment rate, categorized by race, sex, age, and other characteristics, are available. Subaggregates for unemployment are also available and indicate duration of unemployment and reason for unemployment.

3. The Bureau of Labor Statistics also maintains the consumer price index, which reflects prices paid for goods and services purchased by U.S. urban consumers. Unlike the national income account price indexes, it is available monthly.

Concepts for Identification

gross national product
final goods and services
intermediate goods
consumer durable goods
current dollars
constant dollars
imputation
consumption expenditures
gross private domestic investment
government purchases of goods and services
government transfer payments
net exports
consumer durable goods
change in business inventories
personal income
disposable personal Income
national income
net national product
indirect business taxes
capital consumption allowances
proprietors' income
civilian labor force
consumer price index
index number problem

Questions and Problems for Review

1. When the gross national product estimate for the United States is built up from the expenditure side, expenditures for:
a. intermediate product,
b. used cars,
c. newly issued bonds of private corporations, and
d. automobiles newly produced in Japan but purchased by U.S. residents
are not included, except the broker and dealer commissions and fees involved. However:
e. wage and salary payments to government workers,
f. the imputed value of meals provided free to waiters and waitresses as part of their compensation, and
g. the broker and dealer commissions and fees incurred in purchases of securities, real estate, used cars, and the like
are included. Explain why each item is included or excluded.

2. Why is the price index for GNP from the national income accounts referred to as the *implicit* price deflator for GNP?

3. GNP in current dollars was \$286.2 billion for 1950 and \$506.0 billion for 1960. The implicit price deflator for GNP was 53.64 for 1950 (1972 =

100) and 68.67 for 1960. What was the percent increase in output and real income (constant dollar GNP) from 1950 to 1960?

4. GNP in current dollars was $506.0 billion for 1960 and $982.4 billion for 1970. GNP in constant 1972 dollars was $736.8 billion for 1960 and $1,075.3 billion for 1970. What was the percent increase in prices from 1960 to 1970 as reflected by the implicit price deflator for GNP?

5. An automobile was produced in Detroit during 1978 and ended the year in a dealer inventory. It was sold to a final consumer for personal use in February 1979. Indicate the impact of this sequence of events on GNP, gross private domestic investment, and personal consumption expenditures for 1978 and 1979. Is this a sensible treatment from the standpoint of relating to the behavior of aggregate output, employment, and personal consumption expenditures? Why or why not?

6. The U.S. national income accounts for a certain year include the following hypothetical entries:
a. gross private domestic investment = $290 billion,
b. personal income = $1,700 billion,
c. capital consumption allowances = $200 billion,
d. business transfer payments = $10 billion,
e. net exports = $20 billion,
f. personal transfer payments to foreigners = $1 billion,
g. personal consumption expenditures = $1,380 billion,
h. personal tax and nontax payments = $250 billion,
i. subsidies less current surplus of government enterprises = $5 billion,
j. government purchases of goods and services = $310 billion,
k. interest paid by consumers to business = $19 billion,
l. indirect business tax and nontax liability = $150 billion,
m. statistical discrepancy = $5 billion.
Using this information, compute the values for:
a. gross national product,
b. net national product,
c. national income,
d. disposable personal income, and
e. personal saving.

7. Give several examples of persons who may regard themselves as working but who are not counted as members of the civilian labor force by the Department of Labor. Give examples of persons who might regard themselves as unemployed but who would not be counted as unemployed in official statistics.

8. The inflation rate reflected by the consumer price index for recent years has been higher than that reflected by the implicit price deflator for personal consumption expenditures from the national income accounts. Discuss the reasons for this.

References

Ackley, Gardner. *Macroeconomics: Theory and Policy.* New York: Macmillan, 1978, chaps. 2 and 3.

Bailey, M. J. *National Income and the Price Level: A Study in Macroeconomic Theory.* New York: McGraw-Hill, 1971, chap. 12.

U.S. Department of Commerce, Bureau of Economic Analysis. *The National Income and Product Accounts of the United States, 1929–74.* Washington, D.C.: Government Printing Office, 1976.

U.S. Department of Commerce, Bureau of Economic Analysis. "Reconciliation of Quarterly Changes in Measures of Prices Paid by Consumers," *Survey of Current Business* 58 (March 1978): 6–9.

Part 2

The Money Market Ignored

4

A Simple Macroeconomic Model

Aggregate demand for output relative to full-employment output is a key factor in unemployment and inflation problems. When demand fails to support full-employment output, output is fixed at a lower level in the short term, and shortfall unemployment is present. If demand exceeds full-employment output, inflation occurs. The excess demand bids prices upward.

This chapter focuses on a highly simplified macroeconomic model. It contains only producer and consumer sectors—no government sector, no international sector, and no money market. Money is present, of course, providing means of payment and other services, but any effect of the markets for money and securities on the level of expenditures is ignored.

Obviously, the simplified model is incomplete, but it permits the establishment of important macroeconomic concepts in a readily understandable first approximation. It illustrates the determination of equilibrium output and income and represents unemployment and inflation situations. In addition, it is useful for demonstrating the investment multiplier concept. Subsequent chapters add government and international sectors and a money market and emerge with a fairly complete model of the type used by present-day economists for macroeconomic analysis.

Responses of Output and Prices to Aggregate Demand

The general assumption in this chapter and, for the most part, in the illustrative models throughout the book, is that responses of output and prices to demand break cleanly at full employment. If aggregate demand falls short of or just equals full-employment output, output simply adjusts to demand and prices remain constant. If aggregate demand exceeds full-employment output, output is fixed at the full-employment level, since demand will support such a level; and prices rise. Fluctuations in aggregate demand therefore provoke fluctuations in output and employment, with prices remaining constant, when they are confined to the less than full employment range; but they provoke inflation, with output fixed at full employment, when they exceed the full-employment output level.

This assumption obviously is a simplification. In the actual world, output increases slightly when aggregate demand expands at full-employment output, at least in the short term. Moreover, producers adjust prices somewhat when aggregate demand fluctuates within the range of less than full employment. Recall from Chapter 1 that U.S. consumer prices declined substantially in each of the first four years of the Great Depression and have declined by small amounts on an annual basis in two recessions since the end of World War II.

Price and Money-Wage Rigidity

Why do prices not decline when aggregate demand is short of full-employment output? Keynes's observation that worker resistance to money-wage cuts is responsible seems to be correct; money wages are an important element in production costs and therefore in prices.

Resistance may express itself in union opposition to money-wage cuts. But it extends beyond unions. Aware that workers oppose money-wage cuts, employers ordinarily are reluctant to offer them, even when not faced by strong unions, especially during the short term, when the recession may be regarded as temporary. Long-run profit considerations may suggest that inexperienced or inefficient workers be laid off instead, or even that surplus labor be carried for a time. Wage cuts may stimulate union organizing activity to a greater extent than do layoffs, particularly where the layoffs are accompanied by a commitment to recall affected workers when business improves. Wage cuts may alienate valued members of the workforce and perhaps even cause them to quit. Notice that if wage cuts are offered and workers do quit in response, output and employment still decline in the short term, just as in the layoff case, since workers who quit normally spend time in job search before acquiring new positions.

Why do workers oppose money-wage cuts? They regard them as reductions in their real wage, that is, in the purchasing power of their wage. While prices also will be declining during a recession, especially if money-wage cuts are widespread, workers may fail to perceive this in the short term. Moreover, they often fear that money-wage cuts will reduce their wages relative to those of other workers, since they cannot be sure that other workers will receive similar reductions.[1]

Why treat prices as constant when aggregate demand recovers but full employment has not yet been reached? The rationale for this is simpler. Until full employment is reached, an excess supply of labor is present. There is no excess demand for labor to bid money wages up.[2]

Equilibrium Output and Income: The Full-Employment Constraint Ignored

This section begins by ignoring the full-employment constraint on output and acting as if output could adjust fully to any level of demand. The equilibrium condition, therefore, is:

$$Y = E, \qquad 4\text{–}1$$

where:
Y = aggregate output and real income,
E = aggregate real demand, or expenditures,

and prices will be constant.[3] The next section adds a full-employment maximum for output, compares the equilibrium of this section to it, and

[1] For a survey of recent theoretical work into the basis for wage rigidity, see R. J. Gordon, "Recent Developments in the Theory of Inflation and Unemployment," *Journal of Monetary Economics* 2 (April 1976), especially pp. 207–210.

[2] Treating prices as constant if money wages are constant neglects for the moment Keynes's view that prices vary slightly, with money wages constant, as aggregate demand fluctuates within the unemployment range. Chapter 12 examines that view.

[3] You may recall from Chapter 3 that Y always equals E in the national income accounts, since Y is obtained as the sum of the expenditures for it (and also as the sum of the incomes generated in producing it). Equation 4–1 presents $Y = E$ in a different sense. The E refers to desired expenditures rather than to actual expenditures. The economy is in equilibrium when output is just supported by the expenditures producers and consumers desire to make. The expenditures of the national income accounts, which are actual expenditures, equal actual output, whether or not the economy is in equilibrium. For example, if output exceeds desired expenditures, the excess becomes an undesired increase in inventories. Since actual expenditures include the change in business inventories, both desired and undesired, actual expenditures equal actual output.

identifies the situation as the *less than full employment case,* the *full employment with price stability case,* or the *full employment with inflation case,* depending on whether the comparison reveals a shortfall of demand, a demand exactly corresponding with full employment, or an excess of demand.

Other assumptions for this section are that:

$$E = C + I, \quad \text{4–2}$$

$$C = a_0 + bYd = 50 + 0.8Yd, \quad \text{4–3}$$

$$Yd = Y, \text{ and} \quad \text{4–4}$$

$$I = I_0 = 70, \quad \text{4–5}$$

where:
C = real consumption expenditures,
I = real investment expenditures,
Yd = real private disposable income, and
a_0 and I_0 = constants.

Equation 4–2 indicates that aggregate demand, or expenditures, is the sum of consumption and investment expenditures. Since government and foreign sectors are not included in the model, government purchases of final goods and services and net exports of goods and services do not appear as expenditures components.

In Equation 4–3, consumption expenditures depend on private disposable income and vary directly with it. Private disposable income, as Equation 4–4 indicates, is simply total income, since there is no government to levy taxes or make transfer payments. Equation 4–5 specifies investment expenditures as fixed at 70 billion dollars.

The consumption function, Equation 4–3, reflects Keynes's notion that when income changes consumption expenditures change in the same direction, but by less. It requires that changes in disposable income provoke changes in consumption expenditures equal to 0.8 of themselves, since the coefficient of Yd is $b = 0.8$. For example, if $Yd = 200$, $C = 50 + 0.8(200) = 210$. If Yd increases by 100 to 300, C increases from 210 to $C = 50 + 0.8(300) = 290$, or by 80. The ratio of the change in C to the change in Yd is $80/100 = 0.8$. If Yd now increases by an additional 200 to 500, C increases from 290 to $C = 50 + 0.8(500) = 450$, or by 160. The ratio of the change in C to the change in Yd again is 0.8, that is, $\Delta C/\Delta Yd = 160/200 = 0.8$. Table 4–1 summarizes the relationship.

Keynes called $\Delta C/\Delta Yd$ the *marginal propensity to consume.* We shall see in Chapter 4 that the statistical evidence bears out his view that its

Relationship of Consumption Expenditures and Disposable Income, Based on Equation 4–2

Table 4–1

Yd	C	ΔC/Δ*Yd*
0	50	
		80/100 = 0.8
100	130	
		80/100 = 0.8
200	210	
		80/100 = 0.8
300	290	
		160/200 = 0.8
500	450	
		160/200 = 0.8
700	610	
		160/200 = 0.8
900	770	

value falls between zero and one. The particular numbers employed in the hypothetical consumption function in this chapter, that is, $a_0 = 50$ and $b = 0.8$, were chosen for arithmetical convenience.

Y represents both output and real income in the assumptions. These items always have the same value in the model. Whenever output is produced, an equal amount of income is created for the owners of the factors which produced it. The sum of wage, salary, interest, rent, and profit income created always equals the sum of the product.

Computing the Equilibrium

Aggregate demand in the model is found by substituting Equations 4–3 through 4–5 into Equation 4–2:

$$E = C + I$$

$$E = a_0 + bYd + I_0$$

$$E = a_0 + I_0 + bY = 120 + 0.8Y. \qquad \text{4–6}$$

When that is substituted into Equation 4–1, the equilibrium for *Y* emerges as:

$$Y = E$$

$$Y = a_0 + I_0 + bY$$

$$Y - bY = a_0 + I_0$$

$$(1 - b)Y = a_0 + I_0$$

$$Y = \frac{a_0 + I_0}{1 - b} = \frac{50 + 70}{1 - 0.8} = 120/0.2 = 600. \qquad \text{4–7}$$

Checking, if $Y = 600$ is produced, consumption expenditures will be $C = 50 + 0.8(600) = 530$. Adding that to investment expenditures of 70 yields a total demand of 600. Demand supports output.

A Graphic Representation

Figure 4–1 presents the situation graphically. Total demand is represented on the vertical axis. Total output and income appear on the horizontal axis. The total-demand function, labeled $E = 120 + 0.8Y$, plots the demand forthcoming at each level of Y. For convenience, the consumption expenditure function is also plotted. The consumption line falls below the total-demand line by 70, since investment expenditures are 70. The slopes of the two lines are the same. With investment expenditures constant, both

Figure 4–1 **Equilibrium Output and Income**

Equilibrium output and income occur where the total expenditure line intersects the 45° line. When this level of output is produced, demand just supports it.

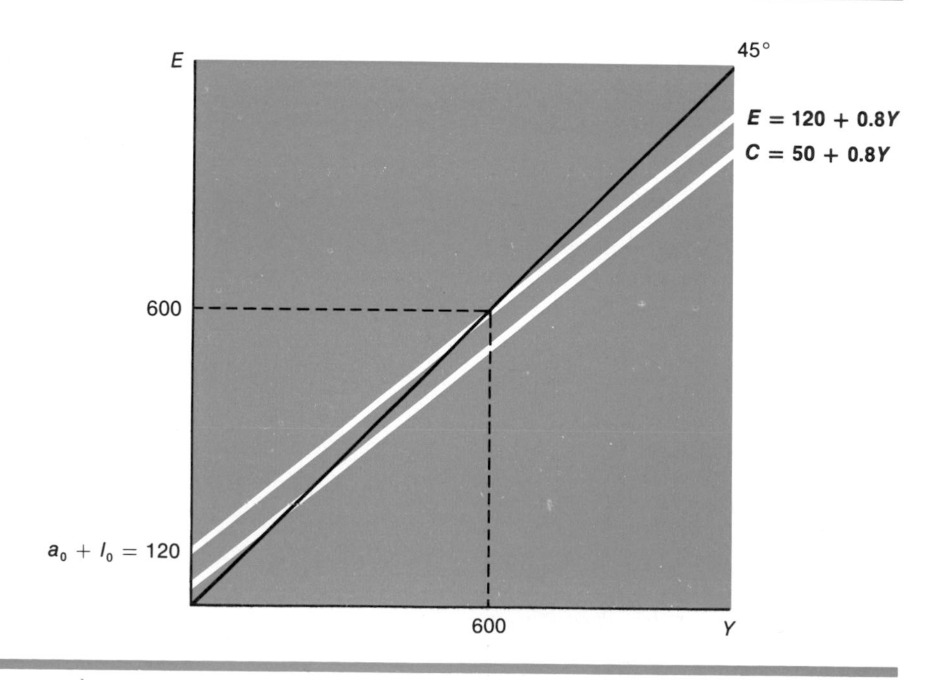

slopes equal the marginal propensity to consume for Y; that is, both $\Delta C/\Delta Y$ and $\Delta E/\Delta Y$ are $b = 0.8$.

Equilibrium output and income occur where the total demand function crosses the 45° line. Since the axes are on the same scale, Y can be read vertically to the 45° line as well as horizontally to the origin. This being the case, E and Y are equal where the total demand function and the 45° line intersect. Demand just supports output. To the left of the point of intersection, the total expenditure line lies above the 45° line, indicating that E exceeds Y. Demand more than supports these levels of output. To the right of the intersection, the 45° line lies above the total expenditure line; that is, output exceeds expenditures. Equilibrium Y occurs at the point intersection, where E just supports Y. The model is in equilibrium in the sense that Y will display no tendency to depart from this value unless the underlying conditions of the model—Equations 4–3 and 4–5—are changed or expanded.

Adding the Full-Employment Constraint

Full-employment output is represented as:

$$Y_f = 1{,}000. \qquad \text{4–8}$$

Taking it as fixed neglects the fact that it grows over time with population and labor force growth and with the capital accumulation required by positive net investment expenditures. Moreover, it is described simply as the output produced by the total labor force less workers frictionally, seasonally, or structurally unemployed (that is, less natural unemployment). Chapter 12 looks at this benchmark for full-employment output more carefully and develops it from labor market equilibrium and from the aggregate production function that relates output to labor and capital goods inputs.

A comparison of the equilibrium Y computed in the preceding section with this full-employment constraint shows that the less than full employment case exists. Whereas equilibrium Y is 600, full-employment Y is 1,000. Output therefore is determined at 600, and prices are constant. Shortfall unemployment is present.

Figure 4–2 presents the situation graphically. The total expenditure line intersects the 45° line to the left of the full-employment line, which rises vertically at $Y_f = 1{,}000$. If full-employment output, $Y_f = 1{,}000$, were pro-

Figure 4–2 **Adding the Full-Employment Constraint**
If the full-employment output of 1,000 is produced, demand will not support it, since the total expenditure line falls below the 45° line at that level of output. Equilibrium output instead is 600, and shortfall unemployment is present.

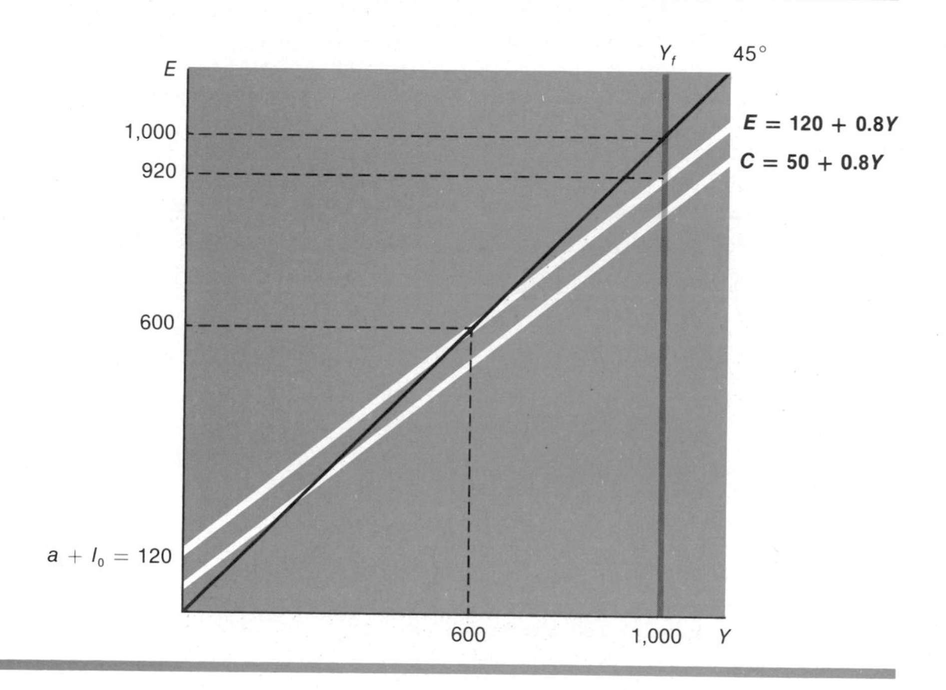

duced, demand would not support it. Total demand, from Equation 4–6 would be:

$$E = 120 + 0.8(1{,}000) = 920.$$

In the graph, the total expenditure line falls below the 45° line by 80 at $Y_f = 1{,}000$.

Notice that the equilibrium income and output is 600 rather than the 920 of demand which would be forthcoming if the full-employment output were produced. If $Y = 920$ were produced, total demand would be smaller than 920, since Y is smaller than 1,000 and demand (specifically consumption expenditures) depends on Y. Output must fall to 600 before demand will support it.

Three Situations

Figure 4–3 presents three levels of investment expenditures, three levels of total demand, and three basic situations. The same three levels for the total expenditure line could be achieved by varying the level of the consumption expenditure function.

Case 1, with $I_0 = 70$, is the less than full employment situation already examined. Demand will not support full-employment output. Output is determined instead at 600, and an unemployment problem exists.

Case 2, with $I_0 = 150$, illustrates the full employment without inflation situation. The total expenditure line and the 45° line intersect at full-employment output. Equilibrium output is:

$$Y = \frac{a_0 + I_0}{1 - b} = \frac{50 + 150}{1 - 0.8} = 200/0.2 = 1{,}000.$$

When the full-employment output of 1,000 is produced, demand, from Equation 4–6, is:

$$E = 50 + 150 + 0.8(1{,}000) = 1{,}000,$$

and just supports it. Output therefore is fixed at the full-employment level and prices are constant at the initial level.

Case 3, with $I_0 = 230$, illustrates the full employment with inflation situation—the *expenditure gap* case. The total expenditure line falls above the 45° line at the full-employment output. When $Y_f = 1{,}000$ is produced, demand, again from Equation 4–6, is:

$$E = 50 + 230 + 0.8(1{,}000) = 1{,}080,$$

yielding an expenditure gap of:

$$E - Y_f = 1{,}080 - 1{,}000 = 80.$$

Under the assumptions made earlier, output is fixed at the full-employment level, since demand will support such an output, and prices rise. This is not an equilibrium situation, of course, since prices are rising.

Notice in Figure 4–3 that the expenditure gap is the vertical distance between the total expenditure line for $I_0 = 230$ and the 45° line at the full-employment output. It is not the horizontal distance between Point A, where the total expenditure line and the 45° line intersect, and the full-

Figure 4–3 **Three Situations**

The model produces situations of shortfall unemployment, full employment with price stability, or full employment with inflation, depending on whether the total expenditure line falls below, on, or above the 45° line at the full-employment output.

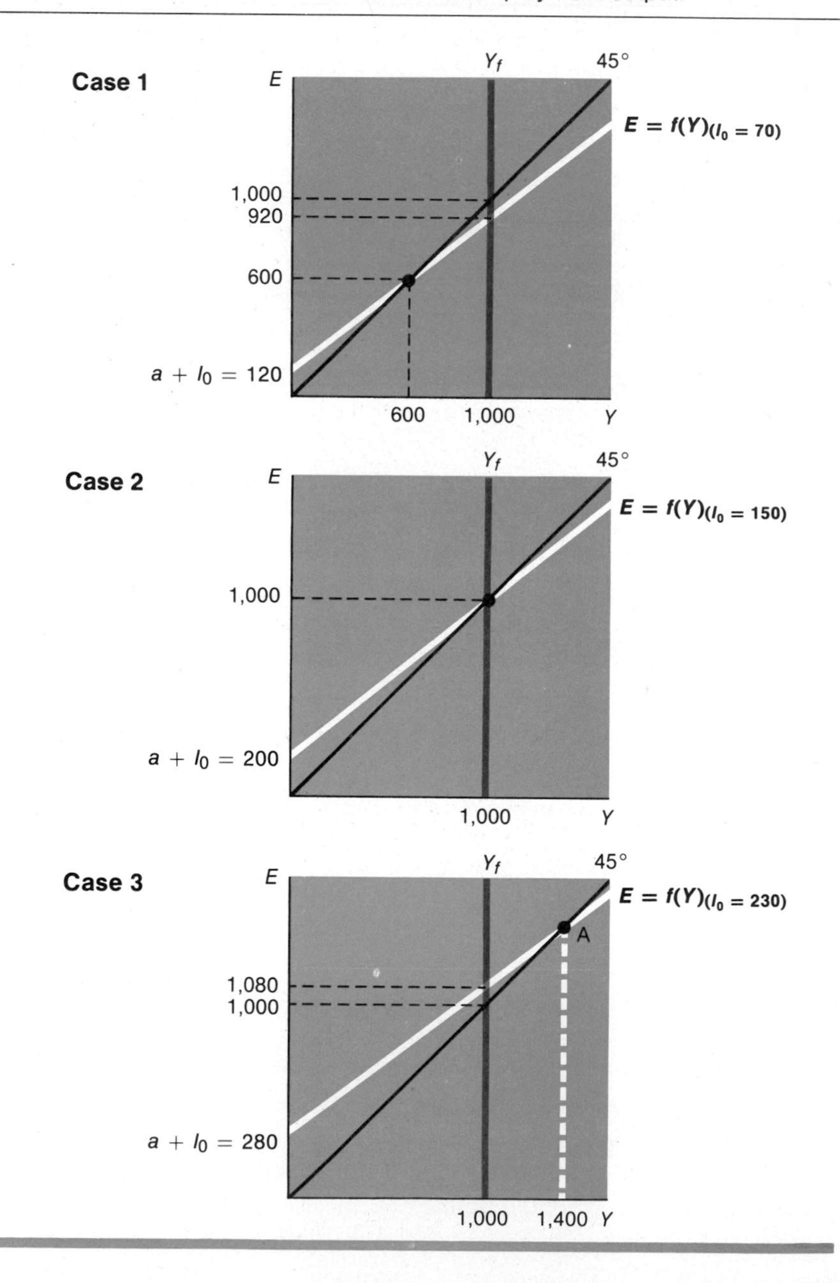

employment line. Point A, with $Y = 1{,}400$, is obtained by substituting into the $Y = E$ condition; that is, equilibrium output, from Equation 4–7, is:

$$Y = \frac{a_0 + I_0}{1 - b} = \frac{50 + 230}{1 - 0.8} = 280/0.2 = 1{,}400.$$

This can be regarded as a trial equilibrium for Y. It indicates the presence of an expenditure gap when it exceeds Y_f, the maximum for Y, but it does not measure the gap. The Y of Point A includes the C which would be forthcoming if output and income could be 1,400. But output and income cannot be 1,400 because they are restricted to $Y_f = 1{,}000$. The horizontal distance between Point A and the Y_f line overstates the expenditure gap by $0.8(400) = 320$—that is, by the C which would be present if the extra Y could be present. The expenditure gap is not 400, but 80, the excess of expenditures at the full-employment output of 1,000.

The Investment Multiplier

In the model just presented, if investment expenditures are 70 rather than 150, equilibrium output and income are 600 rather than 1,000. A decline of 80 in investment expenditures produces a decline of 400 in equilibrium output and income. Keynes described this effect with his *investment multiplier* concept. It occurs because the decline in total expenditures, to which output and income adjust, includes not just the initiating decline in investment expenditures but also the decline in consumption expenditures induced by the lower levels of output and income.

Demonstrating the investment multiplier effect in the model involves obtaining the ratio of a change in equilibrium Y to the change in I_0 provoking it and showing that the ratio is greater than 1. The ratio, that is, $\Delta Y/\Delta I_0$, is called the investment multiplier because it yields the change in equilibrium Y when it is multiplied times the change in I_0. It applies only in the less than full employment cases, where Y responds fully to changes in aggregate expenditures. For example, when I_0 increases at Y_f in the model, the change in Y is zero, since Y is already at its maximum. Prices merely rise.

To obtain $\Delta Y/\Delta I_0$, consider a case where I_0 increases from I_0' to I_0'', so that equilibrium Y increases from:

$$Y' = \frac{a_0 + I_0'}{1 - b} \tag{4–9}$$

to

$$Y'' = \frac{a_0 + I_0''}{1 - b}, \qquad \text{4–10}$$

where Y'', by assumption, does not exceed Y_f.

Subtracting Equation 4–9 from Equation 4–10 produces:

$$Y'' - Y' = \frac{a_0 + I_0''}{1 - b} - \frac{a_0 + I_0'}{1 - b} = \frac{I_0'' - I_0'}{1 - b},$$

or

$$\Delta Y = \frac{\Delta I_0}{1 - b}.$$

This reduces to:

$$\Delta Y/\Delta I_0 = \frac{1}{1 - b}, \qquad \text{4–11}$$

the investment multiplier, when divided through by ΔI_0.

$\Delta Y/\Delta I_0$ must be greater than 1, since b, the marginal propensity to consume from income, is a fraction. Notice also that the multiplier becomes larger as the marginal propensity to consume becomes larger.

Under the assumptions introduced earlier for this model, the marginal propensity to consume is 0.8, and the investment multiplier is 5; that is:

$$\Delta Y/\Delta I_0 = \frac{1}{1 - b} = \frac{1}{1 - 0.8} = 5.$$

Therefore, a reduction of 80 in I_0 produces a change in equilibrium output and income of:

$$\Delta Y = (\Delta Y/\Delta I_0)\Delta I_0 = \frac{1}{1 - b}(\Delta I_0) = 5(-80) = -400.$$

The reduction of 400 in Y equals the initiating reduction of 80 in investment expenditures plus the income-induced change in consumption expenditures of:

$$\Delta C = (\Delta C/\Delta Y)\Delta Y = 0.8(-400) = -320.$$

The Sum of Series Approach

The *sum of series* approach to obtaining the investment multiplier presents the concept in a useful perspective. It involves expressing the increase in equilibrium Y which takes place following a sustained increase in the level of investment expenditures as the sum of the increases which occur as output and income respond to demand, first in the investment goods industries and then in industries producing consumption goods and services.

Specifically, the rise in equilibrium Y is expressed as:

$$\Delta Y = \Delta I_0 + b\Delta I_0 + b^2\Delta I_0 + \ldots + b^{n-1}\Delta I_0, \quad \text{4-12}$$

where ΔI_0 is the first-round rise in output in the investment goods industries, $b\Delta I_0$ is the second-round response, which raises output in the consumption industries, and $b^2\Delta I_0$ and so on are the subsequent rounds of output increases in the consumption industries. The contribution to the rise in equilibrium Y in the second round, for example, is $b\Delta I_0$, since b is the marginal propensity to consume from income and ΔI_0 is the rise in income provoked by the first-round increase in demand. Similarly, the contribution to the increase in equilibrium Y on the third round is $b(b\Delta I_0)$, or $b^2\Delta I_0$, since $b\Delta I_0$ is the rise in income provoked by the second-round increase in demand. Since b is a fraction, the contributions to the change

The Cumulative Response of Y to a Sustained Increase in I_0

Table 4-2

Round	ΔI_0	ΔC	ΔY
1	80.0	—	80.000
2	80.0	64.000	144.000
3	80.0	115.200	195.200
4	80.0	156.160	236.160
5	80.0	188.928	268.928
6	80.0	215.142	295.142
7	80.0	236.114	316.114
8	80.0	252.891	332.891
9	80.0	266.313	346.313
10	80.0	277.050	357.050
.	.	.	.
.	.	.	.
.	.	.	.
n	80.0	320.000	400.000

in equilibrium Y become successively smaller, eventually approaching zero on the $(n - 1)$th round, with n being a number approaching infinity.

Table 4–2 utilizes the sum of series approach to illustrate how, under the numerical assumptions made earlier, an increase in I_0 of 80, from 70 to 150, increases equilibrium output and income by 400, from 600 to 1,000. Investment expenditures must remain at the higher level, of course, if equilibrium Y is to remain at 1,000. If I_0 falls back to 70, equilibrium Y falls back to 600.[4]

A Consumption Expenditure Multiplier

While Keynes regarded investment expenditures as the volatile element in private demand, present-day economists point out that the consumption expenditure function also shifts on occasion. Consideration of this is especially important when expenditures for durable goods by consumers are treated as consumption expenditures, as they are in the U.S. national income and product accounts. Sharp increases in such expenditures seem to have occurred in the United States during 1950, for example, following the outbreak of fighting in Korea. Consumers, with memories of World War II shortages fresh in their minds, rushed to make purchases. On

---

[4] It is not difficult to move from Equation 4–12 to the multiplier statement. To do so, multiply each term in the equation by b, obtaining:

$$b\Delta Y = b\Delta I_0 + b^2\Delta I_0 + b^3\Delta I_0 + \ldots + b^n\Delta I_0. \qquad \textbf{4–12a}$$

Now subtract Equation 4–12a from Equation 4–12 and solve for ΔY, producing

$$\Delta Y - b\Delta Y = \Delta I_0 - b^n\Delta I_0$$

$$(1 - b)\Delta Y = \Delta I_0 - b^n\Delta I_0$$

$$\Delta Y = \frac{\Delta I_0}{1 - b} - \frac{b^n\Delta I_0}{1 - b}.$$

Since b is a fraction, $b^n\Delta I_0/(1 - b)$ approaches zero as n approaches infinity, leaving:

$$\Delta Y = \frac{\Delta I_0}{1 - b},$$

or

$$\Delta Y/\Delta I_0 = \frac{1}{1 - b},$$

the investment multiplier.

several occasions during the past few decades expenditures for personal automobiles have shown fluctuations unrelated to changes in disposable income.

The multiplier principle is as applicable to these shifts as to shifts in investment expenditures. Consider the consumption constant, for convenience; it is apparent that the consumption constant multiplier is the same as the investment multiplier. For example, when the consumption constant increases from a_0' to a_0'' in the model, equilibrium Y rises from:

$$Y' = \frac{a_0' + I_0}{1 - b} \tag{4-13}$$

to

$$Y'' = \frac{a_0'' + I_0}{1 - b}, \tag{4-14}$$

assuming that Y'' does not exceed Y_f. Subtracting Equation 4–13 from Equation 4–14 and dividing the result by $(a_0'' - a_0')$ produces the consumption constant multiplier of:

$$\Delta Y/\Delta a_0 = \frac{1}{1 - b}. \tag{4-15}$$

which is the same as the investment multiplier. When the consumption constant changes, of course, the change in Y is entirely a change in output of consumption goods and services. The first-round change in Y, as well as the subsequent rounds of changes, are responses to changes in consumption expenditures.

A Caution

Remember that the model used in this chapter is a highly simplified one. In the more realistic models of subsequent chapters, the investment multiplier will not necessarily be greater than 1, even for less than full employment situations. It will be dampened by taxes and transfer payments acting as functions of income and by money market effects. Still, the consumption and income relationship is an aggravating influence, taken by itself, and remains so even in the presence of other influences. The simplified model of this chapter is useful in that it clearly expresses this important macroeconomic relationship.

Summary

1. The model used in this chapter is a very simple one, containing only producer and consumer sectors and no markets for money or securities, but it has illustrated a number of important macroeconomic propositions.

2. Most important, a shortfall of aggregate demand, as compared to full-employment output, creates a less than full employment situation, at least in the short term, while an excess of demand creates inflation.

3. Impacts on aggregate output, income, and employment that are caused by fluctuations in investment expenditures or by fluctuations in the consumption function tend to be aggravated by income-induced effects on consumption expenditures, except as interrupted by the full-employment constraint. J. M. Keynes termed this the multiplier effect.

Concepts for Identification

consumption function
marginal propensity to consume
equilibrium output and income
full-employment constraint
natural unemployment
shortfall unemployment
expenditure gap
investment multiplier
sum of series approach
consumption constant multiplier

Questions and Problems for Review

1. The model in this chapter has assumed that money wages are rigid downward in the short term. They do not decline in the presence of a shortfall of aggregate demand. What basis was given for this assumption? Is it an appropriate assumption in terms of real world behavior?

2. Construct a table similar to Table 4–1 to demonstrate that the marginal propensity to consume from private disposable income is constant at 0.9 for the hypothetical aggregate consumption function $C = 50 + 0.9Yd$.

3. Using a graph (but no numbers) and a model similar to the one introduced in this chapter, illustrate a full employment with price stability

situation. Employ the graph to illustrate the effect of a decline in investment expenditures on equilibrium output and real income.

4. Consider a situation where $C = 50 + 0.9Yd$, $I_0 = 40$, $Y = Yd$, and $E = C + I$.

a. Construct a table showing the value of E for the Y values 0, 200, 400, 600, 800, 1,000, and 1,200.

b. Verify that the equilibrium value for Y, without considering a full-employment constraint, is 900.

c. If full-employment output is $Y_f = 1{,}000$, is this a shortfall unemployment, a full employment with price stability, or a full employment with inflation situation?

d. Illustrate the situation graphically, using a figure such as those appearing in Figure 4–3.

5. Beginning with the situation set out in Question 3, what will be the change in equilibrium Y if I_0 declines from 40 to 30? What is the new equilibrium value for Y? Explain why the change in equilibrium Y is greater than the change in I_0.

6. Consider a situation where $C = 50 + 0.9Yd$, $I_0 = 70$, $Y = Yd$, $E = C + I$, and $Y_f = 1{,}000$.

a. Which of the three situations illustrated in Figure 4–3 occurs in this case?

b. Illustrate the situation graphically.

c. Verify that the value of the expenditure gap is 20.

d. Why is the expenditure gap smaller than the trial equilibrium for Y less Y_f?

7. Returning to the assumptions of Question 3—that is, $C = 50 + 0.9Yd$, $I_0 = 40$, $Y = Yd$, $E = C + I$, and $Y_f = 1{,}000$—what will be the change in equilibrium Y if the consumption constant increases from 50 to 55? Is the impact on equilibrium Y different if the disturbance is instead an increase in I_0 from 40 to 45? Is the impact on the equilibrium value for C the same in the two cases?

8. Using the assumptions from Question 6, with the consumption constant back at 50 and I_0 back at 40, construct a table similar to Table 4–2 showing the cumulative change in Y for the first ten rounds following an increase in the consumption constant from 50 to 60. Which of the three situations illustrated in Figure 4–3 occurs in the new equilibrium in this case?

References

Feldstein, M. "Temporary Layoffs in the Theory of Unemployment." *Journal of Political Economy* 84 (October 1976): 937–959.

Goodwin, Richard M. "The Multiplier." In *The New Economics,* ed. Seymour E. Harris. New York: Knopf, 1947, pp. 482–499.

Gordon, Donald F. "A Neo-classical Theory of Keynesian Unemployment." *Economic Inquiry* 12 (December 1974): 431–459.

Gordon, R. J. "Recent Developments in the Theory of Inflation and Unemployment." *Journal of Monetary Economics* 2 (April 1976): 185–219.

Keynes, John Maynard. *The General Theory of Employment, Interest, and Money.* New York: Harcourt, Brace, 1936, chaps. 2–3, 8–10.

Machlup, Fritz. "Period Analysis and Multiplier Theory." *Quarterly Journal of Economics* 54 (November 1939): 1–27.

Morley, Samuel A. *Inflation and Unemployment.* 2d ed. Hinsdale, Ill.: Dryden Press, 1979, chap. 3.

Okun, A. "Inflation: Its Mechanics and Welfare Costs." *Brookings Papers on Economic Activity* 2 (1975): 351–390.

Samuelson, Paul A. "The Simple Mathematics of Income Determination." In *Income, Employment and Public Policy, Essays in Honor of Alvin H. Hansen.* New York: W. W. Norton, 1948, pp. 133–155.

5
Consumption Expenditures

The proportion of aggregate income consumed has remained relatively constant as income has grown over time. However, it tends to rise as the economy moves into recession and decline during cyclical recoveries, since consumption adjusts less at first to changes in income than will be the case eventually.

Chapter 4 employed a consumption function with income as the determinant of consumption expenditures. The marginal propensity to consume from income was specified as a positive fraction and identified as the key factor in the strength of the simple multiplier effect. As the marginal propensity to consume becomes larger the simple multiplier effect becomes larger. Beyond that, little was said about the determinants of consumption expenditures.

This chapter takes a closer look. The next section focuses on the question of whether the proportion of aggregate income consumed tends to diminish in the long term as income increases. Keynes suggested that it does diminish, but the modern view is that it tends to remain constant.

The closing section of the chapter examines the relationship between short-term and long-term consumption functions. It notes that the more modern theories of the consumption function agree with Keynes's view that the marginal propensity to consume from income is smaller in the short term than in the long term and reviews the explanations which have been offered as to why the short-term value is smaller. Representative values for the long-term and short-term marginal propensities to consume are presented.

The Long-Term Consumption Function

Keynes argued that the marginal propensity to consume from income is a positive fraction, as noted earlier. Beyond this, he suggested that the proportion of income consumed, C/Yd, often called the *average propensity to consume,* declines over time as income increases, both for the individual spending unit and for the aggregate of spending units. This occurs, he argued, because providing for the basic necessities consumes a larger proportion of income when income is low. With the real income of spending units increasing over time, spending units consume smaller proportions of their incomes and the aggregate average propensity to consume declines.[1]

In Keynes's view, therefore, the long-term consumption and income relationship, when approximated by a straight line, appears as in Figure 5–1. It takes on the general characteristics of the consumption function presented in Chapter 4, although that actually was a short-term consumption function, designed to explain and analyze cyclical economic behavior. The slope of the line is positive, though less than that of the 45° line, reflecting the positive but fractional marginal propensity to consume. The intercept with the vertical axis is above the origin, reflecting the diminishing average propensity to consume. When the intercept is positive, that is, when the term a_0 in the consumption equation:

$$C = a_0 + bYd \tag{5–1}$$

is greater than zero, C/Yd diminishes as Yd increases. Table 5–1 illustrates this with selected values for C, Yd, and C/Yd drawn from the numerical consumption function $C = 50 + 0.8Yd$ plotted in Figure 5–1.[2]

Figure 5–2 presents a consumption function with a constant average propensity to consume, for contrast. When the linear consumption func-

[1] John Maynard Keynes, *The General Theory of Employment, Interest, and Money* (New York: Harcourt, Brace, 1936), pp. 96–97.

[2] Dividing Equation 5–1 through by Yd produces the average propensity to consume $C/Yd = a_0/Yd + b$. This diminishes as Yd increases if a_0 is greater than zero.

Figure 5–1 **The Average Propensity to Consume Diminishing as Income Increases**

The average propensity to consume diminishes as income increases along a linear approximation to the consumption expenditure and income relationship which has a positive intercept with the vertical axis.

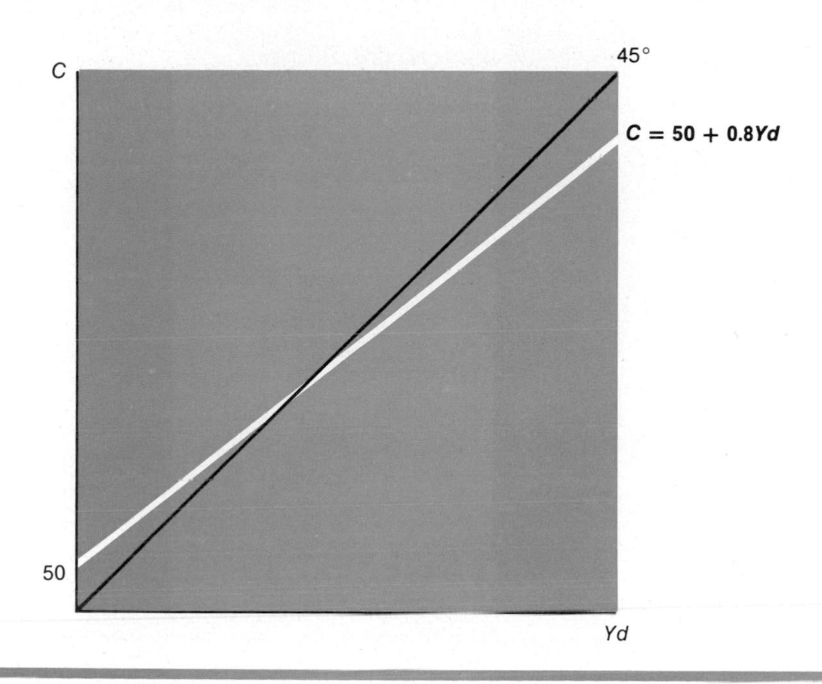

Selected Values for *C, Yd,* and *C/Yd* from the equation C = 50 + 0.80*Yd*

Table 5–1

Y	C	C/Yd
200	210	1.050
400	370	0.925
800	690	0.863

tion passes through the origin, a_0 is zero. Consequently, the consumption function reduces to:

$$C = bYd, \qquad \text{5–2}$$

and C/Yd is constant at b for all values of Yd. Table 5–2 demonstrates this with values for C, Yd, and C/Yd drawn from the numerical function plotted

Figure 5–2 **The Average Propensity to Consume Remaining Constant as Income Increases**

The average propensity to consume is constant as income increases along a linear approximation to the consumption function which passes through the origin.

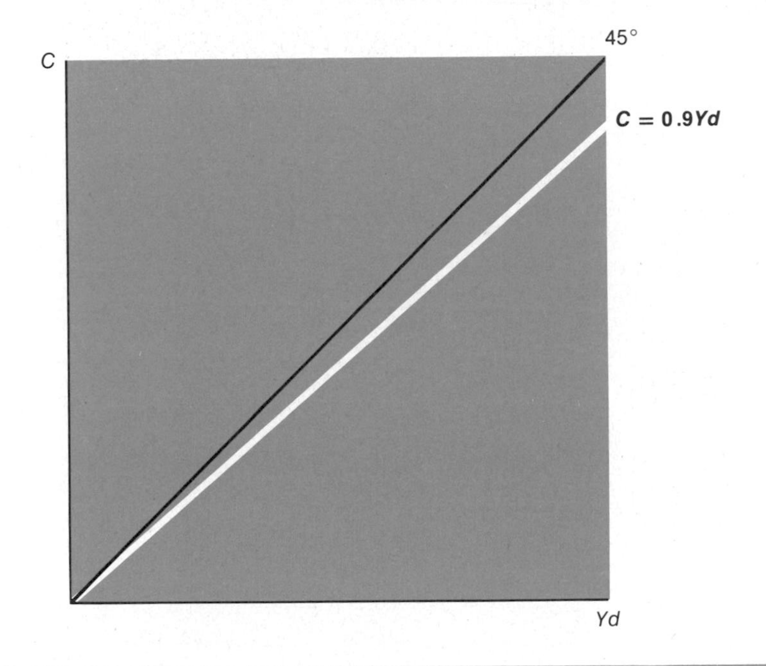

in Figure 5–2. The relationship between C and Yd is proportionate in this case in the sense that a given percent change in Yd provokes an equal percent change in C.[3]

Keynes's view of a diminishing average propensity to consume troubled the economists of the World War II years. If consumption expenditures grow less than in proportion to income as full-employment output and income grow over time, the other components of aggregate expenditures must grow faster than full-employment income if full-employment aggregate expenditures are to be maintained. Since most economists of the day attached dismal prospects to growth in investment expenditures, they

[3] Dividing Equation 5–2 through by Yd produces the average propensity to consume as the constant $C/Yd = b$ for this case. The average propensity to consume and the marginal propensity to consume are equal, since both are equal to b. Consequently, $C/Yd = \Delta C/\Delta Yd$, or $\Delta C/C = \Delta Yd/Yd$. The percent change in C equals the percent change in Yd.

Table 5–2

Selected Values for C, Yd, and C/Yd from the equation $C = 0.9Yd$

Y	C	C/Yd
200	180	0.9
400	360	0.9
800	720	0.9

forecast a return to depression following the war if government purchases were returned to normal peacetime levels. The choice seemed to be between a chronic deficiency in aggregate demand (Alvin Hansen's *secular stagnation*) on the one hand and relative growth in government purchases of goods and services on the other.[4]

Budget Study and Time Series Results

Does the proportion of aggregate income consumed decline as aggregate income increases? Early statistical investigations into the matter produced a puzzle. Budget studies, which examined the proportion of income consumed across the income distribution at a single point in time, revealed that households with higher incomes consumed a smaller proportion of their incomes. The average propensity to consume declined across the income distribution, seemingly supporting Keynes's view of nonproportionality. Table 5–3 illustrates this result with data drawn from a survey of income and spending patterns for 1972 and 1973. Figure 5–3 plots the data and also presents a linear consumption function fitted to them by a regression technique.[5] The positive intercept with the vertical axis is apparent in the figure.

Time series studies, which examined the ratio of aggregate consumption to aggregate income for points widely separated in time, produced a different result. Simon Kuznets, examining the behavior of the average propensity to consume over periods extending from 1869 into the mid-1900s, found that it had not declined appreciably from its nineteenth-century levels even though income had multiplied by several times.[6] Table 5–4 reveals that this result also holds for the period for which U.S. national

[4] For an exposition of the secular stagnation thesis, see Alvin Hansen, "Economic Progress and Declining Population Growth," *American Economic Review* 29 (March 1939): 1–15.

[5] For an exposition of the linear regression technique, see J. Johnston, *Econometric Methods*, 2d ed. (New York: McGraw-Hill, 1972).

[6] Simon Kuznets, *National Product since 1869* (New York: National Bureau of Economic Research, 1946), no. 46.

Table 5–3 **Consumption Expenditures and Disposable Incomes by Income Class of Spending Units, 1973**

Average After-Tax Income[a]	Average Consumption Expenses[a]	Average Propensity to Consume
$ 1,636	$ 3,039.34	1.858
3,347	3,999.69	1.195
4,252	4,531.32	1.066
5,084	5,099.71	1.003
5,928	5,724.97	0.966
6,715	6,147.90	0.916
7,911	6,921.21	0.875
9,491	7,888.79	0.831
11,485	8,889.67	0.774
14,541	10,639.26	0.732
18,370	12,591,46	0.685
30,461	16,737.95	0.549

[a] Figures are averages of after-tax incomes and consumption expenses for gross income classes. Consumption expenses do not include spending for personal insurance and gifts and contributions.

Source: U.S. Department of Labor, Bureau of Labor Statistics, *Consumer Expenditure Survey Series: Interview Survey, 1972–73,* Report 455–4 (Washington, D.C.: Government Printing Office, 1977), pp. 4–7.

income account data are available. The ratio of consumption expenditures to disposable personal income was 0.938 during the business peak year of 1929 and was 0.926 and 0.923, respectively, for 1977 and 1978, two recent business expansion years. The average propensity to consume has remained near its 1929 level though disposable personal income has more than quadrupled over the fifty-year period.

A linear consumption function fitted to the Table 5–4 data takes the form of the equation:

$$C = \$1.51 \text{ billion} + 0.91Yd. \qquad \text{5–3}$$

This function passes approximately through the origin, indicating the proportional relationship. The intercept is positive but, at $1.51 billion, is very small relative to the consumption expenditure data it describes. (The data range from $167.7 billion to $892.2 billion.) Plotted, the function very closely resembles the relationship presented in Figure 5–2.

Figure 5–3 **Consumption Expenditures and Disposable Income by Income Class of Spending Units, 1972–1973 (Thousands of Dollars)**

The proportion of income consumed becomes lower as income becomes higher, looking at average consumption expenditures and average disposable incomes, by income classes, across the income distribution.

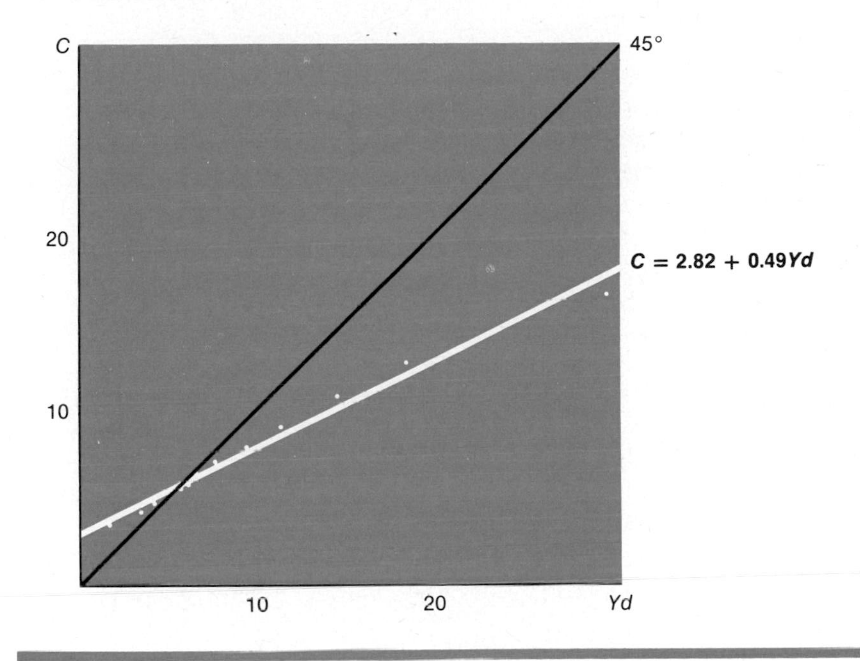

Reconciling the Budget Study and Time Series Results. Early attempts to reconcile the budget study and time series results took the approach that the proportion of income consumed does diminish in the long term as income increases, and for the reason Keynes cited, but that the aggregate average propensity to consume is sustained by factors other than income. These factors stimulated consumption and shifted the consumption and income relationship upward over time. For example, the federal debt grew rapidly relative to aggregate income during the 1930s and early 1940s. Perhaps this stimulated consumption expenditures during those years by causing households to feel wealthier. The top of the U.S. income distribution appears to have leveled somewhat towards the middle during the same period. Perhaps this raised the aggregate

Table 5-4

U.S. Personal Consumption Expenditures and Disposable Personal Income in 1972 Dollars and the Average Propensity to Consume, 1929–1978

Year	Personal Consumption Expenditures	Disposable Personal Income	Average Propensity to Consume
1929	$207.5	$222.3	0.938
1930	193.8	205.2	0.938
1931	187.4	197.3	0.943
1932	170.4	169.9	0.997
1933	167.7	165.6	1.006
1934	175.6	177.7	0.981
1935	186.6	194.5	0.952
1936	205.7	219.0	0.933
1937	212.7	226.9	0.935
1938	208.4	211.9	0.976
1939	220.3	230.1	0.957
1940	230.4	244.3	0.943
1941	244.1	278.1	0.878
1942	241.7	317.3	0.762
1943	248.7	332.2	0.749
1944	255.7	343.9	0.744
1945	271.4	338.6	0.802
1946	301.4	332.4	0.907
1947	306.2	318.8	0.960
1948	312.8	335.5	0.932
1949	320.0	336.1	0.952
1950	338.1	361.9	0.934
1951	342.3	371.6	0.921
1952	350.9	382.1	0.918
1953	364.2	397.5	0.916
1954	370.9	402.1	0.922
1955	395.1	425.9	0.928
1956	406.3	444.9	0.913
1957	414.7	453.9	0.914
1958	419.0	459.0	0.913
1959	441.5	477.4	0.925
1960	453.0	487.3	0.930
1961	462.2	500.6	0.923
1962	482.9	521.6	0.926
1963	501.4	539.2	0.930
1964	528.7	577.3	0.916
1965	558.1	612.4	0.911
1966	586.1	643.6	0.911
1967	603.2	669.8	0.901

Table 5–4
Continued

Year	Personal Consumption Expenditures	Disposable Personal Income	Average Propensity to Consume
1968	633.4	695.2	0.911
1969	655.4	712.3	0.920
1970	668.9	741.6	0.902
1971	691.9	769.0	0.900
1972	733.0	801.3	0.915
1973	767.7	854.7	0.898
1974	760.7	842.0	0.903
1975	774.6	859.7	0.901
1976	819.4	890.1	0.921
1977	857.7	926.3	0.926
1978	891.2	965.5	0.923

Source: The data for personal consumption expenditures and disposable personal income are from President's Council of Economic Advisers, *Economic Report of the President* (Washington, D.C.: Government Printing Office, 1972), pp. 196, 213, 220, 247; and *Economic Report of the President* (1979), pp. 184, 208, 214, 239. The data for 1929–1938 were in 1958 dollars in the source but are presented here adjusted to 1972 dollars.

average propensity to consume, since average propensities to consume may be higher for lower income groups. The percentage of the U.S. population in the young adult and retirement age groups increased sharply during the 1960s. Perhaps this raised the aggregate average propensity to consume slightly during that decade, since those age groups tend to have higher average propensities to consume than the middle-aged group. Urbanization may have been a factor. Urban households tend to spend a greater proportion of their incomes than rural households, other things being the same.

Modern Theories of Consumption

The problem with reconciling the budget study and time series results with these factors is the difficulty in documenting them as the causes of the substantial and continuous upward shift in the consumption and income relationship the data require. Of the factors noted, only urbanization shows a sustained trend dating back to 1869, the beginning date for the Kuznets studies. Milton Friedman, making rough estimates, has argued that urbanization could have produced an increase of 0.02 at most in the aggregate average propensity to consume from 1900 to 1949. Even this increase, he says, was most likely offset by the effects of a concurrent decline in the average size of the U.S. family.[7]

The more modern theories of the consumption function take an opposite approach. They see an automatic tendency for the aggregate average propensity to consume to remain constant in the long term as income increases and reconcile the budget study results with such behavior. The more modern approaches include James S. Duesenberry's *relative income theory;* the *life cycle theory* of Albert Ando, Franco Modigliani, and Richard Brumberg; and Milton Friedman's *permanent income theory.* Duesenberry's theory requires a constant distribution of income for the constant long-term average propensity to consume result. The Ando-Modigliani-Brumberg theory and the Friedman theory require that property net worth grow in proportion to income as income grows over time and that the interest rate remain trendless over time. The reassuring feature of the modern theories, as compared to Keynes's view, is that they offer no compelling reason why the aggregate average propensity to consume should decline as aggregate income grows over time.

The Relative Income Theory

Duesenberry's relative income theory begins with the assertion that in the long term the proportion of its income a household consumes depends on its income relative to those of other households.[8] Position in the income distribution is the key factor. The average propensity to consume increases across the income distribution, from higher to lower incomes, because households emulate the spending patterns of higher-income households. The budget study result reflects a "keeping up with the Joneses" effect.

But suppose aggregate income changes, with the incomes of all households changing proportionately. The average propensity to consume of each household and the aggregate average propensity to consume remain unchanged, because relative incomes are unchanged. This produces the constant average propensity to consume of the time series result. The time series data, then, reflect a situation where aggregate income has grown over time and the distribution of income has remained largely unchanged.

The relative income theory can be illustrated with figures from Table

[7] Milton Friedman, *A Theory of the Consumption Function* (Princeton, N.J.: Princeton University Press, 1957), pp. 120–123.

[8] James S. Duesenberry, *Income, Saving, and the Theory of Consumer Behavior* (Cambridge, Mass.: Harvard University Press, 1949).

5–3. If the income of an individual household increases from $5,928 to $9,491, an increase of 60.1 percent, with the incomes of all other households unchanged, the average propensity to consume of the household will diminish from 0.966 to 0.831, assuming its behavior is typical. But if its income increases by the same amount and the incomes of all other households also increase by 60.1 percent, its average propensity to consume will remain at 0.966. The average propensities to consume of all of the households will remain unchanged in this situation; thus, the associated aggregate average propensity to consume will be unchanged.

The Life Cycle Theory

The life cycle theory was first offered by Franco Modigliani and Richard Brumberg in a joint paper and later updated and extended by Albert Ando and Modigliani in a second paper.[9] Under the theory, individuals schedule consumption according to the total resources they expect to have over the life cycle rather than according to current-period income only. Total resources include current and future labor income and also current net worth of property, which represents current and future property income. In the strict version of the theory, property net worth is consumed during the life cycle. No provision is made for an estate to be passed on to heirs.

Figure 5–4 illustrates the consumption and income streams for a typical individual under the life cycle theory. Since income ordinarily is higher during the middle working years than during the young adult and retirement years, the consumption stream is smoothed relative to the income stream.

This relationship provides a ready explanation for the budget study result. The figure shows that individual average propensities to consume will be higher during the young adult and retirement years than during middle age, because of the smoothing of the consumption stream relative to the income stream. Since individuals in the young adult and retirement years tend to have lower than average incomes at any point in time, they cluster toward the low end of the income distribution, and average propensities to consume tend to be higher at that end.

How does the life cycle theory explain the constant average propensity to consume of the time series result? It simply assumes that the utility

[9] Franco Modigliani and Richard Brumberg, "Utility Analysis and the Consumption Function: An Interpretation of Cross-Section Data," in *Post-Keynesian Economics,* ed. Kenneth K. Kurihara (New Brunswick, N.J.: Rutgers University Press, 1954), pp. 388–436; and Albert Ando and Franco Modigliani, "The 'Life Cycle' Hypothesis of Saving: Aggregate Implications and Tests," *American Economic Review* 53 (March 1963): 55–84.

Figure 5–4 **Life Cycle Income and Consumption**

According to the life cycle theory, consumption depends on life cycle income rather than exclusively on current income. For the typical spending unit, utility maximization involves smoothing the consumption stream relative to the income stream, since income tends to be higher in middle age than during the young adult and retirement years.

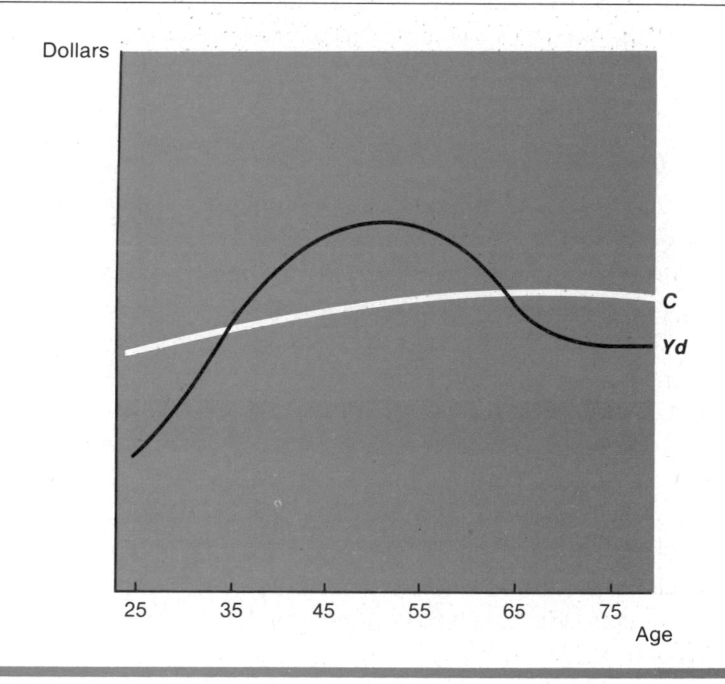

functions of individuals are such that the consumption they plan for each remaining year of their life cycle, including the current one, is proportionate to the total resources they anticipate over their remaining life cycle. When income changes, individuals do not immediately regard life cycle total resources as changing proportionately, but they will gain such a perception eventually if the change in income is maintained. Hence, consumption will eventually change proportionately to income.

Actually, in the strict version of the life cycle theory, individuals do regard future income from labor as changing proportionately with current period income from labor immediately. It is the property net worth component of life cycle total resources which is not perceived as varying proportionately with current period income. But property net worth tends to grow proportionately to labor income over time, where the interest rate is trendless. Property income is also growing in proportion to property net worth and labor income in this situation, since property income is the yield on property net worth. Therefore, a change in income does ultimately involve a proportionate change in total resources and consumption.

The Permanent Income Theory

Milton Friedman's permanent income theory is similar to the Ando-Modigliani-Brumberg life cycle theory in that it sees consumption as depending on a more permanent form of income than current period income. Also, like the life cycle theory, it deals with consumption rather than consumption expenditures. Consumption differs from consumption expenditures in that it includes only the consumption (or depreciation) of consumer durable goods rather than the total expenditures for them. The long-term movements of the two series are very similar, of course.

Under Friedman's theory, planned consumption depends on permanent income rather than actual income. *Permanent income* is the component of actual income regarded by the spending unit as reflecting its basic earnings potential and as arising from its property net worth and its personal attributes (such as skills and personality).[10] Since these same factors determine life cycle income, the permanent income and life cycle theories obviously are very similar in overall approach.

Formally, the theory separates actual consumption and income in the current period into *permanent* and *transitory* components. For income, the permanent component is as defined above, while the transitory component reflects deviations from permanent income arising from such things as illness, weather, and cyclical movements in economic activity. Permanent consumption is essentially planned consumption, at least planned in the sense of the longer-term scheme of things, while transitory consumption reflects unexpected expenditures arising from sickness, accidents, and the like.

Friedman assumes that the utility functions of individual spending units are such that permanent consumption bears a proportionate relationship to permanent income, if other factors affecting consumption are constant. The consumption equation for the individual spending unit is:

$$Cp + k(r, w, u)Yp, \qquad 5\text{–}4$$

where Cp and Yp are current-period permanent consumption and permanent disposable income and where k, the proportion of income con-

[10] Friedman, *Consumption Function,* p. 21.

sumed, depends on *r*, the rate of interest, on *w*, the ratio of property net worth to permanent income, and on *u*, an "other factors" variable which reflects such things as tastes and preferences, age, family size, and urban-rural designation. Aggregated, this produces the time series result of a fairly constant aggregate average propensity to consume, since transitory movements in consumption and income tend to cancel out in the long term, and since other factors, including the interest rate and the ratio of property net worth to permanent income, tend to be trendless over time.

Friedman, like the pre-Keynesian economists, sees *k*, and therefore consumption, as varying inversely with the interest rate. (This relationship is considered more carefully in Chapter 7.) He sees consumption as varying directly with *w*. This occurs because property net worth is fairly liquid in many of its forms and offers a better reserve for meeting unforeseen needs for funds than does expected future income from labor.

How does Friedman reconcile the constant long-term aggregate average propensity to consume with the budget study result of a diminishing average propensity to consume across the income distribution? He points out that, moving across the income distribution for a normal year, low income spending units who believe that their permanent incomes exceed their actual incomes will outnumber those who believe that the opposite is the case. The reverse will be true among high income spending units, and middle income units will be divided roughly equally between the two attitudes. Since consumption depends on permanent income, a cross-section of the income distribution, relating actual consumption to actual income, will show average propensities to consume declining as income rises. This explanation can incorporate the life cycle explanation, since many of the households with temporarily low incomes can be thought of as spending units in the low income years of the life cycle, and vice versa. But Friedman's explanation goes beyond that. It encompasses situations in which spending units are receiving actual incomes above or below their permanent incomes because of such things as good or bad fortune.

Relationship of Short-Term and Long-Term Consumption Functions

Keynes suggested that the change in consumption provoked by a change in income would be smaller at first than subsequently.[11] In effect, the

[11] Keynes, *General Theory*, p. 97.

marginal propensity to consume from income would be smaller in the short term than in the long term. The time series data offer some support for this view, and the more modern theories of the consumption function have accepted it. The aggregate average propensity to consume rose during each of the five recessions that took place from 1929 through 1954 and during two of the four subsequent recessions, instead of remaining constant in the manner of the long-term relationship.[12] In the case of the two exceptions (1958 and 1970), a decline in the consumption expenditures and disposable income relationship could have been a contributing factor to the recessions.

Figure 5–5 shows the smaller short-term marginal propensity to consume graphically by plotting short-term and long-term consumption functions. The short-term function is flatter, to reflect the smaller short-term marginal propensity to consume. When private disposable income declines from Yd', the short-term decline in consumption expenditures (perhaps occurring within the same year) is read from the short-term function, and the new Yd substituted in. The eventual response in consumption expenditures, after the full adjustment in spending is made, occurs along the long-term function.

Why is the short-term marginal propensity to consume smaller? Keynes argued that it is smaller because spending is influenced for a time by the habitual standard of life. Duesenberry formalized this effect as a second aspect of his relative income theory, stipulating that, when the economy moves into recession, consumption expenditures are sustained by the past peak income achieved. If the distribution of income is constant, the proportion of income consumed is constant as the economy expands along a full-employment trend; but it rises as the economy moves into recession because it is influenced by the standard of life achieved at the past peak income. The proportion of income consumed is influenced by actual income *relative* to past peak income as the economy moves into recession and as economic activity recovers.

Friedman and Ando-Modigliani-Brumberg offer a different explanation for the smaller short-term marginal propensity to consume. According to their theories, when income changes, consumption changes by less in the short term than in the long term because permanent income, or life cycle resources, are not immediately perceived as changing in proportion to the change in current income.

[12] Of course, if consumption expenditures vary inversely with interest rates, as most modern economists believe, reductions in interest rates during these recessions could have contributed to the increases in the average propensity to consume.

Figure 5–5 **Short-Term and Long-Term Consumption Functions**

The short-term consumption function is flatter than the long-term consumption function, reflecting the smaller short-term marginal propensity to consume.

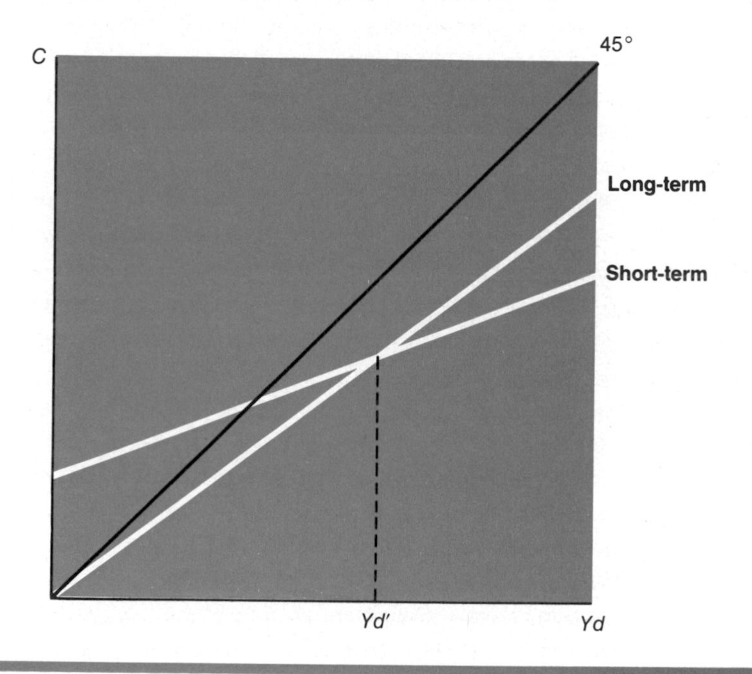

At one point in his consumption study, Friedman estimates that permanent income changes by about one-third of the change in actual income in the same year and requires sixteen additional years for full adjustment.[13] But Friedman's formulation implies that the speed of adjustment varies with the circumstances of the change in current income. The immediate response may be smaller if there is some reason for supposing the change in current income to be cyclical or temporary.

The Ando and Modigliani explanation is less flexible, at least in its strict version. Consumption fails to respond proportionately to a change in

[13] Friedman, *Consumption Function,* p. 147. The change in permanent income equals about 0.7 of the change in actual income by the end of the second year after the current year, however.

income in the short term because the property net worth component of lifetime total resources is fixed in the short term. The labor income individuals expect in future periods varies proportionately with current period labor income; but property net worth responds with a lag. Many economists criticize this formulation as understating the lags involved in expected labor income and overstating the lags for the property component. If aggregate income falls off during an economic recession, it seems unreasonable to require that individuals immediately regard the reduction in labor income as permanent and ignore completely any attending decline in property income. Another criticism of the formulation is that it does not allow for differing effects of differing circumstances.

How Large Is the Marginal Propensity to Consume?

The values estimated for the long-term marginal propensity to consume from disposable income by Friedman and Duesenberry are quite large. Friedman gives us a figure of 0.88 at one point in his study of the consumption function.[14] Duesenberry, in the earlier but still influential study setting out the relative income theory, presents a figure of 0.9. These estimates are similar to the 0.91 presented in Equation 5–3, which was obtained from a simple linear regression of consumption expenditures on disposable personal income for 1929 through 1978.

Of course, the size of the short-term marginal propensity to consume is also of interest to this book, since one of its major concerns is explaining cyclical economic fluctuations. It was for this reason that Chapter 4 employed a short-term consumption function with a positive vertical axis intercept.

A recent version of the MPS (MIT-University of Pennsylvania-Social Sciences Research Council) econometric model presents the aggregate marginal propensity to make consumption expenditures as building to the 0.6 to 0.7 range by the end of four quarters following a maintained increase in disposable personal income.[15] The consumption expenditures equation of the MPS model was evolved from the Ando and Modigliani work on the life cycle theory.

Friedman's work does not provide a direct marginal propensity to consume for consumption expenditures, since his study is in terms of

---

[14] Friedman, *Consumption Function*, p. 147.

[15] William H. Branson, *Macroeconomic Theory and Policy*, 2d ed. (New York: Harper & Row, 1979), p. 205.

consumption, which responds less sharply to changes in disposable income in the short term than do consumption expenditures. However, the short-term responses in consumption implied by Friedman's empirical work are somewhat smaller than those from the original Ando and Modigliani work, which also is in terms of consumption.

Summary

1. In the *General Theory,* J. M. Keynes suggested that the marginal propensity to consume is a positive fraction, and that it is smaller in the short term than in the long term. In addition, he suggested that the average propensity to consume diminishes over time as aggregate income grows.

2. Modern theories of the consumption function accept the first two propositions; however, they see no compelling reason why the average propensity to consume should decline over time as income grows. This is important because a diminishing average propensity to consume complicates the problem of maintaining a full-employment aggregate demand as full-employment output and real income grow over time. In Duesenberry's formulation, the average propensity to consume remains constant over time if the distribution of income remains constant. The Ando-Modigliani-Brumberg theory and the Friedman theory require a constant ratio of property net worth to income and a trendless interest rate in order for the average propensity to consume to remain constant over time.

3. The modern view on the average propensity to consume is consistent with the time series result that the average propensity to consume has not diminished appreciably over widely separated points in time, even though aggregate income has multiplied by several times. However, theories of the consumption function which incorporate a constant long-term average propensity to consume must reconcile it with the budget study result which shows that the average propensity to consume is lower for high than for low income groups at a given point in time.

4. Keynes and Duesenberry attribute the smaller short-term marginal propensity to consume to the influence of past income levels in establishing habits in spending patterns which resist change. Ando-Modigliani-Brumberg and Friedman approach it from the standpoint that consumption depends not just on current income but on life cycle resources or permanent income, which people perceive as changing by less than current income in the short term.

Concepts for Identification

average propensity to consume
marginal propensity to consume
long-term consumption function
time series result
budget study result
short-term consumption function
secular stagnation
relative income theory
past peak income
life cycle theory
permanent income

Questions and Problems for Review

1. Present a graphical representation of a linear approximation to the long-term relationship between consumption expenditures and private disposable income which conforms to J. M. Keynes's view on the matter. What happens to the average propensity to consume as income increases along this function? What rationale did Keynes offer for this behavior?

2. Explain why it might be a problem if the aggregate average propensity to consume diminishes over time as income increases.

3. Working from a table such as Table 5–1 or from footnotes 2 and 3, show that the percent change in consumption expenditures is smaller than the percent change in private disposable income with a linear consumption function if the consumption constant is positive—that is, with a consumption function such as $C = a_0 + bYd$, where $a_0 = 0$ is the case.

4. What is the difference between consumption and consumption expenditures? Which of them builds to its eventual value more slowly when a change in private disposable income occurs? Which is best suited to incorporation into the multiplier effect? Why?

5. Assume that a budget study of spending unit behavior reveals that, on the average, spending units with the disposable incomes listed below on the left make the level of consumption expenditures appearing to the right.

Yd	C
$ 4,000	$ 6,000
8,000	8,000
12,000	10,000
16,000	12,000
20,000	14,000

According to J. S. Duesenberry's relative income theory:

a. What would be the initial and eventual average propensity to consume of a typical spending unit with an income of $12,000 whose income increases to $16,000 while the income of all other spending units remained unchanged?

b. What would be the initial and eventual average propensity to consume of the spending unit if the incomes of all other spending units also increased by one-third?

Apply these experiments to explain how Duesenberry's theory reconciles the budget study and time series results on the relationship between the average propensity to consume and the level of income.

6. The Ando-Modigliani-Brumberg life cycle theory and the Friedman permanent income theory feature long-term consumption functions in which the average propensity to consume remains constant as income increases. Explain how these theories reconcile such a feature with the budget study result that the average propensity to consume diminishes as income increases.

7. According to the life cycle theory, what would happen to the aggregate average propensity to consume at each level of aggregate income as a result of a demographically based increase in the proportion of persons sixty-five years of age and over in the population? How might improvements in benefits under the social security program financed from increases in payroll taxes affect the aggregate average propensity to consume, according to the theory?

References

Ando, Albert, and Modigliani, Franco. "The 'Life Cycle' Hypothesis of Saving: Aggregate Implications and Tests." *American Economic Review* 53 (March 1963): 55–84.

Branson, William H. *Macroeconomic Theory and Policy,* 2d ed. New York: Harper & Row, 1979, chap. 10.

Duesenberry, James S. *Income, Saving, and the Theory of Consumer Behavior.* Cambridge, Mass.: Harvard University Press, 1949.

Friedman, Milton. *A Theory of the Consumption Function.* Princeton, N.J.: Princeton University Press, 1957.

Hansen, Alvin. "Economic Progress and Declining Population Growth." *American Economic Review* 29 (March 1939): 1–50.

Keynes, John Maynard. *The General Theory of Employment, Interest, and Money.* New York: Harcourt, Brace, 1936, chaps. 8–10.

Kuznets, Simon. *National Product since 1869.* New York: National Bureau of Economic Research, 1946, no. 46.

Modigliani, Franco, and Brumberg, Richard. "Utility Analysis and the Consumption Function: An Interpretation of Cross-section Data." In *Post-Keynesian Economics,* ed. Kenneth K. Kurihara. New Brunswick, N.J.: Rutgers University Press, 1954, pp. 388–436.

6

The Government Sector and Fiscal Policies

If aggregate demand is falling short of full-employment output, the government can stimulate demand and reduce unemployment by increasing government purchases, reducing taxes, or increasing transfer payments. Opposite policies can reduce demand and check inflation in situations where demand exceeds full-employment output. The government can attack structural unemployment with specialized fiscal policies such as public service employment programs and job training programs.

This chapter adds a government sector to the model introduced in Chapter 4 and employs the expanded model to demonstrate the operation of discretionary and built-in fiscal policies. The government engages in *discretionary fiscal policies* when it adjusts government purchase, tax, and transfer payment programs to ease unemployment and inflation problems. *Built-in fiscal policies* are the stabilizing effects which occur automatically as tax receipts and transfer payments vary with changes in income. In this chapter, monetary influences are once again ignored.

Discretionary Fiscal Policies

The addition of the government sector to the model proceeds with the initial assumptions that:

$$G = G_0 = 80, \tag{6-1}$$

$$Tx = Tx_0 = 200, \text{ and} \tag{6-2}$$

$$Tr = Tr_0 = 100, \tag{6-3}$$

where:

G = real government purchases of final goods and services,
Tx = real government tax receipts, and
Tr = real government transfer payments.

G includes such things as payments for typewriters for government offices, wage payments to government workers, government construction expenditures, and the like. It is a component of total demand for output, so that total demand now is:

$$E = C + I + G, \tag{6-4}$$

instead of the $E = C + I$ of Chapter 4.

Tx includes tax payments—transfers of income from the private sector to government—of all kinds. Tr, by contrast, involves the transfer of income from government to the private sector. Tr, unlike G, does not represent government payments for newly produced final goods and services. It includes such items as unemployment compensation payments, veterans' benefits, and social security benefits.

With taxes and transfer payments included in the model, private disposable income, Yd, no longer equals Y. Yd now is:

$$Yd = Y - Tx + Tr. \tag{6-5}$$

Rearranging Equation 6–5 yields:

$$Y = Yd + Tx - Tr. \tag{6-6}$$

Total income splits into Yd, the disposable income of the private sector, and $(Tx - Tr)$, the *disposable income* of the government sector.

The assumption that G, Tx, and Tr are independent of the level of income is a simplification made in this section to facilitate the illustration of discretionary fiscal policies. In the section where built-in fiscal policies are discussed, taxes are allowed to vary directly with income, and transfer payments are considered an inverse function of income. These dependencies produce the built-in fiscal policy effects.

Other assumptions remain the same as in Chapter 4. Specifically:

$$I = I_0 = 70, \quad 6\text{–}7$$

$$C = a_0 + bYd = 50 + 0.8Yd, \text{ and} \quad 6\text{–}8$$

$$Y_f = 1{,}000. \quad 6\text{–}9$$

As before, output adjusts to demand and prices remain constant if demand does not exceed full-employment output, but output is fixed at Y_f and prices rise if demand exceeds Y_f.

Equilibrium Output and Income with Government Included

Consumption expenditures now are:

$$C = a_0 + Yd$$

$$C = a_0 + b(Y - Tx + Tr)$$

$$C = a_0 + b(Y - Tx_0 + Tr_0)$$

$$C = a_0 - bTx_0 + bTr_0 + bY, \quad 6\text{–}10$$

so that total demand is:

$$E = C + I + G$$

$$E = (a_0 - bTx_0 + bTr_0 + bY) + I_0 + G_0$$

$$E = a_0 - bTx_0 + bTr_0 + I_0 + G_0 + bY. \quad 6\text{–}11$$

When the appropriate numbers are substituted into these equations, consumption expenditures are found to be:

$$C = 50 - 0.8(200) + 0.8(100) - 0.8Y$$

$$C = -30 + 0.8Y \quad 6\text{–}12$$

and total demand is:

$$E = 50 - 0.8(200) + 0.8(100) + 70 + 80 + 0.8Y$$

$$E + 120 + 0.8Y. \quad 6\text{–}13$$

Equilibrium output and real income, computed with the full-employment constraint on output ignored, are:

$$Y = E$$

$$Y = a_0 - bTx_0 + bTr_0 + I_0 + G_0 + bY$$

$$Y - bY = a_0 - bTx_0 + bTr_0 + I_0 + G_0$$

$$(1 - b)Y = a_0 - bTx_0 + bTr_0 + I_0 + G_0$$

$$Y = \frac{a_0 - bTx_0 + bTr_0 + I_0 + G_0}{1 - b} = 120/0.2 = 600. \quad \text{6–14}$$

Checking, when Y of 600 is produced, demand is:

$$E = 120 + 0.8(600) = 600,$$

consisting of consumption expenditures of:

$$C = -30 + 0.8(600) = 450,$$

investment expenditures of 70, and government purchases of 80. Demand just supports output.

Clearly, this is a less than full employment situation; the equilibrium output is 600, whereas the full-employment output is 1,000. Shortfall unemployment is present.

Figure 6–1 illustrates the situation. At $Y = 600$, the 45° line, representing output and income, intersects the demand function. If Y equaling 600 is produced, demand just supports it. For Y less than 600, E is greater than Y, since the demand line lies above the 45° line. For Y greater than 600, the demand line lies below the 45° line, indicating that demand will not support output.

Discretionary Fiscal Ease

The government can eliminate the unemployment problem described in the example just given by using *discretionary fiscal ease;* it can raise government purchases, raise transfer payments, and reduce taxes, either individually or in combination. An increase in government purchases raises the demand for output directly, since G, like investment or consumption expenditures, is itself a component of demand. An increase in transfer payments or a reduction in taxes raises private disposable in-

Figure 6–1 **Equilibrium Output with the Government Sector Included**

Equilibrium output and real income occur where the total expenditure line intersects the 45° line. The total expenditure line now incorporates government purchases and reflects the influence of taxes and transfer payments on consumption expenditures.

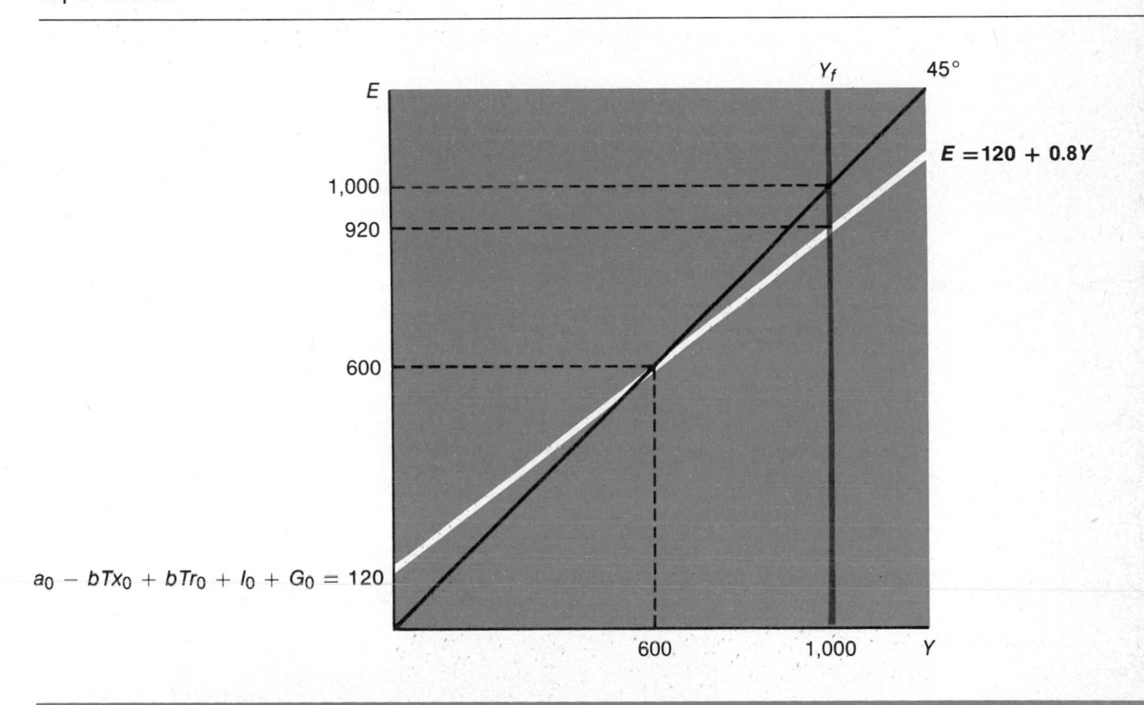

come, and thereby consumption expenditures, since consumption expenditures vary directly with income.

Graphically, an increase in G_0 raises the total demand line in Figure 6–1 vertically by the amount of the increase. Notice that G_0 enters fully into the sum, fixing the intercept of the total demand line with the vertical axis. For example, if G_0 increases from 80 to 85, the intercept moves up from 120 to 125. The total demand line shifts upward by 5 at each level of Y.

On the other hand, if Tx_0 is reduced by 5 or if Tr_0 is increased by 5, the total demand line moves upward only by 4. Private disposable income is higher by 5 at each level of Y, so that C and E are higher by:

$$\Delta C/\Delta Yd(\Delta Yd) = b(\Delta Yd) = 0.8(5) = 4$$

at each level of Y. The demand line shifts vertically by the marginal propensity to consume from private disposable income times the change in private disposable income induced by the changes in tax or transfer payments. Notice that Tx_0 and Tr_0 enter into the intercept of the E line, with the vertical axis preceded by $(-b)$ and (b), respectively.

What increase in G_0 will produce full employment in the model, given the situation illustrated in Figure 6–1? The demand line must shift upward by the deficiency of demand at full-employment output, that is, by:

$$Y_f - (E \text{ at } Y_f) = 1{,}000 - (120 + 0.8[1{,}000])$$
$$= 1{,}000 - 920$$
$$= 80.$$

Figure 6–2 **Discretionary Fiscal Ease for Full Employment**

Increases in government purchases, reductions in taxes, and increases in transfer payments shift the total expenditure line upward and raise equilibrium and real income. They produce full employment by stimulating demand.

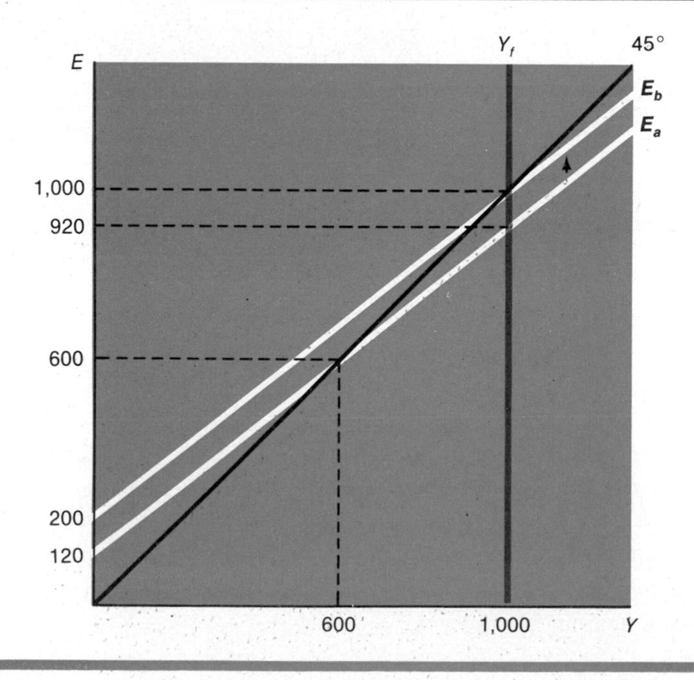

In Figure 6–1, the demand line falls below the 45° line by 80 at $Y_f = 1{,}000$. Therefore, to produce full employment by increasing G_0, the government must increase G_0 from 80 to 160 and maintain it at the new level. Figure 6–2 illustrates the operation. The demand line shifts upward by 80, from E_a to E_b, so that it intersects the 45° line at $Y_f = 1{,}000$. The intercept of the demand line with the vertical axis increases from 120 to 200, reflecting the increase of 80 in G_0.

Checking, when the full-employment Y of 1,000 is produced, demand becomes:

$$E = 200 + 0.8(1{,}000) = 1{,}000$$

and just supports it. Alternatively, with G_0 equal to 160 instead of 80, equilibrium Y is:

$$Y = \frac{a_0 - bTx_0 + bTr_0 + I_0 + G_0}{1 - b} = 200/0.2 = 1{,}000.$$

Since, in the model as it stands, tax and transfer payment policies are weaker than policies involving government purchases, an increase in Tr_0 or a decrease in Tx_0 must be greater than 80 if either is to produce a full-employment situation. Specifically, Tr_0 must be increased by 100 or Tx_0 reduced by 100. These changes increase Yd by 100 at each level of Y and shift the demand line upward by the marginal propensity to consume from disposable income times 100, that is, by:

$$\Delta C/\Delta Yd(\Delta Yd) = b(\Delta Yd) = 0.8(100) = 80,$$

which eliminates the deficiency of demand at full-employment output.

The Fiscal Multipliers

A multiplier process (similar to the one for changes in investment expenditures discussed in Chapter 4) obviously is involved when discretionary fiscal ease is employed. The changes of 80 in G_0, of 100 in Tr_0, and -100 in Tx_0 each produce an increase of 400 in Y. Equilibrium Y increases from 600 to 1,000. As with the investment multiplier, the multiplier effects arise from the induced effect on consumption expenditures which occurs as Y changes.

Multiplier statements for G_0, Tx_0, and Tr_0 can be obtained from Equation 6–14. They are simply the coefficients of the appropriate constants in that equation.[1] They are:

$$\Delta Y/\Delta G_0 = \frac{1}{1-b} = \frac{1}{1-0.8} = 5, \tag{6–15}$$

$$\Delta Y/\Delta Tx_0 = \frac{-b}{1-b} = \frac{-0.8}{1-0.8} = -4, \tag{6–16}$$

and

$$\Delta Y/\Delta Tr_0 = \frac{b}{1-b} = \frac{0.8}{1-0.8} = 4. \tag{6–17}$$

The government purchases multiplier is stronger than the tax and transfer payment multipliers, reflecting the fact already noted that G_0 does not have to change by as much as Tr_0 and Tx_0 to produce an equal impact on Y. Notice also that the government purchases multiplier is the same as the investment and consumption constant multipliers, if these two multipliers are obtained from Equation 6–14. The economics of this situation is easily perceived. Total output and income in the model are indifferent to whether a typewriter is purchased by a private corporation, a household, or a government office. The initial effect on output, employment, and income in the typewriter industry is the same, and the induced effect on consump-

---

[1] For example, the demonstration that the government purchases multiplier is the coefficient of G_0 in Equation 6–14 is parallel to that involving the investment multiplier in Chapter 4. That is, increasing G_0 in Equation 6–14 to G_0' produces a new equilibrium for Y:

$$Y' = \frac{a_0 - bTx_0 + bTr_0 + I_0 + G_0'}{1-b}.$$

Subtracting Equation 6–14 from this equation produces:

$$Y' - Y = \frac{G_0' - G_0}{1-b},$$

or:

$$\Delta Y = \frac{\Delta G_0}{1-b}.$$

Divided through by ΔG_0, this yields Equation 6–15, the government purchases multiplier.

tion expenditures, coming in a series of rounds as income expands, is also the same.

The changes in G_0, Tx_0, and Tr_0 necessary to produce a full-employment equilibrium in the example of the last section can be computed in another way. The required increase of 400 in Y can be divided by the appropriate multiplier. That is, if Equation 6–15, the government purchases multiplier, is true, it must be true that:

$$\Delta G_0 = \frac{\Delta Y}{1/(1-b)}.$$

Therefore, the ΔG_0 required for producing an increase of 400 in Y is:

$$\Delta G_0 = 400/5 = 80.$$

Similarly, from Equation 6–16, it must be true that:

$$\Delta Tx_0 = \frac{\Delta Y}{-b/(1-b)}.$$

Consequently, the change in Tx_0 that will produce the required increase of 400 in equilibrium Y is:

$$\Delta Tx_0 = 400/-4 = -100.$$

By the same token, the change in Tr_0 required for full employment is:

$$\Delta Tr_0 = 400/4 = 100.$$

Discretionary Fiscal Restraint

Discretionary fiscal restraint is the reverse of discretionary fiscal ease. It is used to check expenditure gaps and resulting inflationary pressures. In terms of the model, it involves reductions in G_0, increases in Tx_0, and reductions in Tr_0, employed individually or in combination. (However, governments ordinarily do not consciously employ reductions in transfer payments for cyclical stabilization purposes.)

Figure 6–3 illustrates the fiscal restraint case. The demand line initially is E_a, which reflects the earlier assumptions made here except that I_0 is 230 instead of 70. The trial equilibrium for Y is 1,400, an unattainable Y.

Figure 6–3 **Discretionary Fiscal Restraint to Remove an Expenditure Gap**

Reductions in government purchases, increases in taxes, and reductions in government transfer payments shift the total expenditure line downward. By removing expenditure gaps, they check inflationary pressures.

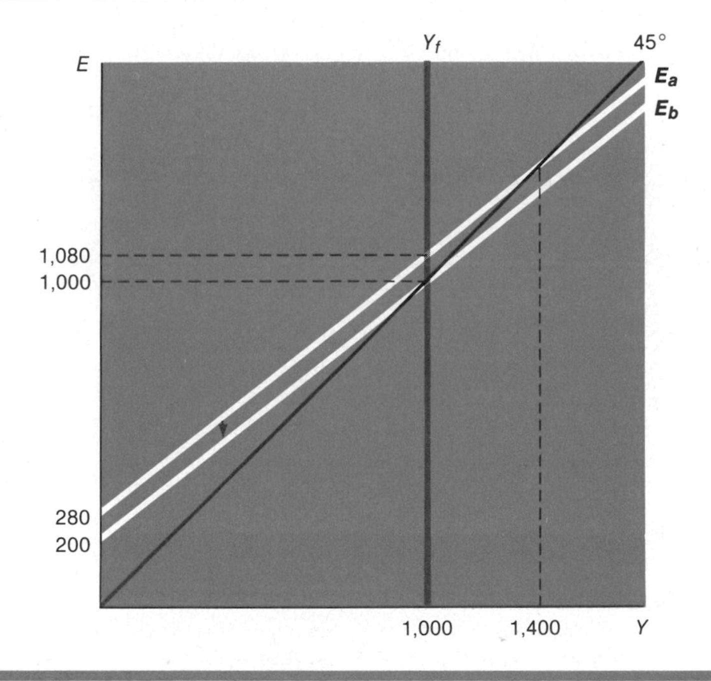

The actual expenditure gap is 80. The demand line, from Equation 6–11, is:

$$E = a_0 - bTx_0 + bTr_0 + I_0 + G_0 + bY$$

$$E = 50 - 0.8(200) + 0.8(100) + 230 + 80 + 0.8Y$$

$$E = 280 + 0.8Y,$$

so that demand at full-employment output is:

$$E = 280 + 0.8(1{,}000) = 1{,}080.$$

Eliminating the expenditure gap with discretionary fiscal restraint requires shifting the demand line downward by 80 to E_b in the figure. This can be accomplished by a reduction of 80 in G_0, an increase of 100 in Tx_0, or, if a reduction in transfer payments is to be used, a reduction of 100 in Tr_0. The rationale is symmetrical with that for the demand deficiency case. Reductions in government purchases shift the demand line downward dollar for dollar. Increases in taxes and reductions in transfer payments reduce *Yd* dollar for dollar at each level of *Y* and shift the demand line downward by the marginal propensity to consume from *Yd* times the changes caused by tax and transfer payments. The multiplier analysis does not apply in the expenditure gap case, strictly speaking, since *Y* remains fixed at Y_f as the gap is removed. No income-induced reductions in *C* occur except those which take place initially if changes in taxes or transfer payments, which induce reductions in *Yd,* are used. The multiplier technique still can be used in the mechanical sense, however, since the correct results for the required changes in G_0, Tx_0, and Tr_0 can be obtained by dividing the appropriate multiplier into $Y_f = 1{,}000$ less the unattainable equilibrium output of $Y = 1{,}400$—that is, into -400.

Choosing the Fiscal Instrument

In the model being used here, government purchase policies are stronger than tax and transfer payment policies, and tax and transfer payment policies are equal in strength, though opposite in sign. These relationships may have some bearing on the selection of a fiscal instrument for use in a given circumstance. For example, in an initial less than full employment situation, using tax and transfer payment policies to produce full employment involves a larger increase in the government deficit or a larger reduction in the government surplus than using increases in government purchases. Similarly, using them to eliminate an expenditure gap involves a larger reduction in the government deficit than using reductions in government purchases.

The relative strength of these policies as determined by the model should not be taken as absolute, however. Several important qualifications must be noted:

1. Transfer payment policies may be roughly equal in strength to policies involving government purchases in many instances. Recipients of unemployment compensation payments or welfare benefits are likely to spend nearly all such income, rather than just a portion of it, as the model implies. In effect, their marginal propensity to consume from disposable income approaches 1. If it reaches 1, the demand line will shift vertically by the full amount of changes in transfer payments received. The effect will be identical to that of changes in government purchases.

2. Tax policies, especially tax increases, may be much weaker than the model implies if they are announced in advance to be temporary counter-cyclical measures. (The Friedman approach to the consumption function, discussed in Chapter 5, suggests this, in any event.) If changes in private disposable income affect consumption only to the extent that they are perceived to be permanent, tax policies known to be temporary may have very little effect on the consumption expenditures and total demand functions. Robert Eisner has argued that the 1968–69 surcharge on U.S. income taxes, in which persons paid their regular federal income taxes plus a surcharge of 10 percent, did not achieve its anti-inflationary objectives because it was advertised widely as temporary.[2]

This effect may be one-sided—that is, it may reduce the strength of tax increases but not that of tax reductions. Households may tend to maintain consumption levels in the face of temporary tax increases, paying the taxes from what would have been savings; but, contrary to the permanent income theory, they may treat temporary tax reductions as windfalls to be used for consumption.

3. The model neglects any effects that changes in government purchases may have on other categories of expenditures. For example, accelerated government expenditures for interstate highways may stimulate private investment expenditures for associated lodging, restaurant, service station, shopping center, and recreational facilities, so that the total impact on output and income may greatly exceed that indicated by the government purchases multiplier of the model. On the other hand, the longer-term effect may be essentially zero. The government purchases may displace expenditures for a private toll road which would eventually have been built or for train and airline facilities. The restaurant, lodging, recreational, and other facilities would have accompanied these displaced private expenditures. Similarly, government construction and operating expenditures for public parks ultimately may be offset by reductions in consumption and investment expenditures for privately produced recreational services. It is probably true, however, that these longer term effects are best neglected when

---

[2] Robert Eisner, "Fiscal and Monetary Policy Reconsidered," *American Economic Review* 59 (December 1969): 897–905.

shorter term counter-cyclical fiscal policy impacts are being considered.

Lags as a Factor

Whatever the relative strength of the fiscal instruments, it is important to note that relative strength is not the only factor to be considered in choosing among them. In most instances, it is not even the most important factor.

What else must be considered? The speed with which impacts on expenditures and employment are achieved is important, since problems must be endured until these impacts are accomplished. Moreover, if lags are a year or more, conditions may be changed so that when impacts finally are achieved they are the opposite of what is needed.

In the United States, the administrative portion of the total fiscal policy lag has been especially important for tax and transfer payment policies. Congress has not given the executive branch discretionary authority over the timing of tax and transfer payment changes, and it seems unlikely that such authority will be granted in the future. Each application requires separate legislation and a separate legislative lag. There is some indication that the precedents established by the 1964 and 1975 tax cuts and the 1968 tax increase have shortened this lag somewhat, however. Chapter 20 elaborates this point.

Government purchases also require legislative authorization, but it has sometimes been possible for the executive branch to vary the rate of expenditures under programs already budgeted. For example, highway expenditures have, on occasion, been accelerated during recession and reduced during inflation. Of course, if Congress presses the "impoundments" issue vigorously and requires that funds be spent in close accord with timetables established in the authorizing legislation, government purchase policies will have the same legislative lag problem as tax and transfer payment policies.

Beyond the legislative lag is the *impact lag*—the lag between the enactment of the change in federal purchases, transfer payments, or taxes and its impact on expenditures and employment. The impact lag is less of a problem for tax and transfer payment changes than for government purchases, as a general rule. Once a tax change is enacted, the effect on disposable income is almost immediate; tax withholding can be changed on the next paycheck. The same is true for transfer payments. The effect on expenditures is distributed over time, but initial impacts may even anticipate the signing of the legislation. Once passage and signing are assured, changes in expenditure levels may occur.

With government construction purchases, however, even initial effects on expenditures and employment are less immediate. It takes time to move expenditures and employment to planned levels, even after changes have been decided on. With new projects, plans must be made, the work must be contracted, and workers must be found and hired. Even with projects already underway, construction procedures may be such as to inhibit rapid changes in the level of expenditure and hiring. Recent programs involving public works projects have had an additional lag problem; time has been consumed in the proposing of projects by municipalities and in the selection of projects to be funded by the federal government.

The Area of Impact as a Factor

A further consideration affecting the choice of a fiscal instrument is that tax and transfer payment policies work by influencing private consumption and investment, whereas government purchase policies involve variations in public consumption and investment. If full employment is achieved via a tax reduction or an increase in transfer payments, private citizens make the decisions as to the additional specific goods and services to be produced and consumed. If government purchases are used instead, the area of government decision-making expands.

Another important factor is that tax and transfer payment policies tend to be general in their impacts on employment, whereas government purchase policies can be directed at employment in particular categories. If personal income taxes are changed or social security benefits are adjusted, the induced change in expenditures tends to fan out over all industries producing consumption goods and services. Increases in government construction expenditures, on the other hand, produce a first-round effect directly on unemployment in the construction industry. Moreover, projects can be placed geographically so as to have their greatest impacts on areas of highest unemployment.

Targeting Structural Unemployment. Increases in government purchases involving expenditures for public service employment or job training programs have the special feature of being able to reduce structural unemployment and may be chosen for that reason. As stated earlier, structural unemployment, and the broader category natural unemployment, does not respond well to increases in overall demand. It arises in mismatches between the requirements of job openings and qualifications of job seekers. Public service employment programs, by hiring structually unemployed workers, can affect this type of unemployment. Recent public service employment programs have been targeted at youths, American Indians, migrant workers, and other worker categories in which structural unemployment is high. Job training programs involve expenditures for such things as federal job training centers and subsidies paid to private employers for hiring and training workers who otherwise would not be hired.[3]

Figure 6–4 presents, at Point A, an initial situation of full employment without inflation and compares the effect of an increase in public service employment expenditures targeted to structural unemployment with the effect of an increase in general government purchases which leaves structural unemployment unchanged. The increase in expenditures is $(E_b - E_a)$ in both cases.

The increase in general government purchases merely shifts the total expenditures line upward from E_1 to E_2. Since it leaves structural unemployment unchanged, it leaves the full-employment line unchanged. Consequently, it creates the expenditure gap $(E_b - E_a)$ and leaves Y unchanged at Y_f. The unemployment rate also is unchanged. This increase in government purchases might be an increase in federal government highway construction expenditures. By assumption, any new hiring it involves represents employment of workers bid away from other employers.

The increase in public service employment expenditures shifts both the total expenditure line and the full-employment line by $(E_b - E_a)$. This quantity represents both the increase in government purchases and an increase in output, since it is an income payment measuring the product of newly hired government workers who previously were structurally unemployed. Y rises to Y_f' and the unemployment rate declines. The entire decline in unemployment is a decline in structural unemployment. Notice that an expenditure gap still occurs. This gap, which is $(E_c - E_b)$, equals the consumption expenditures induced by $(Y_f' - Y_f)$, the income paid to

---

[3] The Works Progress Administration (WPA) of the 1930s was the principal public service employment program of that period, although it was directed as much at shortfall unemployment as at structural unemployment. The same can be said of the Public Employment Program (PEP), authorized in 1971, and the Temporary Employment Assistance program (TEA), authorized in 1974. The Comprehensive Employment and Training Act (CETA), operative since 1974, provides for both public service employment and job training expenditures and is targeted more directly at structural unemployment. Programs initiated during the 1960s and aimed directly at structural unemployment include the Neighborhood Youth Corps (summer employment of youths) and Operation Mainstream (subsidized employment of the elderly).

Figure 6–4 **Increases in General Government Purchases and Increases in Public Service Employment Expenditures Compared**

Increases in public service employment expenditures raise full-employment output and create expenditure gaps when applied in full-employment situations. Increases of the same amounts in general government purchases, applied in the same situations, leave full-employment output unchanged and create larger expenditure gaps.

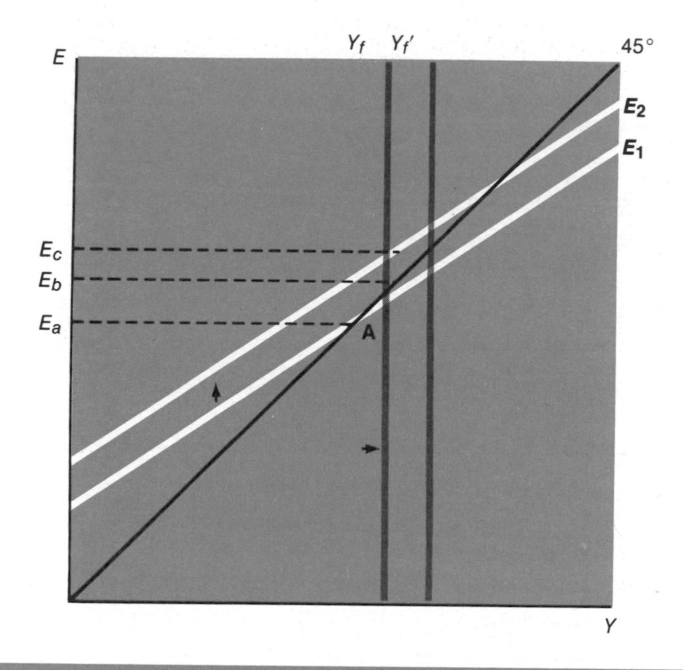

the newly hired government workers. The possible decline in transfer payments to these workers and the offsetting effect on consumption expenditures which would result from it are not considered here.

Built-in Fiscal Policies

The preceding sections of this chapter, whose purpose was to present principles of discretionary fiscal policies, assumed for convenience that taxes and transfer payments were independent of income. In this section, that assumption is relaxed. Taxes become a positive function of income, transfer payments an inverse function of income. An important principle of macroeconomics—the principle of *built-in fiscal policies*—emerges.

When taxes and transfer payments vary with income, they dampen the fluctuations in output, real income, and employment which occur when investment expenditures or some other component of expenditures shift. They do this by dampening the multiplier effect caused by the consumption expenditures and private disposable income relationship. For example, when investment expenditures decline, the decline in private disposable income, on each round and in sum, now falls short of the decline in total income instead of equaling it as it did when taxes and transfer payments were constant. As total income declines, taxes fall and transfer payments rise. This cushions the decline in private disposable income, since private disposable income consists of total income minus taxes plus transfer payments. With the decline in private disposable income dampened, the decline in consumption expenditures is dampened. The impact on equilibrium demand, output, and real income is smaller.

Taxes and Income

Several of the major components of government tax receipts in the United States vary directly either with income itself or with expenditures, which fluctuate with income. The federal government, most state governments, and many municipalities impose taxes directly on incomes. In most cases, the income taxes contain a progressive feature, so that the percentage of income paid in taxes rises as income rises. Aggregate social security tax receipts also vary directly with income. For individuals, social security taxes are a constant portion of income until a prescribed maximum income is reached, and then collections cease. State and local sales taxes and federal excise taxes vary directly with expenditures. The major tax categories which do not vary in an automatic and prescribed way with income or expenditures are property taxes and estate and gift taxes.

The dampening influence of the tax and income relationship is demonstrated by showing that the investment multiplier is smaller when taxes vary with income than when they do not—that is, by showing that a decline in investment expenditures provokes a smaller reduction in equilibrium output and real income when taxes vary with income.

To get the investment multiplier for the case where taxes vary directly with income, replace Equations 6–1, 6–2, and 6–3 of the model with:

$$Tx = Tx_0 + tY = 50 + 0.25Y, \qquad \text{6–18}$$

$$Tr = Tr_0 = 50, \text{ and} \qquad \text{6–19}$$

$$G = G_0 = 250, \tag{6-20}$$

while retaining Equations 6–4 through 6–9. As before, Tx is real taxes, Tr is real transfer payments, and G is real government purchases.

Taxes now vary directly with Y. Figure 6–5 plots the relationship. The slope of the plotting is $\Delta Tx/\Delta Y = t = 0.25$, the marginal tax rate and the coefficient of Y in Equation 6–18.

Figure 6–5 **Taxes as a Function of Income**

As output and real income expand, government tax receipts expand, chiefly as a result of income and sales taxes. Tax receipts would be positive even with output and real income at zero, at least theoretically, since property taxes, estate taxes, and other such taxes do not depend on the level of income.

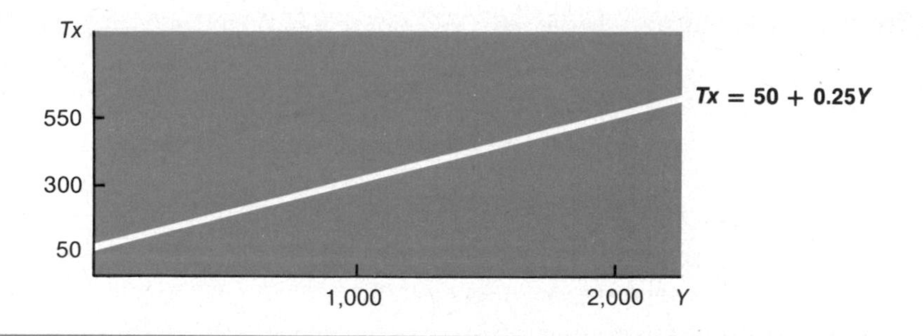

Several simplifications are employed in these calculations. Making the marginal tax rate a constant ignores the progressive element contributed by real-world income taxes. The simplification is useful, however. It permits the investment multiplier to be obtained simply, and nothing of importance is lost. Writing the tax function in real rather than current dollar terms, a further simplification, is of no consequence in this chapter, which is not concerned with the effects of price changes. Treating taxes as positive when income is zero is consistent with property and estate and gift taxes, which are levied even when income is not earned.

These qualifications noted, the demonstration will proceed. Consumption expenditures now are:

$$C = a_0 + bYd$$

$$C = a_0 + b(Y - Tx + Tr)$$

$$C = a_0 + b(Y - [Tx_0 + tY] + Tr_0)$$

$$C = a_0 - bTx_0 + bTr_0 + b(1 - t)Y, \qquad 6\text{–}21$$

so that total demand is:

$$E = C + I + G$$

$$E = a_0 - bTx_0 + bTr_0 + b(1 - t)Y + I_0 + G_0. \qquad 6\text{–}22$$

Equilibrium Y is:

$$Y = E$$

$$Y = a_0 - bTx_0 + bTr_0 + b(1 - t)Y + I_0 + G_0$$

$$Y - b(1 - t)Y = a_0 - bTx_0 + bTr_0 + I_0 + G_0$$

$$[1 - b(1 - t)]Y = a_0 - bTx_0 + bTr_0 + I_0 + G_0$$

$$Y = \frac{a_0 - bTx_0 + bTr_0 + I_0 + G_0}{1 - b(1 - t)} = 370/0.4 = 925, \qquad 6\text{–}23$$

since this Y does not exceed $Y_f = 1{,}000$.

The investment multiplier is the coefficient of I_0 in Equation 6–23, or:

$$\Delta Y/\Delta I_0 = \frac{1}{1 - b(1 - t)} = \frac{1}{1 - 0.8(1 - 0.25)} = 2.5. \qquad 6\text{–}24$$

Compare this with the investment multiplier where taxes are constant, which, as the coefficient of I_0 in Equation 6–14, is:

$$\Delta Y/\Delta I_0 = \frac{1}{1 - b} - \frac{1}{1 - 0.8} = 5. \qquad 6\text{–}25$$

The new multiplier is smaller. Indeed, it must be smaller, even ignoring the numbers, since t will always be a positive fraction. With the particular numbers used here, the multiplier declines from 5 with taxes a constant to 2.5 with a marginal tax rate of 0.25. If I_0 declines by 10, equilibrium Y declines by 25 instead of by 50.

Even with the built-in fiscal policy effect provided by t, the multiplier still depends on the marginal propensity to consume from total income, which, as before, determines the induced effect on consumption expenditures. The multiplier remains $1/(1 - MPC_Y)$, where MPC_Y is the marginal propensity to consume from total income. But the MPC_Y is now $b(1 - t) = 0.8(1 - 0.25) = 0.6$ instead of $b = 0.8$. Now, when total income changes by \$1, private disposable income changes by $(1 - t)\$1 = (1 - 0.25)\$1 =$ 75¢, and consumption expenditures change by $b(1 - t)\$1 = 0.8(1 - 0.25)\$1 =$ 60¢. Before, when Y changed by \$1, Yd also changed by \$1, since taxes were constant, and C changed by $b(\$1) = 0.8(\$1) =$ 80¢.

Transfer Payments and Income

In the United States, transfer payments tend to vary inversely with cyclical movements in real income instead of remaining fixed as the model has required. Unemployment compensation is a major factor in this behavior. As output, real income, and employment fall during a recession, unemployment compensation payments rise. During cyclical recoveries, output, real income, and employment rise and unemployment compensation payments decline. Payments under the federal food stamp program display a similar cyclical association with employment and real income.

This behavior adds to the built-in fiscal policy effects examined in the preceding section. It further dampens the reductions in output, real income, and employment which occur when investment expenditures or some other component of expenditures decline. Now, as total income begins to decline, private disposable income declines by a smaller amount, not only because taxes decline but also because government transfer payments increase. The induced effect on consumption expenditures is further diminished. Fluctuations in union or union-bargained payments to laid-off members have similar effects. They diminish multiplier effects by cushioning impacts on personal disposable income and consumption expenditures.

Discretionary Fiscal Ease with Taxes a Function of Income

Making taxes a function of Y weakens not just the investment multiplier but also the multipliers for discretionary fiscal ease. As the coefficients of G_0, Tx_0, and Tr_0 in Equation 6–23, they now are:

$$\Delta Y/\Delta G_0 = \frac{1}{1 - b(1 - t)} = \frac{1}{1 - 0.8(1 - 0.25)} = 2.5, \quad \text{6–26}$$

$$\Delta Y/\Delta Tx_0 = \frac{-b}{1 - b(1 - t)} = \frac{-0.8}{1 - 0.8(1 - 0.25)} = -2.0, \quad \text{6–27}$$

$$\Delta Y/\Delta Tr_0 = \frac{b}{1 - b(1 - t)} = \frac{0.8}{1 - 0.8(1 - 0.25)} = 2.0, \quad \text{6–28}$$

instead of Equations 6–15, 6–16, and 6–17. They are weaker for the same reason the investment multiplier is weaker—because, with a portion of increases in total income leaking into taxes, income-induced effects on consumption expenditures are lessened.

A multiplier technique for computing the changes in G_0, Tx_0, and Tr_0 required for bringing the economy to full employment was described in an earlier section. If that method is to be used with the model where taxes are functions of income, the new multipliers must be employed. For example, recalling Equation 6–23, the increase in Y necessary for full employment is 75, and the increase in G_0 which will produce that change in Y is $G_0 = 75/2.5 = 30$. The procedure is unchanged if the expenditure gap technique is used, however.

It is important to keep in mind that while these new multipliers are more realistic than the ones they replace, they still are quite incomplete. They omit the transfer payment and income relationship, of course, but, more important, they neglect monetary influences. Part 3 of the book will show that monetary influences reduce the size of the multipliers further by producing offsetting interest rate effects on interest-sensitive expenditures.

Built-in Fiscal Policies and the Government Budget

One result of letting taxes and transfer payments vary with income is that an increase in the government deficit during recession no longer signifies that discretionary fiscal ease has been applied. The *government deficit,* which is government purchases and transfer payments less tax receipts, increases automatically as the economy moves into recession, since taxes diminish and transfer payments increase as income declines.

This has an important implication concerning the wisdom of proposals which would require the federal government to balance its budget at all times. Such a requirement would force the government to apply discretionary fiscal restraint as the economy moves into recession. The government would have to raise taxes, reduce purchases, or reduce transfer payments in order to avoid the deficit which otherwise would arise automatically from built-in fiscal policies. The discretionary restraint would provoke further reductions in aggregate output and income, of course, and worsen the recession. That is just what happened in 1932. The federal government increased taxes to eliminate the deficit which had developed during the depression, thus, presumably, making the depression worse.

Modern economists who are fiscal conservatives ordinarily recommend that the federal government balance its *full-employment budget* rather than its actual budget. The full-employment budget is the budget which occurs—or would occur—with the economy fully employed, given existing government purchase, tax, and transfer payment programs. Balancing this budget permits the deficit which arises automatically during a recession to continue. It rejects fine-tuning the economy with fiscal ease to end recessions but accepts the benefits of built-in fiscal policies.[4]

Figure 6–6 illustrates this position by showing the *government surplus* function. Government surplus is tax receipts less purchases and transfer payments; it is government deficit with the sign reversed. Plotted against Y, it slopes positively, since taxes increase and transfer payments diminish as income increases. The functions of Figure 6–6 are curved to incorporate the progressive feature of the federal income tax.

With the economy in the less than full employment situation represented by Y at Y', the federal government is required to set tax, purchase, and transfer payment programs such that the surplus function is SG_1 in the figure. This yields the actual deficit Sg_a, but the full-employment federal budget is balanced, since Sg would be zero if Y were at Y_f. The government does not return the economy to Y_f with discretionary fiscal ease, which shifts the surplus function to SG_2 and produces the full-employment deficit Sg_b. But neither does it apply discretionary fiscal restraint to balance the government's actual budget. This would require shifting the surplus function to SG_3, which balances the actual budget at Y'', it is assumed, and produces the positive full-employment surplus Sg_c in the process.

[4] See Milton Friedman, "A Monetary and Fiscal Framework for Economic Stability," *American Economic Review* 38 (June 1948): 254–264. See also Committee for Economic Development, *Taxes and the Budget: A Program for Prosperity in a Free Economy* (New York: Committee for Economic Development, November 1947).

Figure 6–6 **Government Surplus and Aggregate Income**

Because taxes increase and transfer payments diminish as income increases, the government surplus is a positive function of income. With the curve labeled SG_1 in the figure, government purchase, tax, and transfer payment programs are such that the full-employment government budget is balanced. With SG_2, the government has a full-employment deficit; with SG_3, a positive full-employment surplus.

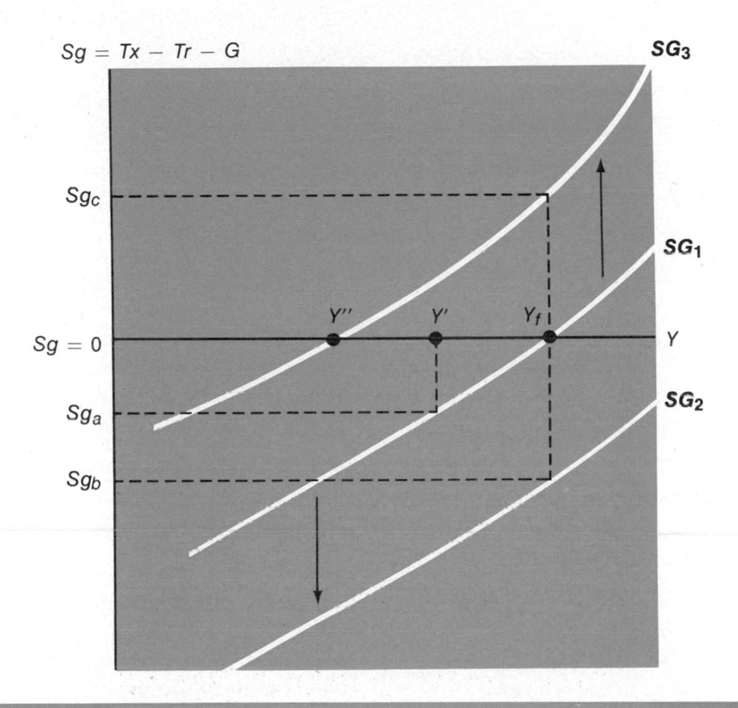

Summary

1. The government can employ discretionary fiscal policies to ease unemployment and inflation problems. Discretionary fiscal policies involve adjustments in government purchase, tax, and transfer payment programs.

2. In choosing the specific discretionary fiscal policy instrument to be used in a particular situation, matters such as the strength of the

instrument, the lags it involves, the precise area of expenditures it affects, and whether it affects structural unemployment may be important.

3. Even if the government does not employ discretionary fiscal policies to counter impacts of reductions in private demand on aggregate output, income, and employment, such impacts are diminished to some extent by the built-in fiscal policy effects which arise from the dependencies of taxes and transfer payments on income and employment levels.

4. A government which balances its full-employment budget is accepting the benefits of built-in fiscal policies during recessions but rejecting the use of discretionary fiscal policies as instruments to counter declines in private demand. A government which balances its budget regardless of the state of the economy is rejecting the benefits provided by built-in fiscal policies during recessions as well. It applies discretionary fiscal restraint as the economy moves into recession, worsening the recession.

Concepts for Identification

discretionary fiscal policies
built-in fiscal policies
discretionary fiscal ease
government purchases multiplier
transfer payment multiplier
tax constant multiplier
discretionary fiscal restraint
trial equilibrium for **Y**
legislative lag
impact lag
full-employment government budget
government surplus function
full-employment surplus

Questions and Problems for Review

1. Identify the three general discretionary fiscal policy actions the government can employ to move a less than fully employed economy towards full employment.

2. If the economy is fully employed but the level of structural unemployment is unsatisfactory, what policies can government employ to reduce the level of structural unemployment? What would be the effect of a general cut in personal income taxes in this situation?

3. Using a graphical representation (but no numbers) and a model such as that presented in this chapter, illustrate a less than full employment situation. Employ the graph to illustrate the effects of the three general discretionary fiscal policy instruments in placing the economy in the full employment with price stability situation.

4. Consider an economy where $E = C + I + G$, $Yd = Y - Tx + Tr$, $C = 20 + 0.75Yd$, $Tx = 50 + 0.2Y$, $Tr = 70$, $G = 180$, $I = 89$, and $Y_f = 1{,}000$. Prices rise if an expenditure gap is present but otherwise fixed. Equilibrium occurs where $Y = E$.

a. Is this a less than full employment situation, a full employment with price stability situation, or a full employment with inflation situation?

b. Show that the equilibrium for Y is 760. Show that the equilibrium for C is 491. Demonstrate that aggregate expenditures just support output at the equilibrium output.

c. Show that the increase in G which will move the economy to the full employment with price stability situation is 96. Show that the increase in Tr which would be required for that is 128. What change in the tax constant (Tx_0) would be required? Explain why the required increase is smaller for G than for Tr.

d. Discuss factors which might be considered in choosing among the three fiscal instruments.

5. With the economy in the initial situation set out in Question 4:

a. Verify that the government's deficit is 48.

b. Show that the government's full-employment budget is balanced.

c. Verify that the government's full-employment deficit will be larger if transfer payments rather than government purchases are used to move the economy to full employment.

d. Show that consumption expenditures will be larger and government purchases smaller in the full-employment equilibrium if transfer payments rather than government purchases are used to produce full employment.

6. Adjust the initial conditions set out in Question 4 so that investment expenditures are 200 rather than 89.

a. Is this a less than full employment situation, a full employment with price stability situation, or a full employment with inflation situation?

b. Show that the decrease in G which would place the economy in the full employment with price stability situation is 15. Show that the required increase in the tax constant is 20.

c. Show that the trial equilibrium for Y in the initial situation with investment expenditures at 200 is 1,037.5. Demonstrate that the actual expenditure gap is 15.

7. Return to the initial conditions of Question 4, but make investment expenditures 185 rather than 89.
a. Show that this is a full employment with price stability situation.
b. Demonstrate that an expenditure gap of 7.5 appears if the government raises its purchases by 30 for some purpose and finances the purchase with an increase of 30 in the tax constant. Explain why this occurs. Show that an increase of 40 in the tax constant would maintain the full employment with price stability situation when G increases by 30.
c. With G and Tx_0 at their initial levels, show that an increase of 24 in Tr would maintain the full employment with price stability situation in the face of a decline in investment expenditures from 155 to 137. What would the equilibrium for Y be if no action were taken?
d. Beginning again with the initial full employment with price stability situation, assume that government raises public service employment expenditures by 10, with all of the increase being wage and salary payments to newly hired government workers who previously had been structurally unemployed. Assume that transfer payments are unchanged. Explain why the new full-employment output is 1,010. Show that the increase in the tax constant which would be required to maintain a full employment with price stability situation is 8.

8. Explain why the decline in equilibrium Y caused by a decline in investment expenditures of a given amount is smaller if government tax receipts vary directly with income than if taxes are a constant.

References

Committee for Economic Development. *Taxes and the Budget: A Program for Prosperity in a Free Economy.* New York: Committee for Economic Development, November 1947.

Eisner, Robert. "Fiscal and Monetary Policy Reconsidered." *American Economic Review* 59 (December 1969): 897–905.

Friedman, Milton. "A Monetary and Fiscal Framework for Economic Stability." *American Economic Review* 38 (June 1948): 254–264.

Musgrave, R. A. *The Theory of Public Finance.* New York: McGraw-Hill, 1959, chap. 18.

Musgrave, R. A., and Miller, M. H. "Built-in Flexibility." *American Economic Review* 38 (March 1948): 122–128.

Okun, A. M., and Teeters, N. H. "The Full Employment Surplus Revisited." *Brookings Papers on Economic Activity* 1 (1970): 77–116.

Pechman, Joseph A. *Federal Tax Policy.* 3rd ed. Washington, D.C.: Brookings Institution, 1977.

President's Council of Economic Advisers. "The Full Employment Surplus Concept." In *Annual Report of the Council of Economic Advisers,* Washington, D.C.: Government Printing Office, January 1962, pp. 78–81.

Salant, W. A. "Taxes, Income Determination, and the Balanced Budget Theorem." *Review of Economics and Statistics* 39 (May 1957): 152–161.

Samuelson, Paul A. "The Simple Mathematics of Income Determination." In *Income, Employment and Public Policy: Essays in Honor of Alvin H. Hansen.* New York: W. W. Norton, 1948, pp. 133–155.

Part 3

Adding the Money Market

7

Investment Expenditures

Aggregate investment expenditures vary inversely with the rate of interest. This chapter examines the reasons for that relationship. It identifies several channels by which changes in interest rates influence investment expenditures and discusses their importance. A closing section looks briefly at interest rate effects on consumption expenditures.

In Part 2 of the book, where monetary influences were ignored, equilibrium output and income occurred when desired expenditures just supported output. The equilibrium condition was $Y = E$, with Y being aggregate output and income and E being aggregate desired expenditures. Money was present in Part 2, of course, performing its functions as a means of payment, a store of value, and so on, but any effect the money market had on the level of expenditures was neglected.

This part of the book moves closer to the actual world with the addition of a money market to the model. Equilibrium Y now will require not only that expenditures equal output, but also that the community be willing to hold the supply of money the monetary authority is providing. For example, if the supply of money exceeds the demand for it, the model will not be in equilibrium, even though expenditures may be just supporting output. With an excess supply of money present, wealth-holders will be shifting wealth from money to other assets—for example, to time deposits in thrift institutions, government securities, private sector debt securities, corporate stock, and the like. This will bid down the "interest" yields on these assets and stimulate interest-sensitive expenditures. Output, prices, or both will respond to the increase in expenditures, with the mix of the response between the two depending on the proximity of the economy to full employment. For equilibrium output and prices, desired expenditures must equal output *and* money demand must equal money supply. Otherwise, output or prices will be changing, even if growth factors are neglected.

Chapter 10 illustrates the equilibrium for aggregate output, prices, the interest rate, and the other macroeconomic variables in a model which includes a money market. The model is a modified version of the model used in Part 2. Investment and consumption expenditures vary inversely with the interest rate, instead of being insensitive to it. These relationships provide the channel by which money market effects influence aggregate expenditures, output, and prices. A money demand function is added, with the demand for real money balances varying inversely with the interest rate and directly with real income. The money supply appears as a constant fixed by the monetary authority.

The first order of business is to discuss the theoretical and empirical basis for these relationships, however. This chapter discusses the interest rate as a determinant of investment expenditures, and a closing section expands the earlier discussion of the consumption function to include the role of the interest rate. In Chapter 8, Federal Reserve control of the U.S. money supply is examined. Chapter 9 explores the determinants of the demand for money, highlighting the roles of the level of income and the interest rate. Part 4 of the book then employs the model developed in Chapter 10 to analyze sources of unemployment and inflation problems and the mechanics of government stabilization policies.

Investment Expenditures and the Interest Rate

Business firms combine raw materials, capital goods, and labor in order to produce the goods and services that ultimately will generate revenues and profits for the firm. If the addition of a capital good through an investment expenditure offers an expected rate of return on its purchase price that exceeds the cost of the funds required to finance the purchase by enough to justify the risks involved, the profit-oriented firm makes the investment expenditure.

The cost of funds for financing is reflected by the interest rate on securities, which represents both the cost of borrowed funds and the *opportunity cost of internal funds*. The opportunity cost of internal funds (that is, of retained past earnings) refers to the return that could be earned on the funds if they were placed in securities instead of being used for financing. Keynes called the expected rate of return on the purchase price of a capital good the *marginal efficiency of capital*. Today, it is more often called the *marginal efficiency of investment*, or the *internal rate of return*.

How is this profitability test relevant to the inverse relationship between the interest rate and investment expenditures illustrated by the investment demand schedule of Figure 7–1? At a given rate of interest—for example, at r_a in the figure—a certain set of investment opportunities will meet the test, and the related flow of investment expenditures, I_a, will be forthcoming. At a lower rate of interest, additional investment opportunities will meet the test, and the flow of investment expenditures will be larger. At a

Figure 7–1 **The Investment Demand Schedule**

Aggregate investment expenditures vary inversely with the rate of interest. As the rate of interest declines, the flow of investment expenditures expands.

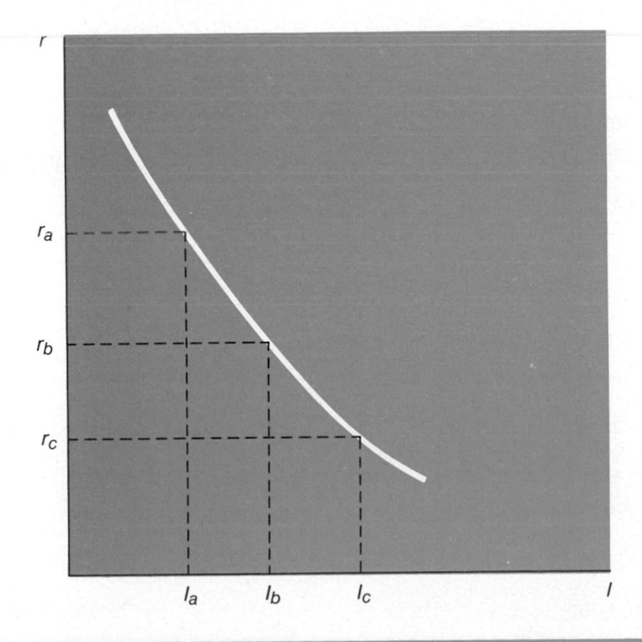

still lower rate of interest, investment expenditures will be still larger. This effect of the interest rate on investment expenditures which results from comparing the marginal efficiency of investment to the interest rate will be referred to here as the *marginal efficiency of investment effect.*

Computing the Marginal Efficiency of Investment

While it is easy to see the role of the marginal efficiency of investment concept in the investment expenditures and interest relationship, computing the marginal efficiency of investment, or MEI, is a fairly complicated matter. It is simple only for the unrealistic case of a capital good with a productive life of one year or for the totally implausible case of the capital good which never wears out.

To take the first mentioned case as a beginning point, consider the example of a machine which has a purchase price of $c_0 = \$100{,}000$ and produces a single expected return of $R_1 = \$116{,}000$ at the end of one year. This investment opportunity obviously provides an MEI of 16 percent, since $16,000, which is the return over purchase price, is a yield of 16 percent on the $100,000 invested for one year—that is:

$$\text{MEI} = \frac{R_1 - c_0}{c_0} = \frac{\$116{,}000 - \$100{,}000}{\$100{,}000} = 0.16 \qquad \text{7–1}$$

Table 7–1 presents the pertinent facts in this calculation. Notice that R_1, the expected return, is the difference between the expected increase in the firm's revenues and the expected increase in its costs (excluding deprecia-

Table 7–1 Computing the Marginal Efficiency of Investment

Expected increase in total revenue for the firm (125,000 units at $2 per unit)		$250,000
Expected increase in total costs for the firm		134,000
Additional labor costs	$55,000	
Additional materials costs	67,000	
Additional taxes	3,000	
Additional miscellaneous costs	9,000	
Expected return over costs, excluding depreciation and financing costs		116,000
Purchase price of the machine		100,000
Expected return less purchase price ($116,000 less $100,000)		16,000
Marginal efficiency of investment ($16,000/$100,000)		0.16

tion and financing costs) which result from adding and employing the machine. For example, the expected increase in the firm's total revenue is the product of the expected increase in output in units and the expected sales price for the output.

In the more general case of the investment good with purchase price c_0 expected to earn returns of $R_1, R_2, \ldots,$ and R_n in years 1 through n, the MEI is the interest rate, or discount rate, in the present value (PV) formula:[1]

$$PV = \frac{R_1}{1 + r} + \frac{R_2}{(1 + r)^2} + \ldots + \frac{R_n}{(1 + r)^n}, \quad 7\text{-}2$$

which makes the present value of the returns equal to the purchase price of the good earning them. In other words, the MEI is given by:

$$c_0 = \frac{R_1}{1 + \text{MEI}} + \frac{R_2}{(1 + \text{MEI})^2} + \ldots + \frac{R_n}{(1 + \text{MEI})^n}. \quad 7\text{-}3$$

The relationship among expected yield, expected returns, and purchase price in Equation 7–3 can be clarified by looking at the equation in terms of the one-year investment case just discussed. In this case, Equation 7–3 reduces to:

$$c_0 = \frac{R_1}{(1 + \text{MEI})},$$

since $R_2, \ldots,$ and R_n are zero. This can be rewritten as:

$$c_0(1 + \text{MEI}) = R_1$$

or

$$c_0 + \text{MEI}(c_0) = R_1$$

or

$$\text{MEI} = \frac{R_1 - c_0}{c_0}.$$

[1] The present value of R_1 is $PV_1 = R_1/(1 + r)$, since PV_1 placed for one year at r becomes R_1—that is, $PV_1(1 + r) = R_1$. The present value of R_2, available after two years, is $PV_2 = R_2/(1 + r)^2$, since PV_2 becomes $PV_2(1 + r)$ when left at interest for one year and $PV_2(1 + r)(1 + r) = R_2$ when left at interest a second year. Similarly, the present value of R_n is $PV_n = R_n/(1 + r)^n$. Therefore, the present value of the stream of returns $R_1, R_2, \ldots,$ and R_n is $PV = PV_1 + PV_2 + \ldots + PV_n$, or Equation 7–2.

This is the same as Equation 7–1, which was used in computing the MEI of 16 percent in the example.

The Present Value Method

The present value method offers an alternative approach to the investment decision, one which is computationally simpler and, in the view of many experts in the field of finance, more advantageous for theoretical reasons as well. In the MEI approach just discussed, the MEI emerges as the solution for interest rate in the present value formula after purchase price is substituted for PV. This MEI is then compared to the r representing financing costs, and, if:

$$\text{MEI} > r, \tag{7–4}$$

the investment opportunity is regarded as profitable and the investment expenditure is made. For example, with the machine purchase detailed in Figure 7–1, where the marginal efficiency of investment was computed at 16 percent, the purchase will be made if the interest rate representing financing costs is 5 percent. (Premiums required for risk bearing are not taken into account here.)

In the present value approach, the interest rate representing financing costs is substituted into the present value formula and the solution for present value is obtained and compared to the purchase price of the investment good. Again neglecting risk, if:

$$\text{PV} > c_0, \tag{7–5}$$

the investment opportunity is deemed profitable and the investment expenditure is made. To illustrate with the machine purchase example of Table 7–1, the present value of the expected returns on the machine, from Equation 7–2, is:

$$\text{PV} = \frac{R_1}{1 + r} = \frac{\$116{,}000}{1.05} = \$110{,}476.19,$$

again assuming financing costs of 5 percent. Since this amount exceeds the purchase price of $c_0 = \$100{,}000$, the purchase is made.[2]

[2] The most convenient way of allowing for risk is to add a risk premium of a given percent to the r which is compared to the MEI and used in computing the PV.

Obviously, any investment opportunity which is profitable under one test is profitable under the other.[3] And this is the important feature for the purposes at hand—establishing the basis for the investment demand schedule, which presents the dollar sum of all profitable investment opportunities at each rate of interest.

Ranking Profitable Investment Opportunities

The MEI and PV approaches differ in that they may give a different profitability ranking to the investment opportunities falling within the profitable group. This can be an important matter for real-world firms, which may be choosing between profitable opportunities instead of exploiting all such opportunities, perhaps because funds available at given financing costs are limited. For example, internal funds, which are available in fixed amounts, often are cheaper than external funds. Or the internal funds may be regarded as cheaper. They do not dilute control for existing owners, as do new stock issues, and do not increase the fixed interest charges the firm must pay whether or not it prospers, as do new bond issues.

Economists often prefer the present value approach because it takes the interest rate into account in the ranking of profitable opportunities. For example, an opportunity which has its returns concentrated in early years may have a higher PV than one with returns concentrated in later years if the interest rate is high, but a lower PV if the interest rate is low. The MEI, by contrast, does not change as the interest rate changes. Advocates of the PV approach argue that the interest rate should be taken into account because it is a better measure than the MEI of the yields at which the returns accruing during the life of the investment good can be reinvested.

Table 7–2 illustrates these points by presenting MEI and PV values for two investment opportunities, both involving a purchase price of $c_0 =$ \$100. The MEI is larger for Opportunity B than for A and is independent of whether the rate of interest is 5 percent or 18 percent, since the interest rate is not used in computing the MEI values. As to the PV values, Opportunity B, which has its returns concentrated in the early period, has the higher PV at the higher rate of interest, but the lower PV at the lower rate of interest.[4]

[3] It is apparent from Equations 7–2 and 7–3 that PV must equal c_0 if MEI equals r. Therefore, if MEI is greater than r, PV must be greater than c_0, since, from Equation 7–3, c_0 becomes smaller as MEI becomes larger.

[4] In ranking profitable investment opportunities under the PV approach, the PVs need to be divided by purchase prices when purchase prices differ.

Table 7–2 MEI and PV Values for Two Investment Opportunities

Opportunity (c_0 = \$100)	R_1	R_2	MEI		PV	
			r = 5%	r = 18%	r = 5%	r = 18%
A	0	\$144	20%	20%	\$130.61	\$103.42
B	\$125	0	25%	25%	\$119.05	\$105.93

While both opportunities are profitable under either test and under either rate of interest, the tests differ as to which opportunity is the most profitable when the interest rate is 5 percent. Advocates of the PV ranking point out that the MEI test, in designating Opportunity B as the more profitable when the interest rate is 5 percent, is assuming that the \$125 received in the first year can be invested for the second year at 25 percent, or at least at more than 15.2 percent. Only in that case would it accumulate to more than the \$144 of Opportunity A by the end of the second year. The PV advocates feel that r = 5 percent is a better indicator of the likely reinvestment yield for the \$125.

In the table, the PV values are computed by substituting into the formula:

$$PV = \frac{R_1}{1 + r} + \frac{R_2}{(1 + r)^2}.$$

The MEI value for Opportunity A is 20 percent, since:

$$c_0 = \frac{0}{1 + MEI} + \frac{\$144}{(1 + MEI)^2}$$

reduces to:

$$(1.20)^2 \$100 = \$144.$$

The MEI value for Opportunity B is 25 percent since:

$$c_0 = \frac{\$125}{1 + MEI} + \frac{0}{(1 + MEI)^2}$$

reduces to:

$$(1.25)\$100 = \$125.$$

Are Net Investment Expenditures Actually Independent of the Interest Rate?

The point sometimes is made, as a criticism of both the MEI approach and the PV approach to the investment demand schedule, that net investment expenditures are zero in full equilibrium and therefore are independent of the interest rate, rather than inversely related to it as both approaches imply. The idea is that in full equilibrium the actual capital stock equals the optimum capital stock; thus, net investment, which is the increase in the capital stock, must be zero. The only reason for investment expenditures to bear an inverse relationship to the interest rate in long-term equilibrium is that as the interest rate becomes lower, the optimum capital stock becomes higher (capital goods are substituted for labor in production), and therefore the demand for replacement capital goods increases. Gross investment expenditures would then vary inversely with the interest rate; but net investment expenditures, which omit the replacement capital goods, would not.

The answer to this criticism is that the MEI and PV approaches present a situation short of long-term equilibrium where the optimum capital stock exceeds the actual capital stock and where interest costs are balanced off against rising short-term supply prices in the capital goods industries to determine the rate at which the optimum level for the capital stock is approached. As the investment expenditure rate and the rate of production of capital goods become higher, purchase prices of capital goods become higher, especially in the short term. As the interest rate becomes lower, higher purchase prices for capital goods can be tolerated under either the MEI or PV tests, and the investment expenditures rate can be higher. Both net and gross investment expenditures are thus inversely related to the interest rate.

The Results of Empirical Studies

Producers' plant and equipment expenditures have accounted for about 70 percent of total gross private domestic investment expenditures during recent years. Residential construction expenditures have accounted for 25 to 30 percent, and the net change in business inventories has fluctuated between plus and minus 10 percent.

Statistical investigations establish that plant and equipment expenditures are inversely related to the interest rate. However, these expenditures appear to be relatively interest-insensitive in the aggregate, and substantial lags are involved in their response to the interest rate. Charles Bischoff, who was instrumental in developing the investment expenditure equations of the Federal Reserve–MIT model, has estimated the elasticity of aggregate U.S. plant and equipment expenditures with respect to the corporate bond rate (the percent change in the expenditures divided by the percent change in the interest rates) to be about −0.5, with the major portion of the impact accumulating within two to three years.[5] This means, for example, that a reduction in the corporate bond rate from 10 to 8 percent, which is a 20 percent reduction, would raise the level of plant and equipment expenditures by about 10 percent within two to three years. The Bischoff estimate agrees substantially with the estimate provided several years earlier by John Kareken and Robert Solow.[6]

Statistical studies indicate that residential construction expenditures are more sensitive to interest rates, especially in the short term. A simulation with the 1969 version of the Federal Reserve–MIT model indicates that an increase in bank reserves produces, through interest rate effects, a percent increase in residential construction expenditures more than fifteen times as great after four quarters as the percent increase it provokes in plant and equipment expenditures. After four years, the percent increase in residential construction expenditures is still more than twice as great.

While all of the impact on residential construction expenditures is an interest rate effect, not all of it is the marginal efficiency of investment effect described earlier. That is, not all of it proceeds from a comparison of the expected marginal efficiency of investment, explicit or implicit, with the cost of financing housing purchases, which, essentially, is the mortgage interest rate. In the 1969 version of the Fed–MIT model mentioned above, more than one-third of the first-year impact on residential construction expenditures is a *credit rationing effect.*

The credit rationing effect, which is applied by mortgage lenders, involves supplementing impacts of adjustments in mortgage interest rates on mortgage borrowing with adjustments in the non-price terms of mortgage lending—down payment requirements, the number of years of the loan (which affects monthly payments), loan-to-income ratios, creditworthiness standards, and so on. Or the credit rationing effect may simply involve "bare shelf" rationing.

The credit rationing effect is interest-induced, however, and therefore is

[5] C. W. Bischoff, "Business Investment in the 1970s: A Comparison of Models," *Brookings Papers on Economic Activity,* vol. 1 (Washington, D.C.: Brookings Institution, 1971).

[6] J. Kareken and R. M. Solow, "Lags in Monetary Policy," in *Stabilization Policies,* Commission on Money and Credit (Englewood Cliffs, N.J.: Prentice-Hall, 1963), p. 38.

an interest rate effect and contributes to the interest sensitivity of investment expenditures portrayed in the investment demand schedule. The greater portion of mortgage credit, particularly home mortgage credit, is extended by commercial banks, savings and loan associations, and mutual savings banks, and is financed with savings deposits and other time deposits. Since the yields these institutions pay on such deposits are inflexible relative to interest rates at large, the amount of funds they have available for mortgage lending fluctuates sharply as the general structure of interest rates rises and falls. Wealth-holders shift funds away from time deposits as interest rates at large rise and toward them as general interest rates fall. The institutions ration their available funds in part by varying mortgage interest rates, which produces a marginal efficiency of investment effect; but they also apply the non-price forms of rationing.

The yields paid on time deposits by banks and thrift institutions are inflexible relative to interest rates at large in part because the federal government imposes ceilings on the yields and adjusts the ceilings sluggishly and in part because of the way the institutions adapt to their situation of financing long-term mortgage assets with shorter-term time deposits. When mortgage interest rates increase, the institutions can obtain the higher yields only on new mortgage lending, for the most part; but higher time deposit yields must be paid fairly promptly on a large portion of time deposits. Unless the institutions are willing to speculate cyclically on interest rate movements, they will not be able to raise the time deposit yield by as much as the rise in mortgage interest rates. Moreover, mortgage interest rates are long-term interest rates and fluctuate by a smaller amount cyclically than do yields on the short-term assets which are in the most direct competition with time deposits. Recent trends toward indexing interest payments on outstanding mortgages to market interest rates and toward a longer average term for time deposit liabilities have eased this situation somewhat, but the situation still exists.

Consumption Expenditures and the Interest Rate

Today's economists regard consumption expenditures as varying inversely with interest rates. This view contrasts sharply with the early Keynesian position that interest rates do not influence consumption expenditures significantly; however, it is similar to the pre-Keynesian view. The classical economists, noting that the interest rate is the return for saving, assumed that as the return for saving increases, saving will increase and consumption will fall. Today's economists recognize marginal efficiency of investment effects and interest-induced wealth effects as additional channels contributing to a relationship between the interest rate and consumption expenditures.

The Return for Saving Effect

The *return for saving effect* is actually a price effect. To say that an increase in the interest rate has increased the return for saving is to say that it has improved the price at which current consumption can be exchanged for future consumption. If the interest rate is 5 percent, $100 of present consumption given up returns $105 of consumption at the end of one year. If the interest rate is 10 percent, $100 of consumption given up returns $110 of consumption one year from now. Therefore, a given amount of present consumption can be exchanged for a larger amount of future consumption as the interest rate is higher. Future consumption becomes cheaper. In concluding that an increase in the interest rate will reduce current consumption, the classical economists were assuming that the higher interest rate will induce a substitution of future for current consumption in much the same way as a reduction in the price of beef may induce a substitution of beef for poultry in the household budget.

The Marginal Efficiency of Investment Effect on Consumption Expenditures

The marginal efficiency of investment effect, considered earlier in its role as a channel for interest rate effects on investment expenditures, is also important in consumer expenditures for durable goods, since conceptually they are expenditures for household investment goods. Consumer durable goods—personal automobiles, television sets, furniture, household appliances—are not consumed immediately in their entirety, but produce consumption services for several years.

It is true that consumer durable goods ordinarily do not produce returns which are received explicitly in dollars; but the same is true of residential construction expenditures for owner-occupied housing, and those expenditures have been treated as subject to marginal efficiency of investment effects. The expected returns on such goods are the amounts which would have to be paid for the services they produce if the services were purchased on the market. These expected returns, together with the purchase price of the goods, indicate a marginal efficiency of investment that can be compared with the cost of financing the purchase, either the interest rate on consumer credit or the amount that can be earned on accumulated savings placed elsewhere.

Therefore, the rationale for the inverse relationship between the volume of consumer expenditures for durable goods and the interest rate is the same as that set out earlier for investment expenditures. As the interest rate becomes higher, fewer opportunities for buying consumer durable goods provide marginal efficiencies of investment which exceed financing costs by enough to justify their purchase, and the volume of consumer expenditures for durable goods declines.

This effect differs from the return for saving effect in that, while it involves impacts on consumption expenditures, it does not necessarily involve impacts on consumption, which is what the return for saving effect influences. Consumption includes only the portion which actually is consumed during the current period. The marginal efficiency of investment effect influences consumption expenditures for durable goods but not necessarily the consumption of services of such goods. For example, a reduction in the interest rate through the marginal efficiency of investment effect might induce a household to buy a car rather than to rent one or go by bus, cab, train, or plane. It might induce a household to buy a washer or dryer instead of renting the services of such appliances at a self-service laundry. Consumption of transportation or laundry services is not necessarily affected—the services are being consumed whether the household buys or rents them. However, consumption may be affected, since owning investment goods may broaden consumption opportunities for households.

The Interest-Induced Wealth Effect

The *interest-induced wealth effect* proceeds on the notion that consumption and consumption expenditures depend on household wealth as well as on disposable income and on the interest rate through the return for saving and the marginal efficiency of investment channels. As the interest rate declines, wealth increases, and an interest-induced wealth effect stimulates consumption. Households feel wealthier and as a result increase their consumption spending.

Why does wealth vary inversely with the interest rate? Wealth, in the aggregate, is chiefly the stock of capital goods plus land. Its value is the present value of the income streams associated with these assets. While financial claims are often thought of as wealth, they are not included in the measure of aggregate wealth, for the most part. Either they cancel out as assets to some but debts to others, or they are claims against the real assets just noted.

If human capital as well as property capital is included in the wealth measure, as Milton Friedman has suggested it should be, community wealth can be represented as:

$$\text{Wealth} = \frac{Y_p}{r}, \tag{7-6}$$

where Y_p is permanent net national product and represents roughly the aggregate income expected to accrue to the community's human and property capital perpetually into the future, and where r is the rate of interest.[7] To include only property capital in the wealth measure, exclude labor income from the numerator and restrict it to the property income components of net national product. Either way, wealth varies inversely with the interest rate. It is the present value of expected income and varies inversely with the interest rate at which future income is discounted. In the simulations of the 1969 version of the Federal Reseve–MIT model referred to earlier, the wealth on which the interest-induced wealth effect works is the market value of corporate stock, which represents the equity claim against corporation-held real capital goods. As the interest rate declines, stock prices increase, and consumption expenditures rise. In the model simulation, approximately one-third of the total first-year interest rate effect on aggregate expenditures is accounted for by the interest-induced wealth effect on consumption expenditures. Many economists feel that the model overestimates the effect, but almost all feel that the effect is important.

The more recent MPS (MIT–University of Pennsylvania–Social Sciences Research Foundation) version of the model applies the interest-induced wealth effect to residential construction expenditures—that is, to investment expenditures—as well. The rationale is that the ability to make down

[7] Milton Friedman, "The Quantity Theory of Money—A Restatement," in *Studies in the Quantity Theory of Money,* ed. Milton Friedman (Chicago: University of Chicago Press, 1956), pp. 4–5.

Equation 7–6 is an application of Equation 7–2, the present value formula, which reduces to PV = R/r for the case where R is the same in each period and accrues perpetually into the future. To demonstrate this, set each of the Rs in Equation 7–2 equal to R, multiply every term in the equation by $1/(1 + r)$, and subtract the original equation from the result. The remainder reduces to PV = R/r, since the last term on its right-hand side approaches zero as n approaches infinity. Hint:

$$1 - \frac{1}{1+r} = \frac{1+r}{1+r} - \frac{1}{1+r} = \frac{r}{1+r}.$$

payments on housing purchases depends on stock market wealth. This reinforces the inverse relationship between the interest rate and investment expenditures.

Summary

1. The marginal efficiency of investment effect is the basic channel for interest rate effects on investment expenditures. As financing costs decline, there is an increase in the volume of investment opportunities offering expected yields enough in excess of financing costs to justify bearing the risks involved; therefore, investment expenditures increase. Credit rationing effects, which are interest-induced, are an important supplementary channel for residential construction expenditures. Interest-induced wealth effects may be a factor in residential construction expenditures as well.

2. Today's economists regard consumption expenditures as inversely related to interest rates. The major channels for interest rate effects on consumption expenditures include return for saving, marginal efficiency of investment, and interest-induced wealth effects.

Concepts for Identification

money market
marginal efficiency of investment
investment demand schedule
present value method
interest inelastic
non-price terms of mortgage lending
MPS model

Questions and Problems for Review

1. Describe each of the following channels for interest rate effects on expenditures. Indicate the categories of expenditures for which each is important.

a. MEI effect.
b. Credit rationing effect.
c. Interest-induced wealth effect.
d. Return for saving effect.

2. A firm is considering purchasing a machine costing $500,000. It expects the machine to have a productive life of one year and a salvage value of zero at the end of that period. It estimates that the machine will add 1,000 units to its output (sales price $800 per unit) and increase its costs by $250,000, excluding depreciation and financing costs. Verify that the marginal efficiency of investment for this machine purchase is 10 percent.

3. Show that the present value to the firm of the machine in Question 2 is $523,809.52 if the interest rate reflecting the firm's financing cost is 5 percent. Neglecting risk, is the machine a profitable investment opportunity for the firm?

4. A firm estimates that an investment opportunity available to it will produce a stream of returns over costs other than depreciation and financing costs of R_1 = $10,000, R_2 = $12,000, R_3 = $15,000, and R_4 = $4,000 at the ends of years 1 through 4, where the R_4 return includes any salvage value of the opportunity at the end of the fourth year. Show that the present value of this investment opportunity to the firm is $33,010.04 when the interest rate reflecting the firm's financing costs is 10 percent.

5. A firm is considering two investment opportunities, each involving an initial investment amount (purchase price) of $100,000. The firm expects that the first opportunity will produce a single return over costs (other than depreciation and financing costs) of R_1 = $135,000 at the end of the first year. It estimates that the second opportunity will produce a zero return at the end of the first year but a single net return—R_2 = $156,250—at the end of the second year. Show that, with risk considerations neglected:
a. Both opportunities are profitable under either the MEI or PV tests if the interest rate reflecting financing costs is r = 20 percent.
b. The first opportunity is the more profitable of the two under either the MEI or the PV tests when the interest rate reflecting financing costs is 20 percent.
c. The more profitable opportunity is the first under the MEI test but the second under the PV test when the interest rate reflecting the firm's financing costs is 12 percent.
Assume that the firm has only $100,000 available at the 12 percent financing cost, and nothing beyond that at less than a 40 percent cost. Which investment opportunity should the firm pursue? Explain your answer.

6. Verify that Equation 7–2, the PV formula, reduces to PV = R/r in the special case where R is the same in each period and is received in perpetuity (forever). Footnote 6 of this chapter will help in this verification.

7. Explain why it is meaningful to represent a nation's wealth as $20,000 billion if its permanent net national product is regarded as $1,000 billion and the rate of interest regarded as appropriate for discounting future income is 5 percent.

8. Separating the subaggregate "durable goods" from the expenditure component "personal consumption expenditures" is useful because it allows analysts to treat expenditures for consumer durable goods as investment expenditures if they wish. Discuss.

References

Alchian, A. A. "The Rate of Interest, Fisher's Rate of Return over Cost, and Keynes' Internal Rate of Return." *American Economic Review* 45 (December 1955): 938–943.

Bischoff, C. W. "Business Investment in the 1970s: A Comparison of Models." *Brookings Papers on Economic Activity* (1971).

de Leeuw, Frank, and Gramlich, Edward M. "The Channels of Monetary Policy." *Federal Reserve Bulletin* 55 (June 1969): 472–491.

Evans, Michael K. *Macroeconomic Activity.* New York: Harper & Row, 1969, chaps. 4 and 5.

Fisher, Irving. *The Rate of Interest.* New York: Macmillan, 1907.

———. *The Theory of Interest.* New York: Macmillan, 1930.

Hirshleifer, J. "On the Theory of Optimal Investment Decisions." *Journal of Political Economy* 66 (August 1958): 329–352.

Keynes, John M. *The General Theory of Employment, Interest, and Money.* New York: Harcourt, Brace, 1936, chap. 11.

Modigliani, Franco. "The Channels of Monetary Policy in the Federal Reserve–MIT–University of Pennsylvania Econometric Model of the United States." In *Modeling the Economy,* edited by G. A. Renton for the Social Sciences Research Council. London: Heineman Educational Books, 1975, pp. 240–267.

8

The Supply of Money

The Federal Reserve controls the United States money supply by influencing the reserves of member banks of the Federal Reserve System and by adjusting the reserve requirements these banks must meet. The equilibrium money supply changes by a multiple of the impacts the Federal Reserve achieves on member bank reserves and excess reserves.

This chapter takes a second step toward adding a money market to the model by looking at the determinants of the money supply. Specifically, it examines how the Federal Reserve controls the U.S. money supply by affecting bank reserves and reserve requirements.

Until fairly recently, when economists spoke of the money supply, they most often meant cash plus demand deposits in commercial banks. That is the money supply the Federal Reserve labels *M-1* in its statistical money supply series. The definition of money included only cash and demand deposits in commercial banks because they were the principal assets used as a means of payment and therefore were the most liquid assets.

This book employs a slightly broader definition of money supply, one which retains the means of payment criteria but recognizes that recent regulatory changes have broadened the category of assets which provide means of payment services. In effect, the definition used here is the Federal Reserve's *M-1+* money supply definition, which essentially consists of the M-1 money supply plus regular commercial bank savings deposits held by individuals and nonprofit institutions, though it includes a number of minor items as well. Table 8–1 indicates the composition of the M-1+ money supply as of November 1978.

Table 8–1 **The Federal Reserve's M-1+ Money Supply, November 1978**

	Billions of dollars	Percent
Cash[a]	$ 97.4	16.63
Commercial bank demand deposits[b]	265.5	45.33
Commercial bank savings deposits[c]	220.0	37.56
Other checkable deposits[d]	2.8	0.48
M-1+ money supply	$585.7	100.0

[a]This item refers to holdings of the nonbank public (everyone except the U.S. Treasury, the Federal Reserve banks, and commercial banks).

[b]This item refers to holdings of the nonbank public, less cash items in the process of collection and Federal Reserve float.

[c]This item includes about $2 billion in NOW accounts at commercial banks.

[d]This item includes NOW accounts at mutual savings banks, savings and loan associations, and credit unions; demand deposits at mutual savings banks and savings and loan associations; and credit union share draft accounts. (Checkable deposits are those that can be spent by check.)

Source: "Money Stock Measures and Components," *Federal Reserve Bulletin* 65 (January 1979): A14.

Regular commercial bank savings deposits have always been moneylike in the sense that they can be converted to demand deposits or cash with very little trouble and expense. During recent years, they have become much more moneylike. In 1975, the Federal Reserve authorized member commercial banks to permit transfers between demand and savings deposits by telephone. In late 1978, they went further and authorized member banks to enter into arrangements with individuals whereby funds can be transferred between regular savings deposits and demand deposits automatically as needed to cover checks drawn on the demand deposits. Obviously, such arrangements permit individuals to use savings deposit balances as means of payment. The interest paid on the savings deposits provides them with the incentive to do so, unless the interest is offset by special bank charges.

The minor items that make up part of the M-1+ money supply include negotiable order of withdrawal (NOW) accounts at commercial banks and thrift institutions (mutual savings banks, savings and loan associations, and credit unions), demand deposits at thrift institutions, and credit union share draft accounts. The NOW accounts are savings deposits on which checks can be drawn directly. At the end of 1978, they had been authorized only for commercial banks and thrift institutions in New England and New York state while demand deposits at thrift institutions were confined chiefly to state-chartered mutual savings banks and savings and loan associations in New York state. Credit union share draft accounts, on which checks can be drawn, are authorized for federally chartered credit unions. Notice from Table 8–1 that the checkable deposits at thrift institutions accounted for less than 0.5 percent of the M-1+ money supply as of November 1978. They can be expected to grow in relative importance, however, since, for the most part, they appeared during the 1970s.

The M-1+ money supply does not include commercial bank time deposits and certificates with specified maturity dates. Checks cannot be drawn directly on these accounts, and they do not qualify for the automatic transfer of funds arrangements. Consequently, they do not serve as a direct means of payment.

The M-1+ money supply also excludes credit cards, since it includes only assets. Credit cards, like checks, can be used to effect transactions, but they are not assets in the explicit sense.

The major implication of including savings deposits in the money supply is that interest then can be earned on money. The fact that, in practice, the yields on savings deposits are inflexible relative to those on other assets greatly narrows the circumstances in which this is important for macroeconomic analysis, however. *It still is true that money becomes less attractive as a store of wealth as general interest rates rise and more attractive as interest rates at large fall.*

The next section takes a preliminary look at the determinants of the money supply and the techniques of money supply control. A simplified banking system which has only demand deposits is discussed first. Then a subsequent section adds commercial bank savings deposits and illustrates money supply determination and control with savings deposits counted as money.

Federal Reserve Money Supply Control

To see how the Federal Reserve controls the U.S. money supply, consider first a highly simplified situation in which commercial banks are all members of the Federal Reserve System, hold no excess reserves, and have no savings or other time deposit liabilities. Money deposits in thrift institutions are neglected. Under these conditions, the size of the money supply depends on the amount of the reserves of member banks, the reserve requirements for demand deposits set by the Federal Reserve for member banks, and the cash holdings of the nonbank public.

For example, if cash holdings are $50 billion, member bank reserves are $10 billion, and reserve requirements for demand deposits are 10 percent, then the equilibrium money supply is $150 billion, since the $10 billion of reserves will support $100 billion of demand deposits when reserve requirements for demand deposits are just being met. That is, equilibrium demand deposits are:

$$\mathrm{DD} = \mathrm{BR}/q_d = \$10 \text{ billion}/0.10 = \$100 \text{ billion}, \qquad 8\text{–}1$$

where:
DD = demand deposits,
BR = bank reserves, and
q_d = reserve requirements for demand deposits.[1]

Excess reserves, which are bank reserves less required reserves, are zero in this situation, since required reserves are 0.10($100 billion) = $10 billion and just equal bank reserves.

Of course, it is a simplification to assume that banking equilibrium occurs when excess reserves are zero. It is true that banks are reluctant to hold excess reserves, since member bank reserves earn no interest, and since virtually risk-free, interest earning assets such as U.S. Treasury short-term securities are available.[2] But banks ordinarily hold small precautionary balances of excess reserves to guard against suffering a shortage of reserves when check clearings run against them for a time, when withdrawal demands are abnormally high, or when other factors cause their reserve positions to deteriorate. This practice will be discussed in more detail later in the chapter.

The Instruments of Monetary Control

The Federal Reserve has three instruments of monetary control for affecting the U.S. money supply. By engaging in open-market operations and by

[1] Equation 8–1 is derived as follows: Banking equilibrium, in the simple system set out above, occurs when excess reserves are zero—that is, when ER = BR − RR = 0, where ER is excess reserves and RR is required reserves. This can be rewritten as RR = BR, or (since RR = q_dDD) as q_dDD = BR. Therefore, DD equals BR/q_d.

[2] Member bank reserves include the vault cash of member banks plus their deposits at Federal Reserve banks. The Federal Reserve has recommended that Congress permit it to pay interest to member banks on their reserve deposits, but this recommendation had not been acted upon at this writing.

adjusting the interest rate at which it lends reserves to member banks, it affects member bank reserves. By varying the reserve requirement percentages member banks must meet, it affects the amount of deposits a given amount of reserves will support.

Open-Market Operations

When the Federal Reserve engages in *open-market operations,* it buys or sells U.S. government securities in the open market, adding to or diminishing the quantity of such securities in the asset portfolios of the Federal Reserve banks. Open-market purchases increase aggregate bank reserves in the amount of the purchases. Open-market sales have the reverse effect, diminishing bank reserves in the amount of the sales.

Table 8–2 reflects the impact of a $1,000 purchase of U.S. government securities on the balance sheets of the Federal Reserve banks and commercial banks. In this example, the securities are purchased from a nonbank security dealer, though the purchase may be from a commercial bank portfolio. The Federal Reserve pays for the securities by giving the nonbank dealer a check for $1,000 drawn on the Federal Reserve banks. The dealer collects on the check by depositing it in a demand deposit account at a commercial bank. The bank collects by forwarding the check to the Federal Reserve banks, in effect depositing the check in its member bank reserve account with the Federal Reserve banks.

Table 8–2

An Open-Market Purchase

Federal Reserve Banks (Aggregate)

Assets		Liabilities and Net Worth	
U.S. securities	+$1,000	Member bank reserve deposits	+$1,000

Commercial Banks (Aggregate)

Assets		Liabilities and Net Worth	
Member bank reserves	+$1,000	Demand deposits	+$1,000

As a result, the Federal Reserve banks have an increase of $1,000 in their asset item "U.S. Government securities" and an offsetting increase in their liability "member bank reserves." The combined balance sheets for all commercial banks show an increase of $1,000 in the asset item "member bank reserves" and an offsetting increase in the liability item "demand deposits." The important point is that member bank reserves have increased by the amount of the open-market purchase. The equilibrium money supply increases by \$9,000 more, or by \$10,000 in all, since, with reserve requirements at 10 percent, the \$1,000 in additional reserves will support \$10,000 in additional demand deposits. That is, since, from Equation 8–1:

$$DD = BR/q_d,$$

then:

$$\Delta DD = 1/q(\Delta BR) = (1/0.1)\$1{,}000 = \$10{,}000. \quad 8\text{–}2$$

Dividing Equation 8–2 through by ΔBR while holding cash constant produces the *money supply multiplier:*

$$\Delta m/\Delta BR = \Delta DD/\Delta BR = 1/q_d = 1/0.10 = 10, \quad 8\text{–}3$$

where m is the money supply. This indicates that the change in the equilibrium money supply will be ten times the change in bank reserves when reserve requirements for demand deposits are 10 percent and cash is constant.

Table 8–3 reflects the reductions in member bank reserves which occur with an open-market sale of U.S. government securities by the Federal Reserve. In this case, the Federal Reserve sells \$1,000 in U.S. government securities from the portfolio of the Federal Reserve banks to a nonbank security dealer and accepts in payment a check drawn on a commercial bank demand deposit account. The Federal Reserve banks collect on the check by reducing the member bank reserve account of the commercial bank on which it was drawn by \$1,000. Then they send the check to the bank in question, indicating to the bank the reduction in its reserve

Table 8–3 **An Open-Market Sale**

Federal Reserve Banks (Aggregate)

Assets		Liabilities and Net Worth	
U.S. securities	–\$1,000	Member bank reserve deposits	–\$1,000

Commercial Banks (Aggregate)

Assets		Liabilities and Net Worth	
Member bank reserves	–\$1,000	Demand deposits	–\$1,000

account and allowing the bank to reduce the demand deposit account of the dealer who purchased the securities.

The important point is that member bank reserves are reduced by the amount of the open-market sale. The equilibrium money supply diminishes by ten times that amount, including the reduction in demand deposits occasioned by the open-market sale itself.

Changes in the Discount Rate

When the Federal Reserve adjusts the interest rate at which it lends reserves to member banks, the effect on member bank reserves is less direct and less certain. Impacts on bank reserves occur only to the extent that these *discount rate* adjustments induce banks to vary the amount of their borrowings from the Federal Reserve banks. The inducement is the change in the cost of borrowed reserves relative to what can be earned on funds placed in loans and securities.

If a reduction in the discount rate does induce banks as a whole to increase their indebtedness to the Federal Reserve, then borrowed reserves and hence total reserves increase. Table 8–4 reflects the balance sheet entries for an increase of $1 million in borrowed reserves. The equilibrium money supply increases by $10 million, of course, since $1 million of reserves supports $10 million of deposits. Similarly, if an increase in the discount rate induces banks to reduce their borrowings at the Federal Reserve banks by $1 million, member bank reserves decrease by $1 million and the equilibrium money supply decreases by a multiple of that.

Table 8–4

An Increase in Member Bank Borrowing

Federal Reserve Banks (Aggregate)

Assets		Liabilities and Net Worth	
Member bank borrowings	+$1,000,000	Member bank reserve deposits	+$1,000,000

Commercial Banks (Aggregate)

Assets		Liabilities and Net Worth	
Member bank reserves	+$1,000,000	Borrowings from Federal Reserve banks	+$1,000,000

Changes in Reserve Requirements

The third instrument of monetary control, adjustments in reserve requirements, does not affect the amount of bank reserves but changes the amount of deposits supportable by existing reserves. For example, in the earlier illustration, the equilibrium money supply was $150 billion, based on $50 billion of cash, $10 billion of bank reserves, and reserve requirements of 10 percent. The bank reserves supported equilibrium demand deposits of $100 billion.

If the Federal Reserve were to reduce the reserve requirement percentage to 5 percent, the equilibrium money supply would rise to $250 billion, assuming that there was no change in cash holdings. The $10 billion of bank reserves would then support $200 billion of demand deposits.

Of course, in practice, the Federal Reserve would never engage in so large a change in reserve requirements. Increases or decreases in reserve requirements, when they occur, ordinarily are on the order of 0.25 or 0.5 percent (as from 7 percent to 7.25 or 7.5 percent). Even a change of 0.25 percent involves a change of several billion dollars in the equilibrium money supply. That is a very large impact for money and credit markets to absorb.

Open-Market Operations: The Principal Tool

Open-market operations are the primary instrument of monetary control in the United States, especially for day-to-day management of the money supply. Their great advantage is flexibility. They can effect small and precise impacts on member bank reserves, and their course can be changed even within a single day if conditions warrant it.

By contrast, even small adjustments in reserve requirements have large impacts on the equilibrium money supply, as demonstrated earlier, and the instrument is not well suited to frequent use. Adjustments in the discount rate are capable of achieving quite small impacts on member bank reserves, but the impacts are uncertain and delayed, since they require banker decisions as to the level of borrowings.

Another advantage of open-market operations is that their implementation can be unannounced; thus, the sometimes unpredictable effects of an announcement can be avoided. It is difficult to ascertain the direction of monetary policies by observing the level of open-market purchases or sales, since many factors affecting member bank reserves are present on a given day, and data on the volume of member bank reserves are available only with a lag.

On the other hand, changes in discount rates and reserve requirements must be announced, and the effects of these announcements can be a problem. They are not entirely predictable, and they can be perverse. For example, a reduction in the discount rate, a highly visible indicator of a move towards monetary ease, may even reduce investment expenditures for a time if it creates expectations that interest rates will decline still further in the future. Businessmen may hold off on investment expenditures, anticipating even more favorable financing costs in the future. Of course, on occasion, the Federal Reserve has wished to signal its intent to the market and has used adjustments in reserve requirements or discount rates with that in mind.

The Federal Reserve rarely has adjusted reserve requirements as often as twice within a single year and has used adjustments in the discount rate chiefly as a back-up for open-market operations in recent years. Discount rates are tied informally to the yield on U.S. government short-term securities and to the *federal funds rate* (the interest rate banks pay when they borrow excess reserves from other banks). Thus, changes in interest rates provoked by open-market operations do not occasion spreads between the discount rate and other interest rates which induce changes in borrowed reserves and offset the effects of the open-market operations. Indeed, the Federal Reserve generally has followed a policy of discouraging member banks from borrowing from the Federal Reserve banks for purposes other than covering temporary shortages of reserves. This obviously blunts the use of adjustments in discount rates as an instrument for effecting changes in member bank reserves and the equilibrium money supply.

Deposit Expansion by Banks

Now that the three ways in which the Federal Reserve affects the equilibrium money supply have been pointed out, this section will explain the mechanism by which the banking system changes deposits and moves to the new equilibrium money supply when these instruments are applied. For example, in the illustration in which an open-market purchase of $1,000 raised aggregate bank reserves and deposits by $1,000 initially and supported a total increase of $10,000 in the equilibrium money supply when reserve requirements were 10 percent, how did the additional $9,000 of deposits come into being?

Basically, the movement to the new equilibrium money supply occurs as banks, finding themselves with more excess reserves than they want to keep on hand, seek to improve their earnings by placing the extra excess reserves, which earn no interest under present institutional arrangements, in loans and securities. Deposits are created in the process of lending out the excess reserves or using them to purchase securities.

To see how this works, disaggregate the simplified commercial banking system of the preceding section into a system containing a large number of individual banks, each of which, for convenience, has an initial balance sheet identical to that presented in Table 8–5 for Bank A. This represents a banking system which is providing the equilibrium money supply (continuing the earlier assumptions that banks hold zero excess reserves when in equilibrium and that reserve requirements are 10 percent). Excess reserves are zero for each bank, since each bank has $1,000,000 in reserves and 0.10($10,000,000) = $1,000,000 in required reserves.

Table 8–5 Bank A Balance Sheet

Assets		Liabilities and Net Worth	
Member bank reserves	$1,000,000	Demand deposits	$10,000,000
		Borrowings	$100,000
Loans and securities	$9,500,000	Net worth	$400,000
Total	$10,500,000	Total	$10,500,000

Assume that the Federal Reserve now disturbs this banking equilibrium with an open-market purchase of $1,000, with the seller of the security being paid with a check from the Federal Reserve drawn on the Federal Reserve banks. The seller of the security deposits the check in its demand deposit account in Bank A. Bank A's reserves and deposits both increase by $1,000, as shown in Step 1 of Table 8–6, and Bank A has excess reserves of $900. Whereas Bank A's reserves have increased by $1,000, its required reserves have increased by only 0.10($1,000) = $100.

Bank A will now seek to increase its earnings by lending out these excess reserves or placing them in securities. If it lends out the excess reserves—accepting a loan, or promissory note, into its asset portfolio and creating a deposit liability in favor of the borrower—the effects are as indicated in Step 2 in Table 8–6. Bank A's assets and deposits increase by $900, the asset increase occurring in loans.

The process does not stop here, of course. The borrower has borrowed for a purpose, perhaps to buy building materials, and will draw a check against the newly created deposit in favor of the seller. Unless the seller converts the check to cash, the check will return as a deposit to a bank somewhere in the system, probably to a bank other than Bank A. If Bank B is the bank receiving the deposit, as denoted in Step 3 of Table 8–6, Bank B's deposits will increase by $900; and, after the check is cleared through the Federal Reserve banks back to Bank A, Bank B's reserves will have increased by $900, Bank A's reserves will have diminished by $900, and

Deposit Expansion

Table 8–6

Bank A

Assets		Liabilities and Net Worth	
Member bank reserves		Demand deposits	
(1)	+$1,000	(1)	+$1,000
(3)	−$900	(2)	+$900
Loans and securities		(3)	−$900
(2)	+$900		

Bank B

Assets		Liabilities and Net Worth	
Member bank reserves		Demand deposits	
(3)	+$900	(3)	+$900
(5)	−$810	(4)	+$810
Loans and securities		(5)	−$810
(4)	+$810		

Bank C

Assets		Liabilities and Net Worth	
Member bank reserves		Demand deposits	
(5)	+$810	(5)	+$810
(7)	−$729	(6)	+$729
Loans and securities		(7)	−$729
(6)	+$729		

Bank D

Assets		Liabilities and Net Worth	
Member bank reserves		Demand deposits	
(7)	+$729	(7)	+$729

Bank A will have reduced its deposit liability to the drawer of the check by $900. On the liability side of the combined balance sheets for the Federal Reserve banks, member bank reserve deposits of $900 will have been transferred from Bank A to Bank B.

Bank A is now in equilibrium in the sense that it again has zero excess reserves, but Bank B now has excess reserves of $900 − 0.10($900) = $810. The process of expansion continues in Step 4 of Table 8–6 as Bank B lends out these excess reserves by making a loan and creating an offsetting deposit liability in favor of the borrower. A check drawn on this deposit is returned as a deposit to another bank in the system, Bank C, and cleared back through the Federal Reserve banks to Bank B. This returns Bank B to equilibrium, with excess reserves of zero, but Bank C now has excess reserves of \$810 − 0.10(\$810) = \$729. Bank C now lends out these excess reserves, the proceeds are spent and deposited in Bank D, and so on.

The important point here is that if each bank in the system loans out or places in securities any excess reserves it possesses, demand deposits for all banks will accumulate toward a \$10,000 total increase, since the additional reserves provided to the system by the open-market purchase will support \$10,000 of additional demand deposits in equilibrium. Referring again to Table 8–6, notice that Bank A retains the increase of \$1,000 in deposits created by the open-market purchase. Bank B retains the \$910 increase in deposits it received from the check drawn on the deposit created by Bank A. Bank C retains the \$729 increase in deposits it received from the check drawn on the deposit created by Bank B, and so on. Table 8–7 shows the increases in deposits recorded on the balance sheets of the first four banks in the system and indicates their accumulation toward the total increase in deposits for all banks of \$10,000.[3]

Of course, instead of employing excess reserves by making loans and creating offsetting deposit liabilities in their own banks, as in the above example, banks may purchase securities or make loans and make payment with cashier's checks drawn against themselves or with checks drawn against their reserve deposits in Federal Reserve banks. The deposit expansion process is the same in these cases except that the creation of deposits occurs as the checks are deposited in the receiving banks rather than on the books of the banks employing the excess reserves.

Reflection on the process of deposit expansion makes it clear why banks having excess reserves cannot themselves make loans and create deposits equal to a multiple of their excess reserves. If a bank lends out its excess reserves, and all the deposits created in making the loan leave the bank and are deposited in another bank, the lending bank ends up with zero excess reserves. Each lending bank ends up in this situation in our

---

[3] The expansion of demand deposits proceeds by a sum of series process exactly analogous to the investment expenditures multiplier process examined in Chapter 4. The increase in deposits is the sum of increments occurring on successive rounds, with each increment being a constant fraction of the increment occurring on the preceding round. The fraction in this case is $(1 - q_d)$. The change in equilibrium demand deposits is given by:

$$\Delta DD = \Delta BR + (1 - q_d)\Delta BR + (1 - q_d)^2\Delta BR + \ldots + (1 - q_d)^{n-1}\Delta BR.$$

When this equation is multiplied through by $(1 - q_d)$ and the result is subtracted from it, the remainder reduces to $\Delta DD = \Delta BR/q_d$ as n (that is, the number of banks) approaches infinity. This is the same as Equation 8–2, presented earlier.

Deposit Expansion Summary

Table 8–7

Bank	Change in Deposits
Bank A	+$1,000.00
Bank B	+910.00
Bank C	+729.00
Bank D	+656.10
•	•
•	•
•	•
•	•
•	•
•	•
Bank *n*	0
Aggregate	+$10,000.00

example. If a bank loaned out more than its excess reserves, and the deposits it created left, the bank would end up with a shortage of reserves.

Contraction

When the Federal Reserve acts to diminish the equilibrium money supply through open-market sales, increases in the discount rate, or increases in reserve requirements, the commercial banking system participates in the process by contracting rather than expanding demand deposits. These Federal Reserve operations, when imposed on a banking system with zero excess reserves, create negative excess reserves which must be eliminated through deposit contraction. Equation 8–2 works as well for the open-market sale as for the open-market purchase. A change in bank reserves of –$1,000, provoked by an open-market sale of $1,000 to the nonbank public, requires a total change in demand deposits outstanding of $\Delta DD = \Delta BR/q_d = -\$1{,}000/0.10 = -\$10{,}000$.

To accomplish this, the banking system as a whole sells off $9,000 worth of loans and securities to the nonbank public (including maturing loans sold back to their issuers) and simply reduces demand deposits by the checks drawn on them to purchase the securities. These deposits disappear. This, plus the initial reduction in deposits of $1,000 provoked by the open-market sale itself, provides the total contraction of $9,000 in deposits. Ordinarily, the security sales must be made to the nonbank public if they are to improve the aggregate banking reserve position. Sales of securities to other commercial banks usually are paid for by shifting reserves from buying bank to selling bank without affecting deposit liabilities of either. This leaves aggregate bank reserves, deposit liabilities, and excess reserves unchanged.

Notice also that whereas the banking system *can* increase loans and securities and therefore deposits when the monetary authority provides it with excess reserves, it *must* sell off loans and securities and eliminate deposits when the authority produces a shortage of reserves. In this sense, the expansion and contraction processes are not quite symmetrical.

Allowing for Savings Deposits

If the banking system of the preceding sections is modified to permit commercial banks to have savings deposits, then the determinants of the

Table 8–8 **Member Bank Reserve Requirements by Type and Size of Deposit (in Millions of Dollars), December 31, 1978**

	Reserve Requirement (Percent of Deposits)
Demand deposits	
0–2 million	7.00
Over 2–10 million	9.50
10–100 million	11.75
100–400 million	12.75
Over 400 million	16.25
Time deposits	
Savings deposits	3.00
Other	
0–5 million maturing in:	
30–179 days	3.00
180 days to 4 years	2.50
4 years or more	1.00
Over 5 million, maturing in:	
30–179 days	6.00
180 days to 4 years	2.50
4 years or more	1.00

Each deposit interval applies to that part of the deposits of each bank. For example, a bank with $10 million of demand deposits would be required to hold 7 percent reserves against the first $2 million and 9.5 percent against the next $8 million. (Required reserves would be $140,000 + $760,000 = $900,000.)

Source: "Member Bank Reserve Requirements," *Federal Reserve Bulletin* 65 (January 1979): p. A9.

money supply and the money supply multiplier change. This is the case, in any event, if reserve requirements for savings deposits differ from those for demand deposits, as in the United States, where the requirements for demand deposits are higher (See Table 8–8).

As before, the money supply depends on cash holdings, bank reserves, and reserve requirements for demand deposits, but now it also depends on reserve requirements for savings deposits and the ratio of savings to demand deposits. For example, if:

CU = cash = $10 billion,
BR = bank reserves = $12.4 billion,
q_d = reserve requirements for demand deposits = 0.10,
q_s = reserve requirements for savings deposits = 0.03, and
T = SD/DD = the ratio of savings to demand deposits = 0.8,

the equilibrium value for total deposits, D = DD + SD, is:

$$\text{D} = \text{DD} + \text{SD} = \frac{(1 + T)\text{BR}}{q_d + q_s T} = \frac{(1 + 0.8)\$12.4 \text{ billion}}{0.10 + 0.03(0.8)} = \$180 \text{ billion.} \qquad \text{8–4}$$

Total deposits are divided into $100 billion for demand deposits and 0.8($100) = $80 billion for savings deposits. This makes excess reserves zero and produces banking equilibrium, since required reserves are:

$$\text{RR} = q_d \text{DD} + q_s \text{SD} = 0.10(\$100 \text{ billion}) + 0.03(\$80 \text{ billion}), \qquad \text{8–5}$$

which just equals BR = $12.4 billion.[4] The $180 billion of total deposits plus the $10 billion of cash produce a total money supply of $150 billion.

---

[4] The formula for total deposits (Equation 8–4) is derived as follows. Banking equilibrium occurs where ER = BR − RR = 0, or RR = BR, as before. Substituting from Equation 8–5, this is:

$$q_d \text{DD} + q_s \text{SD} = \text{BR}.$$

Since SD = T(DD), this becomes:

$$q_d \text{DD} + q_s T(\text{DD}) = \text{BR},$$

or

$$(q_d + q_s T)\text{DD} = \text{BR},$$

and yields the equilibrium for demand deposits as:

The point being made here is that the money supply depends on *CU*, BR, and q_d, as before, but now it depends on q_s and T as well.[5]

From Equation 8–4, it is apparent that, when savings deposits are included as money, the money supply multiplier is:

$$\Delta m/\Delta \text{BR} = \Delta \text{D}/\Delta \text{BR} = \frac{1 + T}{q_d + q_s T} = 1.8/0.124 = 14.516. \qquad 8\text{–}6$$

This assumes that cash holdings are constant and that deposit holders adjust their savings deposits to maintain a constant savings to demand deposit ratio as demand deposits change.

Recognizing savings deposits expands the instruments of monetary control. An adjustment in reserve requirements for either savings or demand deposits will change the equilibrium money supply.

Complications

While the money supply models employed in the preceding sections have been valuable for highlighting the essential factors involved in money supply control, the actual money supply process involves a number of complicating factors in the United States. This section recognizes several such factors, though it does not illustrate them with calculations.

First, whereas the assumption here has been that banks hold no excess reserves when in equilibrium, U.S. commercial banks actually hold precautionary balances of excess reserves as a hedge against being caught short of reserves when factors beyond their control—such as cash withdrawals or an adverse balance of check clearings—cause their reserve positions to deteriorate. These balances of *desired excess reserves* re-

$$\text{DD} = \frac{\text{BR}}{q_d + q_s T}.$$

The equilibrium for total deposits therefore is:

$$\text{D} = \text{DD} + \text{SD}$$

$$\text{D} = \text{DD} + T(\text{DD})$$

$$\text{D} = (1 + T)\text{DD}$$

$$\text{D} = \frac{(1 + T)\text{BR}}{q_d + q_s T}.$$

[5] This is true even if savings deposits are not counted as money, since savings deposits claim a portion of the available reserves.

duce the money supply that a given level of bank reserves will support, since fewer reserves are available for supporting demand and savings deposits.

A second complication is that U.S. commercial banks have time deposit liabilities other than regular savings deposits. These are the time deposits with specified maturity dates. Since these deposits claim a portion of reserves, but are not money in the M-1+ sense, they also reduce the money supply supportable by a given level of reserves.

Is the Money Supply a Positive Function of the Interest Rate?

The money supply has been considered here as a constant fixed by Federal Reserve policies. However, two important factors contribute to the view that it may be a positive function of the interest rate.

First, as interest rates available on loans and securities increase, reserves borrowed from the Federal Reserve by member banks may increase, since, if adjustments in discount rates lag for a time, it becomes more profitable for banks to borrow in order to lend. If borrowed reserves increase, total reserves increase, and a larger volume of deposits can be supported. The Federal Reserve discourages member banks from borrowing to expand loans, but some such borrowing occurs.

Second, as interest rates rise, banks tend to reduce their holdings of excess reserves, since interest rates measure the cost of holding these reserves—that is, interest rates reflect what can be earned by placing assets in loans and securities rather than in excess reserves. Therefore, with excess reserves declining as interest rates rise, a greater proportion of total bank reserves is available for supporting demand and savings deposits, and the equilibrium money supply rises.

This positive relationship between the money supply and the interest rate is not assured, however. A third factor has worked against such a relationship more often than not during recent years. During the 1970s, bank savings deposits have tended to decline relative to demand deposits and other time deposits when interest rates are high and to increase relative to these deposits when interest rates are low. This occurs because savings deposits are quite liquid and have yields which are inflexible relative to interest rates at large. Since reserve requirements are higher for demand deposits than for savings deposits, and since other time deposits are not counted as money, this behavior of savings deposits works against the positive money supply and interest rate relationship.

In any event, this book will continue to treat the money supply as a constant. Under ordinary circumstances, the Federal Reserve can fix the supply of money within very narrow limits, at least in terms of average balances over relatively short periods of time, simply by compensating for interest rate effects with open-market operations. Treating the money supply as a constant emphasizes this fact. Moreover, it greatly simplifies macroeconomic analysis, and at very little cost in terms of realism.

Complications for the Money Supply Multiplier

The earlier representation of the money supply multiplier must also now be amended. For example, an open-market purchase of U.S. government securities was earlier said to increase the equilibrium money supply by $(1 + T)/(q_d + q_s T)$ times the open-market purchase. In fact, since money holders tend to allocate their money holdings between cash and deposits in a fairly stable ratio, cash withdrawals tend to occur at commercial banks as deposits expand. These cash withdrawals reduce commercial bank reserves dollar for dollar, since they are paid either from the vault cash commercial banks hold, which counts as member bank reserves, or from cash the banks secure by making withdrawals from their member bank reserve deposits at the Federal Reserve banks. Therefore, a portion of the excess reserves created by open-market purchases is eliminated through cash withdrawals as deposits expand. The total expansion of deposits is dampened. It will be dampened further if the desired excess reserves of bankers expand as total deposits expand.

The factors which contribute to an association between the money supply and the interest rate often enter into the size of the money supply multiplier. Interest rates ordinarily decline as the money supply expands in response to an open-market purchase, since banks lower lending interest rates or bid up interest yields on securities as they loan out excess reserves or place them in securities. Interest rates rise as banks sell off securities and restrict lending in the process of contracting deposits.

Regardless of these complications, it is still true that the instruments of monetary control occasion impacts on the U.S. equilibrium money supply which are multiples of impacts on bank reserves and excess reserves. And it is still true that the multiplier involved depends on reserve requirements for deposits. The point here is that it also depends on induced changes in cash outstanding, borrowed bank reserves, desired excess reserves, and ratios of savings deposits to demand deposits and other time deposits. Money and banking textbooks often present more complicated money supply multipliers which take some of these factors into account.

Nonmember Banks and Thrift Institutions

A final complication is that the member banks of the Federal Reserve system to which our models have applied account for only two-thirds of the deposits of the actual M-1+ money supply. Nonmember commercial banks and thrift institutions account for the remainder, and these institutions are not directly subject to the Federal Reserve's instruments of monetary control. The Federal Reserve can fix the aggregate of reserve deposits at the Federal Reserve banks with precision, but nonmember banks and thrift institutions are not required to hold their reserves in this form. Moreover, changes in reserve requirements for member banks do not apply to nonmember banks and thrift institutions. Strictly speaking, the models used here represent money supply determination and control only for cash plus member bank deposits.

The proportion of total M-1+ deposits accounted for by member commercial banks declined from well over 80 percent in 1950 to 67.9 percent in June 1978. Most of the loss was to nonmember banks, since thrift institutions accounted for less than 1 percent of the M-1+ deposits by the later date. The loss resulted chiefly from financial disadvantages associated with Federal Reserve membership, which have discouraged membership and encouraged conversion to nonmember status. Reserve requirements imposed by state laws for nonmember banks usually are lower than Federal Reserve requirements, and often they permit a portion of reserves to be held as interest bearing deposits in other banks.

The Federal Reserve authorities are sensitive to the problem the declining number of member banks poses for monetary control. They have recommended legislation to require that all institutions issuing M-1+ deposits be subject to reserve requirements for such deposits and that the reserves be held at Federal Reserve banks. To date, M-1+ deposits at nonmember banks have not behaved so as to offset the impact of monetary policies on deposits of member banks, but the nonmember bank deposits are noticeably less sensitive to monetary policies.

Summary

1. The Federal Reserve controls the U.S. money supply by affecting member bank reserves with open-market operations and adjustments in discount rates and by adjusting reserve requirements for deposits. Open-market operations are the major instrument of monetary control.

2. Open-market operations affect member bank reserves dollar for dollar and have a multiplier effect on the equilibrium money supply. Because member banks are required to hold only a fraction of their deposits as reserves, each dollar of reserves supports several dollars of deposits.

3. The multiple expansion of deposits comes about as commercial banks lend out excess reserves or place them in securities and create demand deposits in the process. Multiple contraction of deposits, forced when monetary authorities induce shortages of reserves, comes about as the banking system sells off loans and securities to the nonbank public and reduces the demand deposits of the purchasers as payment.

Concepts for Identification

M-1 money supply
M-1+ money supply
means of payment
demand deposits
commercial banks
thrift institutions
regular savings deposits at commercial banks
time deposits with specific maturity dates
NOW accounts
credit cards
member bank reserves
reserve requirements
required reserves
excess reserves
desired excess reserves
open-market operations
discount rate
equilibrium money supply
money supply multiplier
nonmember banks

Questions and Problems for Review

1. Assume that all commercial banks are members of the Federal Reserve System, hold no excess reserves when in equilibrium, and have no savings or other time deposit liabilities. Checkable deposits in other financial institutions are zero. Show that if cash outstanding is $100 billion, if member bank reserves are $30 billion, and if reserve requirements for demand deposits are 15 percent, the equilibrium money supply is $300 billion. Verify that excess reserves are zero when the money supply is at this level.

2. Using the money supply multiplier appropriate to the banking system of Question 1 (cash remains fixed at $100 billion), show that an open-market purchase of $15 million of U.S. government securities by the Federal Reserve increases the equilibrium money supply by $100 million. Verify that excess reserves will be zero for the banking system when demand deposits change by this amount. Explain why commercial bank holdings of loans and securities will have expanded by only $85 million comparing the new and former equilibriums.

3. Illustrate the initial impact of the open-market purchase in Question 2 on the combined balance sheets of all commercial banks and explain how the banking system brings about the new equilibrium money supply.

4. Discuss the advantages of open-market operations as compared with adjustments in reserve requirements and changes in the discount rate as an instrument for bringing about changes in the equilibrium money supply.

5. Retain the assumptions of Question 1—including $CU = \$100$ billion, BR = $30 billion, and $q_d = 0.15$—but now allow for savings deposits in commercial banks and count them in the money supply. T, the ratio of savings to demand deposits, is 0.5, and q_s, the reserve requirement for savings deposits, is 0.02. Verify that in this situation the equilibrium money supply is $381.25 billion. Show that excess reserves for the banking system are zero when the money supply is at this level.

6. Verify that the value of the money supply multiplier is 9.375 for the economy of Question 5. Show that an open-market purchase of $10 million will increase equilibrium savings deposits by $31.25 million.

7. Illustrate the impact on the combined balance sheets of all commercial banks, equilibrium to equilibrium, if the banking system of Question 5 is disturbed by an open-market sale of $100 million. Explain how the banking system restores equilibrium in this case.

8. Explain why the money supply multiplier is smaller if the community holds cash in a fixed ratio to its demand deposits.

9. Explain why the U.S. money supply might be expected to be a positive function of the rate of interest in the absence of Federal Reserve action to neutralize such a relationship.

10. Why does it make sense to use the M-1+ money supply in macroeconomics instead of restricting the money supply to cash and demand deposits in commercial banks? Would it make still greater sense to include commercial bank time deposits with specified maturity dates in the money supply? Explain.

References

Board of Governors of the Federal Reserve System. "A Proposal for Redefining the Monetary Aggregates." *Federal Reserve Bulletin* 65 (January 1979): 13–42.

Jordan, Jerry L. "Elements of Money Stock Determination." *Federal Reserve Bank of St. Louis Review* 51 (October 1969): 10–19.

Kaufman, George G. "Federal Reserve Inability to Control the Money Supply: A Self-fulfilling Prophecy." *Financial Analysts Journal* 28 (September–October 1972): 20–26.

Klein, John J. *Money and the Economy.* 4th ed. New York: Harcourt Brace Jovanovich, 1978, chaps. 3–14.

Poole, William, and Lieberman, Charles. "Improving Monetary Control." *Brookings Papers on Economic Activity* 2 (1972): 293–335.

Smith, W. L. "The Instruments of General Monetary Control." *National Banking Review* 1 (September 1963): 47–76.

9
The Demand for Money

This chapter examines the determinants of the demand for real money balances. It focuses on the roles of real income and interest and considers whether the function relating these determinants to real money balances demanded is stable or subject to shifts.

In macroeconomics, the *demand for money* means the decision to hold wealth in money rather than in other assets. This being the case, economists who have formulated theories of the demand for money have found it useful as a point of departure to pose the following question. Why do wealth-holders place a portion of their wealth in money when they can place it instead in assets such as bonds, stocks, and real estate, which ordinarily earn a higher rate of return? The answer, of course, is that money possesses characteristics and provides services not available in these other assets.

The classical economists, whose views prevailed before Keynes's break with tradition occurred, emphasized the *transactions motive* for holding money. They pointed out that money serves as a means of payment. It offers convenience in effecting transactions. Cash and demand deposits can be exchanged directly for goods, services, and securities. Commercial bank savings deposits convert readily to cash or demand deposits, with little trouble (no trouble where automatic transfer to demand deposits plans are in force) and no transaction costs.

Emphasizing the transactions motive, the classical economists emerged with a theory in which real money balances demanded bore a stable, proportionate relationship to total transactions as well as to aggregate income, which varied directly with total transactions. Since money receipt and money payment streams were not perfectly synchronized within economic units, money balances arose in bridging the gaps between receipts and payments. As income and total transactions became higher, the money balances required for bridging the gaps between receipts and payment streams became higher, and proportionately so.

Keynes incorporated the transactions motive into his theory of money demand and added precautionary and speculative motives, emphasizing the latter. The result was a theory in which money balances demanded bore a very unstable relationship to income, with the speculative motive being the primary source of the instability. Because of it, money balances demanded were extremely sensitive to the interest rate on securities, as well as to the level of income, and the *money demand function* relating money demanded to interest and income was subject to shifts.

Modern theories of money demand have put less emphasis on the speculative motive than Keynes and the early Keynesians. These theories provide alternative rationales for a money demand and interest rate relationship but, compared to Keynes, suggest a much smaller interest sensitivity and a much more stable money demand function. One approach points out that the optimum size of the money balance held to satisfy the transactions and precautionary motives varies inversely with the interest rate on securities. Another approach, favored by Milton Friedman, simply views money as a consumer and producer good providing utility and productive services. In this approach, interest and income enter into the demand for money in much the same way as relative prices and income enter into the demand for other consumer and producer goods.

The Transactions Motive and the Role of Income

An illustration is useful in demonstrating the transactions motive as a source of the influence of income on money balances demanded. Consider the highly simplified situation in which an economy consists solely of households and producers, and the only money transactions are the expenditures for final output and the income payments for factor services which are exchanged between households and producers. Producers make income payments of $120 billion per month to households at the beginning of the first day of the month, and households return this to producers in expenditures for final output at the rate of $4 billion per day, paid at midday, on each day of the thirty-day month.

In this situation, average daily money balances for households and producers combined—that is, aggregate average daily money balances—are $120 billion on each day of the month, as illustrated in Figure 9-1, exactly equal to the aggregate output and income of $120 billion per month. Average daily money balances for households decline from $118 billion on the first day of the month ($120 billion until midday,

Figure 9-1 **Transactions Money Holdings**

In this hypothetical and highly simplified model of payment and receipt streams, aggregate transactions money balances demanded over the payment period diminish for households, increase for firms, and remain constant for households and firms combined.

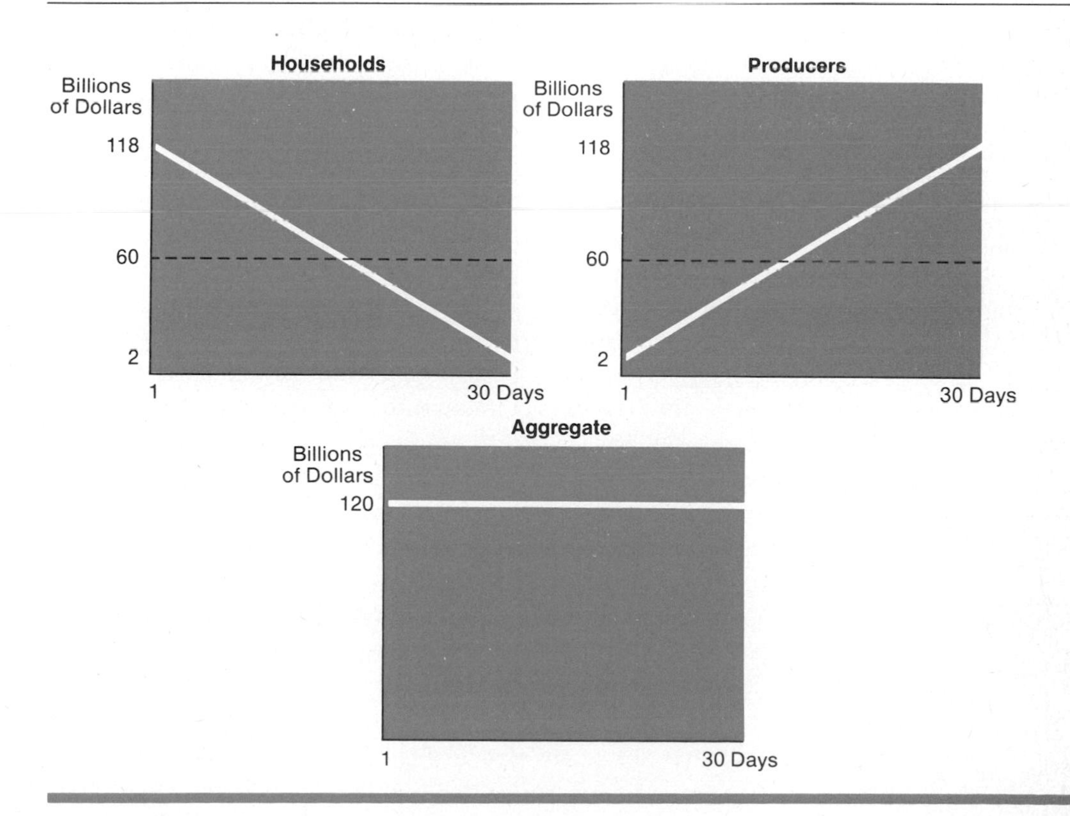

$116 billion after midday) to $2 billion for the thirtieth day of the month ($4 billion until midday, zero after midday), as illustrated in the upper left-hand portion of the figure. Average daily money balances of producers are the exact mirror image of those for households, rising from $2 billion for the first day (zero until midday, $4 billion after midday) to $118 billion for the thirtieth day. As a result, average daily money balances for households and producers combined (in the lower portion of the figure) are $120 billion for each day of the month, which exactly equals aggregate output and income for the month.

The important point of the example is that aggregate money balances held for transaction purposes depend on aggregate output and income and vary directly with them. If aggregate output and income double to $240 billion, with the time sequence of the payment and receipt streams unchanged, household average money balances will decline from $236 billion to $4 billion over the month, producer average money balances will mirror this, and aggregate average money balances will be $240 billion, still equal to aggregate output and income. Indeed, money balances demanded for transaction purposes will vary proportionately with income, producing the classical money demand function described earlier. Money balances demanded depend on output and income and bear a stable, proportionate relationship to them.

Obviously, the payment and receipt streams of the real world do not display the uniformity of those in the example just cited. The length of the income period differs greatly among households, and, in most cases, an individual household receives income from several sources with differing payment periods. Wages may be received monthly and dividend income quarterly. Some income, such as that on savings accounts or imputed income from meals provided, involves no money payment at all. Insofar as expenditure streams are concerned, often a large portion of expenditures are concentrated in a few days of the month—perhaps near payday, when mortgage payments, car payments, credit card company payments, and the like are made—instead of being distributed equally. Moreover, the example entirely neglects receipts from security sales and the money transactions which occur as product passes through the several stages of production.

Still, refinements to take these matters into account do not in themselves violate the basic property of the model, a stable and proportionate relationship between money balances demanded and income. Proportionality and stability in the money demand function require regularity, not uniformity, in payment and receipt streams. The classical economists emphasized that the time distribution of payment and receipt streams depends on the customs and habits of the community, and that these change only gradually over time.

The Speculative Motive and the Role of Interest

Keynes cited three motives for holding money balances, adding the precautionary and speculative motives to the transactions motive.[1] The *precautionary motive* is closely related to the transactions motive; it simply recognizes that households, firms, and governments in general will not be content to see their money balances fall to zero at a point during the receipt-payment period but instead will hold a margin against unforeseen variations in the receipt or payment stream. Keynes recognized that transactions balances and precautionary balances could theoretically be influenced by the interest rate; but he neglected such an influence in his presentation and regarded both types of balances as bearing an essentially proportionate relation to income.

The *speculative motive* is the source of Keynes's view that money demand is highly sensitive to the interest rate on securities and that the money demand function is unstable. The demand for speculative money balances arises from expectations that interest rates will rise in the future. Keynes argued that wealth-holders who expect interest rates to rise significantly will place wealth in money rather than securities, because to expect interest rates to rise is to expect the prices at which securities can be sold to fall, generating losses on securities.

For example, a bond which pays $40 per year in perpetuity to the holder (a bond which never matures) sells for $1,000 when the market rate of interest on such securities is 4 percent, since $40 in perpetuity is a yield of 4 percent on $1,000—that is, $40/$1,000 = 0.04. If the market interest rate rises to 5 percent, however, this security can be sold for only $800, since $40/$800 = 0.05. No one will pay more than $800 for such a security when the market interest rate is 5 percent, because a similar security is available elsewhere in the market for that price. In effect—ignoring transaction costs, risk premiums, and any interest yields which are available on money—wealth will be transferred from the bond to money at the point at which the expected market value loss on the bond from interest rate increases exceeds the interest or dividend payment,

[1] John Maynard Keynes, *The General Theory of Employment, Interest, and Money* (New York: Harcourt, Brace, 1936), chap. 15.

making the expected net yield on the bond inferior to the zero yield on money.

Notice that wealth-holders who expect the interest rate to rise from 4 to 5 percent should sell the bonds even if they expect the interest rate to return eventually to 4 percent. Neglecting the interest payment earnings, the holders would have $1,000 per bond after the interest rate had risen and then returned to its former level if their wealth had remained in the bonds. But if the bonds had been sold for $1,000 each prior to the rise in the interest rate and then repurchased for $800 after the interest rate had risen to 5 percent, the wealth-holders would again have bonds worth $1,000 each plus $200 per bond in profit after the interest rate returned to 4 percent.

How did Keynes get from these considerations to a theory in which money demand varies inversely with the interest rate? He argued that as the interest rate falls a larger proportion of wealth-holders expects it to rise in the future rather than remain unchanged or fall, and consequently a larger proportion of wealth is placed in money instead of securities. Indeed, Keynes offered the view that there exists a low but still positive rate of interest at which no one will hold securities rather than money, since everyone will expect interest rates to rise by enough to eliminate via market value losses the extra interest or dividend payments available on securities. This is Keynes's famous *liquidity trap.* Once the interest rate has fallen to this level, the monetary authority can force it no lower. Increases in the money supply will simply be added to money holdings. The demand for money is infinite.

Figure 9–2 illustrates the relationship between money balances demanded and interest as envisaged by Keynes, complete with liquidity trap. For the purposes of the figure, the level of Y is held constant at Y' along the curve. This liquidity preference curve will shift to the right for higher levels of Y, reflecting the influence of the transactions and precautionary motives for holding money balances. The liquidity trap will remain at the same level, however.

How does the speculative motive produce a money demand function which is unstable, that is, a situation where the volume of money balances demanded at various interest and income combinations is changeable? Since speculative money balances demanded at each interest rate depend on wealth-holders' expectations as to future interest rates, any shift in expectations will shift speculative balances held at each interest rate. For example, if there is an increase in the portion of wealth-holders expecting interest rates to rise by enough to produce net losses on securities, the speculative demand for money balances will increase. The

Figure 9–2 **The Liquidity Preference Curve**

According to Keynes, aggregate money balances demanded become larger as the interest rate becomes lower because the proportion of wealth-holders placing wealth in money rather than bonds expands as the interest rate declines. At some low but still positive rate of interest the demand for money becomes infinite, since no one will hold bonds.

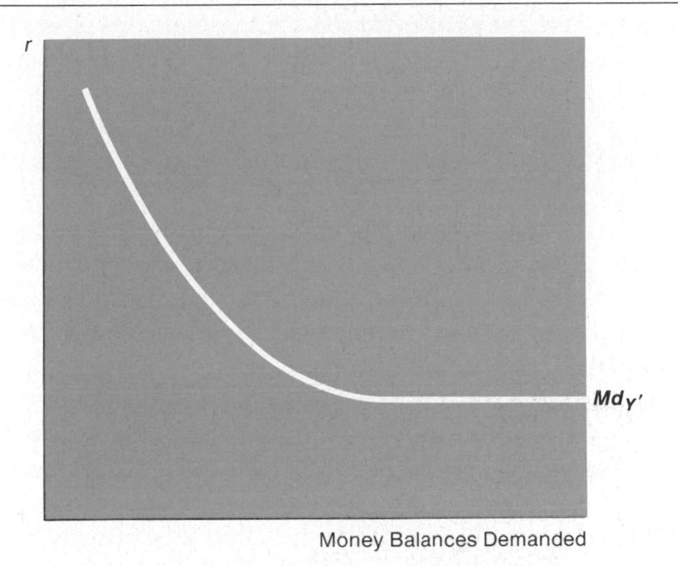

liquidity preference curve of Figure 9–2, relating to income Y', will shift to the right. Keynes's money demand function, like his investment expenditure function, depends on expectations and hence is changeable.

James Tobin has criticized the Keynesian approach to the money demand and interest relationship because it implies that wealth beyond that held in money to satisfy transactions and precautionary motives will, for the individual, be placed either all in money or all in securities.[2] Tobin regards this as implausible and demonstrates that, where expectations as to future changes in interest rates are probabilistic (a 10 percent chance of this, a 30 percent chance of that), individuals likely will diversify their speculative wealth between money and securities, balancing the greater expected return of a portfolio weighted toward securities against the greater risk such a weighting entails.

[2] James Tobin, "Liquidity Preference as Behavior towards Risk," *Review of Economic Studies* 25 (February 1958): 65–86.

The Tobin formulation does more than provide a rationale for diversified speculative portfolios for individuals, however. It provides additional reasons why money demand may relate inversely to interest rates. Aggregate money demand may expand as interest declines not only because individuals revise upward their expectations as to future changes in interest rates, as argued by Keynes, but also because the lower interest rates provide less incentive to risk bearing, that is, to security holding. Moreover, since security prices rise as interest rates fall, the total value of wealth rises, providing a wealth effect which may induce more money holding.

Current Approaches to the Demand for Money

The diminished emphasis modern approaches place on the speculative motive results in part from the failure of statistical investigations to substantiate its suggestions that money demand is highly interest sensitive and that the money demand function is volatile. There is a theoretical problem with the motive as well, however.

Most wealth which is shifted on the basis of the speculative motive shifts between long-term securities and short-term securities such as U.S. Treasury bills rather than between long-term securities and money. Interest still is earned on the short-term securities, and their market prices vary little when the interest rate changes. A $100,000 U.S. Treasury bill which matures next week will sell for very close to $100,000 today regardless of what happens to the interest rate, since the bill will produce $100,000 next week. To the extent that the speculative motive does cause wealth to shift between long-term and short-term securities, money balances are not involved. The speculative motive does not enter into money holding or money demand interest sensitivity.

Of course, if commercial bank savings deposits are included in the money supply, interest can be earned on money as well as on short-term securities. This gives some support to the idea of a speculative motive for money holding. But savings deposits are not convenient vehicles for the large blocks of funds which are essential to an important role for the speculative motive in money holding. They involve greater default risk than U.S. Treasury bills, since they are federally insured only to $40,000. Moreover, it is easier to ask a security dealer to sell bonds and buy bills, which will be stored for you, than to ask that bonds be sold and to arrange for the placement of the proceeds in a savings deposit.

With the diminished importance of the speculative motive in current theories, the emphasis has shifted elsewhere insofar as the rationale for an interest rate and money demand relationship is concerned. The interest rate enters as a determinant of optimum transactions and precautionary money balances or, more generally, as the opportunity cost to be equated to the utility or productivity value of money holdings at the margin.

The Interest Rate and Transactions Money Balances

The earlier discussion of the transactions motive for holding money assumed that funds which arose as a result of differences between receipt and payment streams simply were left in money balances. These funds became *transactions money balances.* Actually, business firms or government units which regularly have such funds on hand in large amounts are likely to place them in short-term securities, such as U.S. Treasury bills, large-denomination certificates of deposit of commercial banks, or commercial paper issued by well established nonbank corporations.

The tendency for firms and government units to place such funds in securities when it is profitable to do so provides a rationale for an inverse relationship between the interest rate and transactions money balances. As the interest rate rises, the period for which funds must be available in order for earnings from placing the funds in securities to exceed the transaction costs of such placement shortens. More transactions funds are placed in securities instead of being left in money, and, as a result, average transactions money balances decline.

To see how this works, consider the case of a profit-oriented firm which has $2 million in temporary funds on a regular basis, a million available for two weeks and a second million available for one week. Assume that the transaction cost of placing the funds in securities is 0.125 percent, half for buying the securities and half for selling.[3] The firm earns no interest on money holdings since savings deposits are restricted to individuals and nonprofit institutions.

In this situation, the firm will invest only the million available for two weeks if the interest rate is 6 percent but will invest both millions if the interest rate is 8 percent. A million dollars invested at a 6 percent annual rate earns $2,243.60 when invested for two weeks and $1,121.20 when

[3] William J. Baumol and James Tobin have provided more general proofs. See W. Baumol, "The Transactions Demand for Cash: An Inventory Theoretic Approach," *Quarterly Journal of Economics* 66 (November 1952): 545–556; and J. Tobin, "The Interest Elasticity of Transactions Demand for Cash," *Review of Economics and Statistics* 38 (August 1956): 241–247.

invested for one week.[4] The million available for two weeks earns more than the $1,250.00 cost of investing (0.00125 times $1 million) but the million available for one week does not. At the 8 percent annual interest rate, both millions can be profitably invested. A million dollars invested at 8 percent earns $2,964.40 when invested for two weeks and $1,481.10 when invested for one week. Therefore, if the interest rate rises from 6 to 8 percent, the firm invests both millions, rather than just the million available for two weeks, and its average transactions money balance declines.

The Interest Rate and Precautionary Money Balances

Precautionary money balances also may be influenced significantly by the interest rate. These balances, as stated earlier, are held so that assets will not have to be sold, or funds borrowed, to cover shortages arising from unforeseen variations in the receipt and payment streams. It seems plausible that wealth-holders will reduce precautionary money balances, and thus bear more risk of suffering a shortage, as market interest rates rise relative to what can be earned on money, which is zero, or the relatively inflexible yields on savings deposits.

---

[4] The formula associating annual interest rate and revenue earned from investment for periods of less than one year is complicated by the necessity of allowing for compounding of interest. In the example, the amount earned for two weeks is more than twice the amount earned for one week because of the interest earned in the second week on the first week's interest. Revenue earned is:

$$X[(1 + r)^{1/p} - 1],$$

where:

X = the amount invested in securities,
r = interest rate, at annual rate, and
$1/p$ = the fraction of a year for which the funds are invested.

Consequently, the condition for profitability is:

$$X[(1 + r)^{1/p} - 1] > uX,$$

where u is the transaction cost as a percentage of the amount invested.
This reduces to:

$$[(1 + r)^{1/p} - 1 > u,$$

from which it is apparent that an increase in the interest rate permits a reduction in the fraction of a year for which funds are available. An increase in r compensates for a decrease in $1/p$. Obviously, this is a difficult formula to solve. It is best to use a financial table or a preprogrammed computer.

Milton Friedman's Approach

Milton Friedman approaches the demand for money by regarding money simply as a consumer and producer good, a good which never wears out.[5] As a consumer good, money provides utility to the holder. As a producer good, it is a factor of production. The services provided by money—convenience in effecting transactions, security, and so on—obviously are the same as those incorporated into transactions, precautionary, and speculative motives, but the emphasis is on utility and productive services provided rather than on motives. For simplicity, Friedman ignores the possibility of interest earnings on money in his analysis. This involves no loss of generality insofar as yields on money are inflexible relative to general market interest rates.

Consumers are regarded as allocating wealth among money balances and other assets. Thus, in the application of consumer demand theory to money holding, wealth, rather than income, enters the budget constraint. Optimum money holdings occur when the utility of the services of the last dollar of money held equals the utility of what can be purchased with the interest yield from a dollar placed in other assets. Money holdings are characterized by diminishing marginal utility and hence experience a diminishing marginal rate of substitution compared with other assets in consumer preferences.

Consumer demand for money balances emerges as varying inversely with interest and directly with income. As the interest rate declines, more money is demanded for two reasons. First, more money must be held to depress the marginal utility of money holding and bring it into line with the lower opportunity cost of holding money. Second, since wealth is the present value of expected income, with the interest rate as the discount factor (that is, wealth equals expected income divided by the interest rate), wealth increases as the interest rate declines, so that more of all assets, including money balances, are held.

Why do money balances demanded expand as income increases? As income increases, expected income, and hence wealth, increases, so that again more of all assets, including money, can be held. As with the consumption function, Friedman uses permanent income rather than measured income as the appropriate income variable, so that responses of money demand to income are delayed. Friedman prefers to suppress

[5] Milton Friedman, "The Quantity Theory of Money—A Restatement," in *Studies in the Quantity Theory of Money*, ed. Milton Friedman (Chicago: University of Chicago Press, 1956).

the transactions and income association insofar as the consumer demand for money is concerned, dealing explicitly with the income-induced wealth effect only.

Producer demand for money balances also varies inversely with interest and directly with income. Producers employ money balances in the production process to the point where the productivity of the marginal dollar of money balances equals the interest rate, which is what could be earned if the dollar were placed instead in securities. As more money balances are added to the production process, with other factors constant, the marginal productivity of money balances diminishes. Thus, as the interest rate increases, a smaller amount of money balances is employed because the marginal productivity of money balances must be increased to bring it into line with the higher opportunity cost.

What is the source of the role of income in producer money demand? As aggregate income and output increase, more of all factors of production, including money balances, are required to support the higher level of production.

Statistical Results

A substantial effort has gone into statistically estimating the money demand function during the past several decades. Regression techniques, the same as those used for estimating the consumption and investment functions, have been the basic device employed. The features of greatest interest concern the extent to which real money balances demanded are sensitive to real income and interest and the extent to which the functional relationship between real money demand and the two variables is stable.

How sensitive is money demand to income? David Laidler has concluded that the income elasticity of money demand was somewhat larger than unity (1.0) in the United States during 1900–1940, and somewhat smaller than unity during 1946–1965.[6] Unity, as applied to the income elasticity of money demand, means that a given percent change in real income provokes the same percent change in real money balances demanded. Laidler's work therefore suggests that there have been economies of scale in money holding in the United States since World War II. Less money is needed, in proportion to real income, as real income increases.

---

[6] D. E. W. Laidler, *The Demand for Money: Theories and Evidence*, 2d ed. (New York: Dun-Donnelley, 1977), pp. 148–149.

How sensitive is money demand to interest? Laidler estimates that the interest elasticity of money demand (percent change in money demand divided by percent change in the interest rate) falls between −0.2 and −0.6 for the long-term rate of interest and between −0.12 and −0.15 for the short-term rate of interest, if time deposits are included in the money definition.[7] These figures indicate that money demand is interest inelastic. That is, changes in the interest rate provoke smaller percentage changes in money demand.

Milton Friedman has used an elasticity estimate, apparently for the long-term rate of interest, which implies a slightly smaller sensitivity of money demand to interest.[8] Franco Modigliani, Robert Rasche, and J. Phillip Cooper, in a joint paper undertaken in connection with estimating the money demand equation of the neo-Keynesian Federal Reserve–MIT model, present empirical estimates relating to the short-term rate of interest which imply a money demand interest sensitivity slightly higher than that indicated by the Laidler range.[9]

F. M. Goldfeld's work on money demand suggests that the money demand function is fairly stable, at least in the absence of technological innovations such as telephonic transfers of funds, automatic transfer plans, and the like.[10]

In sum, the statistical literature confirms real income and the interest rate as determinants of real money balances demanded. However, it does not document either the great sensitivity of money demand to interest or the highly volatile money demand function suggested by Keynes and the early Keynesians.

Summary

1. The classical economists emphasized the transactions motive for holding money balances in their theory of the demand for money and emerged with a view in which money balances demanded bear a stable and proportionate relationship to income.

---

[7] Ibid., pp. 133–134.

[8] Milton Friedman, "Interest Rates and the Demand for Money," *Journal of Law and Economics* 9 (October 1966): 73.

[9] F. Modigliani, R. Rasche, and J. Cooper, "Central Bank Policy, the Money Supply, and the Short-term Rate of Interest," *Journal of Money, Credit, and Banking* 2 (May 1970): 166–218.

[10] F. M. Goldfeld, "The Demand for Money Revisited," *Brookings Papers on Economic Activity* 3 (1973): 577–638; and "The Case of the Missing Money," *Brookings Papers on Economic Activity* 3 (1976): 683–730.

2. Keynes added precautionary and speculative motives for holding money balances and produced a theory in which money balances demanded are highly sensitive to interest and the function relating money balances demanded to interest and income is volatile.

3. Current approaches deemphasize the speculative motive and imply a smaller interest sensitivity of money demand and a more stable money demand function. Emphasis is placed on the interest rate as the opportunity cost of holding money balances, a cost which enters into the determination of optimum transactions and precautionary money balances or which is compared to the utility or productivity of a dollar of money balances at the margin.

4. Statistical investigations confirm both real income and the interest rate as determinants of real money balances demanded, but document neither the substantial interest sensitivity nor the substantial volatility Keynes and the early Keynesians perceived in the money demand function.

Concepts for Identification

demand for money
transactions motive
speculative motive
precautionary motive
liquidity preference curve
liquidity trap
perpetual bond
interest elasticity of money demand
income elasticity of money demand
money demand function

Questions and Problems for Review

1. Explain why aggregate real money balances demanded on the basis of the transactions motive might be expected to vary directly with aggregate real income and inversely with interest rates.

2. Describe the effect on the money demand function (M-1+ balances) of:

a. A trend toward increased use of credit cards for making purchases.

b. A reduction in the minimum denomination of short-term United States government securities from $10,000 to $1,000.

3. The federal government imposes ceilings on the interest rates which can be paid on both regular savings deposits and other time deposits of commercial banks. Explain the effect on the quantity of real M-1+ money balances demanded if the ceilings on the other time deposits are raised but those on regular savings deposits left unchanged during a period of high and rising interest rates.

4. Explain the effect on the demand for demand deposits plus cash if competition among commercial banks forces them to lower charges imposed on savings deposits held under plans which automatically transfer funds between savings deposits and demand deposits as needed for covering checks drawn on the demand deposits. What would be the likely effect of this lowering of charges on the M-1+ money supply, assuming that the Federal Reserve maintained bank reserves, reserve requirements, and the discount rate unchanged?

5. Explain Keynes's speculative motive as a basis for:
a. Sensitivity of real money balances demanded to general interest rates.
b. A liquidity trap at a positive rate of interest.
c. Volatility in the money demand function relating real money balances demanded to real income and general interest rates.

6. Apply Equation 7–2 from Chapter 7 to show that the market price of a bond which pays $50 per year for four years (beginning at the end of the year commencing today) and which also pays a maturity value of $1,000 at the end of the fourth year is $1,036.30 today if the market rate of interest on such securities is 4 percent today. What will be the loss in market value on this security if the market rate of interest on it suddenly rises to 5 percent? What would be the loss in market value of a bond paying $50 per year forever if the market rate of interest on such bonds rose from 4 to 5 percent? Why is the loss greater on the perpetual bond than on the bond which matures in four years?

7. Milton Friedman's approach to the demand for money is to consider the utility or productive services provided by money balances rather than specific motives for holding money. Using Friedman's approach, explain why:
a. Real money balances demanded by households decline as interest rates rise.
b. Real money balances demanded by households rise as real incomes increase.

c. Real money balances demanded by firms increase as interest rates decline.
d. Real money balances demanded by firms increase as output and real income increase.

8. Assume that statistical estimation of the money demand function has indicated that aggregate real money balances demanded would rise from $100 billion to $110 billion if the interest rate declined from 4 to 3 percent with aggregate real income unchanged. Verify that this relationship indicates an interest elasticity of money demand of -0.4.

9. The statistical evidence suggests that the money demand function (real money balances demanded at various interest rate and real income combinations) declined sharply during 1975 and 1976 when the M-1 money definition is used but not when the M-1+ money definition is used. Explain how the introduction of NOW accounts and telephone transfers of funds between commercial bank savings and demand deposits during the mid-1970s may have contributed to this phenomenon.

References

Baumol, William J. "The Transactions Demand for Cash: An Inventory Theoretic Approach." *Quarterly Journal of Economics* 66 (November 1952): 545–556.

Branson, William H. *Macroeconomic Theory and Policy.* New York: Harper & Row, 1979, chap. 12.

Friedman, Milton. "The Quantity Theory of Money—A Restatement." In *Studies in the Quantity Theory of Money,* edited by Milton Friedman (Chicago: University of Chicago Press, 1956, pp. 3–21.

———. "A Theoretical Framework for Monetary Analysis." *Journal of Political Economy* 78 (March–April 1970): 193–219.

Goldfeld, S. M. "The Demand for Money Revisited." *Brookings Papers on Economic Activity* 3 (1973): 577–646.

Keynes, J. M. *The General Theory of Employment, Interest, and Money.* New York: Harcourt, Brace, 1936, chap. 15.

Laidler, D. E. W. *The Demand for Money: Theories and Evidence.* 2d ed. New York: Dun-Donnelley, 1977, chaps. 3–8.

Modigliani, Franco. "Liquidity Preference and the Theory of Interest and Money." *Econometrica* 12 (January 1944): 45–88.

Modigliani, Franco; Rasche, Robert; and Cooper, J. Phillip. "Central Bank Policy, the Money Supply, and the Short-term Rate of Interest." *Journal of Money, Credit, and Banking* 2 (May 1970): 166–218.

Tobin, James. "The Interest Elasticity of Transactions Demand for Cash." *Review of Economics and Statistics* 38 (August 1956): 241–247.

———. "Liquidity Preference as Behavior towards Risk." *Review of Economic Studies* 25 (February 1958): 65–86.

10

Equilibrium with the Money Market Included

An equilibrium involving aggregate output, the price level, and the interest rate occurs where expenditures just support output and the demand for real money balances just equals the real money supply. The IS-LM model illustrates this equilibrium. Less than full employment and full employment with price stability equilibriums are presented, and the expenditure gap situation is shown.

This chapter adds a money market to the models of Part 2 and illustrates macroeconomic equilibrium with the money market included. As noted at the beginning of Chapter 7, money was present in the Part 2 models, performing its function as a means of payment and so on, but its influence on the level of expenditures was neglected.

In this chapter, the channels by which monetary influences cause direct effects on expenditures will be confined to interest rate effects on investment and consumption expenditures. Later chapters will note briefly that interest rate effects appear to be significant for state and local government construction purchases as well and will consider the case where consumption purchases are directly sensitive to the size of the real money supply.

The macroeconomic equilibrium of this chapter is an equilibrium in the sense that output, price level, interest rate, level of employment, and other macroeconomic variables display no tendency to change during the short term to which it pertains. It is not an equilibrium in the broader sense that all markets clear. As in the Part II models, excess supply exists in the labor market when equilibrium occurs at less than full employment.[1] In these cases, the equilibrium depends on price and money wage rigidity.

Equilibrium in the Expanded Model

The expanded model will include the modified relationships:

$$I = f(r) \qquad \text{10–1}$$

and

$$C = f(Yd, r), \qquad \text{10–2}$$

where both I and C vary inversely with r. In addition, it includes the new equations:

$$Ms = Md, \qquad \text{10–3}$$

$$Ms = m/P, \qquad \text{10–4}$$

$$m = m_0, \qquad \text{10–5}$$

and

$$Md = f(Y, r), \qquad \text{10–6}$$

where Md varies directly with Y and inversely with r. In these equations:

r = the interest rate;
Ms = the real money supply, or real money balances;
m = the money supply (non–price deflated); and
Md = real money balances demanded.

---

[1] Economists who define *equilibrium* as a situation where all markets are clearing therefore treat the less than full employment equilibriums of this chapter as disequilibrium situations. See R. W. Clower, "The Keynesian Counter-Revolution: A Theoretical Appraisal," in *The Theory of Interest Rates*, ed. F. H. Hahn and F. P. R. Brechling (London: Macmillan, 1965); and Robert J. Barro and Herschel I. Grossman, "A General Disequilibrium Model of Income and Employment," *American Economic Review* 61 (March 1971): 82–93.

Investment and consumption expenditures now are functions of the interest rate. They become larger as the interest rate becomes smaller. The interest rate is simply a weighted average of the costs of funds raised through issue of securities (bonds, stocks, loans, mortgages, and so on) and savings deposits. From the point of view of the purchaser of these assets, of course, it reflects yields anticipated on funds placed in them. The rationales for these relationships were discussed in detail in Chapters 7, 8, and 9.

For investment expenditures, the profit maximizing principle is the essential factor involved. Firms make investment expenditures if they estimate that the yields to be earned on them will exceed the costs of the funds required for financing plus a margin for risk bearing. As the interest rate falls, the cost of financing investment expenditures falls, and a larger portion of existing investment opportunities appears profitable. The volume of investment expenditures planned by producers therefore rises. With housing expenditures, the credit rationing effect is important.

For consumption expenditures, several factors appear to be involved, including the pre-Keynesian notion that consumption increases as the interest rate declines because households save less and consume more as the return for saving diminishes. Modern views place more emphasis on a marginal efficiency of investment effect on expenditures for consumer durable goods and on an interest-induced wealth effect which presents consumption expenditures as increasing in response to the increases in security prices accompanying reductions in security yields. These effects were discussed in detail in Chapter 7.

Equation 10–3 is the equilibrium condition for the money market. When it is added to the model, macroeconomic equilibrium requires not just that demand support output (that is, not just that Y equal E) but also that the community be willing to hold as money the volume of real money balances available for holding.

The money supply, represented by m, conforms to the Federal Reserve's M-1+ money supply definition. It is the government's monetary control variable. It is fixed by the monetary authority at m_0, which is the money supply corresponding to a banking system in equilibrium with a fixed level of desired excess reserves. Chapter 8 explained how the U.S. monetary authority controls the U.S. money supply by influencing bank reserves and reserve requirements and how it depends upon commercial banks to move to the loaned-up position for demand deposits by shifting any extra excess reserves to loans or securities. For the most part, these details of money supply operations remain in the background in this chapter, emerging only where they are useful. Notice that the term *money supply* is used for the version which is not price deflated, while the price deflated version is the *real money supply*.

Md, real money balances demanded, reflects the real wealth the community wishes to hold in money rather than in alternative forms such as bonds, stocks, and buildings. According to Equation 10–6, *Md* depends on Y and r, varying directly with Y and inversely with r. Chapter 9 discussed the rationales for these relationships.

The other assumptions of the model remain as in Chapter 6. Consumption expenditures vary positively with private disposable income. The marginal propensity to consume from such income is a fraction. Private disposable income is total income minus taxes plus transfer payments. Taxes vary directly with income. Transfer payments are a constant. Government purchases of final goods and services are a constant. All of these relationships are defined in real terms.

Also retained is the assumption that responses of output and prices to demand break cleanly at full employment. If demand exceeds full-employment output, output is fixed at full-employment output and prices rise. If demand equals full-employment output or falls short of it, output adjusts to demand and prices are constant. Worker resistance to money wage cuts prevents prices and money wages from declining in the demand shortfall case. The assumption that prices are constant if money wages are constant is a simplification, as before.

The illustration of macroeconomic equilibrium follows the technique employed in the earlier models. The first equilibrium computation ignores the full-employment constraint and proceeds as if output could adjust fully to any level of demand forthcoming at existing prices. The following conditions apply:

$$Y = E \qquad \text{10–7}$$

and

$$m_0/P_x = Md, \qquad \text{10–8}$$

where P_x is the existing price level. Next, this Y is compared to Y_f, and the result generalized. If this trial equilibrium for Y does not exceed Y_f, it is the equilibrium for Y, and prices are constant at P_x. If the trial Y exceeds Y_f, it indicates an expenditure gap, and prices rise. Now, however, with a money market included, the model finds equilibrium even in the expenditure gap case. Prices come to equilibrium at a level above the initial level, inflation ceases, and output is fixed at full-employment output.

Equilibrium with the Full-Employment Constraint Ignored

When the $Y = E$ condition is applied, there is no longer a single solution for Y, but a series of combinations of Y and r in which Y increases as r diminishes. This occurs because investment expenditures and consumption expenditures increase as the interest rate declines.

Figure 10–1 illustrates the relationship. The lower portion of the figure presents the familiar aggregate expenditures and income relationship of earlier chapters. Now, however, instead of a single upward-sloping line representing the relationship, there are three such lines, one for each of three selected rates of interest. As the interest rate declines from r_a to r_b to r_c, the total expenditure line shifts upward, reflecting the increases in investment and consumption expenditures which occur with reductions in the interest rate. For interest rate r_a, the total expenditure line intersects the 45° line at Y_1, indicating that demand supports an output of Y_1—that is, the $Y = E$ condition determines an output of Y_1. With the interest rate lower, at r_b, the total expenditure line is higher, intersecting the 45° line at Y_2. When the interest rate is still lower, at r_c, the point of intersection is at Y_3, which, of course, is a still larger Y.

The schedule collecting the r and Y combinations appears in the upper portion of the figure. It slopes downward from left to right, reflecting the fact that Y rises as r falls. Traditionally, this schedule is called the *IS* curve, and it is so labelled here. While it plots Y for each r, bear in mind that it also reflects the E for each r, since it is constructed on the assumption that Y adjusts to E. It plots the combinations of Y and r at which Y equals E. Notice that the increase in Y which accompanies the reduction in r from r_a to r_b along the *IS* curve is greater than the vertical shift in the total expenditure line in the lower portion of the figure. This is the case because the increase in E and Y along the *IS* curve includes not just the direct responses of investment and consumption expenditures to the interest rate, which are reflected in the vertical shift in the total expenditure line, but also the income-induced effect on consumption expenditures which occurs as Y increases.

Which of the r and Y combinations of the *IS* curve yields the trial equilibrium for Y? Equilibrium occurs at the combination which also produces equilibrium in the money market.

The *LM* curve of the right-hand portion of Figure 10–2 traces the r and Y

Figure 10–1 A Graphic Construction of the *IS* Curve

As the interest rate becomes lower, interest-sensitive expenditures become greater and support higher levels of output and real income.

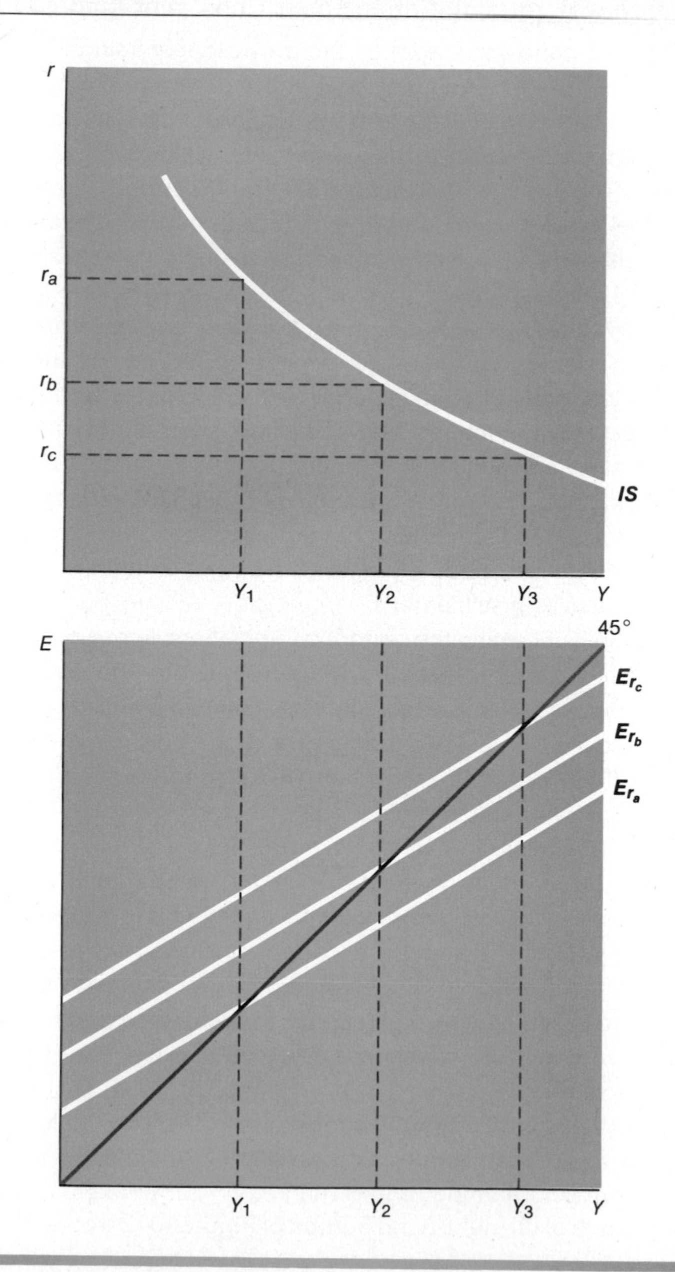

Figure 10–2 **Constructing the *LM* Curve**

The *LM* curve represents money market equilibrium for a given real money supply. It presents combinations of the interest rate and the level of output and real income at which the demand for real money balances just equals the real money supply.

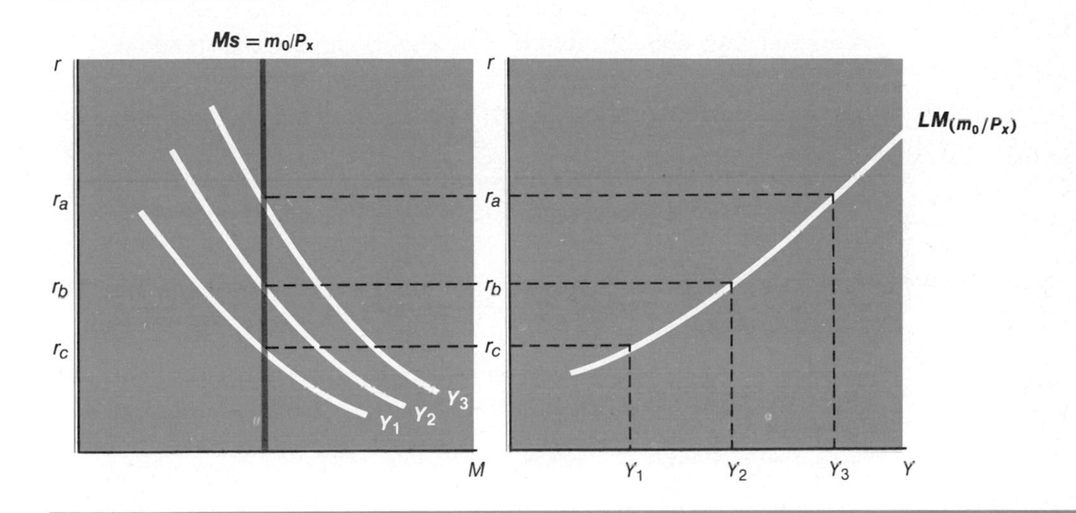

combinations which equilibrate the money market. It presents the combinations at which the demand for real money balances equals the supply of real money balances. This curve must slope upward, since m_0/P_x is fixed and r and Y produce offsetting influences on Md. For example, taking any point on the *LM* curve so that m_0/P_x equals Md initially, an increase in Y must be balanced by an increase in r if m_0/P_x is to remain equal to Md. That is, the increase in Y, which causes Md to increase, must be accompanied by an increase in r, which causes Md to decline, if Md is to remain unchanged and equal to the unchanged m_0/P_x. (Recall from Equation 10–6 that Md varies directly with Y and inversely with r.)

Figure 10–2 generates the *LM* curve graphically. The supply of real money balances is a vertical line at m_0/P_x on the horizontal axis in the left-hand portion of the figure. It is vertical because m_0/P_x does not vary with r. The demand for real money balances appears as a set of three downward-sloping lines, one for each of three selected values of Y. The downward slopes of the lines reflect the inverse variation of Md with r. Md increases as r declines, with Y fixed. The rightward shifts of the Md lines for successively higher levels of Y reflect the positive association of Md with Y.

Md becomes higher as *Y* becomes higher, with *r* fixed. Money market equilibrium occurs where the money demand lines intersect the money supply line. If *Y* is at Y_3, *r* must equal r_a if money demand is to equal money supply. For Y_2, *r* must be at r_b. For Y_1, *r* must be at r_c.

Figure 10–3 puts the *IS* and *LM* curves together and illustrates the model equilibrium with the full-employment constraint ignored. It occurs at Point A, where the curves intersect. Only at this combination of *r* and *Y* do expenditures support output while money supply equals money demand. At any other combination, either expenditures do not exactly support output (the point is off the *IS* curve), or money demand does not equal money supply (the point is off the *LM* curve), or neither condition holds (the point is not on either curve).

Consider Point B in the figure, for example. The economy in this state is

Figure 10–3 **Equilibrium with the Full-Employment Constraint Ignored**

Assuming for the moment that output can adjust to any level of expenditure, equilibrium occurs where the *IS* and *LM* curves intersect. Only at this point does expenditure just support output and the demand for real money balances just equal the real money supply.

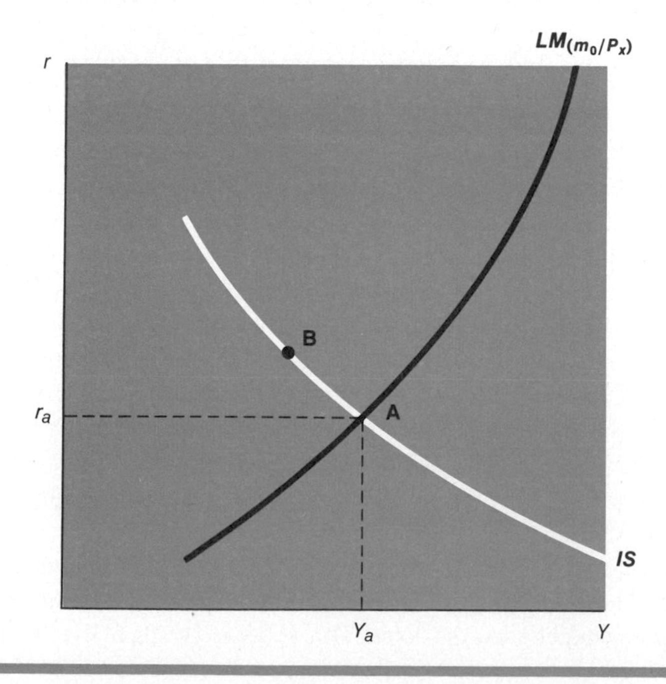

at a point on the *IS* curve, so demand just supports output. The economy is not in equilibrium, however, since Point B is not on the *LM* curve. Money supply exceeds money demand at Point B. The interest rate and output combination at Point B does not induce the community to hold the existing supply of real money balances.

What forces will propel the economy toward the equilibrium at Y_a and r_a if it is initially at Point B? It can be assumed that the excess money supply at Point B will force the interest rate down as holders of the excess money balances shift them to securities.[2] The lower interest rate will expand investment and consumption expenditures and thereby total expenditures, output, and real income. At r_a and Y_a, money demand will have expanded to the point where the community will be willing to hold the existing money supply, and, at the same time, expenditures will support output.

Equilibrium with the Full-Employment Constraint Considered

This section imposes the full-employment constraint on the trial equilibrium of the preceding section, stipulating that the fully employed economy produces an output of:

$$Y = Y_f. \qquad \text{10–9}$$

Y_f, as before, is a constant, consistent with the natural rate of unemployment.

Figure 10–4 presents three basic situations.

In Situation 1, shortfall unemployment is present. The computed Y falls to the left of the full-employment line. This indicates that expenditures will not support full-employment output. Output and real income adjust to the intersection of the *IS* and *LM* curves, and an unemployment problem results. Prices remain constant at the existing level.

Situation 2 represents full employment without inflation. The intersection of the *IS* and *LM* curves falls exactly on the full-employment line. Expenditures at existing prices just support full-employment output. Full-employment output therefore prevails, and prices remain constant.

Situation 3 represents the expenditure gap. The intersection of the *IS*

[2] Recall that the position of the *LM* curve reflects the equilibrium money supply m_0. The excess supply of money at Point B may be either excess money balances or excess reserves of banks. In either form it presumably presses the interest rate down as the excesses are exchanged for loans and securities.

Figure 10–4 **Three Basic Situations**

When the *IS* and *LM* curves intersect to the left of the full-employment line, shortfall unemployment is present. If the intersection is exactly on the full-employment line, full employment occurs and prices are stable. If it falls to the right of the full-employment line, an expenditure gap is present at existing prices, and prices rise.

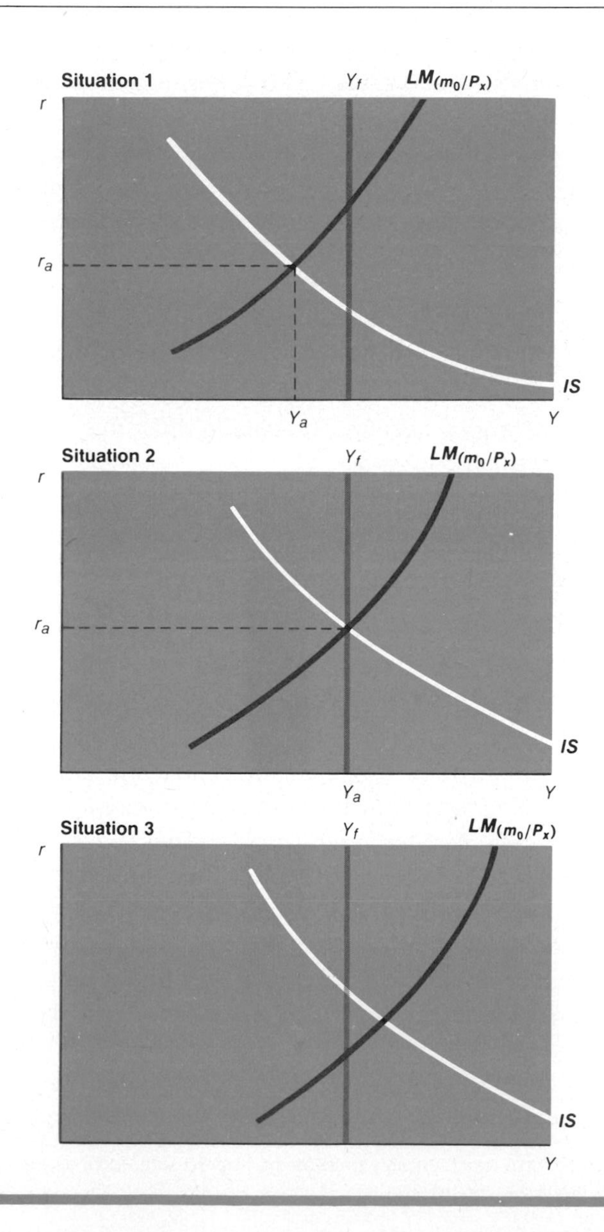

and *LM* curves to the right of the full-employment line indicates that expenditures at existing prices exceed full-employment output. Output is fixed at full-employment output in this situation, since expenditures will support it, and prices rise.

Figure 10–5 reflects the eventual equilibrium for the expenditure gap case. As prices rise, real money balances decline and the *LM* curve shifts to the left. Equilibrium occurs when prices have risen by enough to cause the *LM* curve to intersect the *IS* curve at Point B, where the *IS* curve intersects the full-employment line. At Point B, the expenditure gap is eliminated and inflation ceases. The economy is in full macroeconomic equilibrium. Y equals Y_f, r equals r_b, and P equals P_x'. Expenditures just support full-employment output, and money demand equals money supply.

Figure 10–5 **Equilibrium for the Expenditure Gap Case**

When an expenditure gap is present at the existing price level, prices rise. Equilibrium is restored when the decline in the real money supply has shifted the *LM* curve to the left by enough to close the expenditure gap.

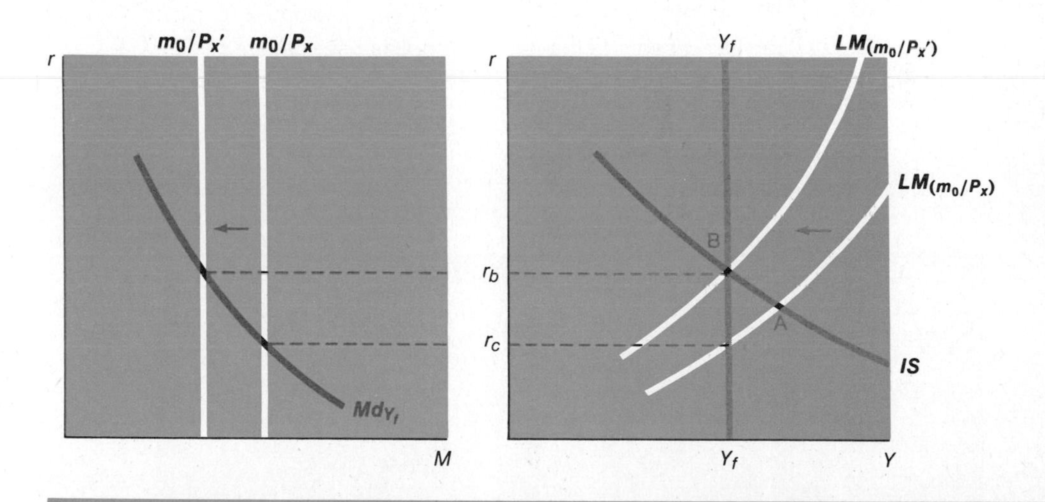

Why does the *LM* curve shift to the left when prices rise and the real money supply declines? Recall that the *LM* curve plots combinations of Y and r at which the real money supply equals real money balances demanded. It must shift to the left when the real money supply declines, since money market equilibrium requires that real money balances demanded also decline, and this situation requires a higher interest rate for each level of Y.

Figure 10–6 illustrates the mechanics of this leftward shift in the *LM* curve in isolation from the complications of the *IS* curve. The left-hand portion of the figure presents the relationship between the real money balances demanded and the interest rate for Y_a, a selected level of output and real income. This curve slopes downward, since the relation between *Md* and r is inverse. Also in the left-hand portion is the real money supply bar for m_0/P_x, where P_x is an initial price level. In the case of Y_a, the interest rate must be r_a if real money balances demanded are to equal real money supply m_0/P_x. This combination of r and Y generates Point A in the right-hand portion of the figure, a point on the *LM* curve for m_0/P_x.

When prices rise to P_x', the real money supply falls to m_0/P_x', and the real money supply bar moves to the left, as in the left-hand portion of Figure 10–6. With Y at Y_a, r now must be at r_a' if real money balances demanded are to equal the real money supply. This produces Point A′ in

Figure 10–6 **The *LM* Curve Shifting to the Left When Prices Rise**

The *LM* curve must shift to the left when prices rise, because increases in prices reduce the real money supply. The interest rate must be higher for each level of output and real income if real money balances demanded are to be smaller and equal to the smaller real money supply.

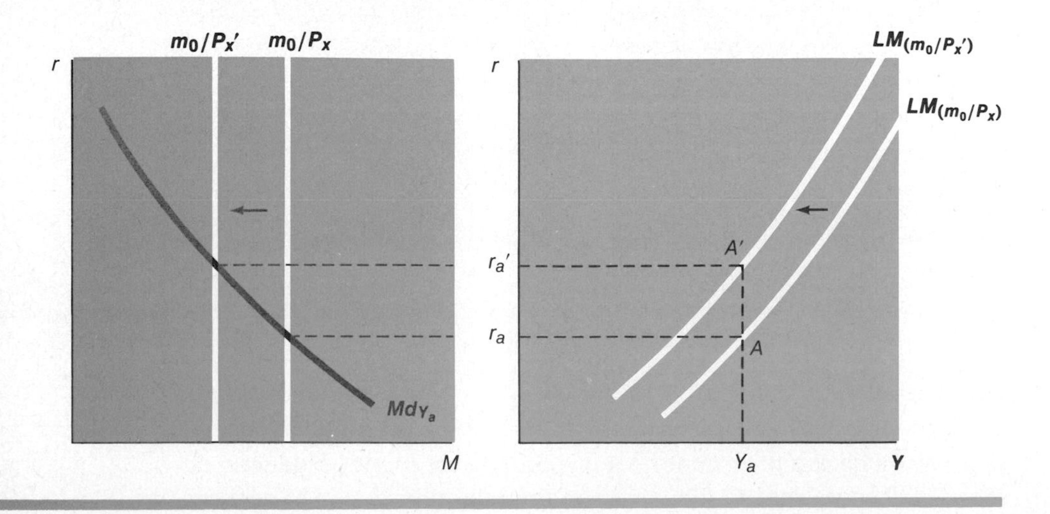

the right-hand portion of the figure, a point on the new *LM* curve corresponding to real money supply m_0/P_x' and the higher price level P_x'. The new *LM* curve must be to the left of the original one, since Point A′ is directly above Point A.

Returning to Figure 10–5, it is useful to note that, whereas the intersection of the *IS* and *LM* curves to the right of the full-employment line indicates the presence of an expenditure gap, it does not measure the gap in the sense of reflecting the excess demand for output actually present in the market. This intersection, Point A in Figure 10–5, presents the total expenditures which would be forthcoming at P_x if Y could also be at that level; but Y cannot be at such a level because it is restricted to Y_f. However, an expenditure gap must exist when P is P_x, since r_c, the interest rate at which the money market is in equilibrium for Y_f and P_x, is below r_b, the interest rate at which expenditures just support Y_f. An excess supply of real money balances exists at r_b when P is P_x, so that r is forced below r_b, and desired expenditures exceed full-employment output.

The Saving and Investment Approach to the *IS* Curve

The *IS* curve was obtained above from the *total expenditure approach*—that is, by application of the condition $Y = E$, where E is the sum of consumption expenditures, investment expenditures, and government purchases of final goods and services.

Often, the *IS* curve is obtained with the *saving and investment approach,* which converts the consumption expenditure function and government purchases of final goods and services into the aggregate saving function and applies the condition $I = S$.[3] Given the macroeconomic definition of saving, the approaches are equivalent.

In the macroeconomic sense, saving is income less consumption. Consumption, in this usage, includes not just private consumption expenditures but also government consumption purchases. Saving is not accumulated wealth, built up over many periods; it is a flow, the difference between income and consumption-like expenditures within a particular period.

Given this definition, aggregate saving is:

$$S = Y - (C + G) \qquad \text{10–10}$$

[3] The saving and investment approach was employed by John R. Hicks, who presented the *IS* curve to the literature. He labeled it *IS,* reflecting his approach, and the label has endured. See J. R. Hicks, "Mr. Keynes and the Classics: A Suggested Interpretation," *Econometrica* 5 (April 1937): 147–159.

in the model, since aggregate income is Y. It is the sum of private sector saving, which is:

$$Sp = Yd - C, \qquad \text{10–11}$$

where:

$$Yd = Y - Tx + Tr, \qquad \text{10–12}$$

and government saving, which is:

$$Sg = Tx - Tr - G.^{4} \qquad \text{10–13}$$

But I also is $Y - (C + G)$ if Y equals E. That is:

$$Y = E$$

$$Y = C + I + G$$

$$I = Y - (C + G). \qquad \text{10–14}$$

Substituting Equation 10–14 into Equation 10–10, $Y = E$ becomes $I = S$. To require that saving equal investment expenditures is to require that output and real income equal total expenditures, given the definition of saving.

Figure 10–7 presents a graphic illustration of the derivation of the *IS* curve by the saving and investment approach. The *IS* curve, on the right, derives from the saving and investment schedules, on the left. The saving schedules slope positively, since households save more and consume less from given levels of income as the interest rate increases. The schedules move to the right for higher levels of Y, since saving and income are positively associated. Both government and private saving vary di-

---

[4] That is:

$$S = Sp + Sg$$

$$S = (Yd - C) + (Tx - Tr - G)$$

$$S = (Y - Tx + Tr - C) + (Tx - Tr - G)$$

$$S = Y - (C + G).$$

Figure 10–7 **The Saving and Investment Approach to the *IS* Curve**

From the perspective of the saving and investment approach, the *IS* curve presents combinations of *r* and *Y* at which saving equals investment expenditures. *Y* must become higher as *r* becomes lower if saving is to expand and match the greater investment expenditures associated with the lower interest rate.

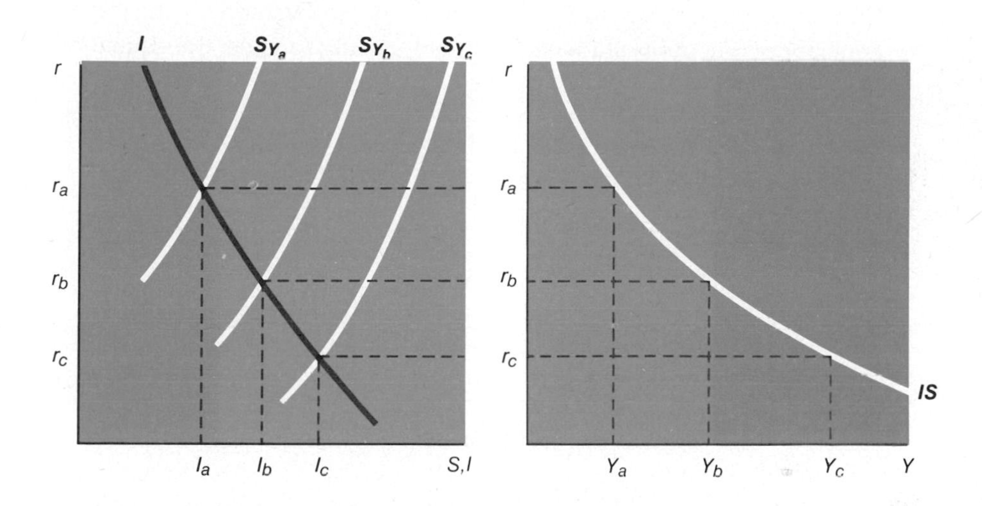

rectly with *Y*. An increase in *Y* is divided into an increase in *Tx*, which becomes an increase in *Sg*, and an increase in *Yd*, which is divided into an increase in *C* and an increase in *Sp*.[5]

A single investment expenditure curve appears in the left-hand portion of Figure 10–7, since investment expenditures do not depend on *Y* in the model. It slopes downward, reflecting the inverse association between investment expenditures and interest rate.

The points of intersection of the *S* and *I* schedules generate the *IS* curve, to the right. For example, as the interest rate declines from r_a to r_b, investment expenditures increase from I_a to I_b. *Y*, then, must increase from Y_a to Y_b so that *S* can increase and remain equal to *I*. The *IS* curve plots the combinations of *Y* and *r* at which aggregate savings equals

[5] Recall that $Yd = Y - Tx + Tr$, or $Y = Yd + Tx - Tr$, in the model. This being the case, an increase in *Y* must divide into an increase in *Yd* and an increase in *Tx*, given the fact that transfer payments are a constant and that the marginal tax rate is a positive fraction.

aggregate investment expenditures. Notice that Y must increase by enough to shift the saving schedule horizontally by more than the increase in I, since saving declines as the interest rate declines.

Numerical Illustrations of Equilibrium

Numerical illustrations are not essential for understanding the model equilibrium, but many students find them useful. Consider the equations:

$$E = C + I + G, \qquad \text{10–15}$$

$$C = a_0 + bYd - sr = 50 + 0.8Yd - 1000r, \qquad \text{10–16}$$

$$Yd = Y - Tx + Tr, \qquad \text{10–17}$$

$$Tx = Tx_0 + tY = 50 + 0.25Y, \qquad \text{10–18}$$

$$Tr = Tr_0 = 75, \qquad \text{10–19}$$

$$G = G_0 = 230, \qquad \text{10–20}$$

$$I = I_0 - ir = 200 - 1000r, \qquad \text{10–21}$$

$$Ms = m_0/P = 200/P, \qquad \text{10–22}$$

$$Md = L_0 + kY - qr = 50 + 0.2Y - 1000r, \text{ and} \qquad \text{10–23}$$

$$Y_f = 1{,}000. \qquad \text{10–24}$$

The innovations introduced in this chapter appear in Equation 10–16, the consumption expenditure function; Equation 10–21, the investment expenditure function; and Equations 10–22 and 10–23, which give money supply and money demand. The consumption and investment expenditure functions present these expenditures as varying inversely with the interest rate. The interest responsiveness of C and I are given by the coefficients of r in the equations—that is, they are:

$$\Delta C/\Delta r = -s = -1000 \qquad \text{10–25}$$

and

$$\Delta I/\Delta r = -i = -1000. \qquad \text{10–26}$$

Therefore, the direct effect of an interest rate increase of one percentage point in the model, as from 0.05 to 0.06, is that consumption expenditures and investment expenditures each will decline by $10 billion. The particular numbers in the model are chosen for arithmetic convenience, as in earlier models, but they are realistic to the extent that early versions of the Federal Reserve–MIT model present the direct effects of interest rate changes on consumption and investment expenditures as being roughly equal.

Equation 10–22 gives the money supply as fixed at 200 and indicates that the real money supply varies inversely with the price level.

Equation 10–23 gives the demand for real money balances as varying directly with Y and inversely with r. The income responsiveness of money demand is:

$$\Delta Md/\Delta Y = k = 0.2 \qquad \text{10–27}$$

and the interest responsiveness of money demand is:

$$\Delta Md/\Delta r = -q = -1000. \qquad \text{10–28}$$

An interest rate increase of one percentage point, again as from 0.05 to 0.06, therefore provokes a decline of 10 in Md. L_0 is simply the money demand constant. At a zero rate of interest, some wealth would presumably be held in money rather than securities or capital goods even if income were zero.

The model equilibrium can be found exactly as in the earlier portion of the chapter. First a trial equilibrium for comparison to Y_f is computed from the conditions:

$$Y = E \qquad \text{10–29}$$

and

$$Ms = Md, \qquad \text{10–30}$$

where:

$$Ms = m_0/P_x, \qquad \text{10–31}$$

with $P_x = 1.0$ the existing price level.

The consumption expenditure equation now is:

$$C = a_0 + bYd - sr$$

$$C = a_0 + b(Y - [Tx_0 + tY] + Tr_0) - sr$$

$$C = a_0 - bTx_0 + bTr_0 + b(1 - t)Y - sr = 70 + 0.6Y - 1000r, \quad \text{10–32}$$

so that the total expenditure equation is:

$$E = C + I + G$$

$$E = a_0 - bTx_0 + bTr_0 + b(1 - t)Y - sr + I_0 - ir + G_0,$$

or:

$$E = E_0 + b(1 - t)Y - (i + s)r = 500 + 0.6Y - 2000r, \quad \text{10–33}$$

where:

$$E_0 = a_0 - bTx_0 + bTr_0 + I_0 + G_0 = 500, \quad \text{10–34}$$

the total expenditure constant, is introduced for convenience. Substitution of Equation 10–33 into the $Y = E$ condition produces the *IS* schedule as:

$$Y = E$$

$$Y = E_0 + b(1 - t)Y - (i + s)r$$

$$(i + s)r = E_0 + [1 - b(1 - t)]Y$$

$$r = \frac{E_0 - [1 - b(1 - t)]Y}{i + s} = \frac{500 - 0.4Y}{2000} = 0.25 - 0.0002Y. \quad \text{10–35}$$

The *LM* schedule for the existing price level emerges when Equations 10–23 and 10–31 are substituted into Equation 10–30. That is, the *LM* schedule is:

$$Ms = Md$$

$$m_0/P_x = L_0 + kY - qr$$

$$qr = L_0 - m_0/P_x + kY$$

$$r = \frac{L_0 - M_0/P_x + kY}{q} = -0.15 + 0.0002Y. \quad \text{10–36}$$

The trial equilibrium for Y results when the LM schedule is substituted into the IS schedule, or vice versa. It is:

$$-0.15 + 0.0002Y = 0.25 - 0.0002Y$$

$$0.0004Y = 0.40$$

$$Y = 1000.$$

Since the trial equilibrium for Y does not exceed Y_f, the trial Y is the equilibrium Y and prices remain fixed at the existing level. That is, $P_x = 1.0$ is the equilibrium for P.

The equilibrium interest rate can be found by substituting the equilibrium Y of 1,000 into either the IS or LM equation and solving for r. Employing the IS equation yields equilibrium r of:

$$r = 0.25 - 0.0002(1000) = 0.05 = 5 \text{ percent.}$$

Checking, when Y equals 1,000 and r equals 0.05, total expenditures are:

$$E = 500 + 0.6(1000) - 2000(0.05) = 1000,$$

consisting of:

$$C = 70 + 0.6(1000) - 1000(0.05) = 620,$$

$$I = 200 - 1000(0.05) = 150,$$

and

$$G = 230.$$

Demand just supports output. Md is:

$$Md = 50 + 0.2(1000) - 1000(0.05) = 200,$$

so that the demand for real money balances just equals the real money supply of $m_0/P_x = 200$.

Figure 10–8 illustrates the equilibrium. It occurs at Point A, where the LM curve relating to price level $P_x = 1.0$ and the IS curve for $I_0 = 200$ intersect. The IS and LM intersection falls exactly on the full-employment line, indicating a situation of full employment and price stability.

Figure 10–8 **Numerical Illustrations of Equilibrium**

For $I_0 = 200$ and $P = 1.0$, the *IS* and *LM* curves intersect at the Y_f line, yielding full employment, price stability, and an interest rate of 5 percent. $I_0 = 280$ produces an expenditure gap at $P = 1.0$. Equilibrium requires $P = 1.25$ and $r = 9$ percent.

10–32

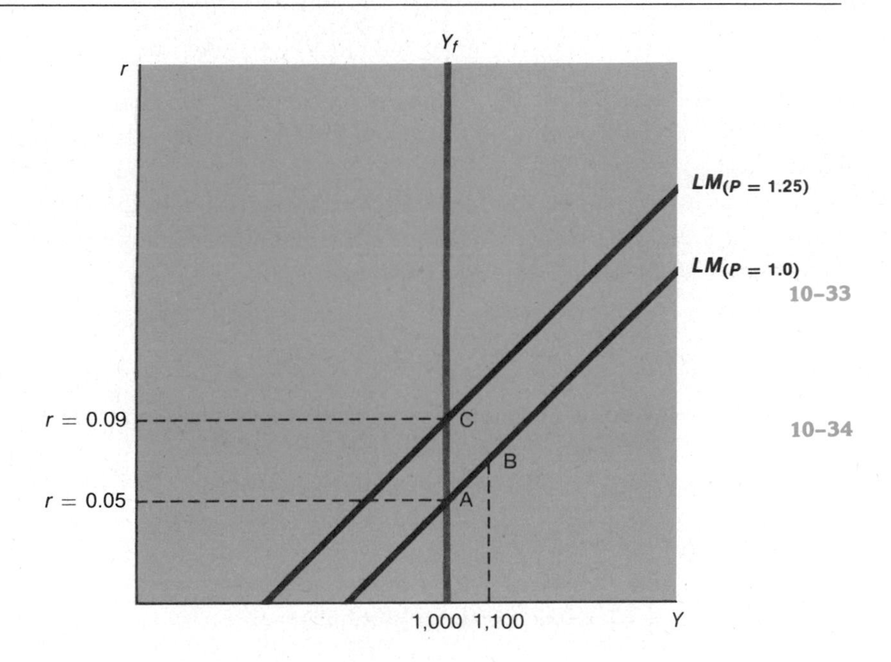

10–33

10–34

10–35

Saving and Investment in the Numerical Example

The *IS* schedule can be obtained by the saving and investment approach, as indicated earlier in the chapter. This involves deriving the aggregate saving equation and substituting it, along with the investment expenditures equation, into the condition $I = S$.

The aggregate saving equation is:

$$S = Y - (C + G)$$

$$S = Y - [a_0 - bTx_0 + bTr_0 + b(1 - t)Y - sr + G_0]$$

$$S = -a_0 + bTx_0 - bTr_0 - G_0 + [1 - b(1 - t)]Y + sr$$

10–36

$$S = -300 + 0.4Y + 1000r.$$

It is the sum of the private saving equation:

$$Sp = Yd - C$$

$$Sp = -a_0 + bTx_0 - bTr_0 - Tx_0 + Tr_0 + (1 - b + bt - t)Y + sr$$

$$Sp = -45 + 0.15Y + 1000r$$

and the government saving equation:

$$Sg = Tx - Tr - G$$

$$Sg = Tx_0 - Tr_0 - G_0 + tY = -255 + 0.25Y.$$

Substituting Equation 10–37 and Equation 10–21 into the $I = S$ condition gives the IS schedule obtained earlier with the $Y = E$ condition. It is:

$$I = S$$

$$200 - 1000r = -300 + 0.4Y + 1000r$$

$$r = \frac{500 - 0.4Y}{2000} = 0.25 - 0.0002Y.$$

In the equilibrium of $Y = 1{,}000$ and $r = 0.05$, aggregate saving of:

$$S = -300 + 0.4(1000) + 1000(0.05) = 150$$

equals aggregate investment expenditures of:

$$I = 200 - 1000(0.05) = 150.$$

Private saving of:

$$Sp = -45 + 0.15(1000) + 1000(0.05) = 155$$

finances investment expenditures of 150 plus the government deficit of:

$$Sg = -255 + 0.25(1000) = -5.$$

The Expenditure Gap Case

The expenditure gap case can be illustrated by increasing I_0 in Equation 10–21 from 200 to 280. This renders investment expenditures:

$$I = I_0 - ir = 280 - 1000r,$$

so that E_0, adjusting Equation 10–34, is 580, and the *IS* schedule is:

$$r = \frac{580 - 0.4Y}{2000} = 0.29 - 0.0002Y.$$

The trial equilibrium for Y now is:

$$-0.15 + 0.0002Y = 0.29 - 0.0002Y$$

$$0.0004Y = 0.44$$

$$Y = 1100,$$

the *LM* schedule for $P_x = 1.0$ being unchanged.

Since the trial equilibrium for Y exceeds $Y_f = 1{,}000$, an expenditure gap is present. Figure 10–8 illustrates this situation. The new *IS* schedule, labeled ($I_0 = 280$), intersects the *LM* schedule for $P_x = 1.0$ at Point B, which is beyond the Y_f line. Under the assumptions used here, prices must rise until the *LM* curve has moved enough leftward to intersect the new *IS* schedule at the Y_f line. This occurs at Point C.

Equilibrium r can be found by substituting $Y_f = 1{,}000$ into the *IS* schedule for $I_0 = 280$ and solving for r, since equilibrium will occur where the *IS* schedule intersects the full-employment line. The solution is:

$$r = 0.29 - 0.0002(1000) = 0.09 = 9 \text{ percent.}$$

This is the r which produces total expenditures just sufficient to purchase the full-employment output.

Equilibrium P is the P which causes the money market to be in equilibrium at $r = 0.09$ and $Y_f = 1{,}000$. To obtain it, substitute those values into the *LM* schedule with P expressed as a variable and solve for P. Making the appropriate adjustments in Equation 10–36 yields:

$$r = \frac{L_0 - m_0/P + kY}{q}$$

$$0.09 = \frac{50 - 200/P + 0.2(1000)}{1000}$$

$$P = 1.25.$$

What is the expenditure gap which causes P to rise from 1.0 to 1.25? It is the 80 of I_0 added to create it. The interest rate increase of 0.04, from $r = 0.05$ to $r = 0.09$, produces an offsetting effect on investment and consumption expenditures of:

$$\Delta(I + C) = \Delta I/\Delta r(\Delta r) + \Delta C/\Delta r(\Delta r)$$

$$\Delta(I + C) = -1000(0.04) - 1000(0.04)$$

$$\Delta(I + C) = -80,$$

and just eliminates this gap. Saving and investment expenditures are each 190 in the new equilibrium. Consumption expenditures are 580.

Summary

1. The addition of a money market to the model yields a general equilibrium involving interest and prices as well as output, real income, and real expenditures.

2. The *IS* and *LM* curves, imposed upon a graph which includes the full-employment line, offer a useful representation of the equilibrium.

3. The *IS* curve can be developed by either the total expenditure approach or the saving and investment approach.

Concepts for Identification

IS curve
LM curve
full-employment constraint
excess money supply
expenditure gap
saving
private saving
government saving
aggregate saving
saving and investment approach

Questions and Problems for Review

1. Explain why the *IS* curve must slope downward, given the assumptions of the model in this chapter. Explain why the *LM* curve must slope upward.

2. Using the model in this chapter, illustrate graphically:
a. A less than full employment equilibrium.
b. An equilibrium involving full employment and price stability.
c. An expenditure gap situation.

3. Extend the graphical illustration of the expenditure gap situation of Question 2 to show the eventual equilibrium which will prevail in this case. Explain how the equilibrium comes about.

4. Assume that an r and Y combination prevails which places the economy on the IS curve but to the right of the LM curve. The Y is short of full-employment Y. Explain why r might be expected to rise, and Y to fall, in this situation.

5. The economy finds itself with an r and Y combination which places it on the LM curve but to the left of the IS curve. Assume that the point of intersection of the IS and LM curves is to the left of the full-employment line. Explain why Y and r might be expected to rise in this situation.

6. Explain why aggregate saving must vary directly with Y and directly with r given the definitions of aggregate, private, and government saving and the assumptions relating to the consumption function, the government budget items, and private disposable income employed in this chapter.

7. Demonstrate that $I = S$ must be true if $Y = E$ is true, given the definitions for aggregate saving, private saving, and government saving offered in this chapter.

8. Show that if I_0 is 120 rather than 200 in the numerical illustration (Figure 10–8) in this chapter, equilibrium Y is 900. What is the equilibrium interest rate for this case? Verify that real money balances demanded equal the real money supply and that total expenditures just support output at this Y and r combination.

9. What is the equilibrium for Y, r, and P if I_0 is 80 instead of 200 in the numerical illustration in this chapter? Check your answer by demonstrating that Y equals E and m_0/P equals Md at the computed Y and r combination.

10. Verify that if I_0 is 350 rather than 200 in the numerical illustration, the equilibrium values are $Y = 1{,}000$, $r = 12.5$ percent, and $P = 1.60$. Show that $Y = E$ and $m_0/P = Md$ in this equilibrium.

11. With $Ms = m_0/P_x = 200/1.0$ and $Md = 50 + 0.2Y - 1000r$, the *LM* curve is $r = -0.15 + 0.0002Y$.

a. Verify that the *r* and *Y* combinations:

Y	*r*
800	0.010
925	0.035
975	0.045

fall on this *LM* curve.

b. Select an *r* and *Y* combination which falls to the left of this *LM* curve and verify that an excess supply of money exists at the combination.

c. Pick an *r* and *Y* combination to the right of the *LM* curve and show that an excess demand for money is present at the combination.

12. With I_0 at 200, the equation for the *IS* curve was $r = 0.25 + 0.0002Y$ in the numerical illustration.

a. Find three points on this curve by solving the equation for *r* at selected levels of *Y* and show that *Y* equals *E* and *I* equals *S* at each of the three points.

b. Pick an *r* and *Y* combination to the left of this *IS* curve and show that aggregate expenditures exceed output and investment expenditures exceed aggregate saving at the combination.

c. Select an *r* and *Y* combination to the right of the *IS* curve and show that *Y* exceeds *E* and *S* exceeds *I* at the combination.

References

Barro, R. J., and Grossman, H. I. "A General Disequilibrium Model of Income and Employment." *American Economic Review* 61 (March 1971): 82–93.

Clower, R. W. "The Keynesian Counter-Revolution: A Theoretical Appraisal." In *The Theory of Interest Rates,* edited by F. H. Hahn and F. P. R. Brechling. London: Macmillan, 1965.

Hicks, John R. "Mr. Keynes and the Classics: A Suggested Interpretation." *Econometrica* 5 (April 1937): 147–159.

Laidler, D. E. W. *The Demand for Money: Theories and Evidence.* 2d ed. New York: Dun-Donnelley, 1977, chap. 1.

Smith, Warren L. "A Graphical Exposition of the Complete Keynesian System." *Southern Economic Journal* 23 (October 1956): 115–125.

Part 4

Unemployment, Inflation, and Stabilization Policy

11

Fluctuations in Aggregate Demand

Fluctuations in aggregate demand are a primary source of unemployment and inflation problems —most economists would say the primary source. They arise from shifts in the expenditure functions, often called **real disturbances**, *or from shifts in the money supply or in the money demand function, which are called* **monetary disturbances**. *Graphically, the real disturbances are shifts in the* **IS** *curve, the monetary disturbances shifts in the* **LM** *curve.*

Chapter 10 added a money market to the model developed in Chapters 4 and 6 and illustrated macroeconomic equilibrium with monetary influences present. It presented inflation and less than full employment situations, but it did not indicate how such situations arise or how the government can act with discretionary monetary and fiscal policies to improve them.

These matters are the business of this chapter and Chapters 12 and 13. This chapter employs the model developed in Chapter 10 to illustrate fluctuations in aggregate demand as sources of unemployment and inflation problems. Chapter 12 elaborates the supply sector of the model and considers aggregate supply disturbances as sources of unemployment and inflation problems. Chapter 13 begins by presenting the simple mechanics of monetary and fiscal policies in the model and ends by considering the broader question of whether such policies by themselves can provide satisfactory results in the post-1970 U.S. economy, when unemployment and inflation have been simultaneous problems, judged by earlier standards.

Real and Monetary Disturbances

In the model situation in which aggregate demand is just supporting full-employment output, a decline in aggregate demand produces an unemployment problem. Output simply adjusts to demand and prices are constant. An increase in aggregate demand in the same initial situation produces an expenditure gap and inflation. Indeed, an increase in aggregate demand produces an expenditure gap and inflation even if it occurs in an initial less than full employment situation, if it carries beyond the full-employment level.

With a money market present, fluctuations in aggregate demand can originate in monetary disturbances as well as in the real disturbances of earlier models. *Monetary disturbances* refers to shifts in the money supply, that is, shifts in:

$$m_0, \qquad \text{11–1}$$

and shifts in the money demand function:

$$Md = f(Y, r). \qquad \text{11–2}$$

These disturbances introduce excess supplies or demands for money, affecting aggregate demand, or expenditures, through interest rate effects on interest-sensitive expenditures. It is important to notice that a shift in the money demand function (Equation 11–2) means changes in real money balances demanded at various Y and r combinations, not changes in real money balances demanded which come about because of changes in Y and r.

Real disturbances include shifts in the investment expenditure function:

$$I = f(r), \qquad \text{11–3}$$

shifts in the consumption expenditure function:

$$C = f(Yd, r), \qquad \text{11–4}$$

changes in the level of government purchases:

$$G_0, \qquad \text{11–5}$$

and changes in the level of consumption expenditures induced by shifts in the tax function:

$$Tx = f(Y) \qquad 11\text{–}6$$

or in transfer payments:

$$Tr_0. \qquad 11\text{–}7$$

These disturbances contribute to fluctuations in aggregate demand as in the models in Chapters 4 and 6. Shifts in the investment expenditure function, the consumption expenditure function, and the level of government purchases directly affect the demand for output, since they themselves are expenditures for final goods and services. Shifts in the tax and transfer payment functions induce changes in consumption expenditures by affecting private disposable income.[1]

Shifts in government purchases and transfer payments and in the tax function often are discretionary fiscal policy applications, of course, intended to check unemployment and inflation problems. They also can be sources of such problems, however. Shifts in government purchases associated with wars and their aftermaths rank among the most severe real disturbances of U.S. economic experience. The tax function can shift as a side effect of tax reform. Transfer payments have grown over time independently of stabilization policy objectives. Even when government purchases, tax, and transfer payment changes occur as conscious applications of discretionary fiscal policies, they can be destabilizing rather than stabilizing if they are too large or poorly timed. Consequently, both public and private sector real disturbances are considered here as sources of unemployment and inflation problems.

A shift in the investment expenditure function (Equation 11–3) means a change in the level of planned investment expenditures at each rate of interest, not changes in planned investment expenditures which occur because the interest rate changes. Similarly, a shift in the consumption expenditure function (Equation 11–4) is a change in consumption expenditures for given r and Yd combinations, not changes in consumption expenditures which occur because r and Yd change. A shift in the tax

[1] Fluctuations in the demand for domestically produced output also can arise from changes in foreign demand for domestic exports or from shifts in domestic demand between domestically produced and imported goods and services. A detailed demonstration of these effects is presented in Chapter 19, which incorporates the foreign sector into the model.

function (Equation 11–6) means a change in taxes at each level of Y, not changes in taxes which occur because Y changes.

This distinction between shifts in functions and changes in economic aggregates which occur within the functional relationships is an important one in macroeconomics. The shifts in the functions and in the government purchases, government transfer payment, and money supply constants are disturbances to equilibrium. They set up new equilibriums involving new equilibrium values for economic aggregates. They produce changes in output, employment, and prices. Changes in the expenditure components, in taxes, or in money balances demanded which come about because income and the interest rate vary are not disturbances to equilibrium (unless the relevant functional relationship also is shifting). They are the product of the disturbances which have caused income and the interest rate to vary.

Real Disturbances as Sources of Shortfall Unemployment

When the investment or consumption expenditure functions decline, when government purchases fall, or when consumption expenditures decline because the government has increased the tax function or diminished transfer payments, aggregate demand declines in the model and aggregate output and real income decline in response. The unemployment rate rises.

Figure 11–1 illustrates the case where these disturbances occur in the initial model situation with aggregate demand just supporting full-employment output. In the graph, they cause the *IS* curve to shift to the left, so that the equilibrium for Y shifts from Y_f to Y_b. The *IS* curve, it will be recalled, reflects both aggregate expenditures and aggregate output and real income at each interest rate, since it is plotted on the assumption that output and real income adjust fully to expenditures. Therefore, when the expenditure functions decline for any sector or when reductions in expenditures are induced by tax function increases or transfer payment reductions, aggregate expenditures are smaller at each rate of interest, and the *IS* curve shifts to the left. The new equilibrium for Y and r occurs where the new *IS* curve intersects the unchanged *LM* curve. The *LM* curve is unchanged because the money supply and the money demand function, by assumption, are unchanged. The only disturbance is the real disturbance.

Figures 11–2 and 11–3 illustrate the mechanics of the leftward shift in the *IS* curve caused by the real disturbances.

Figure 11–1 **Real Disturbances as Sources of Shortfall Unemployment**

When real disturbances shift the *IS* curve to the left in an initial full employment and price stability situation, output and the interest rate decline. Shortfall unemployment appears.

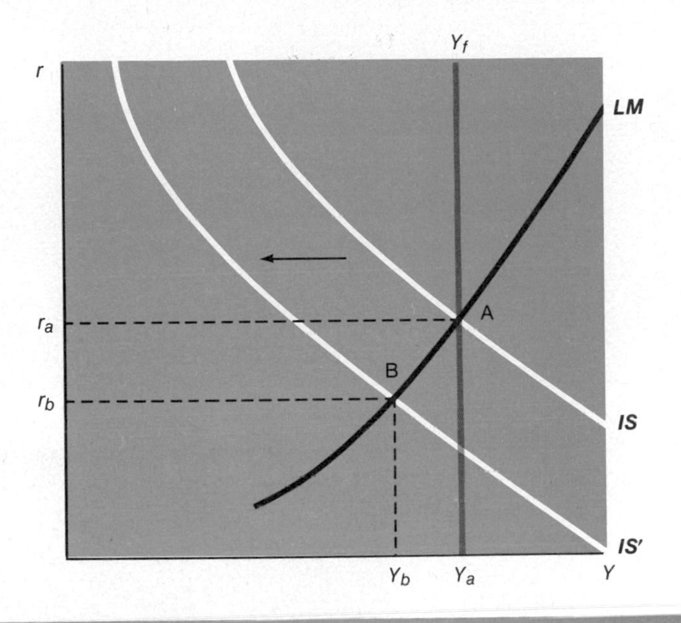

the investment expenditure function. The upper left-hand portion of the figure identifies reference points on new and old investment expenditure schedules at interest rate r_a so that the upper right-hand portion of the figure can show the impact on the *IS* curve. The decline in the investment expenditure function reflects a situation where producers, for some reason, have decided to make a smaller amount of investment expenditures at each rate of interest. When the investment expenditure schedule declines, I at r_a falls from I_a to I_a'. The total expenditure schedule corresponding to r_a in the lower portion of the figure then falls from E_{r_a} to $(E_{r_a})'$ producing a reduction in the E and Y forthcoming at r_a from Y_a to Y_a'. This information is accumulated in the upper right-hand portion of the figure, which shows the *IS* schedule shifting to the left.

Notice that the leftward shift in the *IS* schedule exceeds the leftward shift in the investment demand schedule. The *IS* schedule shift includes not

Figure 11–2 **A Decline in the Investment Expenditure Function**

If producers for some reason reduce the level of investment expenditures they wish to make at each rate of interest, the *IS* curve shifts to the left. Total expenditures support a lesser output at each rate of interest.

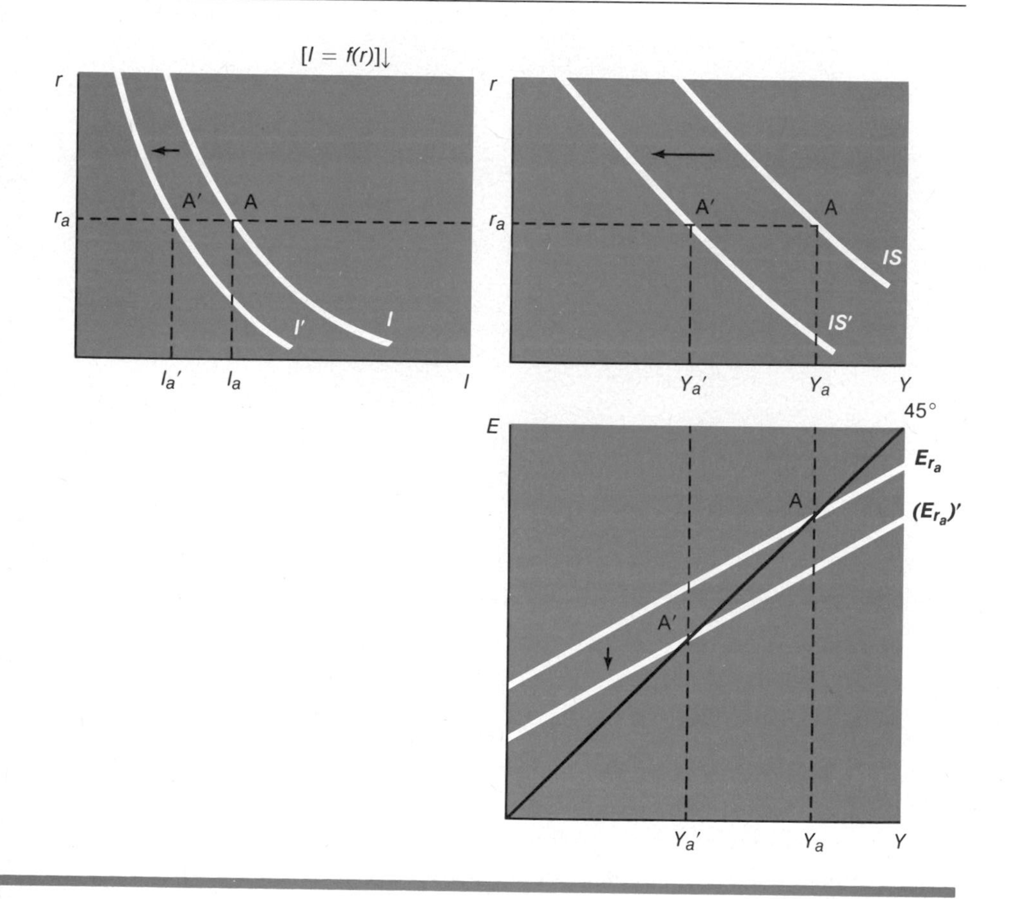

only the decline in I at r_a, which is the vertical decline in the total expenditure line in the lower portion of the figure, but also the induced effect on C which occurs as Y declines. The leftward shift in the IS curve in fact reflects the simple Keynesian multiplier effect examined in earlier chapters. It is:

$$\Delta Y = \frac{1}{1 - MPC_Y}(I_a - I_a'), \quad \text{11–8}$$

Figure 11–3 **A Decline in the Consumption Expenditure Function, a Decline in Government Purchases, a Decline in Transfer Payments, or an Increase in the Tax Function**

If the consumption function declines, if government purchases decline, if the tax function increases, or if transfer payments decline, the *IS* curve shifts to the left. Total expenditures support a smaller level of output at each rate of interest.

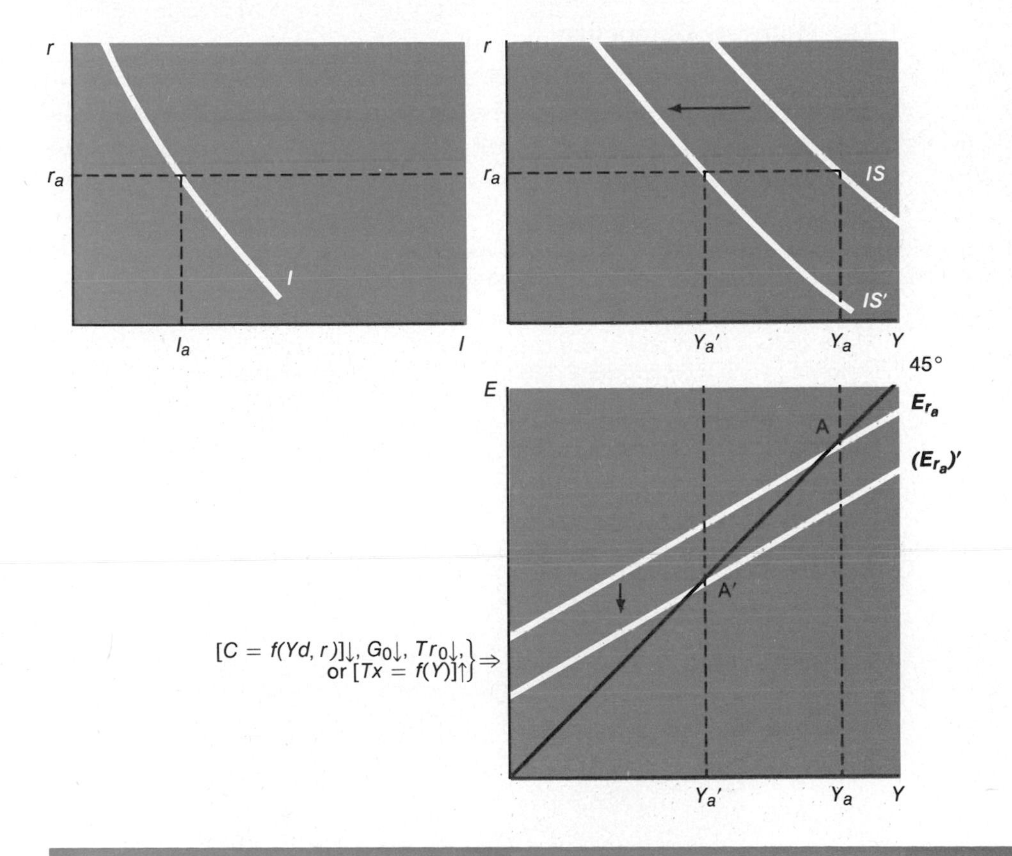

where MPC_Y is the marginal propensity to consume from *Y*, or $b(1 - t)$, if the tax function is spelled out as in Equation 6–18 of Chapter 6.

Figure 11–3 illustrates the leftward shift in the *IS* curve caused by the other real disturbances. In this illustration, the investment expenditure schedule, at the upper left, is unchanged. The total expenditure line for r_a in the lower portion of the figure shifts downward because of one of the other real disturbances. It reflects a decline in the consumption expenditure function (Equation 11–4), a decline in G_0, an increase in the tax function (Equation 11–6), or a decrease in Tr_0. Expenditures support Y_a' instead of Y_a at r_a, and the *IS* curve, at the upper right, moves to the left. Again, the leftward shift in the *IS* curve reflects the vertical decline in the total expenditure function for r_a, in the lower portion of the figure, times the simple multiplier of Equation 11–8.

The Monetary Dampener

Monetary influences automatically dampen the declines in equilibrium output, real income, and employment which occur in response to the real disturbances just examined. As noted above, when the total expenditure line in the lower portion of Figures 11–2 and 11–3 declines by a given

Figure 11–4 **The Monetary Dampener**

The money market dampens the decline in equilibrium output which occurs when one of the expenditure functions declines. Following such a disturbance, the interest rate must decline if the money market is to remain in equilibrium. The decline in the interest rate stimulates interest-sensitive expenditures and cushions the impact on output.

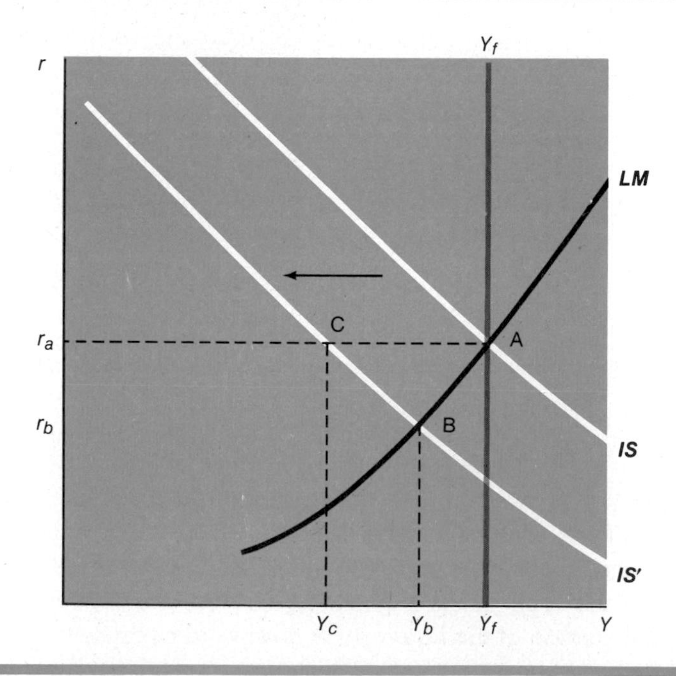

amount at interest rate r_a, the *IS* curve shifts to the left by this amount times the simple multiplier effect. This was the decline in equilibrium *Y* in the models in Chapters 4 and 6, which neglected money market effects on expenditures.

With the money market included, equilibrium *Y* declines by a smaller amount. Figure 11–4 illustrates the point. When the *IS* curve shifts from *IS* to *IS'* as a result of a real disturbance, equilibrium *Y* declines not from Y_f to Y_c, which is the leftward shift in the *IS* curve, but by the smaller amount Y_f to Y_b. When *Y* declines, *r* must decline if the money market is to remain in equilibrium. The decline in *Y* causes real money balances demanded to diminish, so that *r* must decline and produce a compensating increase in *Md* if money balances demanded are to remain unchanged and equal to the unchanged money supply. The lower *r* stimulates investment and consumption expenditures and partially offsets the effects of the initial spending disturbance. The money market thus dampens the decline in equilibrium *Y*.

Notice that while the *IS* curve has shifted to the left because of a decline in the investment function or an increase in the aggregate saving function, it is not an excess of saving over investment expenditures which prevents Point C from being an equilibrium by bidding interest rates down. Saving equals investment expenditures at Point C, since Point C is on the new *IS* curve. It is the excess supply of real money balances which bids interest rates on securities down if the economy is at Point C, as wealth-holders attempt to shift money balances to securities or other assets which earn more than money does.

Monetary Disturbances as Sources of Shortfall Unemployment

When the money supply declines or the money demand function (Equation 11–2) increases in the model situation of full employment without inflation, aggregate demand for output declines, and shortfall unemployment appears. Graphically, these disturbances provoke a leftward shift in the *LM* curve, as from LM_1 to LM_2 in Figure 11–5. Equilibrium *Y* declines from Y_f to Y_b in the figure. If the disturbances occur when shortfall unemployment already is present, aggregate demand still declines, and unemployment increases.

Reductions in the money supply and increases in the money demand function operate by creating a shortage of money balances at r_a and Y_f, the initial equilibrium values for *r* and *Y*. As wealth-holders exchange securities for money in an effort to build up money balances, interest rates on securities rise and interest-sensitive expenditures decline. As output and real income respond to these effects, income-induced effects on consumption expenditures are added, aggravating the decline in demand. In Figure 11–5, equilibrium is restored at Point B, where the higher r and lower Y have diminished money balances demanded by enough to restore money market equilibrium.

Figure 11–6 presents the mechanics of the leftward shift in the *LM* curve following a reduction in money supply. The left-hand portion of the figure presents the relationship of money balances demanded and the interest rate for Y_a, a selected level of output and real income. For money supply m_0 and real money supply m_0/P_x, the interest rate must be at r_a if money demand is to equal money supply for Y_a. This r and Y combination generates Point A in the right-hand portion of the figure and the *LM* curve corresponding to it, labeled m_0/P_x. If money supply now is reduced to m_0',

Figure 11–5 **A Monetary Disturbance as a Source of Shortfall Unemployment**

A reduction in the money supply or an increase in the money demand function shifts the *LM* curve to the left, reducing equilibrium output and causing the equilibrium interest rate to rise.

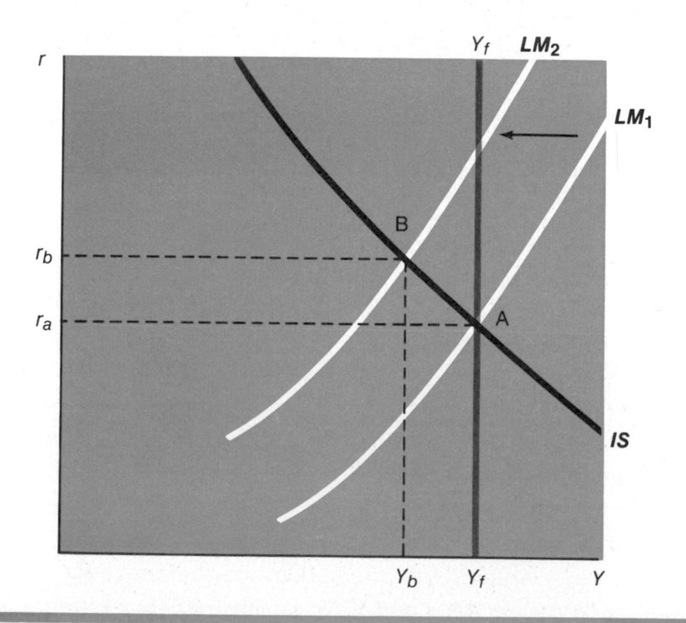

Figure 11–6 **A Decrease in the Money Supply**

When the money supply declines, the *LM* curve shifts to the left. The interest rate must be higher for each level of output and real income in order for money balances demanded to be smaller and equal to the smaller money supply.

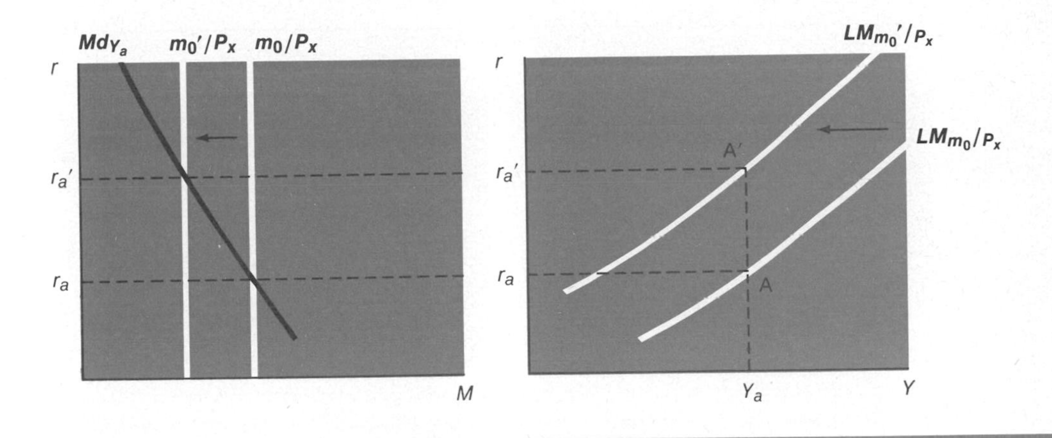

and real money supply to m_0'/P_x, the interest rate must rise to r_a' if the money market is to be in equilibrium for Y_a. Point A, the initial reference point for locating the *LM* curve, shifts to Point *A'*, and the *LM* curve shifts to the left.

The description here of the process by which nominal money supply reductions raise interest rates and reduce interest-sensitive expenditures is a considerable abbreviation of the process by which these effects actually occur. Reductions in the U.S. money supply occur mainly through impacts on bank reserves and excess reserves, as described in Chapter 8. The shortage of money, in the physical sense, is mainly a shortage of the bank reserve base for m_0, the equilibrium money supply; and the security sales which drive interest rates on securities up are sales made by banks in an effort to improve their reserve positions.

Figure 11–7 illustrates the leftward shift in the *LM* curve caused by an increase in the money demand function. The left-hand portion of the figure presents the initial money demand schedule corresponding to Y_a, labeled MD_{Y_a}. Given money supply m_0/P_x, this schedule generates LM_1, the initial *LM* curve, in the right-hand portion of the figure. When the money demand function increases, the money demand schedule corresponding to Y_a shifts to the right, to MD_{Y_a}', since wealth-holders now

Figure 11–7 **An Increase in the Money Supply Demand Function**

If the community decides to hold a larger portion of its wealth in money at each *r* and *Y* combination, the *LM* curve shifts to the left. The interest rate must be higher for each level of *Y* in order for the community to be willing to hold the unchanged money supply.

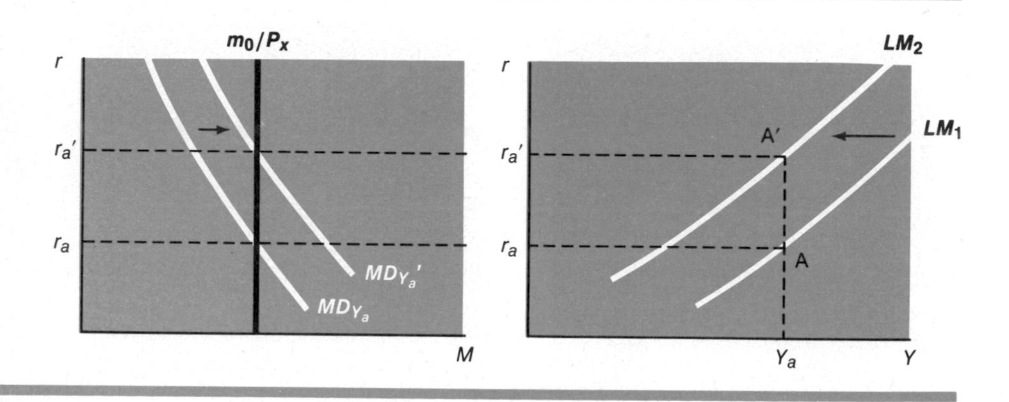

demand more money balances at each *r* and *Y* combination. The interest rate now must be higher, at r_a', for money market equilibrium, with *Y* at Y_a. The reference point locating the *LM* curve moves from Point A to Point A′, indicating a leftward shift in the *LM* curve.

The mechanism by which increases in the money demand function raise interest rates and discourage interest-sensitive expenditures is straightforward. Desiring more money balances, wealth-holders simply exchange securities for money, bidding security prices down and interest rates on securities up.

Real Disturbances as Sources of Inflation

If the investment or consumption expenditure functions increase, if government purchases increase, or if increases in consumption expenditures are induced by a reduction in the tax function or an increase in the transfer payment function, aggregate demand increases. If this occurs in the situation in which demand initially just supports full-employment output, an expenditure gap opens up and prices rise.

Figure 11–8 reflects the situation graphically. The real disturbances shift the *IS* curve to the right, from IS_1 to IS_2, so that it intersects the *LM* curve

Figure 11–8 **Real Disturbances as Sources of Inflation**

When real disturbances shift the *IS* curve to the right in an initial full employment and price stability situation, an expenditure gap opens up and prices rise. Equilibrium is restored when the decline in the real money supply has shifted the *LM* curve to the left by enough to close the expenditure gap.

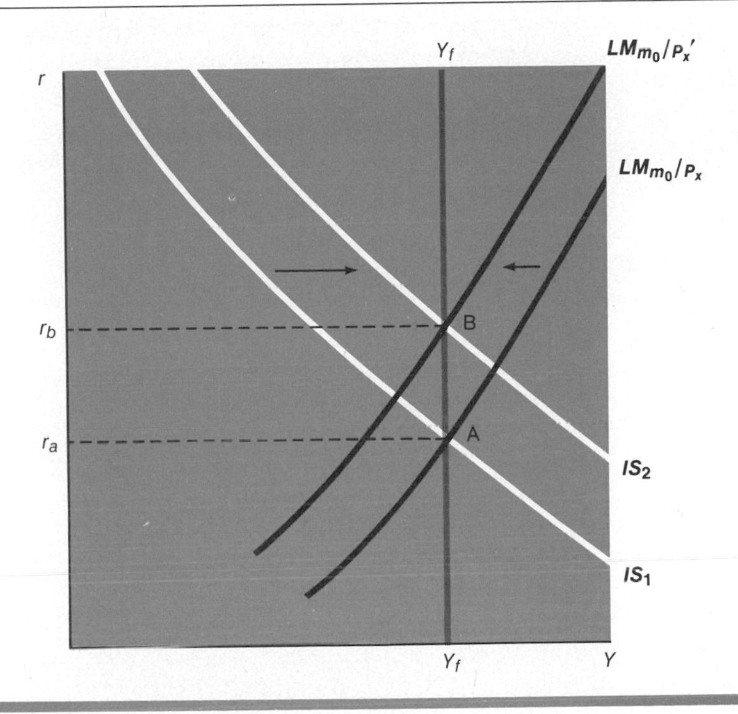

for P_x, the initial price level, to the right of the full-employment line, indicating an expenditure gap. Prices then rise, reducing the real money supply and shifting the *LM* curve to the left until the expenditure gap is eliminated. This occurs at price level P_x'. Equilibrium is reestablished, but inflation has occurred.

Figure 11–9 illustrates the rightward shift of the *IS* curve which occurs with an increase in the investment expenditure function. The procedure is the reverse of that already examined for the decline in the investment expenditure function, but it is useful to trace the mechanics again. In the left-hand portion of the figure, the investment expenditure schedule shifts to the right, yielding I_a' rather than I_a at interest rate r_a. The *E* and *Y* relationship corresponding to r_a shifts upward in the lower portion of the

Figure 11–9 An Increase in the Investment Expenditure Function

When the investment demand schedule shifts to the right, the *IS* curve shifts to the right. Demand supports a higher level of output at each rate of interest.

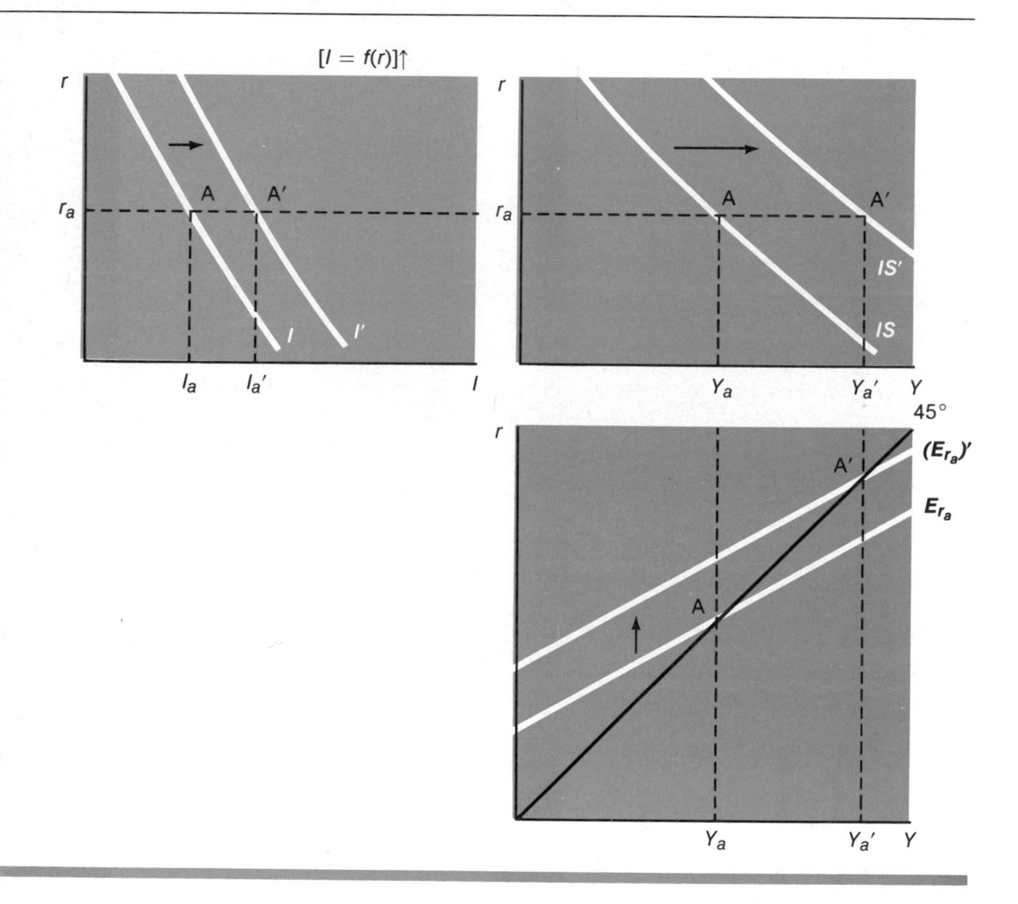

figure, reflecting the larger flow of investment expenditures at r_a. E now supports a Y of Y_a' rather than Y_a for interest rate r_a, producing the rightward shift in the *IS* curve pictured in the upper right-hand portion of the figure.

The upward shift in the E and Y relationship for r_a could have been produced by an increase in the consumption expenditure function, an increase in government purchases, a reduction in the tax function, or an increase in the transfer payment function rather than by an increase in the investment expenditure function. Figure 11–10, which presents the E and

Figure 11–10 An Increase in the Consumption Expenditure Function, an Increase in Government Purchases, an Increase in Transfer Payments, or a Decline in the Tax Function

When the consumption expenditure function increases, when government purchases or transfer payments increase, or when the tax function declines, the *IS* curve shifts to the right. Demand supports a greater output at each interest rate.

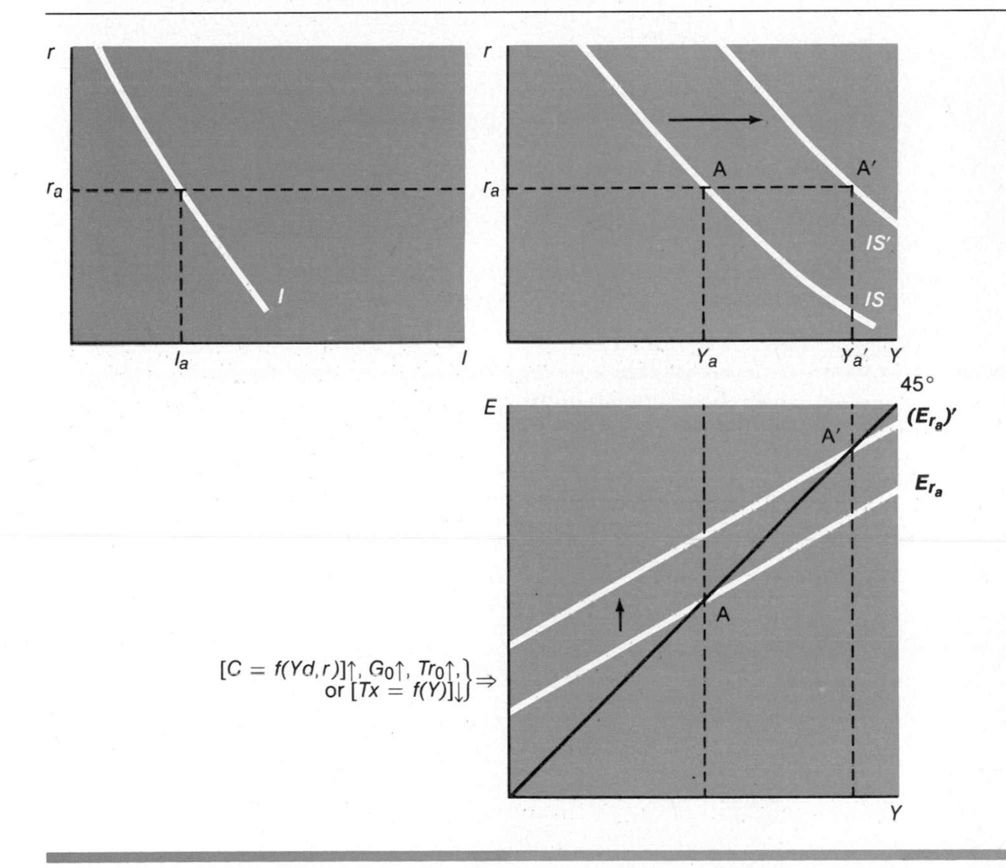

Y relationship for r_a shifting upward, with the investment schedule fixed, illustrates these cases.

There is an important difference between the case where the rightward shift in the *IS* curve results from an increase in the investment expenditure function and the case where it results from one of the other real disturbances. If the investment expenditure function increases at full employment, investment expenditures will be greater in the new equilibrium than in the old. If one of the other real disturbances is involved, investment expenditures will decline. Aggregate output, which is unchanged at full-employment output, is reallocated toward investment expenditures and capital goods accumulation in the one case and toward government purchases or consumption expenditures in the other. Investment expenditures will be greater in equilibrium when the investment expenditure function increases at full employment, since consumption expenditures will be lower because the interest rate is higher, and $Y = C + I + G$ will be unchanged. Investment expenditures will be smaller if one of the other real disturbances is involved, since the interest rate will be higher and the investment expenditure function, by assumption, will be unchanged.

Monetary Disturbances as Sources of Inflation

An increase in the money supply or a decrease in the money demand function (Equation 11–2), also produces an increase in aggregate de-

Figure 11–11 **An Increase in the Money Supply as a Source of Inflation**

An increase in the money supply, coming in an initial full employment and price stability situation, shifts the *LM* curve to the right, opens up an expenditure gap, and causes prices to rise. Equilibrium is reestablished when the increase in prices has reduced the real money supply to its initial level, so that the *LM* curve is in its original position and the expenditure gap closes.

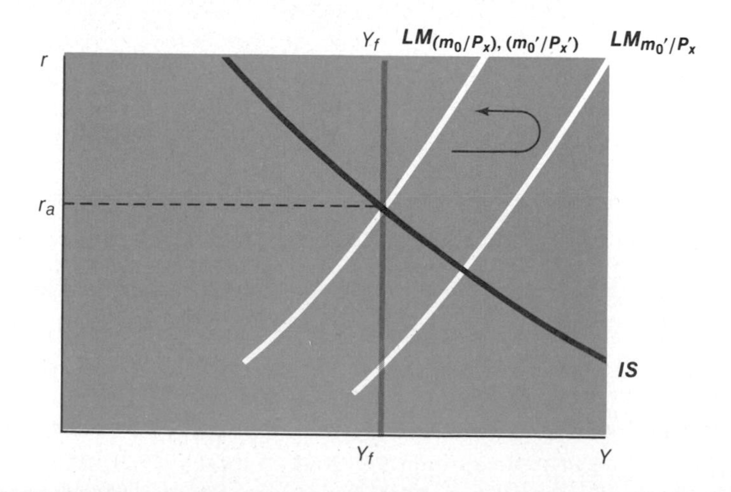

mand in the model. When these disturbances occur in a fully employed economy, an expenditure gap appears, and prices rise, if the gap is not eliminated through discretionary stabilization policies. Figure 11–11 illustrates the money supply increase, while Figure 11–12 illustrates the decrease in the money demand function. Either disturbance causes the *LM* curve for P_x to shift to the right and produces an intersection of the new *LM* curve with the unchanged *IS* curve to the right of the full-employment line, indicating an expenditure gap.

For the increase in the money supply, in Figure 11–11, the old and new *LM* curves are labeled m_0/P_x and m_0'/P_x, respectively, indicating that the shift was caused by an increase in the money supply from m_0 to m_0'. For the decrease in the money demand function, in Figure 11–12, both the initial and new *LM* curves have the m_0/P_x label, since the money supply has not changed.

In both cases, the new equilibriums, in the absence of discretionary stabilization policies, occur when prices have risen by enough to move the *LM* curves back to their initial positions, where the *IS* curve is again

Figure 11–12 **A Decrease in the Money Demand Function as a Source of Inflation**

When the demand function for money declines with the economy in an initial full employment and price stability situation, the *LM* curve shifts to the right, an expenditure gap appears, and prices rise. Equilibrium is restored when the decline in the real money supply shifts the *LM* curve leftward by enough to close the expenditure gap.

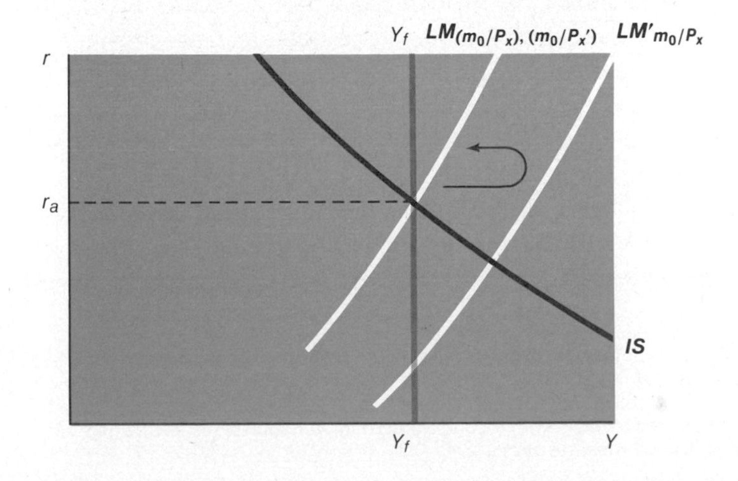

intersected at the full-employment line. This involves real money balances m_0'/P_x', with prices having risen in proportion to the money supply increase, for the increase in money supply case, and m_0/P_x' for the decrease in money demand case.[2] In both cases, the rate of interest is unchanged in equilibrium.

The economics of the initial rightward shift in the *LM* curve accompanying either the money supply increase or the money demand function decrease is that an excess supply of real money balances is created at the initial Y and r combination. This produces a temporary decline in interest rates on securities, as wealth-holders seek to place the excess money in securities. The decline in interest rates increases desired aggregate expenditures through interest rate effects on investment and consumption expenditures and opens up an expenditure gap. In the absence of discretionary stabilization policies to eliminate the gap, it is eliminated automatically by the increase in prices it produces. As prices rise, the real money supply declines, eliminating the excess supply of real money balances and permitting interest rates to return to their initial level, where aggregate demand again is just sufficient to purchase full-employment output. For the money supply increase case, the excess supply of real money balances which is introduced is ordinarily an excess supply of the bank reserve base of real money balances, and the shift into securities which depresses interest rates on securities temporarily is actually a shift of excess reserves to loans and securities by banks.

The mechanics of the rightward shift in the *LM* curves relating to initial prices which accompanies the increase in money supply and the decrease in the money demand function are illustrated in Figures 11–13 and 11–14.

Figure 11–13 shows that an increase in money supply from m_0 to m_0', with prices at P_x, requires that the interest rate decrease from r_a to r_a' for output and real income Y_a if the money market is to remain in equilibrium. The reference point on old and new *LM* curves, in the right-hand portion of the figure, moves from Point A to Point A′, indicating that the *LM* curve must shift to the right.

Figure 11–14 illustrates the rightward shift in the *LM* curve accompanying the decrease in the money demand function. As money holders decide to hold less cash and demand deposits at each rate of interest, the

---

[2] The percent change in prices must equal the percent change in money supply in equilibrium, since only in that case will the supply of real money balances, m/P, be unchanged. Money market equilibrium requires that m/P be unchanged, since real money balances demanded will not change. With the money demand function given and r and Y unchanged in equilibrium, Md must be unchanged.

Figure 11–13 **An Increase in Money Supply**

When the money supply increases, the *LM* curve shifts to the right. The interest rate must be lower for each level of output and real income in order for money balances demanded to be larger and equal to the larger money supply.

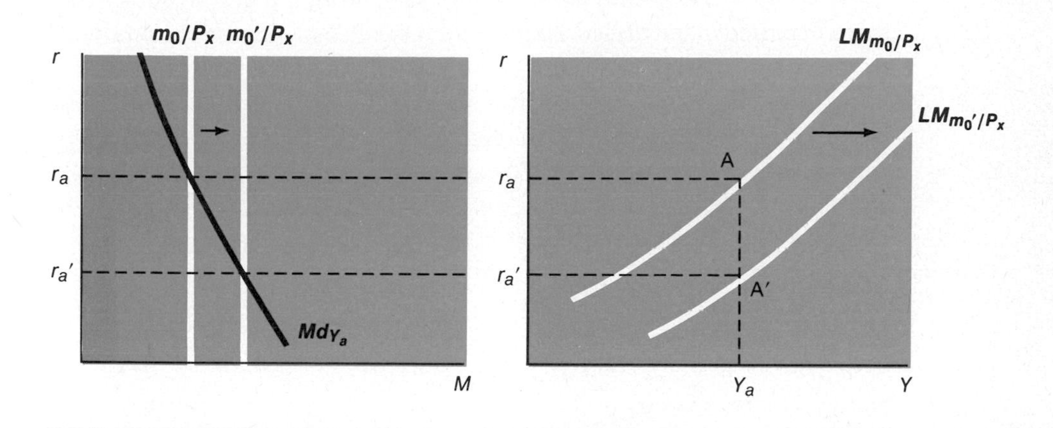

Figure 11–14 **A Decrease in the Money Demand Function**

If the community decides to hold a smaller portion of its wealth in money at each *r* and *Y* combination, the *LM* curve shifts to the right. The interest rate must be lower for each level of *Y* in order for the community to be willing to hold the unchanged money supply.

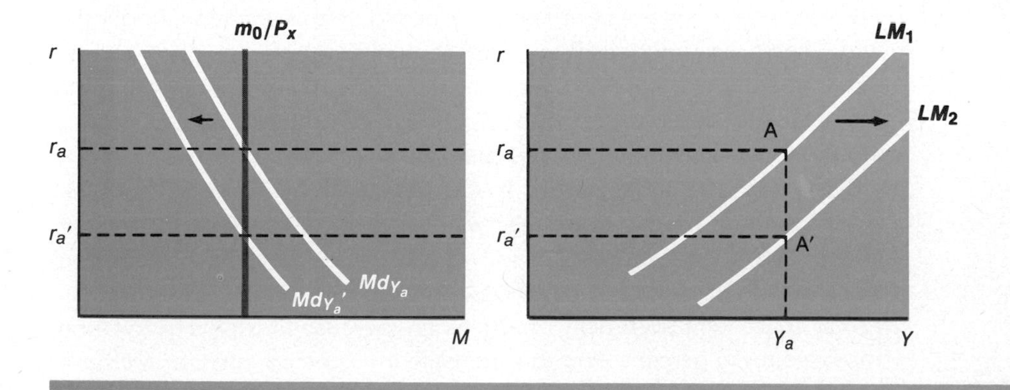

money market equilibrating interest rate must be lower for Y_a, and for any Y, if the money market is to remain in equilibrium. With money supply constant, money holders can be induced to hold money for a given Y only if money demand is stimulated by a lower interest rate. The LM curve must shift to the right.

A decline in the money demand function, though a gradual one, may have occurred in the United States during the 1960s with the rapid growth in the use of credit cards. Effecting transactions with credit cards rather than cash payments permits households to better synchronize their money payment and receipt streams and thereby reduce their average transactions money balances. For example, a household which receives the bulk of its income on the first day of the month can draw a single check on the same day to cover credit card purchases made throughout the preceding month.

Dynamic Money Supply Disturbances and Expected Inflation

Before closing this discussion of aggregate demand disturbances, it is useful to move beyond the once and for all increase in the money supply case discussed in the preceding section and consider a dynamic money supply disturbance, a situation where the monetary authority raises the rate at which it is increasing the money supply from period to period. For example, instead of considering a situation where the money supply is increased by 10 percent and showing that price equilibrium then increases by 10 percent, this section examines the case where the monetary authority begins to increase the money supply at 10 percent per period after numerous periods of holding it constant. In this situation, under the same basic assumptions used earlier, including the neglect of full-employment output growth over time, the economy eventually will settle into a *steady-state equilibrium* in which both prices and the money supply increase at 10 percent per period.

But that is not all that occurs. If prices increase by 10 percent in each period, the community eventually will begin to anticipate a 10 percent inflation rate. Price expectations will *adapt* to price performance. Raising the rate at which the money supply is increased from period to period from zero to 10 percent eventually produces an increase in expected inflation from zero to 10 percent. And this increase in expected inflation will have two results.

First, the market rate of interest, that is, the rate of interest observed in the market, will rise by 10 percent. This occurs because lenders demand such a premium to compensate them for the purchasing power losses from inflation they expect on debt securities, and borrowers are willing to pay the premium. For example, a lender who is willing to lend $100 to get $105 back at the end of a year when prices are expected to remain constant will require $115.50 back if prices are expected to rise by 10 percent, because then it will take $115.50 to buy what $105 would have bought had prices remained constant, since $115.50 is 110 percent of $105.

Borrowers are willing to pay the inflation premium because they are borrowing, for the most part, to finance either purchases of capital goods, on which prices and yields rise with increases in commodity prices, or purchases of debt securities, where market yields rise to reflect the inflation rate. The real rate of interest, which is the market interest rate less the adjustment for purchasing power losses from inflation, remains fixed, as in the case of the once and for all increase in the money supply, where expected inflation was zero. However, the market rate of interest rises by the expected inflation. The relationship which prevails in the steady-state equilibrium is:

$$r = r_r + \%\Delta P, \qquad \text{11–9}$$

where r is the market interest rate (which is the interest rate that has been dealt with in this book), r_r is the real interest rate, and $\%\Delta P$ is the expected and actual inflation rate.[3]

Second, in addition to the permanently higher inflation rate of 10 percent, there is a once and for all increase in prices because real money balances demanded are lower at the higher market interest rate produced by the increase in expected inflation, assuming that interest is not paid on money, or that interest rates on money are inflexible relative to interest rates on other assets. Wealth-holders economize on their real money balances, placing more of their wealth in securities and other assets, where yields can increase to match expected inflation.

[3] Actually, where interest is compounded annually, as is usual, rather than continuously, the relationship is not Equation 11–9 but:

$$r = r_r + \%\Delta P + r_r(\%\Delta P), \qquad \text{11–9a}$$

since the purchasing power adjustment must be applied to the interest earnings as well as to the principal.

Figure 11–15 illustrates how these effects on inflation rate, the market rate of interest, the real rate of interest, and real money balances might occur, adding adjustment lags to make the representation more realistic. In the periods prior to t_{10}, $\%\Delta m_0$ and $\%\Delta P$ are zero, and r and r_r are equal at r_1. With the increase in $\%\Delta m_0$ to 10 percent per period in Period t_{10}, m/P initially rises, reflecting an excess supply of real money balances, r and r_r decline, in response to this, an expenditure gap opens up, and prices begin to rise.

Initially, because of the lags involved in this interest rate effect, $\%\Delta P$ falls short of $\%\Delta m_0$. Eventually, however, $\%\Delta P$ catches up to $\%\Delta m_0$. Indeed, $\%\Delta P$ must surpass $\%\Delta m_0$ for a time before settling to it, either smoothly, as shown, or after fluctuating about it. Prices must increase faster than money supply for a time, not only because $\%\Delta P$ must make up for the earlier lag, but also because real money balances demanded decline as inflation begins to be anticipated. As expected inflation catches up to actual inflation and the new steady-state equilibrium is achieved, the percent change in m_0, actual inflation, and expected inflation all are 10 percent per period, r_r has returned to its predisturbance value, r has risen by 10 percent, and m/P has declined.

Rational Expectations

How soon the steady-state values are achieved following a disturbance depends on the length of the adjustment lags. A number of economists have recently begun to speculate that adjustment occurs fairly rapidly in the real world—much more rapidly than many present-day large statistical models suggest.

Their argument is that economic units apply *rational expectations* rather than the purely *adaptive expectations* implicit in most of these models and in the scenario sketched above.[4] Rational expectations are expectations shaped on the basis of all the information economic units have at their disposal. Therefore, when the monetary authority raises the rate at which it is increasing the money supply from period to period, economic units do not wait until they begin to observe that the inflation rate is increasing to revise upward the inflation rate they expect. They revise it much more quickly than that, because they know, from their

[4] John F. Muth is responsible for the rational expectations hypothesis. See J. F. Muth, "Rational Expectations and the Theory of Price Movements," *Econometrica* 29 (May 1961): 315–335. For a discussion of the application of the hypothesis to macroeconomics, see R. J. Barro and S. Fischer, "Recent Developments in Monetary Theory," *Journal of Monetary Economics* 2 (April 1976), especially pp. 155–163.

Figure 11–15 **A Dynamic Money Supply Disturbance**

If the monetary authority raises the rate at which it is increasing the money supply per period from zero to 10 percent, the model in this chapter settles into an eventual steady-state equilibrium in which prices also are increasing at 10 percent per period. The market rate of interest is higher by 10 percent, the real rate of interest is unchanged, and the real money supply is lower.

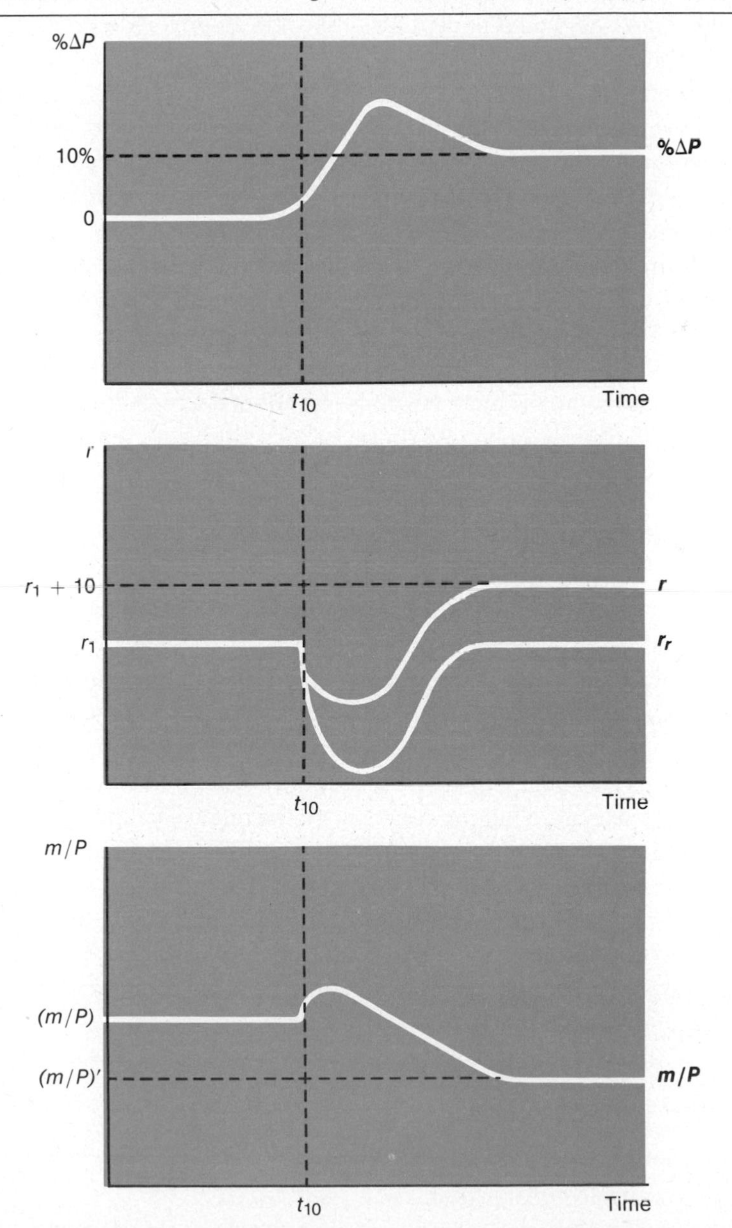

general familiarity with the way in which the economy operates, that a rise in the rate of money supply increase will produce an increase in the inflation rate. As a result, the steady-state values are achieved fairly promptly. For example, if knowledge, and therefore foresight, were perfect, and if prices, wages, and security yields were perfectly flexible upward, the adjustment to steady-state values would be essentially instantaneous.[5] No one would accept less than the steady-state price, money wage, or interest rate, because people would know that these values soon would be available.

Whatever the length of the adjustment lags, the dynamic money supply increase, unlike the once and for all increase in the money supply examined earlier, affects the equilibrium values for market interest rate and real money balances. Moreover, since it reduces equilibrium real money balances, it provokes a more than proportionate increase in prices, comparing points in time before and after the disturbance. It does this because it produces expected inflation, and the effects remain as long as the expected inflation remains. However, in the model sketched here, the dynamic money supply increase does not affect the real rate of interest. In that way, it is like the once and for all money supply increase.

Complications of Distinguishing between Real and Monetary Disturbances

The influence of expected inflation on market interest rates complicates the problem of distinguishing between real and monetary disturbances as sources of inflation and unemployment problems in the actual world. For example, both the inflation rate and market interest rates rose during 1973 and 1974. Did this combination of rising inflation rates and rising market interest rates rule out the possibility that the higher inflation rates were, in significant measure, a lagged response to the relatively rapid growth rates for the money supply which occurred during 1971 and 1972, when effective price and wage controls were in place? This could be concluded if the effects of expected inflation on market interest rates were ignored. In the absence of such effects, an inflation induced by money supply (that is, by a rightward shift in the *LM* curve) would be expected to involve declining or unchanging interest rates.

[5] This is provided that the problem of stability is overcome. For a discussion of this problem, see T. J. Sargent and N. Wallace, "The Stability of Models of Money and Growth with Perfect Foresight," *Econometrica* 41 (November 1973): 1043–1048. Muth argued that the aggregate of rationally formulated expectations is essentially the same as the prediction of the relevant economy theory, which implies very good foresight.

But taking expected inflation effects into account, the increase is consistent with an inflation induced exclusively by money supply. As illustrated in the preceding section, a money supply increase can produce higher market interest rates as well as higher inflation rates if the inflation provokes expectations of inflation.

Summary

1. The model with a money market, like the earlier models which ignored the money market, presents unemployment and inflation problems occurring alternately as aggregate demand fluctuates about full-employment output.

2. Economists often classify the disturbances which lead to fluctuations in aggregate demand as real or monetary, depending on whether they involve shifts in the expenditure functions or shifts in money supply and demand.

3. The real disturbances, which are reflected as shifts in the *IS* curve, include shifts in the investment expenditure function, shifts in the consumption expenditure function, changes in government purchases, and changes in consumption expenditures induced by changes in the tax function and transfer payments. When real disturbances produce declines in aggregate demand, money market effects dampen their impacts on output and employment, as compared with the case where money is absent.

4. In the model used in this chapter, once and for all money supply increases, occurring at full employment, provoke proportionate changes in prices and leave the equilibrium values for the market rate of interest, the real rate of interest, and real money balances unchanged.

5. Dynamic money supply increases, where the monetary authority raises the rate at which it is increasing the money supply from period to period, increase the equilibrium value for the market rate of interest when invoked at full employment, since they raise the equilibrium rate of inflation and the expected rate of inflation. Also, assuming that interest is not paid on money or that interest yields on money are inflexible relative to yields on other assets, the dynamic money supply increases reduce equilibrium real money balances. This means that they provoke more than proportionate increases in prices, comparing points in time before and after they occur.

Concepts for Identification

fluctuations in aggregate demand
real disturbances
monetary disturbances
increases and decreases in the:
- money demand function
- investment expenditure function
- consumption expenditure function
- tax function

monetary dampener
once and for all money supply increase
dynamic money supply increase
expected inflation
market rate of interest
real rate of interest
steady-state equilibrium
rational expectations
adaptive expectations

Questions and Problems for Review

1. Verify the entries in the table which appears below, using *IS* and *LM* curves and the assumptions of the model in this chapter. The changes are changes in equilibrium values. They result from the disturbances listed in the left-hand column. The disturbances are of the once and for all variety and occur with the economy in an initial full employment and price

Disturbance	ΔY	Δr	ΔP	ΔU
Increase in investment expenditure function	0	+	+	0
Decline in money supply	–	+	0	+
Decline in consumption expenditure function	–	–	0	+
Increase in transfer payments	0	+	+	0
Increase in tax function	–	–	0	+
Decline in investment expenditure function	–	–	0	+
Increase in government purchases	0	+	+	0
Increase in private saving function	–	–	0	+
Increase in money demand function	–	+	0	+
Decline in tax function	0	+	+	0
Increase in money supply	0	0	+	0
Increase in consumption expenditure function	0	+	+	0
Decline in money demand function	0	0	+	0

stability situation. The variable U represents the unemployment rate. A plus means an increase. A minus means a decrease. A zero means no change.

2. Construct a table showing what the entries in the table of Question 1 would be if the disturbances occurred in a less than full employment situation and none of the disturbances which increase aggregate demand were strong enough to move the economy quite to full employment. Show what the entries would be if all the disturbances which increase aggregate demand were stronger than needed to move the economy to full employment.

3. A once and for all increase of 10 percent in the money supply, imposed when the model in this chapter is in an initial full-employment equilibrium, will produce a 10 percent increase in the equilibrium value for prices. Explain why this must be true.

4. Explain why the market rate of interest might be expected to rise by 5 percent eventually if the monetary authority increases by 5 percent the rate at which it increases the money supply per period. Why would the equilibrium real money supply be expected to settle to a lower level in this situation?

5. Explain why the market rate of interest and the inflation rate might be expected to achieve their steady-state equilibrium values more quickly following a maintained increase in the rate of increase in the money supply if expectations are formed rationally rather than on a purely adaptive basis.

References

Barro, R. J., and Fischer, S. "Recent Developments in Monetary Theory." *Journal of Monetary Economics* 2 (April 1976): 133–167.

Cagan, Phillip. "The Monetary Dynamics of Hyperinflation." In *Studies in the Quantity Theory of Money,* edited by Milton Friedman. Chicago: University of Chicago Press, 1956, pp. 25–117.

Friedman, Milton, and Schwartz, Anna J. *A Monetary History of the United States, 1867–1960.* Princeton, N.J.: Princeton University Press, 1963.

Jonson, P. D., and Mahoney, D. M. "Price Expectations in Australia." *Economic Record* 48 (March 1973): 50–61.

Laidler, David. "Money and Money Income: An Essay on the 'Transmission Mechanism.' " *Journal of Monetary Economics* 4 (April 1978): 151–191.

Muth, J. F. "Rational Expectations and the Theory of Price Movements." *Econometrica* 29 (May 1961): 315–335.

Rutledge, J. *A Monetarist Model of Inflationary Expectations.* Lexington, Mass.: Lexington Books, 1974.

Sargent, T. J., and Wallace, N. "The Stability of Models of Money and Growth with Perfect Foresight." *Econometrica* 41 (November 1973): 1043–1048.

Taylor, Dean. "A Simple Model of Monetary Dynamics." *Journal of Money, Credit, and Banking* 9 (February 1977): pt. 1, 107–111.

Appendix to Chapter 11
An Alternative Method for Obtaining Shifts in *IS* and *LM* Curves

Readers who find the graphical method for obtaining shifts in *IS* and *LM* curves cumbersome may wish to utilize the algebraic-numerical model of Chapter 10 for the purpose. It yields a very efficient method, and one which provides some insights as well.

Referring back to Chapter 10, substitution of Equations 10–15 through 10–21 into Equation 10–29, the $Y = E$ condition, produced the *IS* curve as:

$$r = \frac{E_0 - [1 - b(1 - t)]Y}{i + s}, \tag{11–10}$$

where:

$$E_0 = a_0 - bTx_0 + bTr_0 + I_0 + G_0. \tag{11–11}$$

Substitution of Equations 10–23 and 10–31 into Equation 10–30, the $Md = Ms$ condition, produced the *LM* curve as:

$$r = \frac{L_0 - M_0/P_x + kY}{q}. \tag{11–12}$$

When the *IS* and *LM* curve equations are rearranged, with Y placed on the left-hand side, the *IS* curve is:

$$Y = \frac{E_0 - (i + s)r}{1 - b(1 - t)} \qquad \text{11–13}$$

and the *LM* curve is:

$$Y = \frac{m_0/P_x - L_0 + qr}{k}. \qquad \text{11–14}$$

Setting r equal to zero in Equation 11–13 produces the reference point B on the *IS* curve in Figure 11–16 as:

$$Y = \frac{E_0 - (i + s)(0)}{1 - b(1 - t)} = \frac{E_0}{1 - b(1 - t)}. \qquad \text{11–15}$$

Similarly, setting r equal to zero in Equation 11–14 yields reference point A on the *LM* curve in Figure 11–16 as:

$$Y = \frac{m_0/P_x - L_0 + q(0)}{k} = \frac{m_0/P_x - L_0}{k}. \qquad \text{11–16}$$

Shifts in the *IS* and *LM* curves caused by monetary and real disturbances now can be perceived directly from the figure by observing their impacts on Points A and B. For example, an increase in the money supply, which is an increase in m_0 in the model, increases the numerator of Point A and shifts Point A and the *LM* curve to the right. An increase in the money demand function, represented by an increase in L_0, the money demand constant, diminishes the numerator of Point A and shifts Point A and the *LM* curve to the left. The slope of the *LM* curve remains the same for both of these disturbances, since the slope, from Equation 11–12, is:

$$\Delta r/\Delta Y = k/q \qquad \text{11–17}$$

and is independent of changes in m_0 and L_0.

If an increase in the investment demand function is introduced as an increase in I_0, the investment demand constant, the numerator of Point B in the figure increases, and Point B and the *IS* curve shift to the right. E_0 increases by the increase in I_0, since I_0 enters into E_0 on a one for one basis. Similarly, increases in G_0 and in a_0, the consumption constant, increase E_0

Figure 11–16 **Shifting the *IS* and *LM* Curves**
($E_0 = a_0 - bTx_0 + bTr_0 + I_0 + G_0$)

If the values for Points A, B, and C are obtained from the algebraic model of Chapter 10, the impacts of shifts in the various relationships underlying the *IS* and *LM* curves on these curves can be perceived by noting their impacts on the points.

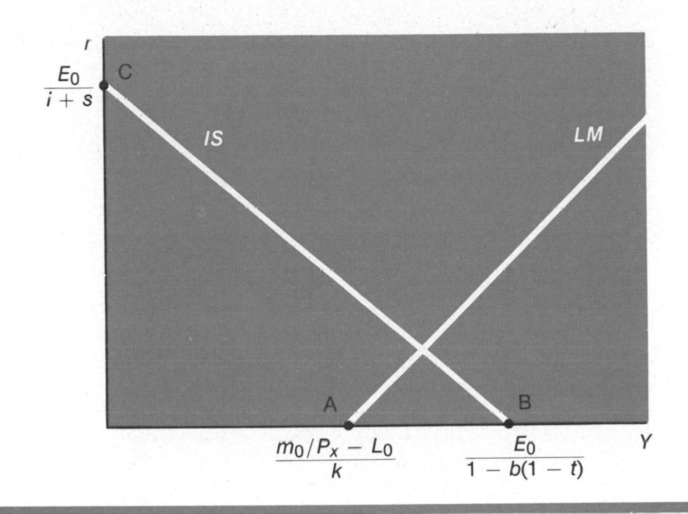

on a one for one basis and shift Point B and the *IS* curve to the right. A tax rebate, which reduces Tx_0, the tax constant, increases E_0 by $b\Delta Tx_0$ and shifts Point B and the *IS* curve to the right. All of these disturbances leave the slope of the *IS* curve unchanged, since the slope of the *IS* curve, from Equation 11–10, is:

$$\Delta r/\Delta Y = -\left\{\frac{1 - b(1 - t)}{i + s}\right\} \tag{11–18}$$

and is independent of the expenditure, tax, and transfer payment constants.

A reduction in *t*, the marginal tax rate, or an increase in *b*, the marginal propensity to consume, does affect the slope of the *IS* curve, however, since *t* and *b* enter into Equation 11–18. Since these changes increase Point B but do not affect Point C, they rotate the *IS* curve to the right on Point C. The value for Point C is obtained by setting *Y* equal to zero in Equation 11–10.

12

The Supply Sector and Supply Disturbances

The aggregate supply curve for output depends on the aggregate production function relating labor input to output, on the supply curve for labor, and on the existing money-wage level. Wage-push inflation, technological advance, reductions in the supply of oil, and shifts in the supply of labor induced by expansions in income-maintenance programs and changes in labor force composition are some of the supply disturbances which affect these determinants and give rise to unemployment and inflation problems.

Most economists regard fluctuations in aggregate demand as the chief source of the severe unemployment and inflation problems the United States economy has experienced in this century. The debate as to the sources of these problems tends to be over whether real or monetary disturbances have dominated in the fluctuations in demand. Was the key factor in the Great Depression of the 1930s the 33 percent decline in the money supply (cash plus commercial bank demand and time deposits) which occurred from the end of 1929 to the end of 1933, or was an independent and substantial decline in the investment expenditure function the more important factor? Perhaps both were important. Did the economic recovery and inflation associated with World War II and its aftermath result chiefly from the 223 percent increase in the money supply which occurred from the end of 1938 to the end of 1945, or was the large increase in government purchases, and later in the investment expenditure function, the more important factor?

Whatever the resolution of this debate—and the issue will be considered more carefully in Chapter 14—it is clear that supply disturbances have contributed to economic stabilization problems on occasion. They appear to have been an important factor in the difficulties of the 1970s, for example, when both unemployment and inflation have been problems at the same time, as judged by earlier standards.

This chapter illustrates the unemployment and inflation impacts of aggregate supply disturbances ranging from wage-push inflation and technological advance to increases in the natural rate of unemployment arising from expansions in income-maintenance programs and the shifting composition of the labor force. The first order of business will be an elaboration of the macroeconomic model developed in earlier chapters, however, since a more elaborate supply sector is useful for conceptualizing supply disturbances. The sections which follow present the market for aggregate output with demand and supply curves plotted against price. The demand curve is constructed from *IS* and *LM* curves, while the supply curve is built up from the aggregate production function and the labor market.

Aggregate Demand and Supply Curves

Figure 12–1 presents the market for aggregate output with the demand and supply for aggregate output plotted against the price level. The demand curve, labeled Y_D, slopes negatively, because of the effect of the price level on the real money supply. As prices become higher, the real money supply becomes lower if the non–price deflated money supply is unchanged. With the real money supply lower, the interest rate must be higher for money market equilibrium to occur. With the interest rate higher, interest-sensitive expenditures, and therefore expenditures as a whole, are lower.

The Aggregate Demand Curve

This relationship is illustrated by Figure 12–2, which presents the aggregate demand curve constructed from the *IS-LM* representation already developed. The figure ignores the full-employment constraint on output and generates the aggregate demand curve of the lower portion by imposing three price levels on the *IS-LM* graph of the upper portion. At price level P_1, the real money supply is m_0/P_1, and the *LM* curve intersects

Figure 12–1 **The Market for Aggregate Output**

The market for aggregate output can be presented as a market with aggregate demand and supply curves plotted against price. Equilibrium price and output occur at the point of intersection of the curves, where output demand and output supply are equal.

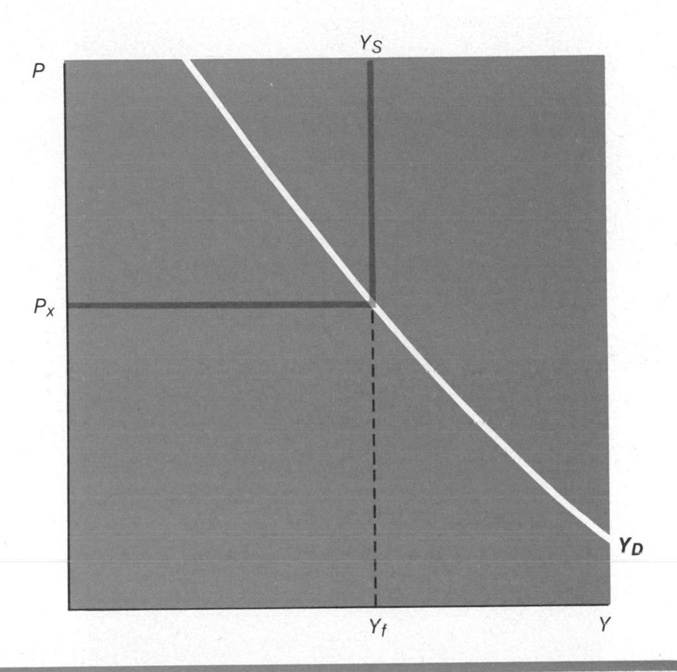

the IS curve at output Y_a. That is, ignoring the full-employment constraint on output and assuming that Y simply adjusts to E, price level P_1 produces an aggregate demand for output equal to Y_a. Recorded below, in the aggregate output market, this produces a point on the aggregate demand curve at P_1 and Y_a.

If prices are higher, at P_2, the real money supply is smaller, at m_0/P_2. The LM curve moves to the left and intersects the IS curve at Y_b. This is recorded in the lower portion of the figure as a second point on the aggregate demand curve. At price level P_2, aggregate output demanded is only Y_b. Similarly, if prices are still higher, at P_3, aggregate output demanded is Y_c, since the LM curve for P_3 intersects the IS curve at Y_c. The combination P_3 and Y_c is a third point on the aggregate demand curve. Increases in the price level reduce the real money supply, raise the interest

Figure 12–2 **Constructing the Aggregate Demand Curve**

As the price level becomes higher, the real money supply becomes smaller, the interest rate which yields money market equilibrium becomes higher, and the demand for aggregate output diminishes.

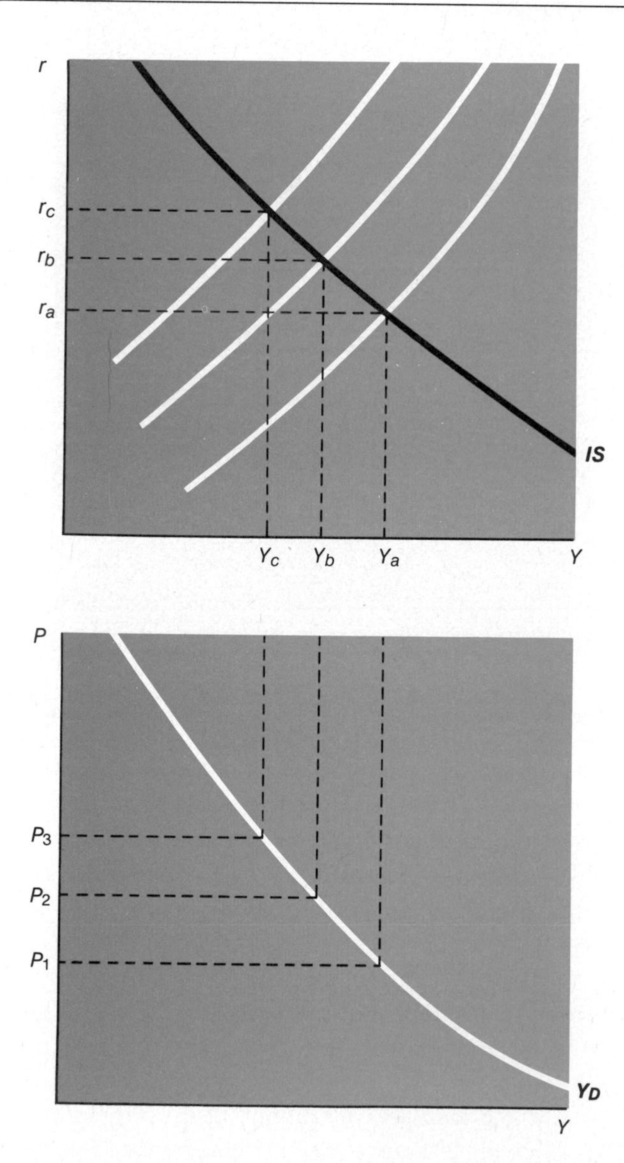

rate, and reduce interest-sensitive expenditures. Aggregate output demanded declines as the price level increases.

The Aggregate Supply Curve

Returning now to Figure12–1, notice that the aggregate supply for output curve, labeled Y_S, is flat at P_x, the existing price level, up to full-employment output and then is vertical. This reflects the assumption made here all along that output supplied simply adjusts to aggregate demand at existing prices until full employment is reached and then remains fixed even though prices rise.

In Figure 12–3, when the IS and Y_D curves decline from IS' and Y_D' to IS'' and Y_D'', perhaps because of a decline in the investment expenditure function, equilibrium Y declines from Y_f to Y_a, the full amount of the decline in aggregate demand at existing prices, and prices remain fixed at P_x. A recovery in the IS and Y_D curves to IS' and Y_D' restores equilibrium output to Y_f with prices still constant at P_x.

In Figure 12–4, an increase in aggregate demand at Y_f, shifting the IS and Y_D curves from IS' and Y_D' to IS'' and Y_D'', provokes an increase in equilibrium prices from P_x to P_x'' and leaves output unchanged at Y_f.

The vertical portion of the aggregate supply curve reflects the full-employment constraint on output imposed by labor market equilibrium and the aggregate production function. The flat portion of the curve reflects the inflexibility of money wages simplification introduced by Keynes. It will soon be demonstrated, however, that representing this portion of the curve as flat rather than sloping upward requires a slight modification of the traditional Keynesian representation.

The Vertical Portion of the Aggregate Supply Curve

Figure 12–5 illustrates the basis for the full-employment constraint on output and the vertical portion of the aggregate supply curve. The upper portion of the figure plots the aggregate production function, showing labor input required for varying levels of output supplied, with the stock of capital goods constant at K_0, which is the existing level. (Capital goods include plant, equipment, and inventories of producers and also residential construction.) N represents labor employment in hours.

The production function slopes positively throughout, indicating that labor employment moves in the same direction as output. The slope

Figure 12-3 **Output Declines, Prices Remain Constant**

The conclusion reached in earlier chapters—that output declines and prices remain constant when aggregate demand declines—implies an aggregate supply of output curve which is horizontal at the existing price level for less than full employment levels of output.

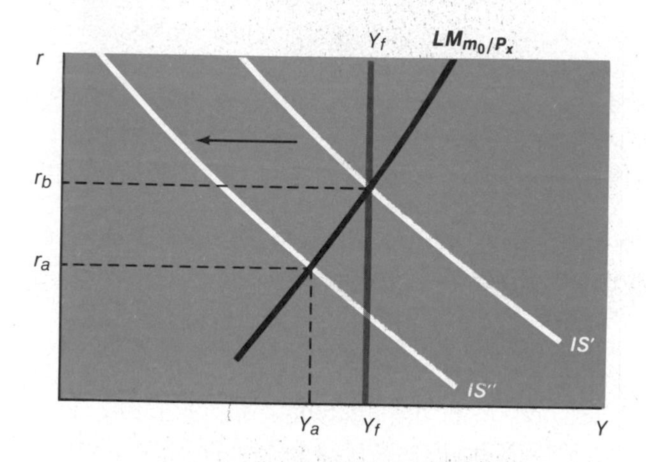

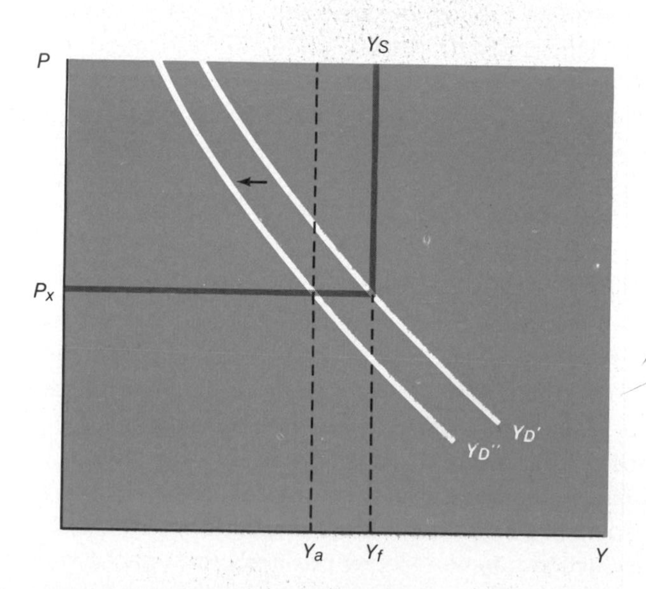

Figure 12–4 **Output Remains Constant, Prices Increase**

The earlier statement that output remains constant and prices increase when aggregate demand increases at full-employment output implies an aggregate supply of output curve which becomes vertical once full-employment output is reached.

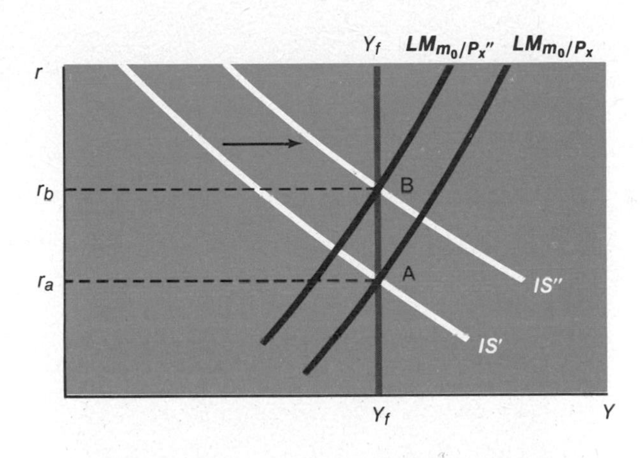

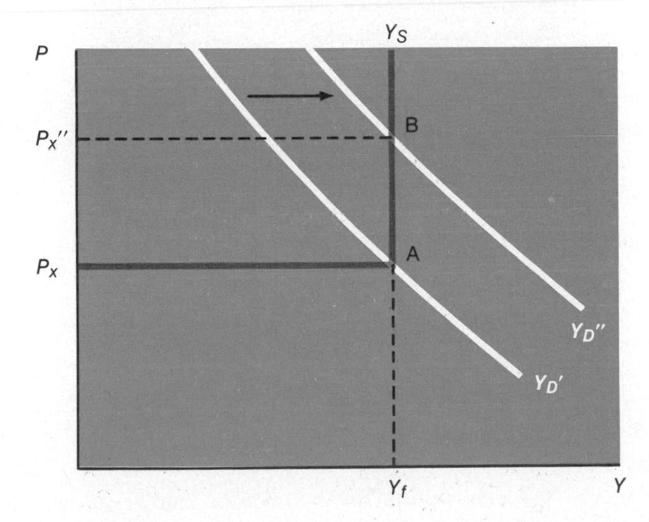

Figure 12–5 **The Full-Employment Benchmark**

Full-employment output occurs at the level of output consistent with labor market equilibrium.

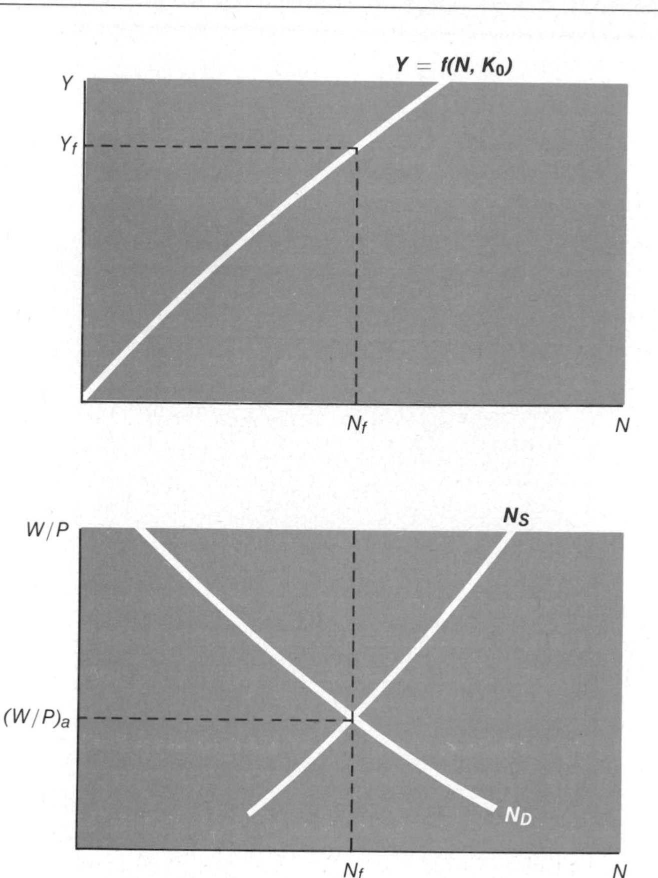

diminishes, however, denoting that the marginal product of labor, that is, $\Delta Y/\Delta N$, diminishes as N is increased with capital constant. As labor is added, output increases, but the increments in output are successively smaller, since capital per hour of labor diminishes.

The lower portion of the figure presents the labor market. The demand for labor curve, N_D, is drawn on the assumption that employers hire labor up to the point where the marginal product of labor is equal to W/P, the real wage paid for labor services. This is the profit maximizing position for employers. It reflects a situation where the last unit of labor hired brings to employers a value just equal to the outlay involved. The demand for labor curve must slope downward, given this profit condition and the aggregate production function in the top portion of the figure. The real wage must decline if more labor is to be demanded, since the marginal product of labor declines as labor is added.

Figure 12–5 shows the supply of labor curve, N_S, as positively sloped, though the curve does not necessarily have this feature. For example, some workers may offer fewer hours of labor per period as the real wage increases, since the same income can be earned with fewer hours of work. It will be assumed here, however, that the cyclical response in the aggregate supply of labor is that more labor is offered as real wages increase, at least in the range relevant for macroeconomic analysis. Higher real wages attract additional entrants into the labor force—homemakers, students, teenagers, and the like—and cause workers who are already employed to offer more hours of work.

Labor market equilibrium occurs where the demand and supply for labor curves intersect. At this point, the quantities of labor services demanded and supplied are equal, and the equilibrium values N_f and $(W/P)_a$ are determined. N_f, inserted into the aggregate production function, yields Y_f, the benchmark for full-employment output and the source of the vertical portion of the aggregate supply of output curve. The assumption for the present will be simply that N and Y remain approximately at N_f and Y_f when aggregate demand for output exceeds Y_f. A total expenditure greater than Y_f induces an effort by producers to expand Y beyond Y_f, but this effort involves an excess demand for labor if real wages equal to marginal products are offered and correctly perceived by workers. Consequently, money wages and prices merely rise when aggregate demand exceeds Y_f, and N, W/P, and Y remain at the values indicated by the labor market equilibrium.

Y_f and N_f are consistent with structural unemployment and normal amounts of frictional and seasonal unemployment, which are excluded from the supply of labor curve. Y_f and N_f thus are consistent with the natural rate of unemployment of from 5 to 7 percent described in Chapter 2.

The Flat Portion of the Aggregate Supply Curve

The flat portion of the aggregate supply of output curve in Figure 12–1 reflects the inflexibility of money wages simplification noted above. Money wages do not decline when aggregate demand declines, because workers resist money-wage cuts. This resistance can show itself formally through union pressure and contracts or informally as the basis of employer reluctance to demoralize and alienate a workforce by imposing money-wage cuts. Money wages do not increase when aggregate demand increases until full employment is passed, since excess demands for output and labor are not present until full employment is passed. Some price inflexibility may occur independently of inflexibility in money-wage costs; but, for present purposes, that possibility is neglected.[1]

Whatever the source of the money-wage inflexibility, the inference that prices are constant if money wages are constant involves some modification of the traditional Keynesian representation. In that representation, prices diminish somewhat when aggregate demand declines and recover when aggregate demand recovers, even though money wages are constant throughout. This occurs because the capital stock is assumed to remain fully employed during fluctuations in output and labor employment. Production adjusts to aggregate demand along the aggregate production function of Figure 12–5. The marginal product of labor increases during demand-induced recessions and diminishes again during recoveries. This being the case, producers can lower prices slightly during the recessions without paying workers more than their marginal products even though wages are constant. Presumably, competition for sales induces them to make the price reductions. When demand recovers, producers must restore prices to their former level if they are to hire the labor necessary to meet the increased demand with expanded output. Otherwise, with money wages constant and the marginal product of labor diminishing, they cannot profitably hire additional labor.

The upper left-hand portion of Figure 12–6 presents the traditional Keynesian aggregate supply curve. The curve slopes upward toward full-employment output. When the aggregate demand curve declines from Y_D' to Y_D'', output falls to Y_1 and prices decline to P_x'. Prices diminish because the marginal product of labor increases as N falls from N_f to N_1, permitting the higher real wage W_x/P_x' to be paid. Money wages are constant at W_x, but the real wage increases from W_x/P_x to W_x/P_x'. If the aggregate demand curve recovers to Y_D', output will return to Y_f, and prices must rise back to P_x if producers are to hire the labor necessary to provide output Y_f.

---

[1] For example, in situations where industries are dominated by a few large competitors, each competitor may be reluctant to reduce prices for fear of setting off a price war in which all firms lose. In addition, the practice of listing prices in catalogs inhibits prompt price adjustments in some cases.

Figure 12–6 **The Keynesian Aggregate Supply Curve**

The traditional Keynesian aggregate supply curve is upward sloping, rather than horizontal, for output levels short of full-employment output. This means that prices vary somewhat when aggregate demand fluctuates within the less than full employment range.

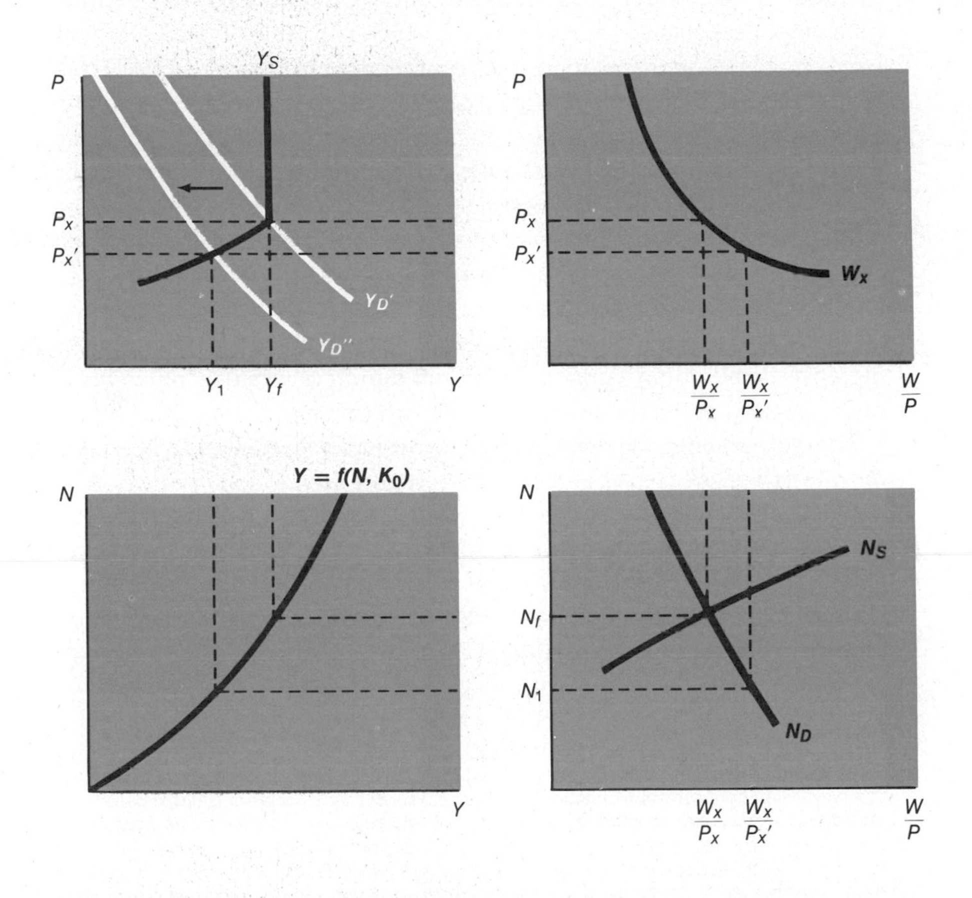

In the construction of the aggregate supply curve for output in the figure, the aggregate production function and the labor market appear in the lower left and lower right-hand portions, respectively, while the curve at the upper right presents the inverse relationship between P and W/P for money wage W_x. In order for the output market to appear upright, the production function and labor market must be placed on their sides.[2]

Available data do not support the upward sloping portion of the Keynesian aggregate supply curve very well. Edwin Kuh, in one study, found no consistent tendency for the real wage to vary cyclically as the Keynesian curve suggests.[3] Moreover, the average product of labor—that is, output per hour of labor input—has tended to decline during declines in aggregate output associated with recessions, which suggests that the marginal product of labor tends to do the same rather than to increase. Notice that the average as well as the marginal product of labor increases as output declines along the aggregate production function of Figure 12–6, since the average product of labor is the slope of a line drawn from a point on the curve through the origin. Apparently, production moves to the left of the aggregate production function of the figure as the economy moves into recession, with both capital and labor being used less efficiently than before. Capacity utilization rates for the capital stock diminish during recessions, indicating that capital as well as labor become unemployed. Moreover, while some workers are laid off during recessions, other workers, especially at the management level, are carried.

The next section will employ the Keynesian aggregate supply curve, despite its weaknesses, in illustrating aggregate supply disturbances. As a convenience, subsequent chapters, for the most part, will return to the simpler, flat portion aggregate supply curve implicit in the models of earlier chapters. Either supply curve is a simplification, over and above matters relating to the cyclical behaviors of the marginal and average products of labor and the real wage.

---

[2] The basis of the Keynesian aggregate supply curve in the production theory of the pre-Keynesian economists is an attractive feature. The demand for labor is derived from the aggregate production function, and labor is paid its real wage. Economists sometimes obtain these characteristics, but still preserve the flat portion aggregate supply curve as a convenience, by assuming that production responds to cyclical fluctuations in aggregate demand with *fixed factor proportions* and *constant returns-to-scale.* This means that when aggregate demand declines by 10 percent and producers respond with a 10 percent reduction in output, both labor and capital inputs are reduced by 10 percent. The marginal product of labor remains constant, the real wage is constant, and prices are fixed if money wages are fixed. Similarly, when aggregate demand recovers, labor and capital are restored in fixed proportions, the marginal product of labor again is constant, and prices need not rise until money wages begin to rise at full employment. David Laidler has used this convenience. See David Laidler, *The Demand for Money: Theories and Evidence* (Scranton, Pa.: International, 1969), p. 3.

[3] See Edwin Kuh, "Unemployment, Production Functions, and Effective Demand," *Journal of Political Economy* 74 (June 1966), especially pp. 246–248.

Money wages are inflexible downward during recessions, but they are not as rigid as these curves imply, at least not during an extremely severe and protracted shortfall of aggregate demand such as existed in the United States during the early 1930s. While it is true that average hourly earnings in manufacturing have not declined on an annual basis since 1933 (a period spanning eight recessions), they did decline by 22 percent during 1929 through 1933 (Figure 12–7). Moreover, a second problem with the curves is that aggregate output is not constrained rigidly to a fixed full-employment level when aggregate demand or supply disturbances create an expenditure gap, as the vertical portions of the curves suggest.

Figure 12–7 **Average Gross Hourly Earnings in Manufacturing in the United States, Current Dollars, 1929–1978**

Money wages declined during each of the four years 1929 through 1933, but have not declined on an annual basis for any year since 1933.

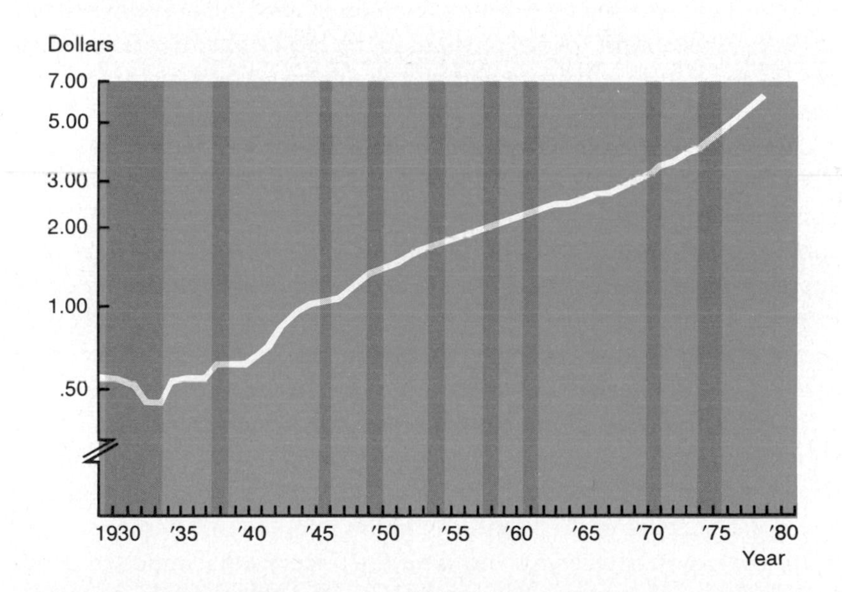

Shaded areas represent business recessions, covering peak to trough, using National Bureau of Economic Research reference dates.

Sources: President's Council of Economic Advisers, ***Economic Report of the President*** (Washington, D.C.: Government Printing Office, 1958), p. 143; and ***Economic Report of the President***, 1979, p. 224.

Aggregate output responds somewhat to inflation, at least in the short term. Chapter 15 will examine the implications of downward flexibility in money wages. Chapter 13 will treat short-term responses to inflation of output that surpasses full-employment output.

Aggregate Supply Disturbances

Before 1970, the aggregate supply disturbances which attracted the most attention among economists and the public at large were cost-push inflation, especially wage-push inflation, and technological advance, though it is not clear that either disturbance had played a major role in U.S. unemployment and inflation problems. Technological advance in agriculture often is cited as a cause of unemployment during the 1930s, but a decline in aggregate demand for output undoubtedly was the major factor in the extremely high general unemployment rates of the period. Wage-push inflation received frequent mention as a factor in the sharp inflation of 1946–1948 and the milder inflations of the 1950s, but most economists cite fluctuations in aggregate demand as the major factor in those inflations.

During the 1970s, shifts in the supply of labor associated with expansions in government income-maintenance programs and changes in the composition of the labor force have emerged as important aggregate supply disturbances. Other disturbances of the 1970s with important supply-side effects for the United States economy include the sharp increase in prices of imported oil administered in late 1973 and early 1974 by the newly effectual cartel of international oil producers and the more gradual rise in prices of other imported goods and services associated with the depreciation of the dollar in foreign exchange markets. The oil shock is a classic instance of cost-push inflation arising from monopoly power, through oil prices undoubtedly would have increased eventually in any event because of the expansion in the international demand for oil relative to known oil reserves. The rise in the price of other imported goods and services caused by the depreciation of the dollar was a significant element in the rise of U.S. consumer prices during the period.

This section examines aggregate supply disturbances as sources of unemployment and inflation problems, using the elaborated model developed in the preceding section for the purpose. It begins with wage-push inflation, moves on to technological advance and reductions in the supply of oil, and closes with an examination of shifts in the supply of labor associated with expansions of income-maintenance programs and changes in the composition of the labor force.

Wage-Push Inflation

The wage-push version of cost-push inflation results from monopoly control over the supply of labor by labor unions across an industry or across several industries. Often, it is represented as follows. Labor leaders, to satisfy union members and to solidify their own positions, seek increases in money wages and fringe benefits in excess of increases in labor productivity. Producers grant such increases under threat of strike or protracted negotiations and pass on the increased costs of production by raising prices. Prices are pushed up by increases in labor costs, rather than rising in response to an increase in demand.

Figure 12–8 illustrates the impact of wage-push inflation. It enters in the lower portion of the figure as an upward shift in the upward sloping portion of the aggregate supply of output curve. Since money wages have risen substantially, producers' costs have increased, and they raise the prices at which they are willing to supply given levels of output.

With the aggregate demand for output curve unchanged, the result is an increase in prices from P_x to P_x' and a decline in equilibrium output from Y_f to Y_b. The aggregate demand curve intersects the new aggregate supply curve at Point B, determining P_x' and Y_b. The result of wage-push inflation, in this illustration, is not only that money wages and prices rise, but also that aggregate output declines and the unemployment rate rises. In the absence of intervention by the stabilization authorities to expand aggregate demand, the wage push produces unemployment as well as inflation.

Why do higher prices produce a decrease in aggregate output demanded along the aggregate demand curve? The reason is the one cited when the curve was constructed. As prices rise, the real money supply declines, the interest rate which maintains money market equilibrium increases, and interest-sensitive expenditures decline. The upper portion of Figure 12–8 illustrates this effect with *IS* and *LM* curves. As prices rise from P_x to P_x', the *LM* curve shifts to the left, reflecting the decline in real money balances. The interest rate rises from r_1 to r_2 to maintain money market equilibrium, and aggregate output adjusts, along the *IS* curve, to the lower level of aggregate output demanded. The decline in aggregate output demanded reflects both the direct interest rate effect on interest-

Figure 12–8 **Wage-Push Inflation**

When wage-push inflation occurs, the upward sloping portion of the aggregate supply of output curve rises. Producers ask a higher price for each level of output because costs have increased. Equilibrium prices rise, and output declines. A shortfall of aggregate demand appears, since demand will not support the former output at the higher price level.

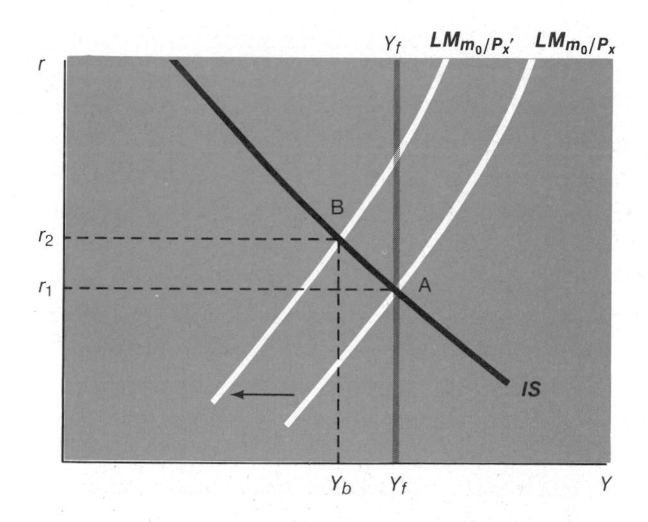

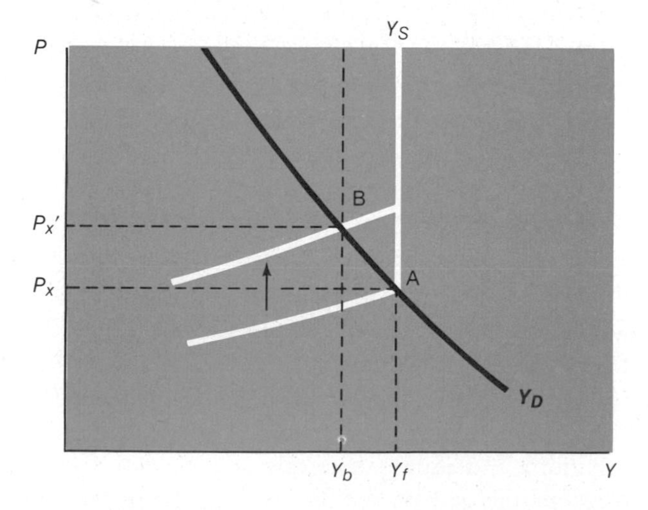

sensitive expenditures and the decline in consumption expenditures induced by the decline in output and real income.

Producer Cost-Push Inflation

Often, it is argued that the large firms which characterize many U.S. industries—such as the steel, automobile, and chemical industries—possess a market power which permits them to raise prices independently of the presence of excess demand, so that cost-push inflation can arise from producers even without a wage push from industry-wide unions.

While there is a basis for arguing that this type of cost-push inflation exists, the conditions under which it occurs are narrower than is often assumed. The basis rests in the result of economic theory that an industry which behaves monopolistically, maximizing the profit of the monopolist or the joint profit of the group of firms acting in concert, will restrict output and raise prices as compared to the case where the industry behaves competitively. Therefore, if industry becomes more monopolistic—that is, more concentrated in a few large firms—cost-push inflationary pressures can occur as the new monopolists restrict output and raise prices.

Concentration among U.S. producers has not increased significantly since the 1920s, but the dollar depreciations of the 1970s have increased the market power of U.S. producers by increasing the dollar price of foreign-produced goods and services, thus reducing foreign competition. This situation has presented the possibility of producer cost-push inflation occurring. In addition, the foreign oil producer cartel restricted output and posted large increases in oil prices in 1973 and 1974 and again in 1979. These increases constituted a cost-push item in the U.S. consumer price index, which includes prices of imported goods and services.

Economists sometimes see wage-push inflation as occurring only on this same basis—increased monopoly power—and discount its significance for that reason. That is, they see it as occurring only when new unions are formed or when existing unions gain additional market power, as the new optimum real wage and employment level combinations are effected. But wage-push inflation need not be as rational as that, or as expert. Given that market power exists, so that a wage push can occur, it may arise simply from the desire of union members for wage gains and from the need of union leaders to satisfy that desire. If this is true, whether wage-push inflation occurs is an empirical matter. Most economists do not see it as having been an important autonomous item in the United States during the 1970s.

Technological Advance

A technological advance is a disturbance which permits a greater amount of output to be obtained with given levels of labor and capital input, measuring the capital input in terms of the reproduction costs of the capital goods involved. Ordinarily, the advance is an improved manner of production arising from a new technique, machine, material, or energy resource, though it can occur gradually from improvement in the quality of labor input from education or immigration. Whatever its source, technological advance shifts the aggregate supply curve to the right and increases full-employment output. In the long term it increases per capita output and real income, provided that full employment is maintained. In the short term it is likely to produce an increase in unemployment, however, and may produce some deflation, though neither of these effects is assured.

Figure 12–9 illustrates the short-term effects of technological advance under conditions of downward wage inflexibility. When the technological advance occurs, the aggregate production function, in the lower left-hand portion of the figure, shifts to the right. More output obtains at each level of labor input, with the capital stock given.

Since the shift in the aggregate production function is presented as increasing the marginal product of labor at each level of N, the demand for labor curve, in the lower portion of the figure, also shifts to the right. The slope of the aggregate production function having declined, the marginal product of labor is higher at each level of labor input. If labor is offered its marginal product, a higher real wage will be offered for each level of labor input; or, what amounts to the same thing, given the diminishing marginal product of labor, more labor will be demanded at each real wage, since the same marginal product prevails at a higher level of labor input. The demand for labor curve shifts to the right.

The aggregate supply curve for output corresponding to money wage W_x, plotted in the upper left-hand portion of the figure, responds to the aggregate production function shift by moving to the right. The aggregate supply curve would shift to the right even if the slope of the aggregate production function remained constant in the relevant range—that is, even if the demand for labor curve did not increase—because the unchanged full-employment level of employment would produce a larger output, as shown by the new aggregate production function. But with the demand for labor curve also shifting, the rightward shift in the aggregate supply of output curve is augmented by the increase in the full-employment level of employment which occurs as the real wage rises. The higher marginal product of labor, evidencing itself in the higher real wage,

Figure 12–9 **Technological Advance**

A technological advance shifts the aggregate production function to the right and ordinarily shifts the demand for labor curve to the right as well. The aggregate supply curve for output shifts to the right. Equilibrium output and full-employment output rise, and prices fall. A shortfall of aggregate demand may appear (as shown in the figure).

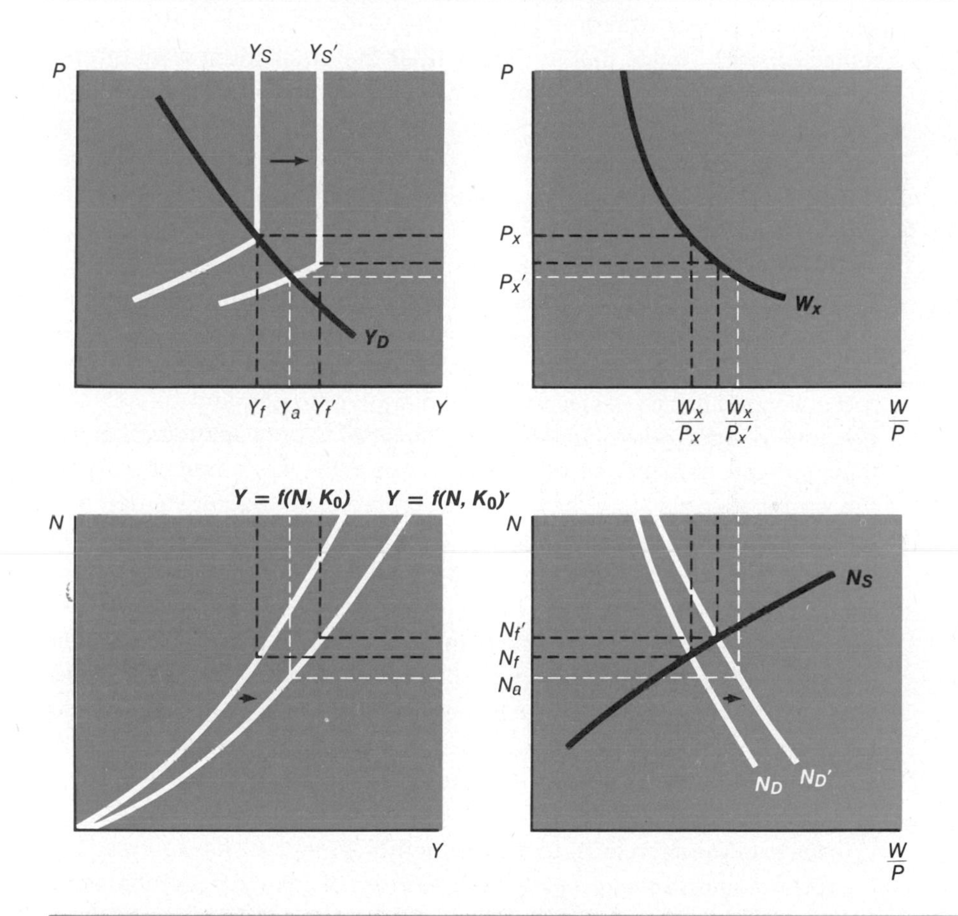

stimulates employment along the supply curve of labor. The full-employment level of output increases both because a given amount of labor input produces a larger output and because the full-employment level of employment increases.

In the situation represented by Figure 12–9, prices decline somewhat, and the unemployment rate increases. Prices decline, with money wages fixed, because the real wage has increased. Output increases from Y_f to Y_a as a result of the price decline, but the increase in Y falls short of the increase in full-employment output to Y_f'. Technological advance has produced technological unemployment.

That is the result traditionally feared by workers and labor unions. Technological advance replaces workers with machines and more efficient processes, divesting workers of jobs. (In the early days of the industrial revolution, workers sometimes destroyed the machines which were to replace them.) Notice that in Figure 12–9 the equilibrium level of employment falls to N_a, which is short of N_f, the original employment level. The equilibrium level of employment has declined. Some workers who were employed before the technological advance are now unemployed, unless a decline in average hours worked per worker accounts totally for the decline in employment.

This decline in employment does not have to occur, however, even during the period in which money wages are fairly rigid downward. Indeed, it is possible that employment will increase and achieve the new higher full-employment level. And that can occur without government action with monetary and fiscal policies to raise the aggregate demand curve. If the demand for aggregate output is highly sensitive to price reductions along the aggregate demand curve, or if conditions in the labor market and with the aggregate production function are favorable, the aggregate demand curve can intersect the new aggregate supply curve above the new full-employment output. Moreover, it is possible that the technological advance will involve an increase in the investment demand schedule because of the capital requirements of the innovation; this increase will shift the aggregate demand for output curve to the right. In that case, prices may even increase. Business cycle theorists such as Joseph Schumpeter felt that the increases in investment expenditures associated with technological advance were an important item in U.S. business recoveries and associated inflations.[4]

In the extreme short term, frictional unemployment will rise as a result of the technological advance, as workers who are displaced from jobs move to the new jobs which appear and incur the hardships this move involves. Moreover, some of the displaced workers may not find new jobs, even if aggregate demand expands and restores full-employment output. Some displaced workers may not possess the skills or the requirements of location or age necessary for the new jobs. They may become perma-

[4] Joseph A. Schumpeter, *The Theory of Economic Development,* trans. Redvers Opie (Cambridge, Mass.: Harvard University Press, 1934).

nently structurally unemployed. In that case, technological advance creates unemployment even if full employment is restored, since it increases the natural rate of unemployment. The affected workers require retraining, relocation, or other specialized programs. An expansion of aggregate demand for output will not reemploy them, at least not efficiently.

Examples of technological advance from U.S. economic experience include the advent of computers, which have displaced many clerical workers and business machine operators; automation in mining, particularly coal mining; and automation in agriculture. In general, electronic computers have not resulted in long-term structural unemployment. The workers involved tend to find that their skills readily transfer to other occupations, and locational factors are not a major problem. Automation in coal mining created significant long-term structural unemployment in the United States during the 1940s and 1950s, since mining skills are less transferable to other occupations than clerical skills, and the workers involved generally had to move to make themselves available for such alternative employment as was available. The same has been true of agriculture.

A Decline in the Supply of Oil

Consider now a supply disturbance involving a decline in the supply of oil, an important energy resource which combines with labor and capital in production. The emphasis here is on a decline resulting from depletion (U.S. oil production peaked during the early 1970s), but the analysis serves as well for declines caused by simple restrictions on oil production imposed by oil producers or from quotas on oil imports imposed by government.

Figure 12–10 illustrates the effects of the disturbance. It appears as a leftward shift in the aggregate supply curve for output corresponding to unchanged money wages, a shift induced by joint leftward shifts in the aggregate production function and the demand curve for labor. Because of the decline in the supply of oil and the increase in its price relative to the price of labor, labor is substituted for oil and alternative energy resources in production, and the average and marginal products of labor decline at each level of labor input. With less energy and energy-using machines to work with, labor is less productive.

Given the unchanged aggregate demand curve for output, prices rise, and output falls. If the demand curve for output intersects the supply curve

Figure 12–10 **A Decline in the Supply of Oil**

A decline in the supply of oil shifts the aggregate supply curve for output to the left. With the demand curve for aggregate output unchanged, prices rise, and output and full-employment output fall.

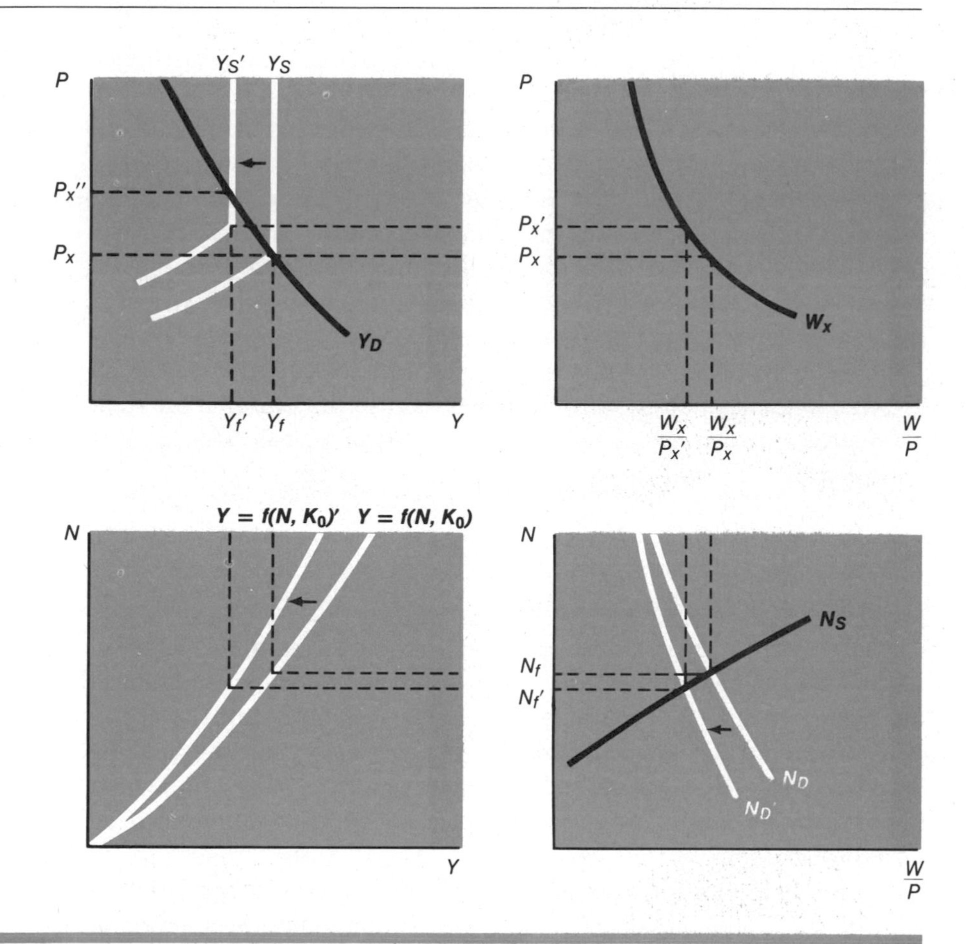

for output to the left of where the supply curve bends, a shortfall of aggregate demand will appear. This does not occur in Figure 12–10. Indeed, in the figure, an expenditure gap occurs at the unchanged money wage. Prices will rise to P_x'', and full employment will prevail. As prices rise above P_x', the money wage increases, shifting the aggregate supply curve for output upward to close the expenditure gap and shifting the money wage bar in the upper right-hand portion of the figure to the right. These shifts are not shown in the figure.

Whether a shortfall of aggregate demand or an expenditure gap occurs at the initial money wage, prices will rise, the real wage will decline, and both equilibrium output and full-employment output will decline. Consequently, per capita real income will decline.

Expansions in Income-Maintenance Programs

Income-maintenance programs include food stamp, unemployment compensation, social security, and other programs which help to maintain income during periods of unemployment or retirement. Since expansions in such programs reduce the burden of unemployment, they may reduce the amount of labor supplied at each real wage—that is, they may reduce the supply curve of labor. If so, they diminish full-employment output, create an expenditure gap, and produce inflation. The inflation is the demand-pull type, since it results from an expenditure gap, but it arises from a supply disturbance rather than an increase in aggregate demand.

To cite examples from the United States experience of the 1970s, the income-maintenance program expansion may involve a rapid expansion in the benefits and the numbers enrolled in a food stamp program, a liberalization in an unemployment program which increases the number of weeks for which benefits can be received and increases the proportion of the labor force eligible for benefits, or a tying of social security benefits to the cost of living.[5]

Whatever the case, the result is illustrated in Figure 12–11. The burden of unemployment is reduced, and the supply of labor curve, in the lower portion of the figure, shifts downward. Frictional unemployment, which is excluded from the labor supply curve, increases, since workers are freer to move between jobs and to spend a greater amount of time in searching for new positions. Moreover, some workers who were working before the program expansion but were near the margin in the labor versus leisure decision may leave the labor force. Some of them may be workers who

---

[5] The average number of persons participating per month in the food stamp program increased from 424,652 in 1965 to 18,526,728 in 1976. The Emergency Unemployment Compensation Act of 1974 extended the number of weeks for which unemployment compensation benefits could be received to fifty-two weeks on a temporary basis, from the twenty-six to thirty-nine weeks which had been the rule prior to that. The act also increased the proportion of workers eligible for such benefits. Social security benefits were cost-of-living indexed in 1978.

Figure 12–11 **A Reduction in the Supply of Labor Induced by Expansions in Income-Maintenance Programs or Changes in Labor Force Composition**

When expansions in income-maintenance programs or changes in labor force composition cause the supply of labor to decline, the aggregate supply curve for output corresponding to initial money wages shifts to the left, an expenditure gap opens up, and prices rise. Full-employment output declines.

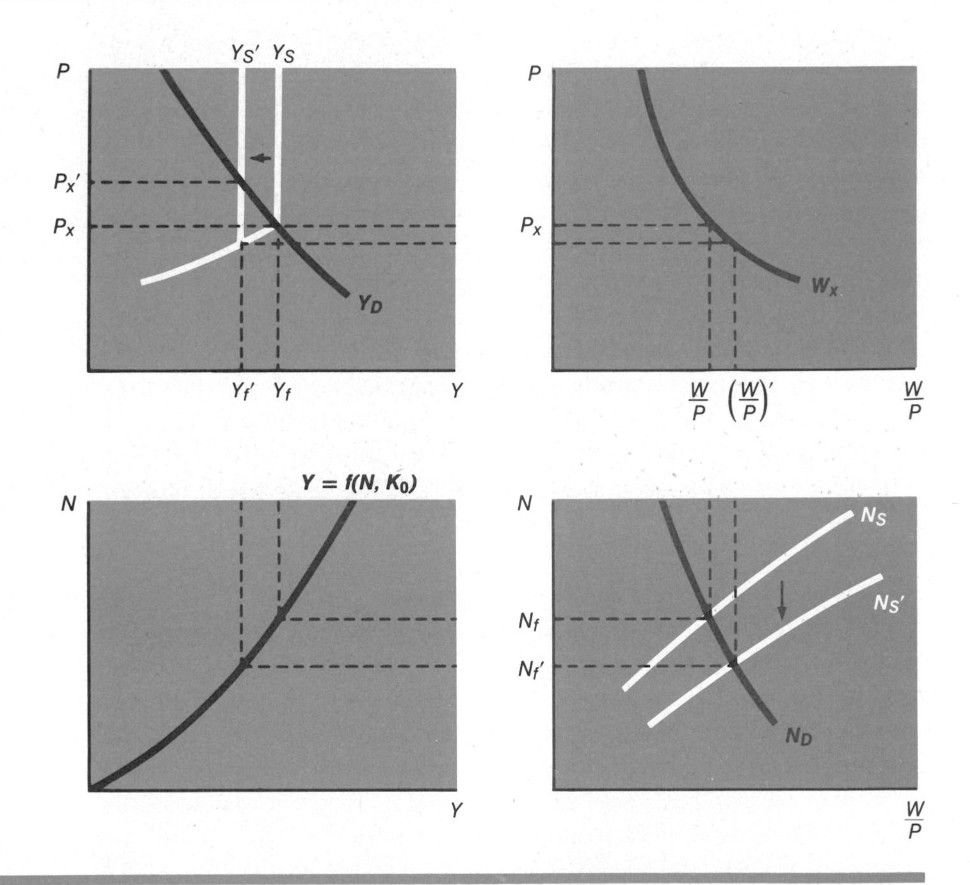

decide to retire earlier than previously planned because of the protection provided to retirement income by the indexed social security benefits.

In terms of Figure 12–11, the full-employment benchmark declines from N_f to N_f', the new point of intersection of the labor demand and supply curves, and the vertical portion of the aggregate supply of output curve, in the upper left-hand portion of the figure, declines from Y_f to Y_f'. With the demand curve for output unchanged, an expenditure gap equal to $Y_f - Y_f'$ opens up, and prices and money wages rise, equilibrium prices rising from P_x to P_x'. In the new equilibrium, the sloping portion of the aggregate supply of output curve will have shifted upward to close the expenditure gap, and the money wage bar in the upper right-hand portion of the figure will have shifted to the right. These shifts, which are not shown in the figure, record the higher equilibrium money wage.

In addition to the increase in prices and money wages, the income-maintenance program expansion produces a lower level of employment and output and a higher real wage. The unemployment rate rises to the extent that the frictional unemployment rate rises, but the increase is in the natural rate of unemployment. The economy remains at full employment.

Shifts in the Composition of the Labor Force

An effect similar to that of expansions in income-maintenance programs occurs if the composition of the labor force shifts toward groups with higher natural unemployment rates, such as teenagers and married women who have been out of the labor force for many years. Because of their inexperience, these groups often have weaker work skills than the average labor supplier and hence are good candidates for natural unemployment of the structural variety. Also, they often are members of multi-worker households, so that they can move between jobs more freely than the average worker and can remain longer in job search, which contributes to the frictional component of the natural unemployment rate. A point sometimes neglected is that an increase in the proportion of married women working can increase the frictional unemployment rate for married men. A married man whose wife enters the labor force becomes a member of a multi-worker household, is freer to move between jobs, at least locally, than before, and thus can be more selective in job search.

If groups with higher natural unemployment rates become more important among total job holders and job applicants, with the total itself taken as fixed for simplicity, the labor supply curve declines (as in Figure 12–11), the vertical portion of the aggregate supply of output curve shifts to the left, and inflation occurs. The economy remains at full employment, but reported unemployment rates increase, since they include natural unemployment. Again, the inflation is of the demand-pull variety, since it results from an expenditure gap, but the factor creating the expenditure gap is a supply disturbance.

Milton Friedman has argued that expansions in income-maintenance programs and shifts in the composition of the labor force have been important contributors to the higher unemployment rates experienced by the United States during the 1970s.[6] Most other economists agree, especially insofar as the effect of increased proportions of teenagers and women in the labor force is concerned, since these proportions are quantifiable.[7]

It helps to see these effects as supply disturbances in a real-world context if, as in Figure 12–12, they are imposed on a growth situation in which aggregate demand *(E)* and full-employment output (Y_f) initially are growing along equal steady-state equilibrium growth paths, producing full employment and price stability. The full-employment labor force (N_f) is growing at a slightly lower rate, if allowance is made for a constant rate of technological advance over time. The figure plots the logarithms of the variables, for convenience, since straight-line plottings of logarithms reflect constant percentage rates of growth.

When the disturbances occur, in Period t_a, the full-employment labor force and full-employment output grow less rapidly for a time, as the higher natural unemployment rate is being achieved, and then settle back to their original growth rates. If the trend factors underlying the growth rate of aggregate demand are undisturbed, including the growth rate of the money supply *(m)*, an expenditure gap appears during the period of slower full-employment output growth, and inflation occurs. In the new steady state, prices will be higher (though the inflation will have ceased), and the unemployment rate, which will be the new natural rate of unemployment, will have increased. The disturbances will have produced a permanently higher unemployment rate and a temporary period of inflation.

---

[6] Milton Friedman, "Nobel Lecture: Inflation and Unemployment," *Journal of Political Economy* 85 (June 1977): 458.

[7] Women comprised 35.2 percent of the U.S. civilian labor force in 1965 but 40 percent in 1975. Teenagers accounted for 7.9 percent in 1965 and 9.5 percent in 1975. In 1975, unemployment rates were 6.7 percent for men twenty years of age and over, 8 percent for women in the same age group, and 19.9 percent for teenagers. (Teenagers include persons sixteen through nineteen years of age, since only persons sixteen years of age and over are included in the civilian labor force.) President's Council of Economic Advisers, *Economic Report of the President* (Washington, D.C.: Government Printing Office, 1979), pp. 216–217.

Figure 12–12 **Expansions in Income-Maintenance Programs and Shifts in Labor Force Composition Imposed on a Growing Economy**

Expansions in income-maintenance programs and shifts in labor force composition can reduce the full-employment labor force and increase the natural rate of unemployment. If they have these effects, they produce a temporary inflation and a permanently higher price level when imposed on a steady-state growth equilibrium featuring full employment and price stability.

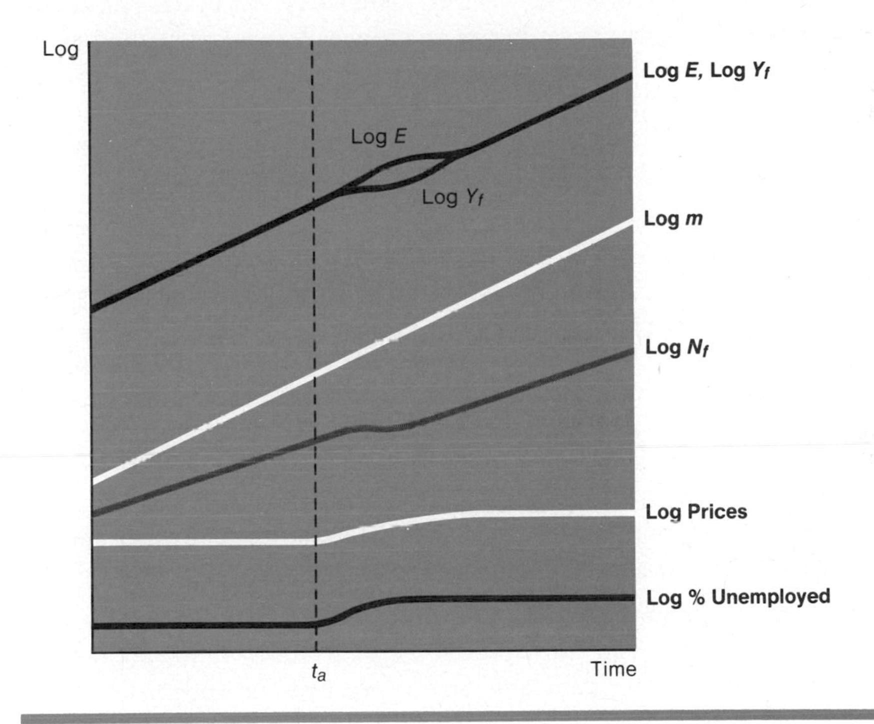

Summary

1. To analyze aggregate supply disturbances, it is useful to utilize an aggregate output market which plots quantities of aggregate output demanded and supplied against price level. The demand curve is constructed from *IS* and *LM* curves, while the supply curve is built from the labor market and the aggregate production function for output.

2. The aggregate supply disturbances which have attracted the most attention in the United States during the past several decades are wage-push inflation, the cost-push inflation involved in the sharp increases in prices of imported oil posted during 1973 and 1974 by the newly effective cartel of international oil producers, technological advance, and labor supply effects of expansions in income-maintenance programs and shifts in labor force composition.

3. Wage-push inflation occurs when unions apply monopoly power over the supply of labor to obtain money-wage gains in excess of productivity increases and producers recover their increased costs by passing on the increases as higher prices. Prices and money wages are pushed up by the exercise of monopoly power rather than being bid up by excess demand. Shortfall unemployment appears if the aggregate demand for output curve is unchanged, since the higher prices reduce the real money supply and diminish interest-sensitive expenditures.

4. A technological advance is an improved manner of production, ordinarily arising from a new technique, machine, material, or energy resource, which permits a greater output to be produced with given quantities of labor and capital inputs. It increases full-employment output and may create shortfall unemployment during the period in which money wages are inflexible downward, depending on such things as the price sensitivity of aggregate output demand and whether the advance increases the demand for investment goods. It may increase the natural rate of unemployment somewhat in any event, since some of the workers who are displaced may be poorly suited for the new jobs which appear and thus may become structurally unemployed.

5. A decline in the supply of oil (or other natural resource which combines with labor and capital in production) will reduce aggregate output and full-employment output and raise prices. The real wage will decline, money wages may rise, and a shortfall of aggregate demand may appear.

6. Expansions in income-maintenance programs tend to increase the natural rate of unemployment, since they reduce the burden of unemployment. Increased proportions of women and teenagers in the labor force produce a similar effect on the natural rate of unemployment, since these groups have higher than average natural unemployment rates. If conditions relating to aggregate demand for output are constant when these two types of disturbances occur, prices rise, since they reduce full-employment output relative to demand. Prices are bid upward by an expenditure gap.

Concepts for Identification

aggregate output market
aggregate production function
labor market
real wage
marginal product of labor
diminishing marginal product of labor
capital stock
constant returns-to-scale
fixed factor proportions
wage-push inflation
producer cost-push inflation
technological advance
income-maintenance programs

Questions and Problems for Review

1. Construct a demand curve for aggregate output from the *IS/LM* diagram. The curve should present quantity demanded as a function of price. What determines the sensitivity of aggregate output demanded to price?

2. Explain the derivation of the vertical portion of the supply curve for aggregate output. Be explicit as to the roles of the supply curve for labor, the aggregate production function, and producers as profit maximizers.

3. Explain why the Keynesian aggregate supply of output curve is upward sloping within the less than full employment range.

4. The assumption that producers respond to fluctuations in aggregate demand for output with fixed factor proportions and constant returns-to-scale yields an aggregate supply of output curve which is flat within the less than full employment range. Explain why this is true.

5. Give several examples of technological advance. In the model used in this chapter, a technological advance can create a shortfall of aggregate demand for output when it occurs in an initial full-employment and price stability situation, though it does not have to do so. Explain what determines whether a shortfall of aggregate demand appears.

6. Discuss technological advance as a source of increases in the natural rate of unemployment. Give examples of technological advance which are especially likely to produce this result.

7. Explain how a decline in the supply of oil resulting from depletion of oil reserves causes a decline in full-employment output and a rise in the general price level.

8. Identify and explain the probable effects of a newly introduced government food stamp program on the natural rate of unemployment, the general price level, and full-employment output.

9. With the economy in a steady-state equilibrium growth path featuring price stability and full employment, a sharp increase in the percentage of married women working occurs. Discuss the effects of this disturbance.

10. Verify the entries in the table below. Assume that the aggregate demand curve for output is fixed in each case. The question marks indicate that the effect cannot be ascertained without further information. The variable *U* represents the unemployment rate.

Disturbance	ΔP	ΔY	$\Delta \% U$	ΔY_f
Technological advance	−	+	?	+
Decline in the supply of oil	+	−	?	−
Expansion of income-maintenance programs	+	−	+	−

References

Bronfenbrenner, M., and Holzman, F. D. "A Survey of Inflation Theory." *American Economic Review* 53 (September 1963): 593–661.

Dunlop, J. T. *Wage Determination under Trade Unions.* New York: A. M. Kelley, 1950.

Eckstein, O., and Wilson, T. "Determination of Money Wages in American Industry." *Quarterly Journal of Economics* 76 (August 1962): 379–414.

Friedman, Milton. "Nobel Lecture: Inflation and Unemployment." *Journal of Political Economy* 85 (June 1977): 451–472.

Hicks, J. R. *The Crisis in Keynesian Economics.* New York: Basic Books, 1974, chap. 3.

Keynes, J. M. *The General Theory of Employment, Interest, and Money.* New York: Harcourt, Brace, 1936, chap. 2.

Kuh, Edwin. "Unemployment, Production Functions, and Effective Demand." *Journal of Political Economy* 74 (June 1966): 238–249.

Laidler, David. *The Demand for Money: Theories and Evidence.* Scranton, Pa.: International, 1969.

Laidler, David, and Parkin, Michael. "Inflation: A Survey." *Economic Journal* 85 (December 1975): 741–809.

Perry, G. "The Determinants of Wage Rate Changes." *Review of Economic Studies* 31 (October 1964): 287–308.

Phelps, E. S. "Money Wage Dynamics and Labor Market Equilibrium." In *Microeconomic Foundations of Employment and Inflation Theory,* edited by E. S. Phelps. New York: Norton, 1970. Reprinted in *Modern Macroeconomics,* edited by P. G. Korliras and R. S. Thorn. New York: Harper & Row, 1979, pp. 213–241.

Schumpeter, Joseph A. *The Theory of Economic Development.* Translated by Redvers Opie. Cambridge, Mass.: Harvard University Press, 1934.

13

Monetary and Fiscal Policies

Monetary and fiscal policies correct unemployment and inflation problems arising from shortfalls of aggregate demand and expenditure gaps by removing the demand shortfalls and expenditure gaps. The poorer unemployment rate and inflation rate combinations of the 1970s appear to reflect more an increase in the natural rate of unemployment than a need for price and wage controls.

This chapter examines the use of monetary and fiscal policies to correct problems of unemployment and inflation. Fiscal policies were examined in Chapter 6, of course, but this chapter considers their impacts with a money market present, chiefly dealing with mechanics and ignoring for the present such things as forecasting problems and uncertainty as to the strength of monetary and fiscal policies and the lags involved in their impacts.

The first part of the chapter employs the *IS–LM* framework to illustrate how unemployment and inflation problems arising from shortfalls of aggregate demand or expenditure gaps can be eliminated with monetary and fiscal policies. The concluding section discusses empirical Phillips curves, examining the explanations which have been offered for them and the implications these explanations convey for policy.

Monetary Policies and Shortfall Unemployment

Figure 13–1 presents a less than full employment situation and illustrates how an increase in the money supply can move the economy to full employment. The aggregate supply curve implicit in the representation is the simplified flat portion aggregate supply curve of Figure 12–1, so that responses of output and prices to fluctuations in aggregate demand again break cleanly at full employment, as in Figures 12–3 and 12–4 as well as earlier discussions. This simplification will be employed in subsequent figures as well, unless otherwise noted.[1]

Figure 13–1 **Monetary Policies and Shortfall Unemployment**

An increase in the money supply causes interest rates to decline and stimulates interest-sensitive expenditures. Applied in a less than full employment situation, it increases equilibrium output and real income and reduces the unemployment rate.

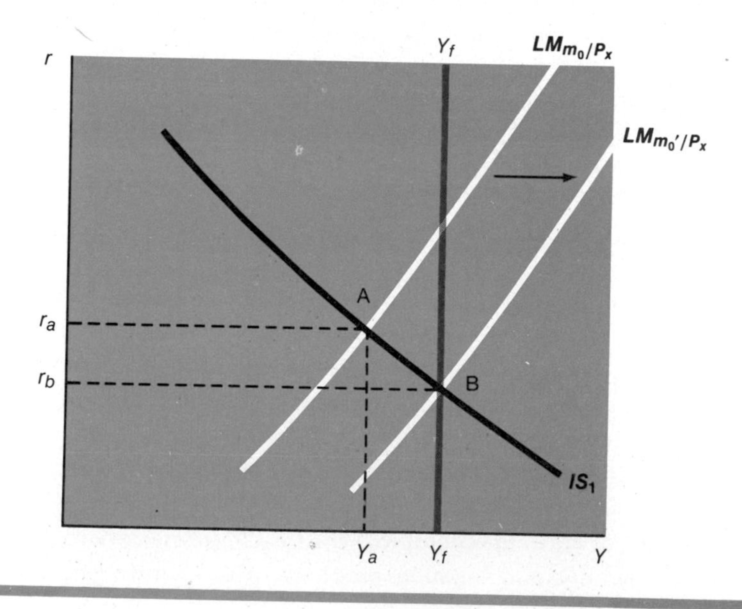

[1] Readers who wish a theoretical basis for this simplification can employ the fixed factor proportion, constant returns-to-scale aggregate production function described in footnote 2 of Chapter 12.

The initial equilibrium is at Point A of Figure 13–1, with IS_1 and LM_{m_0/P_x} indicating a shortfall of aggregate demand and an unemployment problem. Removing the unemployment with monetary policies involves increasing the money supply to m_0', which shifts the LM curve to LM_{m_0'/P_x} so that it intersects the unchanged IS curve at the full-employment line. The new equilibrium is at Point B, where aggregate demand supports full-employment output.

The channel by which monetary policies operate is the same as that described for money supply disturbances in Chapter 11, though that chapter did not explore a case where the money supply increased in a less than full employment situation. The increase in the money supply to m_0' creates an excess supply of real money balances at the initial equilibrium at Point A. Interest rates decline as a result, and interest-sensitive expenditures expand. Income-induced effects on consumption expenditures are added as output and real income expand.

Under the institutional arrangements of the United States, the excess real money supply initially is for the most part an excess supply of the bank reserve base of the money supply, brought about by open market purchases of U.S. government securities by Federal Reserve authorities or by reductions in bank reserve requirements. The actual money supply expands to its equilibrium value as banks loan out excess reserves or place them in securities, expanding demand deposits in the process. Banks lower the interest rates at which they lend to stimulate borrowing, and they bid interest yields on securities down—that is, they bid security prices up—as they purchase securities. Where open-market purchases are employed to provide banks with excess reserves, the purchases themselves cause an earlier impact on security interest yields. If the purchases were made from nonbanks, an initial impact on the money supply also occurs as the sellers deposit their proceeds in banks. In any event, interest rates decline, and interest rate effects are produced on interest-sensitive expenditures.

Frank de Leeuw and Edward M. Gramlich have published simulation results from the 1968–69 version of the Federal Reserve–MIT model to indicate how the interest rate effects of a money supply increase were apportioned among the various categories of expenditures in that neo-Keynesian model.[2] Surprisingly, 43 percent of the total interest rate effect accumulating after one year involved consumption expenditures, the category of expenditures the early Keynesians treated as completely inter-

---

[2] Frank de Leeuw and Edward M. Gramlich, "The Channels of Monetary Policy," *Federal Reserve Bulletin* 55 (June 1969): 472–491.

est insensitive. The effect measured was solely an interest rate effect, since income was held constant in the simulation in order to avoid including income-induced effects on expenditures. Another 51 percent of the first-year impact involved investment expenditures, splitting into 45 percent to residential construction expenditures and 6 percent to business plant and equipment expenditures. The remaining 6 percent of the total first-year interest rate effect involved state and local government construction expenditures, a category of expenditures the model used here has thus far left interest insensitive. After three years, consumption expenditures accounted for 51 percent of the total interest rate effect, business plant and equipment expenditures increased to 16 percent, and residential construction expenditures declined to 26 percent.

De Leeuw and Gramlich divide these interest rate effects into marginal efficiency of investment effects (their term is cost-of-capital effects), which affect all of the categories of expenditures just mentioned; an interest-induced wealth effect, which affects only consumption expenditures; and a credit rationing effect, which affects only residential construction expenditures. A more recent version of the model, now called the MSP model, includes an interest-induced wealth effect on residential construction expenditures.

The mechanisms involved in these three types of effects are as described in Chapter 7. The marginal efficiency of investment effect results from comparing the marginal efficiency of "investment" on investment expenditures, consumption expenditures, and now state and local government construction expenditures with the interest costs of financing.

The interest-induced wealth effect on consumption expenditures occurs as consumption expenditures rise in response to the higher corporate stock prices associated with lower interest rates. As interest rates fall, the present values of the expected future earnings on corporate stocks rise, and the prices of corporate stocks are bid upward. Consumer net worth increases, and consumption expenditures increase.

The credit rationing effect results from sluggish savings deposit interest rates.[3] As the general structure of interest rates declines relative to savings deposit interest rates, funds flood into savings deposits of commercial banks, savings and loan associations, and mutual savings banks. These funds are pushed into loans, chiefly mortgage loans. That is achieved in part by lowering mortgage interest rates, a marginal efficiency of investment effect, but also by easing other terms of lending, a credit rationing

[3] In the upward direction, this sluggishness is enhanced by legal ceilings on the interest yields which can be paid on savings deposits.

effect. Down-payment requirements are lowered, the number of years for which loans are made is increased to lower monthly payments, and general creditworthiness items such as ratios of borrower income to loan amount are eased. As mortgage lending terms are eased, expenditures for new housing expand, since most new housing is financed with mortgages.

Fiscal Policies and Shortfall Unemployment

Full employment also can be achieved with discretionary fiscal ease. As in Chapter 6, it includes increases in government purchases of final goods and services, reductions in taxes, and increases in transfer payments. Each of these shift the *IS* curve to the right, since they produce a greater flow of total expenditures at each rate of interest. In Figure 13–2, for

Figure 13–2 **Fiscal Policies and Shortfall Unemployment**

Applied in a less than full employment situation, increases in government purchases and transfer payments and reductions in the tax function raise the equilibrium levels of output and real income and lower the unemployment rate. The impacts of the policies are offset to some extent by interest rate effects on expenditures, however, since the interest rate must rise if the money market is to remain in equilibrium.

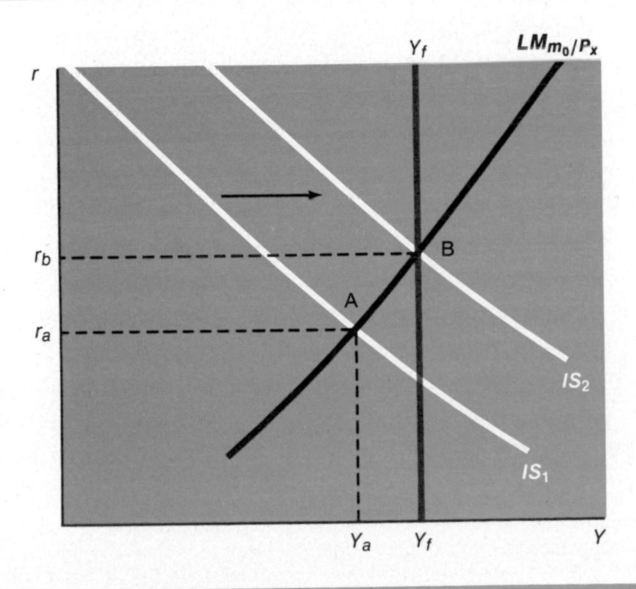

example, Point A indicates a shortfall of aggregate demand and an unemployment situation, but fiscal ease can shift the *IS* curve from IS_1 to IS_2, producing an intersection of the *IS* and *LM* curves on the full-employment line and a full-employment equilibrium at Point B.

The channels by which fiscal ease operates are the same as indicated in Chapter 6. Increases in government purchases of final goods and services are themselves a component of total expenditures and stimulate output directly in the industries providing the goods and services. Reductions in taxes or increases in transfer payments raise private disposable income and stimulate consumption expenditures. In all cases, income-induced effects on consumption expenditures are added as output and real income expand.

Crowding Out

Unlike the Chapter 6 situation, however, here the impacts of fiscal policies are offset somewhat by the increases in interest rates which money market equilibrium requires. As output and real income expand, the demand for real money balances expands, so that the interest rate must be higher if the money market is to remain in equilibrium. The increase in expenditures and output does not equal the full horizontal shift in the *IS* curve, as it would, ignoring the full-employment constraint, if the money market were absent. Only a portion of this impact is felt. The increase in interest rates "crowds out" interest-sensitive expenditures and checks the increase in aggregate demand. It is useful to think of interest rates as rising as securities are sold to build up money balances as output and real income expand.[4]

Mixing Monetary and Fiscal Ease for Full Employment

Combinations of monetary and fiscal policies can be used to effect full employment in the model. For example, in Figure 13–3, beginning with a less than full employment equilibrium at Point A, an increase in the money supply to m_0'', shifting the *LM* curve to the right, can be combined with fiscal ease, shifting the *IS* curve to IS_2, to produce full employment at Point B. In general, beginning with a less than full employment situation, the

[4] The community ends up with the same real money balances in the aggregate, since the real money supply remains unchanged, but the attempt to increase real money balances results in higher interest rates and leaves the community satisfied to hold the same real money supply as before.

Figure 13–3 **Mixing Monetary and Fiscal Ease**

Beginning in a less than full employment situation, full employment can be achieved with a mixture of monetary and fiscal ease. In the new equilibrium, the interest rate will be higher than if only monetary policies had been used and lower than if only fiscal policies had been used.

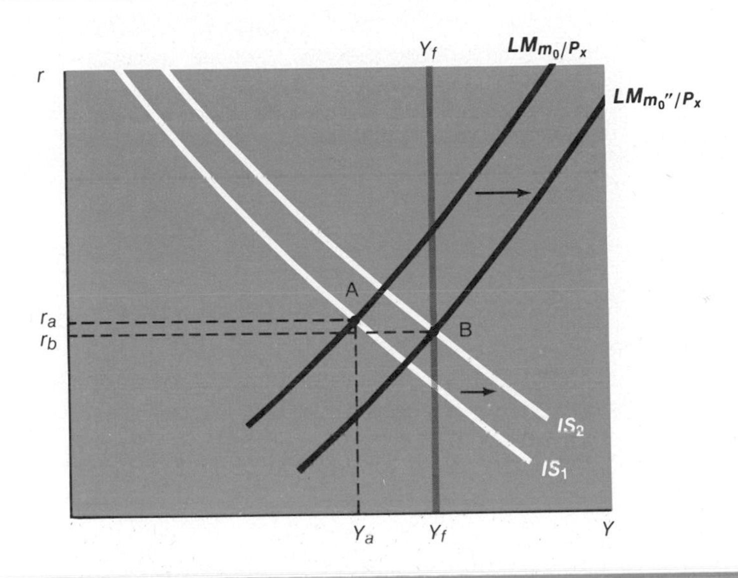

greater the emphasis on monetary policies, the lower the interest rate in the new full-employment equilibrium. This result can be important in choosing the mix of policies in situations where secondary goals sensitive to interest rates must be considered. For example, if the U.S. stabilization authorities, faced with the initial Point A shortfall unemployment situation in Figure 13–3, wish to achieve full employment and price stability and at the same time produce low interest rates in order to have a high level of investment expenditures, they might choose monetary policies over fiscal policies to that end.

Monetary and Fiscal Policies and Expenditure Gap Inflation

Figure 13–4 presents an expenditure gap inflation problem and illustrates the mechanics of coping with it through discretionary monetary and fiscal

Figure 13–4 **Monetary Restraint and Fiscal Restraint**

An expenditure gap can be removed with monetary or fiscal restraint or with a mixture of the two. Graphically, monetary restraint involves shifting the *LM* curve to the left; fiscal restraint involves shifting the *IS* curve to the left.

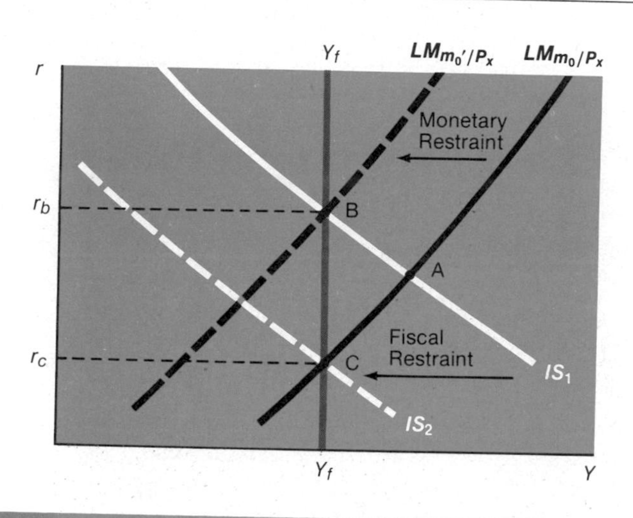

policies. The *IS* curve and LM_{m_0/P_x}, the *LM* curve corresponding to the initial money supply and price level, intersect at Point A, to the right of the full-employment line, indicating an expenditure gap.

Eliminating the expenditure gap through monetary policies involves shifting the *LM* curve to LM_{m_0'/P_x} by reducing the money supply. This obtains an *IS* and *LM* intersection at Point B. Reducing the money supply to m_0' removes the excess money supply which previously existed at Point B, permitting interest rates to rise to r_b, where expenditures just support full-employment output. The expenditure gap, and thus the need for a price increase, is eliminated. The channels of monetary restraint are simply the reverse of those for monetary ease, except that they involve no income-induced effects on consumption expenditures, since real income does not move from Y_f during the process.[5]

Eliminating the expenditure gap with discretionary fiscal restraint involves shifting the *IS* curve from IS_1 to IS_2, so that the *IS* and *LM* intersection at Point C is achieved. At Point C, demand is just purchasing full-

[5] See Jack Vernon, "The Multiplier Concept and Monetary Restraint," *Quarterly Journal of Economics* 88 (May 1974): 330–339.

employment output, and the money market is in equilibrium. Discretionary fiscal restraint involves reducing government purchases of final goods and services, increasing taxes, or, theoretically, reducing transfer payments, all of which shift the *IS* curve to the left. The channels of fiscal restraint are the reverse of those for fiscal ease. Reductions in government purchases diminish the expenditure gap directly, since government purchases are a component of total expenditures. Increases in taxes or reductions in transfer payments reduce private disposable income, which diminishes consumption expenditures. As with monetary restraint, real income remains constant at Y_f during the policy application, ruling out income-induced effects on consumption expenditures, except those which occur on the first round if tax or transfer payment policies are used.

The expenditure gap can also be checked with a combination of monetary and fiscal restraint. An *IS* and *LM* intersection between Points B and C, on the full-employment line, can be achieved by combining a reduction in money supply with the proper measure of fiscal restraint. For that matter, an interest rate above r_b could be achieved, along with full employment and price stability, by combining a little fiscal ease with a large measure of monetary restraint. Or an interest rate below r_c could be obtained, together with full employment and price stability, with a monetary ease and fiscal restraint combination.

Money Supply Effects of Fiscal Policies

The illustrations of fiscal policies in this chapter have ignored the possibility that money supply disturbances can accompany fiscal policies. Specifically, this chapter has presented the *LM* curve as remaining unchanged when fiscal policies are applied. This assumes that someone other than the Federal Reserve banks—specifically, commercial banks or the nonbank public—is the opposite party to the debt transactions the Treasury conducts as a result of the changes in the federal deficit or surplus associated with the fiscal policies.[6] If the Federal Reserve banks accommodate the debt transactions with open-market purchases or sales, bank reserves and the equilibrium money supply are affected, and the *LM* curve shifts.

For example, if fiscal ease is applied in a situation in which the federal budget is initially balanced, it causes a deficit to appear. The Treasury must

[6] The nonbank public includes everyone other than the Treasury, the Federal Reserve banks, and commercial banks.

finance this deficit by issuing and selling U.S. government securities, except in the extreme short run, when it might allow its demand deposit balances to decline. If the Federal Reserve banks accommodate the Treasury funding operation by purchasing U.S. securities in the open market in the amount of the Treasury sales, member bank reserves increase by the amount of the deficit, and the equilibrium money supply increases by a multiple. Monetary ease, in the form of open-market purchases, has accompanied fiscal ease. Both the *IS* and *LM* curves shift to the right, and both shifts contribute to the resulting increase in aggregate demand.

Similarly, if fiscal restraint results in a federal surplus or an increase in an existing surplus, the Treasury will use the proceeds to repurchase U.S. securities outstanding. If the Federal Reserve banks accommodate the debt transactions by selling U.S. securities equal to the Treasury repurchase, member bank reserves decline and the equilibrium money supply declines by a multiple. Monetary restraint, involving open-market sales by the Federal Reserve, has accompanied fiscal restraint.

If, however, the nonbank public or commercial banks are the opposite parties to the debt transactions associated with fiscal policies, there are no effects on bank reserves or the equilibrium money supply. When the federal government incurs a deficit as a result of a fiscal ease operation, the effect of the deficit itself is merely to shift demand deposit liabilities of commercial banks from the Treasury to the nonbank public in the amount of the deficit. The nonbank public receives more from the Treasury in government purchases and transfer payments than it pays to the Treasury in taxes.[7] If the Treasury now finances this deficit by selling U.S. securities to the nonbank public, an exactly offsetting shift of bank demand deposit liabilities occurs. The Treasury deposits checks drawn on demand deposits of the nonbank public in its own accounts in commercial banks, and the banks transfer the ownership of the deposits. The same exactly offsetting shift of demand deposits occurs if the securities are purchased instead by commercial banks, since, if banks were in equilibrium before, with no extra excess reserves, they must sell off securities to the nonbank public to make room for the Treasury securities. In that case, they create deposits in favor of the Treasury as they purchase the Treasury securities,

[7] Whereas the Treasury deposits most of its receipts from taxes and security sales in its accounts in commercial banks, it makes most of its expenditures with checks drawn on its deposits in Federal Reserve banks. However, it replenishes its deposits in Federal Reserve banks regularly with transfers of funds from its deposits in commercial banks, so that the effect of a Treasury deficit is as indicated. The deficit itself transfers commercial bank deposit liabilities from the Treasury to the nonbank public in the amount of the deficit.

and they eliminate deposit liabilities to the nonbank public as they sell off other loans and securities to it to make room for the Treasury securities. The important point is that member bank reserves are unaffected when the nonbank public or commercial banks purchase the Treasury securities, so that the equilibrium money supply is unaffected. The *LM* curve does not shift. Of course, reserves and deposit liabilities may be redistributed among banks as a result of the fiscal operations.

If the model is modified to permit the money supply to vary directly with interest rates, money supply effects accompany fiscal policies, even if the Federal Reserve banks do not accommodate the Treasury debt operations associated with the policies. This occurs because fiscal policies affect interest rates. The money supply expands with fiscal ease, reinforcing it, and contracts with fiscal restraint. However, these are built-in money supply effects, not money supply disturbances. They result from interest rate effects on borrowed bank reserves, desired excess reserves, and perhaps time deposit liabilities. The *LM* curve still does not shift with fiscal policies unless the Federal Reserve accommodates them with open-market purchases or sales. The built-in money supply effects are reflected in the slope of the *LM* curve.

Aggregate Supply Disturbances: Special Problems for Monetary and Fiscal Policies

Monetary and fiscal policies can treat unemployment and inflation originating in either aggregate demand or aggregate supply disturbances. In the case of demand disturbances, policies which influence demand are used to offset fluctuations in demand. Even the interest rate (as well as output, prices, employment, and the unemployment rate) can be stabilized if monetary policies are used to offset monetary disturbances and fiscal policies to offset real disturbances.

In the case of aggregate supply disturbances, there are sometimes special limitations on what can be accomplished with monetary and fiscal policies. For example, Figure 12–11 of Chapter 12 illustrated how a reduction in the supply of labor induced by expansions in income maintenance programs or shifts in the composition of the labor force causes an increase in prices, a reduction in full-employment output, and an increase in the unemployment rate. General monetary and fiscal policies cannot prevent the increase in the unemployment rate, since it is an increase in natural unemployment, and they cannot restore the former full-employment level. They can prevent the increase in prices, however, and they can do so while obtaining the new full-employment output level. Therefore, price stability and full employment still can be achieved.

Figure 13–5, which recreates the disturbance, complete with sloping aggregate supply of output curve, illustrates the point. The disturbance shifts the vertical portion of the aggregate supply of output curve corresponding to initial money wages to the left and creates an expenditure gap. A reduction in the money supply to m_0', shifting the *LM* curve and its associated aggregate demand for output curve to the left, produces an equilibrium featuring P_x, the original price level, and Y_f', the new full-employment output. Prices are prevented from rising to P_x'. In equilibrium, the sloping portion of the aggregate supply of output curve will have shifted upward and will intersect the new demand for output curve at P_x. This shift reflects the increase in money wages to W_x', which must take place to accomplish the higher equilibrium real wage.

A more serious limitation on the stabliizing powers of monetary and fiscal policies occurs with the decline in the supply of oil illustrated in Figure 12–10 of Chapter 12. This disturbance reduces full-employment output and causes prices to increase. Again monetary and fiscal policies cannot restore the former full-employment output. But beyond that, they cannot obtain the new full-employment output without accepting an increase in prices. They can limit the price increase which occurs at full-employment output, but they can maintain the original price level only by provoking a shortfall of aggregate demand. Figure 13–6 recreates the disturbance and illustrates the point.

The disturbance shifts the aggregate supply curve for output corresponding to initial money wages, including its sloping portion, upward and to the left. By shifting the *LM* curve and its associated aggregate demand for output curve to the positions indicated in the figure, monetary restraint can limit the price rise to P_x' and still obtain the new full-employment output. With money wages rigid downward, prices must rise to P_x' to yield the lower full-employment real wage produced by the disturbance. Monetary and fiscal policies can maintain P_x, the original price level, only by creating an equilibrium at Point B in the figure. At Point B, output and employment have been restricted so that the marginal product of labor and the real wage do not decline.

The wage-push inflation disturbance of Chapter 12 (Figure 12–8) is another case in which monetary and fiscal policies have limited effect. When wage-push inflation occurs as described there, money wages become rigid downward at the new higher level, and a shortfall of aggregate demand appears. Monetary and fiscal restraint cannot remove the increases in money wages and prices. If applied, they create a greater shortfall of aggregate demand. Monetary and fiscal ease can restore full

Figure 13–5 **Monetary Policies and a Reduction in the Supply of Labor Induced by Expansions in Income Maintenance Programs or Shifts in Labor Force Composition**

By removing the expenditure gap the disturbances create, monetary restraint can prevent the increase in prices which occurs when expansions in income maintenance programs or shifts in labor force composition cause a reduction in the supply of labor.

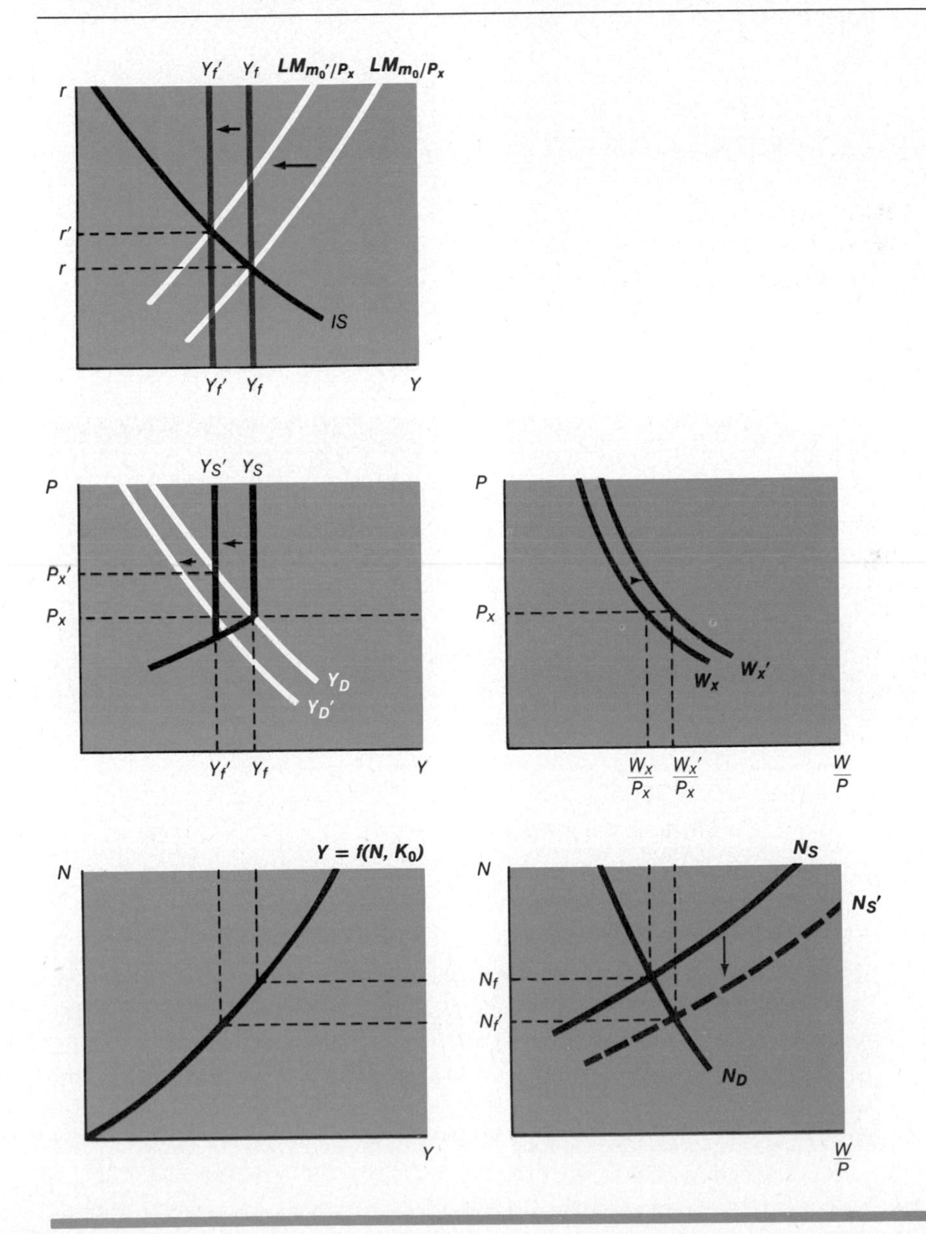

Figure 13–6 **Monetary Policies and a Decline in the Supply of Oil**

Monetary restraint cannot eliminate the price rise which occurs when the supply of oil declines, except by provoking a less than full employment equilibrium.

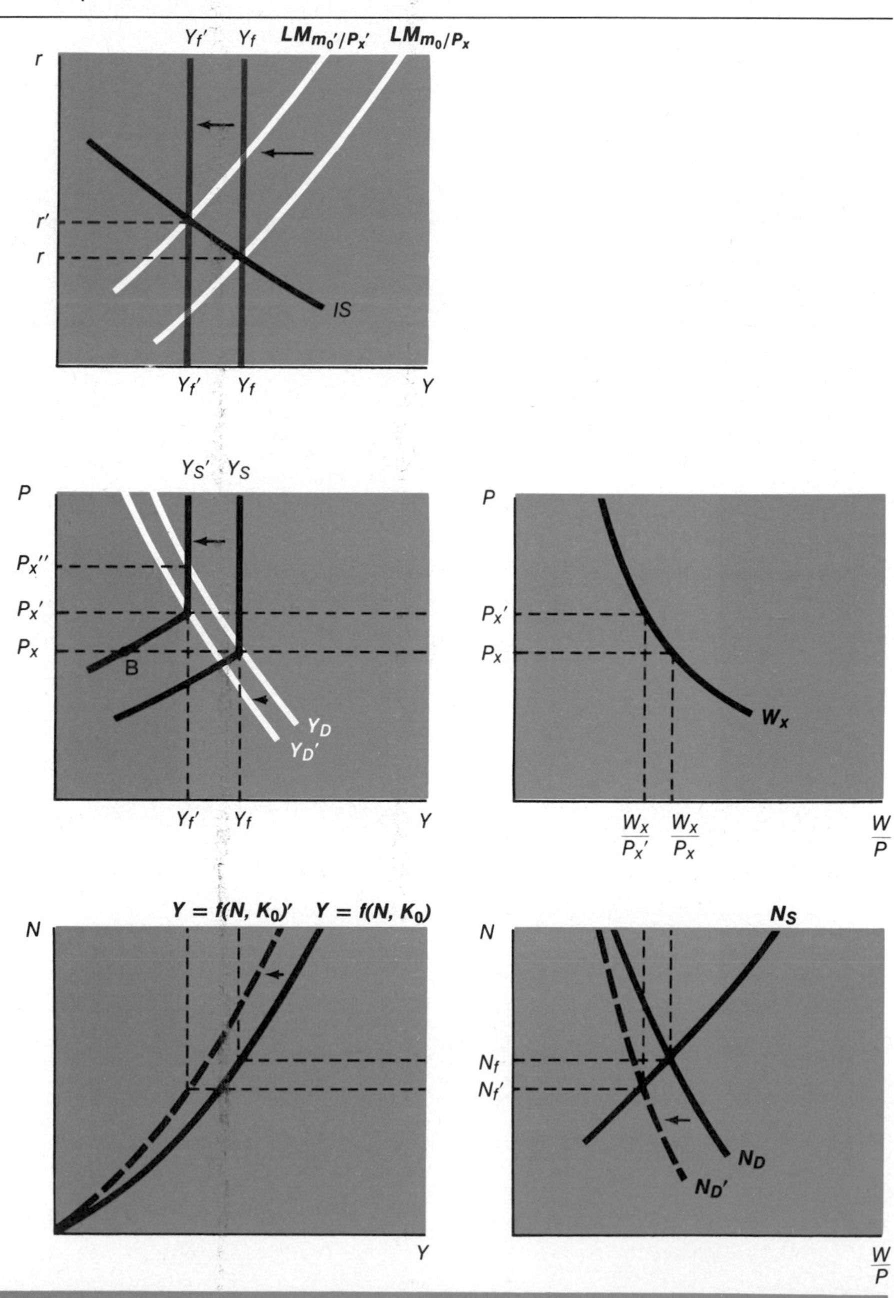

employment, but (as the following sections will explain) that may cause the wage-push pressures to recur.

The Phillips Curve Data: Are Monetary and Fiscal Policies Enough?

In 1958, a British economist, A. W. Phillips, published a paper documenting the empirical relationship which has come to be known as the Phillips curve.[8] Examining data for the percent change in money wages and unemployment rates in the United Kingdom for periods drawn from 1861 through 1957, Phillips noted that a fairly stable relationship existed between the two series: As the unemployment rate decreased, the percent increase in money wages rose. Figure 13–7 illustrates the relationship Phillips documented. The figure plots an equation fitted by R. G. Lipsey to Phillips's annual observations for 1862–1913.[9]

Wage-Push Inflation and the Trade-Off Hypothesis

Many economists interpreted the Phillips curve as evidence that the stabilization authorities are confronted with a trade-off between the unemployment rate and the inflation rate, a trade-off arising from wage-push inflationary pressures. According to the trade-off hypothesis, the strength of wage-push inflation and the percent change in prices which result from it are functions of the economy's proximity to full employment. As aggregate output more closely approaches full-employment output, labor markets tighten. The bargaining position of unions grows stronger as a result, and wage-push inflation produces a higher inflation rate. The stabilization authorities can pick an unemployment rate and achieve it by maintaining the appropriate level of aggregate demand, but they will have to accept the inflation rate wage-push pressures will then produce.

Figure 13–8 illustrates the wage-push trade-off hypothesis. It will be recalled from Chapter 12 (Figure 12–8) that the price increases which accompany wage-push pressures shift the *LM* curve to the left by reducing real money balances if the nominal money supply is constant and that this shift diminishes aggregate expenditures and output through interest rate

---

[8] A. W. Phillips, "The Relationship between Unemployment and the Rate of Change of Money Wage Rates in the U.K., 1861–1957," *Economica* 25 (November 1958): 283–299.

[9] R. G. Lipsey, "The Relationship between Unemployment and the Rate of Change of Money Wage Rates in the U.K., 1862–1957: A Further Analysis," *Economica* 27 (February 1960): 4–5.

Figure 13–7 The Phillips Curve: The Relationship between the Rate of Money Wage Inflation and the Percent Unemployed (Fitted to Data for 1862–1913 for the United Kingdom)

A curve fitted to A. W. Phillips's data for the United Kingdom, 1862–1913, documents his finding that the rate of money-wage inflation rose as the unemployment rate decreased.

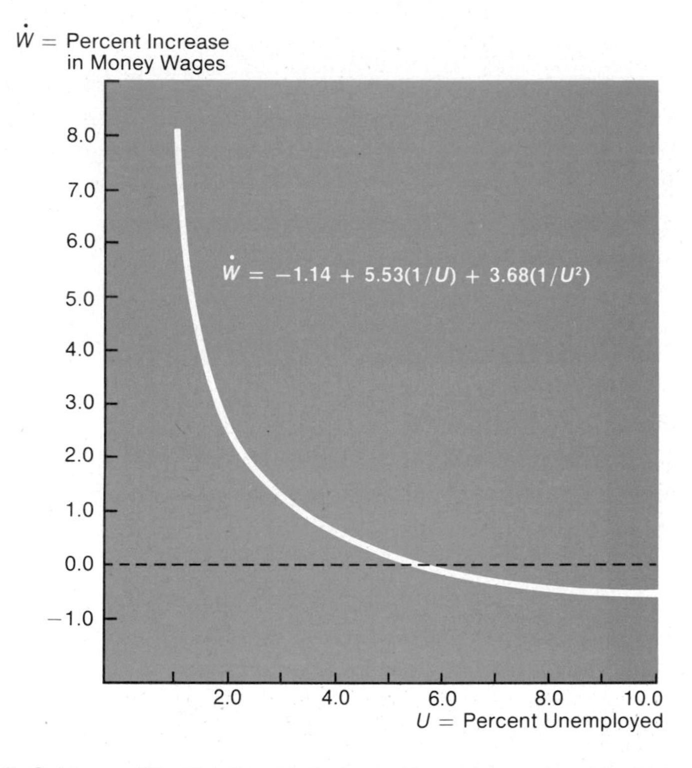

Source: R. G. Lipsey, "The Relationship between Unemployment and the Rate of Change of Money Wage Rates in the U.K., 1862–1957: A Further Analysis," *Economica* 27 (February 1960): 4–5.

effects on interest-sensitive expenditures. Figure 13–8 illustrates how the monetary authority can maintain the *LM* curve at points appropriate to four selected levels of output by increasing the money supply in proportion to the wage-push inflation occurring at the four points. That is, for each of the four *LM* curves presented, the monetary authority is keeping the real money supply, and consequently the *LM* curve, constant. For

Figure 13–8 **The Unemployment and Inflation Trade-Off**

According to the wage-push trade-off hypothesis, the stabilization authorities are faced with a trade-off between unemployment rate and inflation rate. The lower the unemployment rate they target, the greater the inflation rate they must accept.

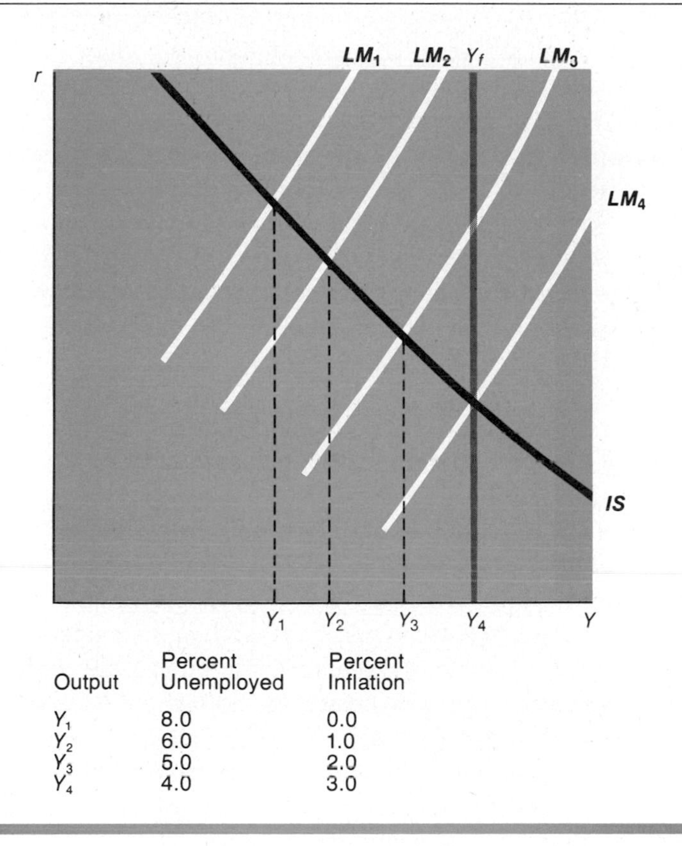

Output	Percent Unemployed	Percent Inflation
Y_1	8.0	0.0
Y_2	6.0	1.0
Y_3	5.0	2.0
Y_4	4.0	3.0

simplicity, the figure ignores the expected inflation effects these permanent inflation rates ordinarily would produce.

At one extreme, the monetary authority can maintain the *LM* curve at LM_1, which, by assumption, involves an 8 percent unemployment rate and enough slack in the labor market so that wage-push inflation is completely absent. Therefore, one possibility open to the monetary authority, recorded in the first row of the table appearing in the figure, is an 8 percent unemployment rate and a zero inflation rate.

Alternately, the money managers can maintain the *LM* curve at LM_2, determining output Y_2, which involves only a 6 percent unemployment rate but tightens labor markets enough that a wage-push inflation rate of 1 percent per year appears. If the *LM* curve is maintained at LM_3 instead, determining output Y_3, the unemployment rate declines to 5 percent, but the wage-push inflation rate is 2 percent per year. If the *LM* curve is maintained at LM_4, output Y_4 is determined, producing the full-employment unemployment rate of 4 percent, but the wage-push inflation rate is 3 percent per year. The stabilization authorities can trade off unemployment against inflation, or vice versa, but they cannot have both full employment and price stability.

The data presented by Phillips fitted very well what many economists of the 1950s regarded as the principal dilemma facing the stabilization authorities. Confronted by powerful unions bargaining on an industry-wide basis so that producers could pass on increased costs with little difficulty, the stabilization authorities could achieve full employment only by validating with monetary or fiscal ease the inflation rate wage-push pressures produced at full employment.

The United States Experience, 1956 through 1978: Were Price and Wage Controls Needed?

Figure 13–9 presents data of the type analyzed by Phillips for the U.S. economy for the years 1956 through 1978.[10] Actually, the figure modifies Phillips's approach in the sense that it plots the unemployment rate against the percent increase in prices rather than the percent increase in money wages. The data for the years 1956 through 1969 conform to the Phillips curve pattern very well. Lower unemployment rates were associated with higher inflation rates for these years. Beginning with 1970, however, the plottings fall to the right of the 1956–1969 curve, presenting combinations of inflation rates and unemployment rates which are much poorer in terms of price and employment goals.

Some of the early interpretations of the post-1969 U.S. experience attributed it to an increase in the strength of wage-push inflationary pressures. In this view, wage-push pressures were stronger at any given unemployment rate; therefore, the inflation rate associated with each

[10] It was discovered in the early 1970s that the U.S. economist Irving Fisher had documented an inverse relationship between the rate of price inflation and the unemployment rate in the United States in a paper published in 1926. See A. Donner and J. F. McCallum, "The Phillips Curve: An Historical Note," *Economica* 40 (August 1972): 322–323. The paper is Irving Fisher, "A Statistical Relation between Unemployment and Price Changes," *International Labour Review* 13 (June 1926): 785–792, reprinted in *Journal of Political Economy* 81 (March–April 1973): 496–502.

Figure 13-9 **The Relationship between U.S. Inflation Rates and Unemployment Rates, 1956–1978**

Data for the U.S. unemployment and inflation rates for the period 1956–1969 conform to the inverse relationship noted by Phillips. The plottings for the 1970s fall to the right of the 1956–1969 relationship, however.

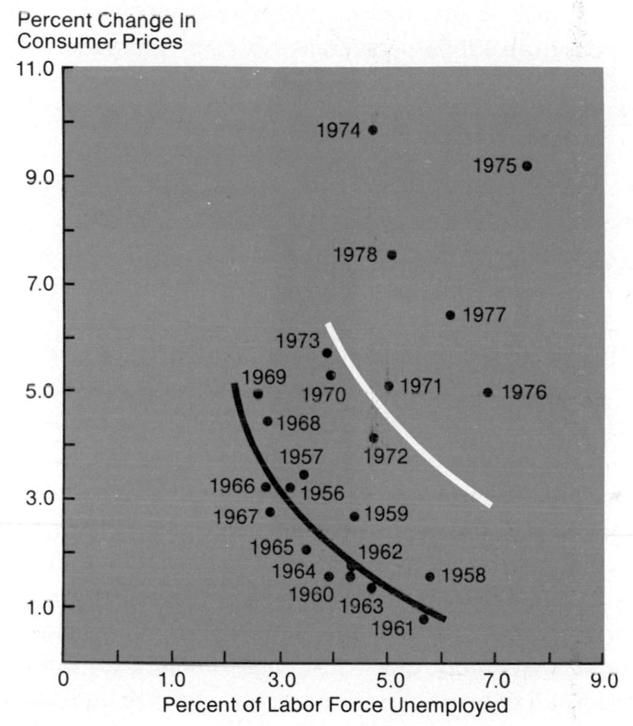

Source: President's Council of Economic Advisers, *Economic Report of the President* (Washington, D.C.: Government Printing Office, 1979), pp. 214, 239.

unemployment rate was greater. The wage-push trade-off between unemployment and inflation existed, but the curve denoting the relationship had shifted outward, possibly to the curve labeled PC_2 in Figure 13–9 by 1970 and 1971.

What was the cause of the stronger wage-push pressure? One possibility was the recent appearance of substantial union power spreading among public employees, offering a new area where gains were to be made and perhaps a fresh militancy as well. Mostly, however, the stronger wage push was attributed to a greater aggressiveness among unions at large, an aggressiveness based in sociological factors. Sir Roy Harrod, the prominent British economist, took this position, arguing that the causes of the wage-price "explosion" of the early 1970s arose from factors akin to such things as student unrest.[11] Gardner Ackley, who was chairman of the President's Council of Economic Advisers under President Johnson during the middle 1960s, suggested that changing social norms had left the community more tolerant of aggressive exercises of market power.[12] Another possibility is that the successes of the civil rights and student movements of the 1960s persuaded labor, or reminded it, that groups acting collectively and aggressively can produce results.

Harrod, Ackley, and others concluded that monetary and fiscal policies would not by themselves be able to provide acceptable price and employment results in the environment of the 1970s. They recommended that monetary and fiscal policies be supplemented with price and wage controls, or, to use the broader term employed by Harrod and Ackley, by *incomes policies,* which control prices and wages but also place direct controls on profits and other forms of property income. They reasoned that the Phillips curve had shifted outward so that it offered only unacceptable combinations of unemployment and inflation rates when monetary and fiscal policies alone were used. Incomes policies were needed to contain wage-push and other cost-push pressures so that monetary and fiscal ease could move the economy to full employment without producing unacceptable inflation rates. This was a discouraging conclusion, since price and wage controls and incomes policies reduce economic efficiency by interfering with the functioning of the price system as an allocator of resources, production, and incomes. The Nixon administration invoked mandatory price and wage controls in late 1971, when inflation seemed to be reappearing even though the unemployment rate had not declined from its peak levels of the 1970 recession.

Demand-Pull Inflation and the Phillips Curve Data

The wage-push trade-off hypothesis, including the view of a stronger wage push during the 1970s, became less persuasive as an explanation for the higher unemployment and inflation rate combinations of the 1970s as the decade unfolded. Most economists today do not see it as having

---

[11] Sir Roy Harrod, with Gottfried Haberler, Robert A. Mundell, Jacques Rueff, and Robert Triffin, "The Issues: Five Views," in *Inflation as a Global Problem,* ed. R. Hinshaw (Baltimore: Johns Hopkins University Press, 1972), p. 44.

[12] Gardner Ackley, "An Incomes Policy for the 1970s," *Review of Economics and Statistics* 54 (August 1972): 219.

been a significant factor in the U.S. experience. Many emphasize instead the expansions in income-maintenance programs and the increases in the proportions of women and teenagers in the labor force, noted in Chapter 12. Figures 12–11 and 12–12 and the discussions relating to them demonstrated that these disturbances increase the natural rate of unemployment and produce a once and for all increase in prices. Moreover, if the stabilization authorities respond to the increase in the natural rate of unemployment by encouraging increases in aggregate demand in persistent attempts to regain former unemployment rates, they produce persistent expenditure gap inflation—that is, demand-pull inflation—and bring about very little long-term effect on unemployment rates.

Cost-push inflation, arising from increases in prices of imported goods and services, especially oil, undoubtedly was a factor in the higher unemployment and inflation rate combinations of the 1970s, especially during 1973 and 1974 and again during 1979. But an increase in the natural rate of unemployment, coupled with an inappropriate demand management policy response to it, appears to have been the major factor.

Rejection of the wage-push trade-off hypothesis as a significant factor means that general price and wage controls were not an appropriate response to the higher unemployment and inflation rates. As demonstrated earlier (in Figure 13–5), monetary and fiscal policies can contain inflationary pressures resulting from a reduction in the supply of labor caused by expansions in income maintenance programs or shifts in labor force composition by removing the expenditure gap the disturbance produces. And they can do so without creating shortfall unemployment. With cost-push inflation centered in import prices, price and wage controls would not have helped.

Milton Friedman has argued that expansive demand management policies have no effect at all on the natural rate of unemployment in the long term. In effect, the long-term Phillips curve is vertical at the natural rate of unemployment in the face of such policies. Figure 13–10 presents two such long-term Phillips curves, one at 4 percent unemployment, relating roughly to the U.S. experience for 1955–69, and one to the right, reflecting the increase in the natural rate of unemployment for the 1970s. The figure plots this 1970s curve at 6 percent unemployment, but it is debatable whether it should fall there, at 5.5 percent as the U.S. Council of Economic Advisers has suggested, or at 7 percent as Herbert Stein has speculated.[13]

---

[13] President's Council of Economic Advisers, *Economic Report of the President* (Washington, D.C.: Government Printing Office, 1977), p. 51; Herbert Stein, "Full Employment at Last?" *Wall Street Journal,* September 14, 1977, p. 22.

Figure 13–10 **Long-Term and Short-Term Phillips Curves**

According to the natural rate hypothesis, there is a short-term trade-off between the unemployment rate and the inflation rate, but no long-term trade-off. In this view, the long-term Phillips curve is vertical at the natural rate of unemployment, which is higher in the 1970s than it was in the 1950s and 1960s.

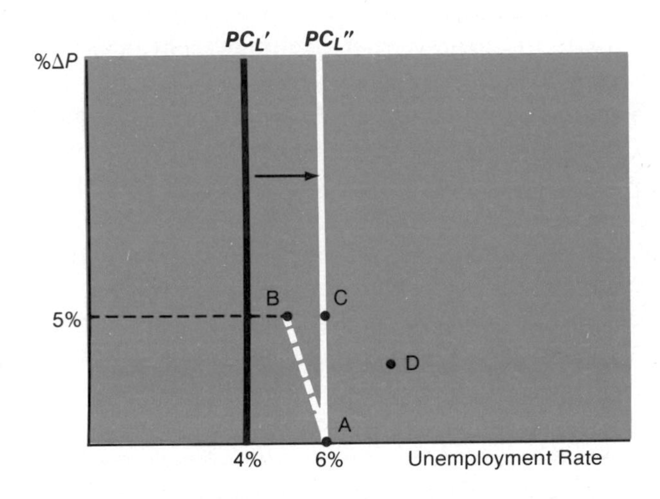

Friedman argues that monetary policies which produce expenditure gap inflation can temporarily lower the unemployment rate below the natural rate, effecting a short-term trade-off between unemployment and inflation, and he explains the trade-off evidenced by the empirical Phillips curve in this way. Workers recognize the money wage increases they receive when making commitments to work, but they temporarily underestimate the price inflation which is occurring because recognizing that inflation requires taking into account the price increases on the many goods and services available for purchase. As a result, according to Friedman, they view the real wage as increasing and increase the quantity of labor services they supply. Producers, correctly recognizing both the higher prices they are receiving for their products and the higher money wages they are paying for labor, see that the real wage is not increasing—in fact, that it can decline—and hire additional labor. Employment rises, and the unemployment rate declines below the natural rate.

In Figure 13–10, an inflation rate increased from zero to 5 percent by a money supply disturbance, with the natural rate of unemployment at 6 percent, might produce a movement from Point A to Point B via this process. In the short term, a trade-off between unemployment and inflation occurs, produced by demand-pull inflation only.

This must be a short-term effect, however, barring the nonsensical case where the inflation accelerates forever. If the 5 percent inflation rate is maintained period after period by the stabilization authorities, workers will come to correctly anticipate it, the supply of labor will be as before, and the natural rate of unemployment will again prevail. We move to Point C in the figure. In the long term, the natural rate of unemployment prevails and is independent of the steady-state inflation rate produced by demand management policies. There is a short-term trade-off between unemployment and inflation, generating the empirical short-term Phillips curve with its observations of unemployment rates below the natural rate of unemployment, but there is no long-term trade-off. The long-term Phillips curve is vertical at the natural rate of unemployment.[14]

It is not necessary to go all the way to the vertical long-term Phillips curve with Friedman to accept the important point that if demand-pull inflation provoked by government is responsible for the higher unemployment rate and inflation rate combinations of the 1970s, price and wage controls are not the appropriate response. Perhaps there is a small measure of wage-push inflationary pressure which produces a permanent but acceptable trade-off between unemployment and inflation as full employment is approached. Perhaps the natural rate of transitory unemployment declines permanently in response to permanent expenditure gaps and inflation rates, because the time between jobs declines for job changers when there is an excess demand for labor.[15]

Whatever the case, unless the wage-push inflation pressures are very

---

[14] For Friedman's description of his natural rate hypothesis, see Milton Friedman, "Nobel Lecture: Inflation and Unemployment," *Journal of Political Economy* 85 (June 1977): 451–472, especially 456–459. E. S. Phelps developed a somewhat similar theory for explaining the Phillips curve data at about the same time. See E. S. Phelps, "Phillips Curve, Expectations of Inflation and Optimal Unemployment over Time," *Economica* 34 (August 1967): 254–281; and "Money Wage Dynamics and Labor Market Equilibrium," in *Microeconomic Foundations of Employment and Inflation Theory,* ed. E. S. Phelps (New York: Norton, 1970).

Chapter 2 defined the natural rate of unemployment pragmatically, calling it the unemployment rate at which increases in aggregate demand for output begin to spill mostly into price and money-wage increases instead of increases in output and employment. Friedman defines it more precisely as the rate consistent with the real forces in the economy and accurate perceptions. He notes that the unemployment rate can be kept below the natural rate in the long term only by accelerating inflation (so that expected inflation never catches up to actual inflation) and can be kept above the natural rate, again in the long term (when money wages are flexible downward), only by accelerating deflation.

[15] Lipsey, "Unemployment and Money Wage Rates," pp. 1–31.

strong, and a major factor in unacceptable unemployment and inflation combinations, there is no need for price and wage controls, unless it is the political one that the electorate simply will not accept monetary and fiscal policies appropriate to acceptable inflation rates when the natural rate of unemployment prevails. Even here, the appropriate response is to reduce the natural rate of unemployment with specific policies addressed to that end rather than to bear the burdens of high inflation rates or price and wage controls.

Notice that Friedman's natural rate hypothesis implies that aggregate output does not remain constant when aggregate demand increases at full employment, as the vertical portion of the aggregate supply of output curves employed in Chapter 12 suggests. Under Friedman's hypothesis, aggregate output expands beyond full-employment output during the period in which workers are underestimating the inflation rate. Moreover, when workers finally adapt their expectations to the inflation rate, output may drop below full-employment output for a time if monetary restraint is applied and the inflation rate slows. In this phase of the adjustment process, workers are overestimating the inflation rate, underestimating the real wage, and temporarily supplying less labor than is consistent with full-employment output. Points such as Point D in Figure 13–10 occur. If the expected inflation induces wage-push inflationary pressures or builds money-wage increases into the economy for a time because many union contracts are for two or three years, this phase of the adjustment process may be lengthened, with the inflation rate sustained for a period and the unemployment effects aggravated. Such factors may have contributed to the persistence of relatively high (though declining) inflation rates throughout the recession extending from November 1973 through March 1975. Wage-push inflation of this type is induced by a prior demand-pull based inflation, of course, and does not imply the need for price and wage controls—at least not permanent controls.

Another complication arises from the fact that if workers formulate their expectations rationally and with perfect foresight, rather than with Friedman's adaptive expectations, the temporary effects on output described above do not occur.[16] Under these conditions, workers at once correctly perceive price inflation, money-wage inflation, and the real wage they are offered for labor services, so that the supply curve of labor is not affected. Aggregate employment and output remain fixed at the levels consistent with the natural rate of employment even in the short term. Of course, to

[16] See T. J. Sargent and Neil Wallace, "Rational Expectations and the Theory of Economic Policy," *Journal of Monetary Economics* 2 (April 1976): 169–183, especially 107–108.

assume perfect foresight probably is going too far. Still, if workers are aware from their knowledge of the economy that prices ordinarily increase along with money wages in situations where increases in worker productivity obviously cannot explain the increases in money wages, the adjustment to the long-term Phillips curve may occur much more rapidly than Friedman's adaptive expectations model suggests. This is a valuable insight, since Friedman at one point speculates that it may require twenty years to fully regain positions on the vertical Phillips curve following a change produced by monetary policies in the steady-state inflation rate.[17]

Summary

1. General monetary and fiscal policies work by influencing aggregate demand. They remove shortfalls in aggregate demand by stimulating demand, and they check inflation caused by expenditure gaps by reducing demand. The interest rate obtained depends on the mix of monetary and fiscal policies used.

2. Fiscal policies are accompanied by money supply disturbances which reinforce them if the Federal Reserve accommodates the Treasury debt operations they require with open-market purchases or sales. Otherwise, associated money supply disturbances do not occur.

3. The unemployment and inflation rate combinations experienced in the United States since 1970 have been much poorer than those experienced during the 1950s and 1960s in terms of price and employment goals.

4. Some of the early interpretations of these poorer combinations saw them as arising from stronger wage-push pressures and concluded that monetary and fiscal policies would have to be supplemented with price and wage controls if acceptable price and employment results were to be achieved.

5. Today, most economists see an increase in the natural rate of unemployment caused by expansions in income-maintenance programs and increased proportions of women and teenagers in the labor force as the principal factor in the higher unemployment rates. They see overly expansive monetary and fiscal policies as the principal factor in the higher inflation rates. In this view, general price and wage controls are not

[17] Milton Friedman, "The Role of Monetary Policy," *American Economic Review* 58 (March 1968): 11.

appropriate. Since the inflation is chiefly the demand-pull type, monetary and fiscal policies can contain it. If the higher natural rate of unemployment is unacceptable, specific fiscal policies targeted to frictional and structural unemployment are the appropriate policy response.

6. Milton Friedman's natural rate hypothesis explains the trade-off between unemployment rate and inflation rate of the empirical Phillips curve as a short-term response to demand-pull inflation, a response arising from worker underestimation of the inflation. In the long term, when both price and money-wage inflation are perceived correctly, the unemployment rate is independent of the inflation rate. The long-term Phillips curve is vertical at the natural rate of unemployment in Friedman's formulation.

Concepts for Identification

crowding out
nonbank public
federal deficit
built-in money supply effects
Phillips curve
trade-off hypothesis
incomes policies
natural rate hypothesis

Questions and Problems for Review

1. Describe the channels by which monetary policies stimulate output and employment when applied in a recession. Start with an open-market purchase or a reduction in reserve requirements and trace the mechanism through to the impacts on output and employment.

2. Explain how the money market checks the strength of fiscal policies applied to stimulate the economy in a recession. Illustrate the effect with *IS* and *LM* curves.

3. Explain why monetary ease might be preferred over fiscal ease to correct a shortfall of aggregate demand if low interest rates are desired.

4. Monetary and fiscal policies can stabilize the interest rate as well as output, prices, employment, and the unemployment rate in the face of aggregate demand disturbances if monetary policies are used to offset monetary disturbances and fiscal policies are used to offset real disturbances. Verify this statement with *IS* and *LM* curves.

5. Explain why an application of fiscal ease has no money supply effect (other than a built-in money supply effect) if the increased federal deficit it involves is financed by Treasury securities purchased by commercial banks or the nonbank public.

6. When the supply of labor declines because of expansions in income maintenance programs or shifts in labor force composition, monetary and fiscal policies can maintain the original price level and achieve equilibrium at the new full-employment output in the process. Demonstrate this statement graphically.

7. Present the wage-push trade-off hypothesis and the natural rate hypothesis as alternative explanations for U.S. Phillips curve type data for 1956 through 1978. Discuss the implications of the two hypotheses for the debate over whether price and wage controls are needed.

8. Explain how the natural rate hypothesis implies that output and real income will move beyond their full-employment levels temporarily when aggregate demand for output increases in a full-employment situation.

9. What happens to the implication drawn in Question 8 if expectations are formulated *rationally* rather than *adaptively* and foresight is perfect? Explain.

References

Ackley, Gardner. "An Incomes Policy for the 1970s." *Review of Economics and Statistics* 54 (August 1972): 218–223.

———. *Macroeconomics: Theory and Policy.* New York: Macmillan, 1978, chaps. 13–15.

Alchian, A. A. "Information Cost, Pricing, and Resource Unemployment." *Western Economic Journal* 7 (June 1969): 109–128.

de Leeuw, Frank, and Gramlich, Edward M. "The Channels of Monetary Policy." *Federal Reserve Bulletin* 55 (June 1969): 472–491.

Donner, A., and McCallum, J. F. "The Phillips Curve: An Historical Note." *Economica* 40 (August 1972): 322–323.

Fisher, Irving. "A Statistical Relation between Unemployment and Price Changes." *International Labour Review* 13 (June 1926): 785–792. Reprinted in *Journal of Political Economy* 81 (March–April 1973): 496–502.

Friedman, Milton. "The Role of Monetary Policy." *American Economic Review* 58 (March 1958): 1–17.

———. "Nobel Lecture: Inflation and Unemployment." *Journal of Political Economy* 85 (June 1977): 451–472.

Gronau, Reuben. "Information and Frictional Unemployment." *American Economic Review* 61 (June 1971): 290–301.

Harrod, R.; with Haberler, Gottfried; Mundell, Robert A.; Rueff, Jacques; and Triffin, Robert. "The Issues: Five Views." In *Inflation as a Global Problem,* edited by R. Hinshaw. Baltimore: Johns Hopkins University Press, 1972, pp. 39–57.

Laidler, David, and Parking, Michael. "Inflation: A Survey." *Economic Journal* 85 (December 1975): 741–809.

Lipsey, R. G. "The Relationship between Unemployment and the Rate of Change of Money Wage Rates in the U.K., 1862–1957: A Further Analysis." *Economica* 27 (February 1960): 1–31.

Lucas, R. E., Jr., and Rapping, L. A. "Price Expectations and the Phillips Curve." *American Economic Review* 59 (June 1969): 342–350.

Mortensen, D. T. "Job Search, the Duration of Unemployment and the Phillips Curve." *American Economic Review* 60 (December 1970): 847–862.

Phelps, E. S. "Phillips Curve, Expectations of Inflation and Optimal Unemployment over Time." *Economica* 34 (August 1967): 254–281.

———. "Money Wage Dynamics and Labor Market Equilibrium." In *Microeconomic Foundations of Employment and Inflation Theory,* edited by E. S. Phelps. New York: Norton, 1970. Reprinted in *Modern Macroeconomics,* edited by P. G. Korliras and R. S. Thorn. New York: Harper & Row, 1979, pp. 213–241.

Phillips, A. W. "The Relationship between Unemployment and the Rate of Change of Money Wage Rates in the U.K., 1861–1957." *Economica* 25 (November 1958): 283–299.

Sargent, T. J., and Wallace, Neil. "Rational Expectations and the Theory of Economic Policy." *Journal of Monetary Economics* 2 (April 1976): 169–183.

Tobin, James. "Inflation and Unemployment." *American Economic Review* 62 (March 1972): 1–18.

Vernon, Jack. "The Multiplier Concept and Monetary Restraint." *Quarterly Journal of Economics* 88 (May 1974): 330–339.

14

Keynesians, Neo-Keynesians, and the Monetarist Propositions

Modern macroeconomics departs from the early Keynesian position in several important respects. Within modern macroeconomics, neo-Keynesian and monetarist positions can be distinguished.

Chapter 1 noted that economists, while agreeing on much of the subject matter of macroeconomics, have differed on important matters. Specifically, differences have existed and continue to exist over such things as the relative importance of real and money supply disturbances in fluctuations in aggregate demand, the extent to which discretionary stabilization policies should be used, and whether fiscal or monetary policies should be emphasized. An early Keynesian viewpoint and a modern viewpoint on these matters were discussed earlier; and, within the latter, a neo-Keynesian position was contrasted with the monetarist propositions offered by Milton Friedman.

According to these distinctions, the early Keynesians, who were concerned mostly with the unemployment problem, viewed real disturbances as the major source of that problem and reserved a special place for shifts in the investment expenditure function. They regarded discretionary stabilization policies by government as essential to acceptable price and employment results, and they recommended emphasis on fiscal policies.

Neo-Keynesians, according to Chapter 1, emphasize both unemployment and inflation problems and see both *IS* curve disturbances and money supply disturbances as important sources of the fluctuations in aggregate demand which contribute to these problems. They retain the early Keynesian view that a program of discretionary stabilization policies by government is desirable; but, unlike the early Keynesians, they see monetary policies as useful elements in the program.

The monetarist propositions on these matters are (1) that money supply disturbances have been the major source of severe fluctuations in aggregate demand, (2) that discretionary stabilization policies of the sort recommended by Keynes and the neo-Keynesians should not be used in ordinary circumstances, and (3) that monetary policies should be emphasized when the activist discretionary policies are used. Milton Friedman has argued that the monetary authority should confine itself to stabilizing money supply growth, with the rate of growth attuned to long-term trends in full-employment output and money demand, unless it is apparent that major disturbances offering a clear and present danger to price and employment goals have occurred.[1] In the usual monetarist representation, discretionary fiscal policies are used only as needed to maintain a balanced, full-employment federal budget.

This chapter interprets these positions with the *IS-LM* model developed in Chapters 7 and 8 and also with the quantity theory of money model. The positions arise in part out of differences in the relative strength accorded to the monetary influences introduced in Chapter 7, differences which depend on differing views as to the interest sensitivity of money demand and expenditures. This is especially true of the distinction between early Keynesian and modern macroeconomics, but there is some reason for believing that it contributes to the split between neo-Keynesian macroeconomics and Friedman's monetarist propositions as well.

The Keynesian Viewpoint

In the view of the early Keynesians, the demand for money balances is quite sensitive to interest rate, while expenditures are not. The speculative motive for holding money is the source of the high interest sensitivity of money demand. As the interest rate falls, a larger portion of wealth is held in money as opposed to securities and other assets because a larger

[1] Milton Friedman, "The Role of Monetary Policy," *American Economic Review* 58 (March 1968): 14–17.

portion of wealth-holders expect interest rates to rise rather than fall in the future. Indeed, at some low but still positive rate of interest, the demand for money balances becomes infinitely interest sensitive, since everyone expects interest rates to rise and produce capital losses on assets other than money. The low estimate of the interest sensitivity of expenditures arises from the Keynesian neglect of interest rate effects on consumption expenditures and the view that such effects are weak and delayed as they apply to investment expenditures.

Figure 14–1 presents *LM* and *IS* curves reflecting the Keynesian attitude about the interest sensitivity of money demand and expenditures and employs them to illustrate the Keynesian propositions relating to sources of fluctuations in aggregate demand and stabilization policy recommendations. The *LM* curves are relatively flat, becoming perfectly flat at a positive rate of interest, while the *IS* curves are relatively steep.

The *LM* curve, recall, presents combinations of r and Y at which the demand and supply for real money balances are equal, with the supply of real money balances being fixed for each curve. They are relatively flat when money demand is highly sensitive to interest rate because in that case a small increase in r compensates for a large increase in Y in keeping Md unchanged and equal to the unchanged real money supply.

The *IS* curves are relatively steep because expenditures expand only slightly as the interest rate falls. Recall that the *IS* curve presents the aggregate expenditure forthcoming at each r, including the income-induced expenditure which occurs as Y expands.

Figures 14–1a and 14–1b illustrate that real disturbances rather than monetary disturbances are the source of the fluctuations in demand which cause severe unemployment problems under the Keynesian assumptions. A fairly substantial monetary disturbance, illustrated in the leftward shift in the *LM* curve in Figure 14–1a, provokes only a small reduction in equilibrium Y, while a real disturbance, pictured in the leftward shift in the *IS* curve in Figure 14–1b, causes a large reduction in equilibrium Y.[2]

Figures 14–1c and 14–1d indicate that fiscal rather than monetary policies are effectual for restoring full employment under the Keynesian assumptions. The figures show the extreme case where the decline in the *IS* curve to *IS'* has placed it in the liquidity trap.

In this situation, monetary policies are completely ineffectual in raising

[2] Readers may satisfy themselves that it is the horizontal rather than the vertical shift in the *LM* and *IS* curves which is proportional to disturbances involving the real money supply, the money demand constant, and the expenditure constants by inspecting Equations 10–35 and 10–36, the equations for the *IS* and *LM* curves.

Figure 14–1 **The Keynesian View**

Under Keynesian assumptions as to money demand and expenditure interest sensitivity, output is much more sensitive to real than to monetary disturbances. Fiscal ease is strong; monetary ease is weak.

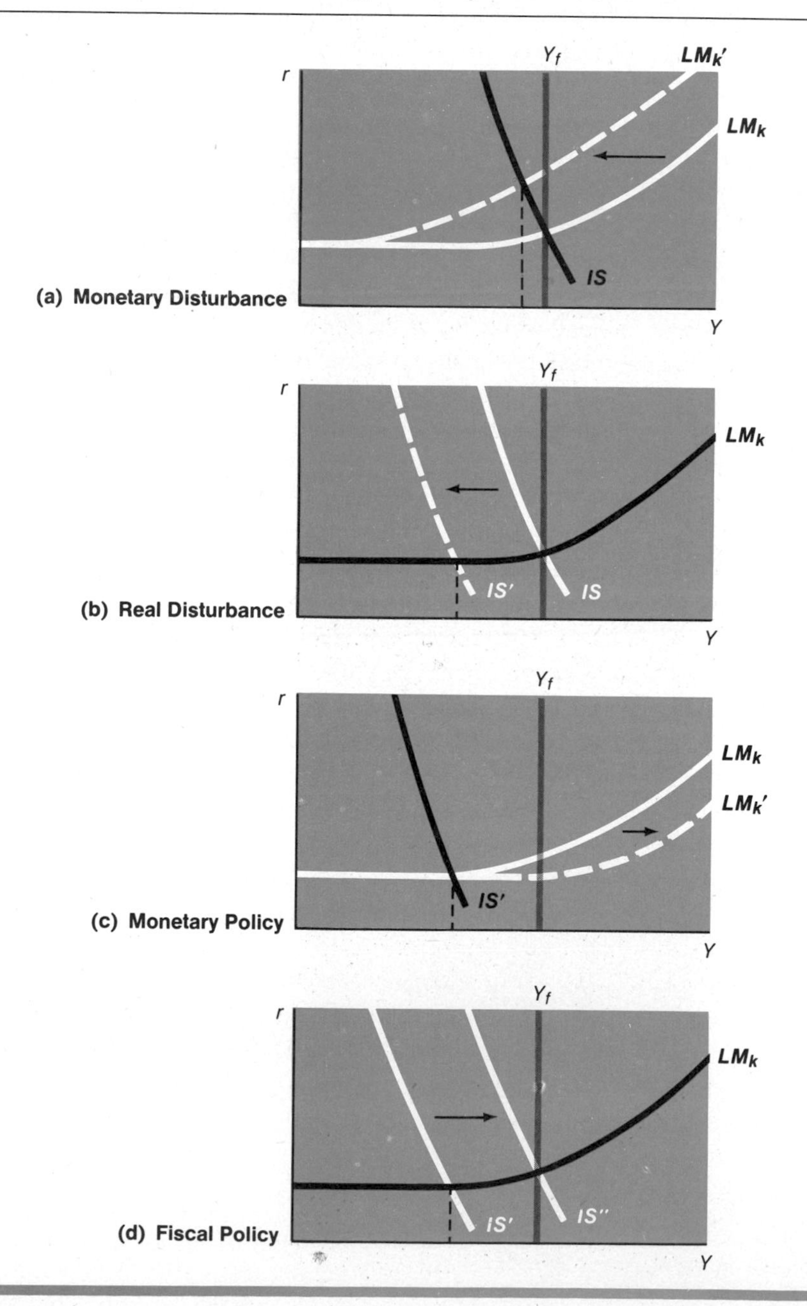

Y. Increased money balances are merely held as money, since the demand for money is infinite in the liquidity trap range. In terms of the graph, the *LM* curve merely shifts outward on itself in the relevant range when the money supply is increased.

Fiscal policies are very strong under the Keynesian assumptions, however. Equilibrium Y increases by virtually the entire horizontal shift in the *IS* curve. Interest rates increase only slightly and produce little offsetting effect on interest-sensitive expenditures.

Modern Views

Modern macroeconomists, for the theoretical and empirical reasons noted in Chapters 5, 7, and 9, see money demand as much less sensitive to interest rate and see expenditures as much more sensitive to interest rate. The *LM* curve is much steeper and the *IS* curve not nearly so steep. Neo-Keynesians, envisaging curves similar to those in Figure 14–2, see both money supply disturbances and real disturbances as important sources of unemployment and inflation problems. Shifts in either curve will occasion significant changes in output and price equilibriums.

Discretionary stabilization policies will improve prices and employment if applied judiciously, in the neo-Keynesian view; and, since both monetary and fiscal policies have strength, both can be used. In effect, monetary influences are strong enough to suggest money supply disturbances as important sources of unemployment and inflation problems, and they are strong enough to suggest monetary policies as a useful stabilization device.[3]

There is one fairly obvious exception to the statement that monetary policies are effective under modern views about money demand and expenditure interest sensitivity. This exception is illustrated in Figure 14–3. If a real disturbance is so severe that the *IS* curve ends up at *IS′* in the figure, even an interest rate of zero will not produce enough aggregate expenditure to support full-employment output. In this case, monetary policies cannot raise output beyond Y_a in the model as presently constituted. A liquidity trap exists at an interest rate of zero (even if none exists at a positive rate of interest), since no one would hold assets with an expected return of less than zero in preference to money. Why lend \$100 to receive \$95 back at the end of a year, when \$100 will be preserved if the

[3] Shifts in the money demand function would also be an important disturbance item with the modern *IS* and *LM* slopes, but most present-day economists do not see this function as subject to severe autonomous shifts (except for those arising in technological innovations in money).

Figure 14–2 **Neo-Keynesian View of *IS* and *LM* Curves**

The neo-Keynesian view differs from the early Keynesian view in that money demand is less sensitive to the interest rate and expenditures are more sensitive to the interest rate. Consequently, in the neo-Keynesian view the *LM* curve is steeper while the *IS* curve is less steep.

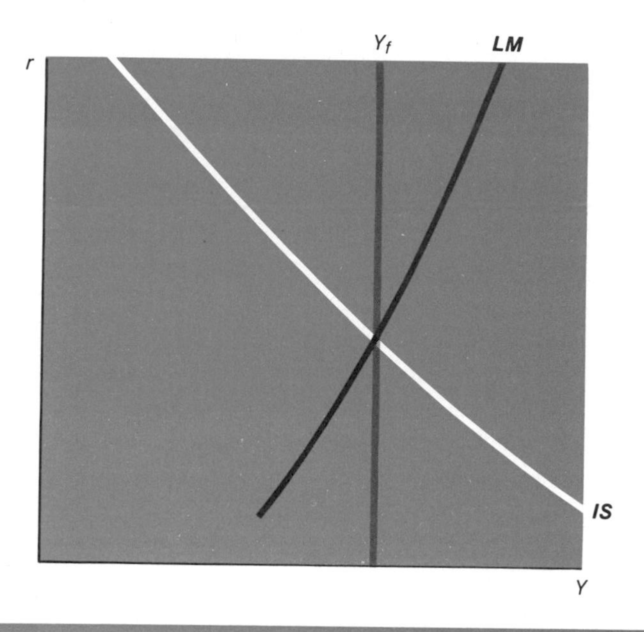

money is simply held? This, therefore, is a situation in which monetary policies would be ineffectual in ending a recession even under modern assumptions as to money demand and expenditure interest sensitivity. The Keynesians were correct on this point, even without the liquidity trap being present at a positive rate of interest.

The Classical Money Demand Function and the Monetarist Propositions

IS and *LM* curves such as those of Figure 14–2 reconcile easily with the neo-Keynesian view. But what of monetarism? Are such curves consistent with monetarist propositions? How do they permit the views that money supply disturbances are the exclusive source of severe fluctuations in aggregate demand and associated unemployment and inflation prob-

Figure 14–3 **The Negative Interest Rate Case**

If the position of the *IS* curve is such that full-employment expenditure requires a negative rate of interest, monetary policies are powerless to increase output, with the model as presently constituted.

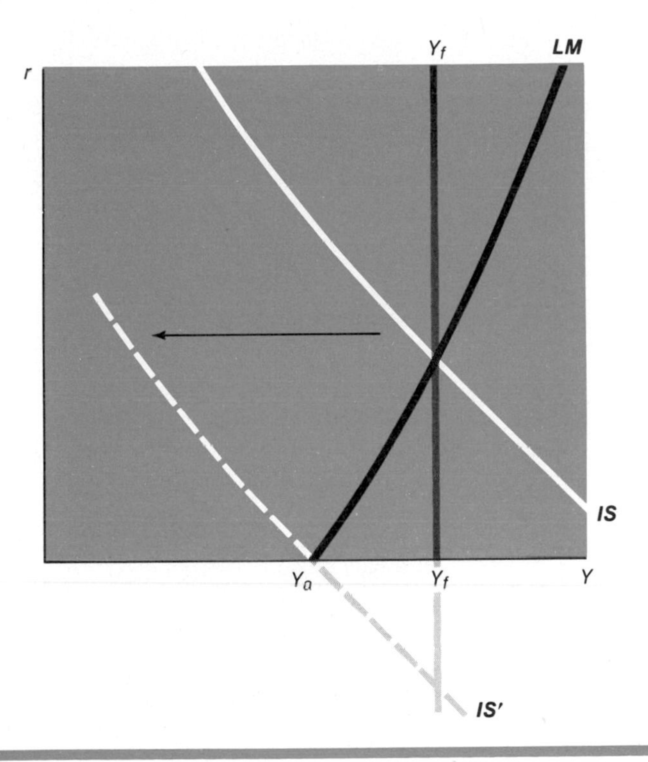

lems, that discretionary policies should not be used in ordinary circumstances, and that fiscal policies are in any event too weak to be useful?

One possibility is that the monetarists do not depend on such curves for their propositions. Often, monetarists are represented as employing the classical demand function for money, discussed in Chapter 9, in which the demand for real money balances bears a constant relation to real income and is entirely interest insensitive. That is, the money demand function is:

$$Md = kY, \qquad 14\text{–}1$$

where k is a constant. In this case, the *LM* curve is a vertical line, as in Figure 14–4a, and does not shift unless the money supply or the price

Figure 14–4 **The Classical Money Demand Function and the Monetarist Propositions**

When the *IS-LM* model is modified to include the classical money demand function, real disturbances, including fiscal policies, leave output and prices unchanged.

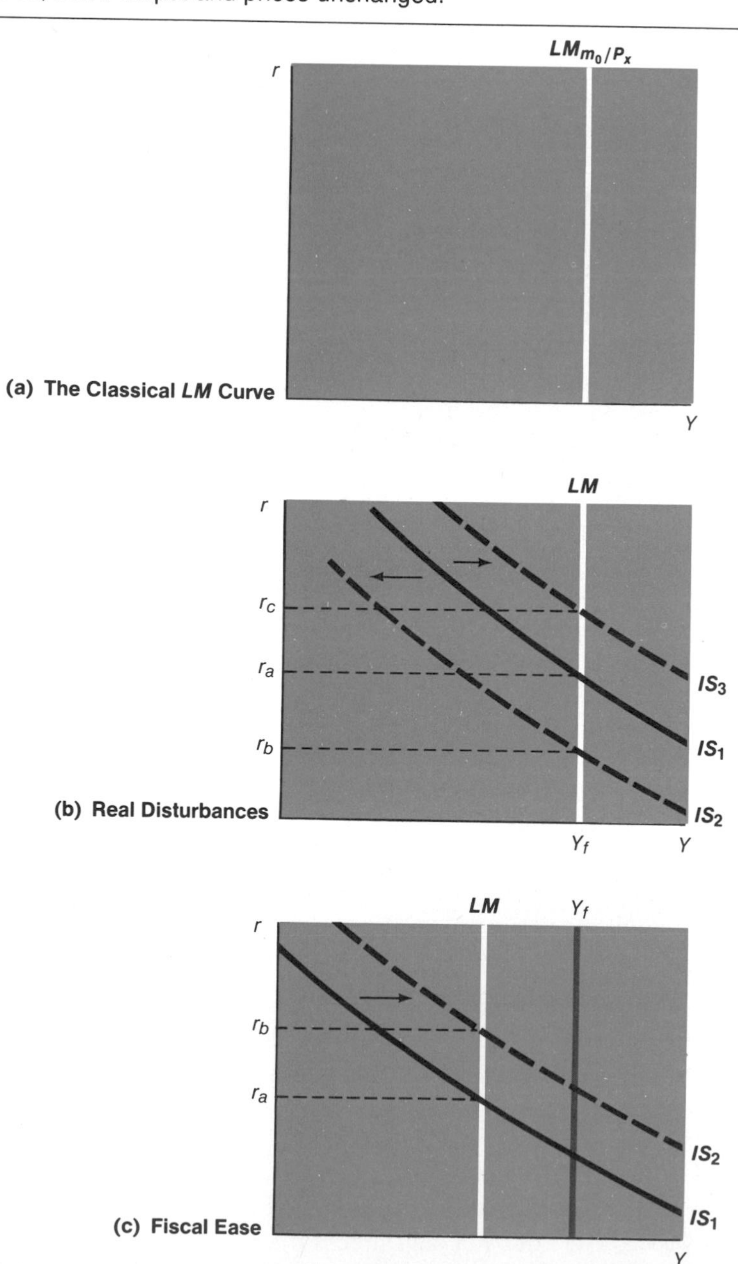

(a) The Classical *LM* Curve

(b) Real Disturbances

(c) Fiscal Ease

level changes. For example, if m_0 and P_x are the existing money supply and price level, money market equilibrium is:

$$m_0/P_x = kY, \qquad \text{14–2}$$

so that the LM curve is a vertical line at a Y of:

$$Y = 1/k(m_0/P_x). \qquad \text{14–3}$$

In this case, the monetarist propositions hold completely, in the absence of aggregate supply disturbances and barring the case where a negative interest rate is required for full-employment expenditure. Shifts in the money supply are the only source of changes in price and output equilibrium, so that a constant money supply—or, allowing for growth trends, constant money supply growth—provides a perfect stabilization result on output and prices. Real disturbances affect interest rate equilibrium but leave price and output equilibriums unchanged. Fiscal policies, which are government-induced real disturbances, have no effect on output or price equilibriums.

Figures 14–4b and 14–4c use the classical money demand function to illustrate the point that real disturbances, including fiscal policies, have no effect on price and output equilibriums. Figure 14–4b shows that real disturbances occurring in a situation where there is full employment and price stability leave the economy in that situation. If the IS curve declines, as from IS_1 to IS_2, the equilibrium interest rate falls from r_a to r_b, but the economy remains at full employment, in equilibrium, even with prices and money wages held rigidly downward. Since the demand for real money balances does not expand as the interest rate declines, an excess supply of money will be present unless the interest rate declines by enough to restore aggregate demand and output to their former levels.

Similarly, if the IS curve shifts from IS_1 to IS_3 in Figure 14–4b, the equilibrium interest rate rises from r_a to r_c, but an expenditure gap does not appear and prices do not rise. Since the demand for real money balances does not decline as the interest rate rises, there is no need for prices to rise to reduce the real money supply.

Figure 14–4c shows that an application of fiscal ease in an initial unemployment situation has no effect on equilibrium output. The interest rate simply rises from r_a to r_b when a fiscal ease application shifts the IS curve from IS_1 to IS_2. The effects of the fiscal operation on spending are exactly offset by an equal reduction in interest-sensitive expenditures. Crowding out is complete.

Figure 14–5 illustrates an exception to the monetarist position that real

Figure 14–5 **The Negative Interest Rate Case and the Classical Money Demand Function**

The negative interest rate case presents an exception to the rule that real disturbances, including fiscal policies, have no effect on output in a model incorporating a classical money demand function.

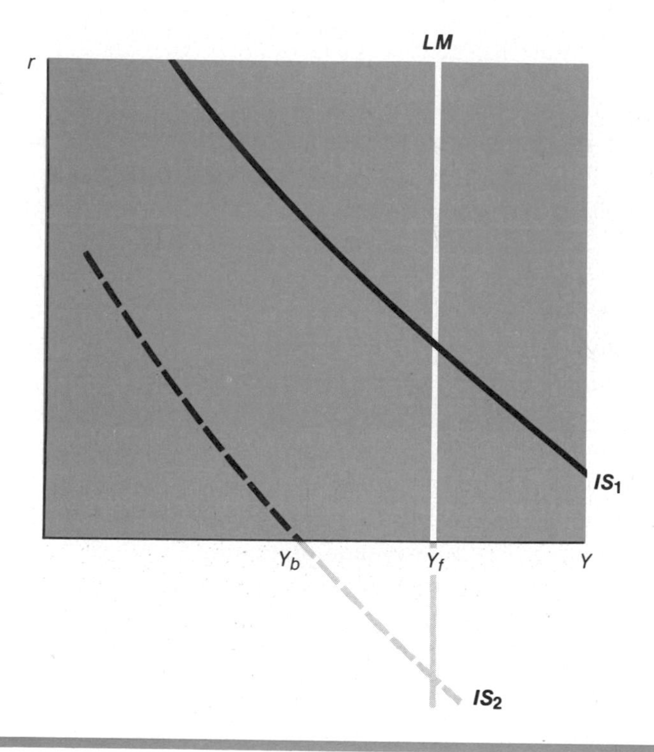

disturbances, including fiscal policies, do not affect output equilibriums. If the *IS* curve shifts from IS_1 to IS_2 in the figure, so that a negative interest rate is required for full-employment output, output declines from Y_f to Y_b, even with the classical money demand function in effect. Moreover, fiscal ease is not powerless in the new situation. Fiscal policies can increase output and restore full employment by shifting the *IS* curve to the right.

Figures 14–6 and 14–7 demonstrate that aggregate supply disturbances also pose an exception to the monetarist propositions, even with the classical money demand function in effect.

In Figure 14–6, when wage-push inflation forces prices upward from P_x

Figure 14–6 **The Classical Money Demand Function and Wage-Push Inflation**

Wage-push pressures produce a shortfall in aggregate demand and an increase in prices even with the classical money demand function present.

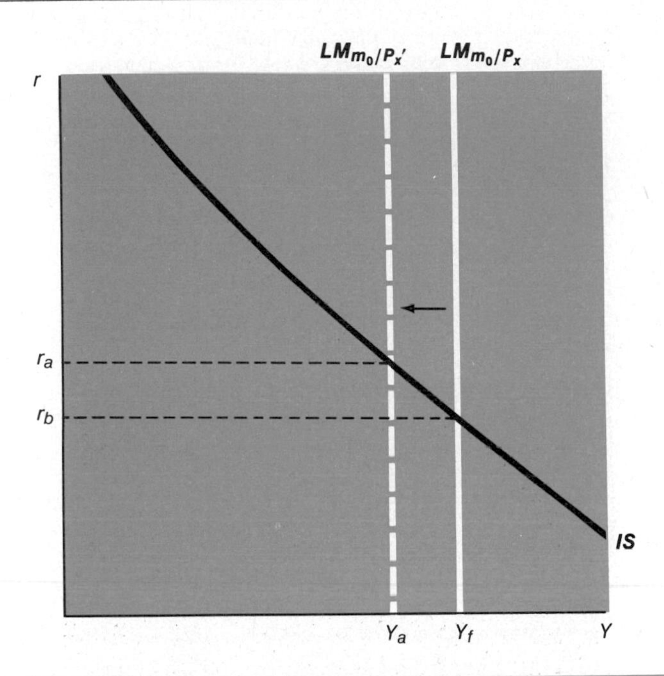

to P_x', the real money supply declines from m_0/P_x to m_0/P_x', the *LM* curve shifts to the left, and equilibrium output falls to Y_a. Prices rise and output falls. A constant m_0 does not produce full employment and price stability.

In Figure 14–7, an increase in the natural rate of unemployment, which shifts the full-employment benchmark to Y_f', produces inflation if the money supply is constant at m_0. Prices rise from P_x to P_x'.

The Quantity Theory of Money Model

While the *IS-LM* model has been used here for expressing the monetarist propositions, and for macroeconomic and monetary analysis in general, monetarists often prefer to use the *quantity theory of money model* for

Figure 14–7 **The Classical Money Demand Function and an Increase in the Natural Rate of Unemployment**

Disturbances which increase the natural rate of unemployment produce inflation, even with the classical money demand function present.

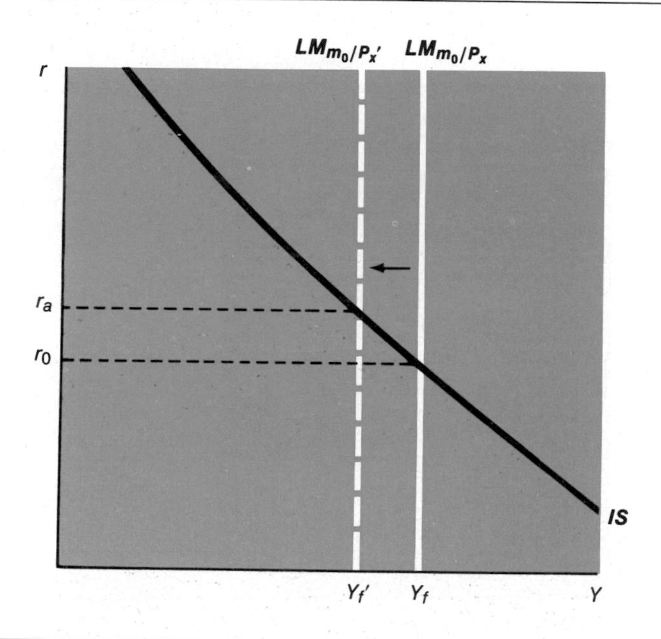

these purposes. It is obtained by substituting the classical money demand function $Md = kY$ into the money market equilibrium condition $m_0/P = Md$ to obtain:

$$m_0 = kPY, \tag{14-4}$$

which is the "cash balances" form of the model, or

$$m_0V = PY, \tag{14-5}$$

which is the "transactions" form of the model, where $V = 1/k$ is defined as the income velocity of money supply circulation. This really is an alternative theory of aggregate demand which permits the factors affecting PY, that is, aggregate money expenditures, to be analyzed in terms of the factors affecting k, the money demand coefficient, or V, its reciprocal.

With the classical money demand function as it is represented here, where k is a constant, V is also a constant, which means that PY is fixed if m_0 is fixed, and the monetarist propositions can be expressed as accruing from constant velocity. Real disturbances, including government fiscal policies, have no effect on price or output equilibrium. Fixing m_0 completely stabilizes prices and output, barring aggregate supply disturbances and the negative interest rate case. The supply disturbances will cause output or price problems, however, even with velocity constant. For example, if wage-push inflation pushes prices up, output must fall if m_0 is constant, since PY will be constant.

Friedman's Monetarism

The classical money demand function of the preceding section, with its implications of a vertical LM curve and a constant velocity, is an exaggeration of Milton Friedman's monetarism. Friedman explicitly says that the demand for real money balances is somewhat sensitive to interest rates, which means that his LM curve has a measure of positive slope, as does the LM curve of Figure 14–2. Or, in terms of the quantity theory of money model, it means that k, and hence V, is not entirely constant but varies somewhat with interest rates. If the IS curve declines, starting at full-employment output, and prices are fixed, output declines somewhat. If the IS curve shifts to the right, starting at full employment, prices rise somewhat. Therefore, velocity, which is $V = PY/M_0$, varies directly with interest rates, since interest rates fall when the IS curve declines and rise when it increases.

These results are not necessarily inconsistent with Friedman's monetarism, since he does not maintain that the monetarist propositions hold completely. His argument is not that money supply disturbances have been the sole source of unemployment and inflation problems. It is that they have been the principal source of severe unemployment and inflation problems. He does not believe that stable money supply growth will provide a perfect price and employment result or that discretionary monetary policies should never be used. Rather, he argues that stable money supply growth most likely will provide a better stabilization result than discretionary policies in ordinary circumstances, granting the difficulties posed for fine-tuning by forecasting problems and by the uncertainty surrounding the strength of the policies and the lags involved in their impacts. Fiscal policies do not have zero strength in Friedman's view. They are weak, however, and the weakness arises from offsetting effects on interest-sensitive expenditures, effects which interfere with the rate of capital stock growth.

Still, there is some evidence that Friedman's money demand function is less interest sensitive than that of many prominent neo-Keynesians, so that considerations of money demand interest sensitivity may enter into his advocacy of the monetarist propositions and the neo-Keynesians' rejection of them. Friedman has used an interest elasticity of money demand of -0.15 in empirical work.[4] This is significantly smaller than the -0.33 to -0.5 range suggested by Franco Modigliani,[5] especially since Friedman is working with the long-term interest rate and Modigliani with the short-term interest rate.

The smaller money demand interest sensitivity is favorable to the monetarist propositions, since real disturbances, including fiscal policies, have smaller impacts on price and output equilibriums as money demand becomes less sensitive to interest rate. Figure 14–8 illustrates this point. The upper portion of the figure shows that a given leftward shift in the *IS* curve provokes a smaller reduction in equilibrium output with the steeper *LM* curve. Similarly, in the lower portion of the figure, with the shift in the *IS* curve to the right at full employment, the steeper *LM* curve will move a shorter distance horizontally in closing the expenditure gap, reflecting a smaller required increase in prices.

Friedman has suggested that differences over the interest sensitivity of expenditures may be a contributing factor to the neo-Keynesian–monetarist split on the monetarist propositions, arguing that many neo-Keynesians have tended to underestimate the interest sensitivity of expenditures by restricting interest sensitivity to investment expenditures.[6] A high interest sensitivity of expenditures is favorable to the monetarist propositions because it reduces the changes in output and price equilibriums which attend real disturbances, with money supply constant. That is, it contributes stability to velocity, just as a low interest sensitivity of money demand does.

Figures 14–9 and 14–10 illustrate this point. Figure 14–9 demonstrates that the reduction in output equilibrium which occurs with a given leftward shift in the *IS* curve is smaller in the lower portion of the figure, where the flatter *IS* curve reflects a higher interest sensitivity of expenditures. In Figure 14–10, the increase in price equilibrium which occurs when the *IS*

---

[4] Milton Friedman, "Interest Rates and the Demand for Money," *Journal of Law and Economics* 9 (October 1966): 73.

[5] F. Modigliani, R. Rasche, and J. Cooper, "Central Bank Policy, the Money Supply, and the Short-Term Rate of Interest," *Journal of Money, Credit, and Banking* 2 (May 1970): 166–218.

[6] Milton Friedman, "Comments on the Critics," *Journal of Political Economy* 80 (September–October 1972): 915–916.

Figure 14–8 **Real Disturbances and Money Demand Interest Sensitivity**

Real disturbances provoke smaller changes in output and price equilibriums when the sensitivity of real money balances demanded to the interest rate is small.

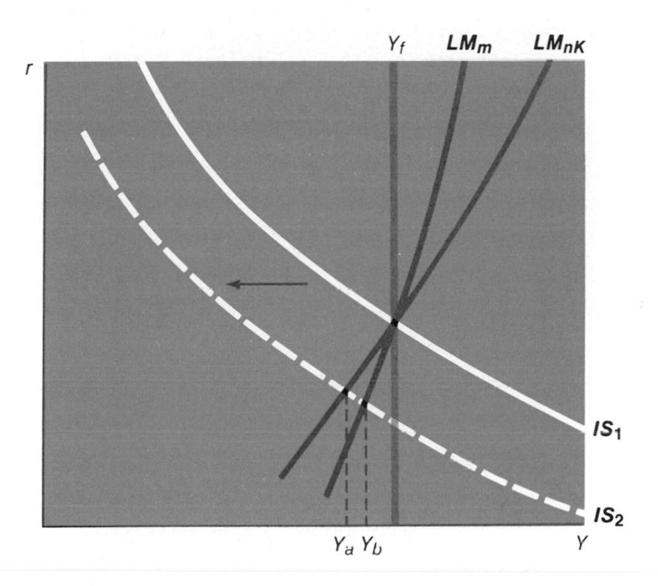

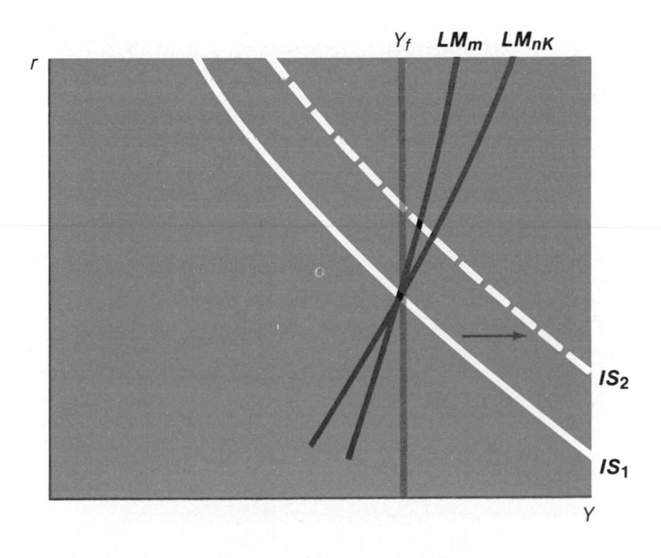

Figure 14–9 **Real Disturbances and Expenditure Interest Sensitivity: Change in Output Equilibrium**

Real disturbances provoke smaller changes in output equilibrium when the sensitivity of expenditures to the interest rate is large.

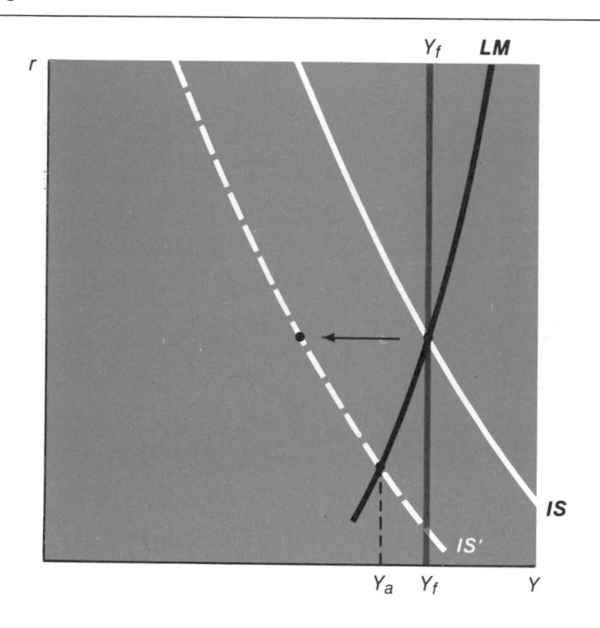

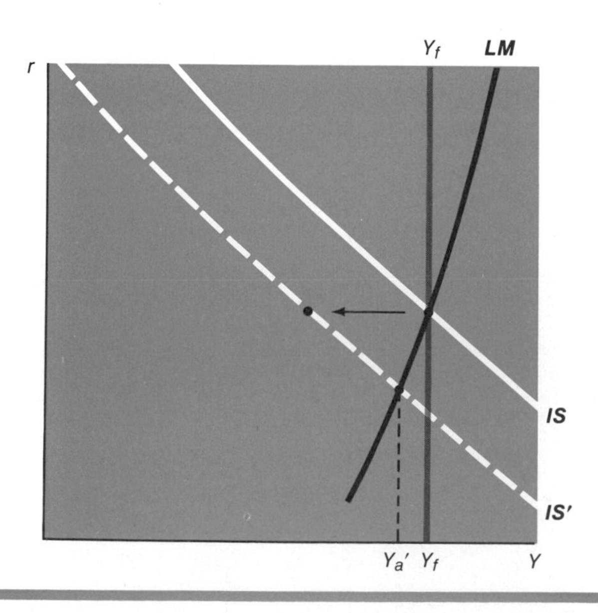

Figure 14–10 **Real Disturbances and Expenditures Interest Sensitivity: Change in Price Equilibrium**

Real disturbances provoke smaller changes in price equilibrium when the sensitivity of expenditures to the interest rate is large.

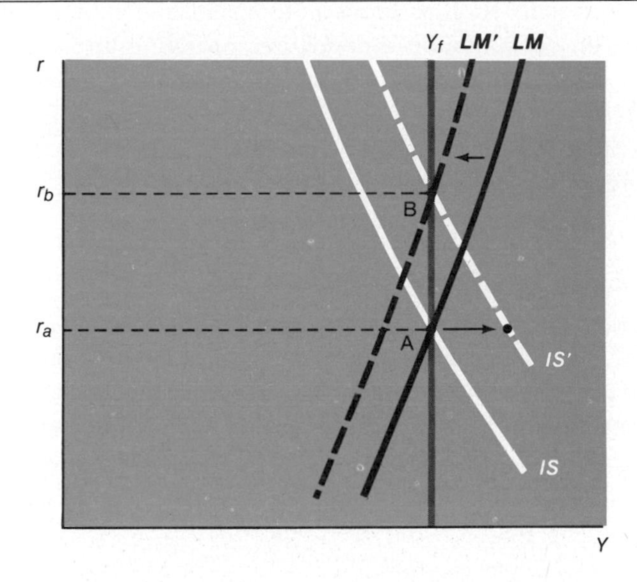

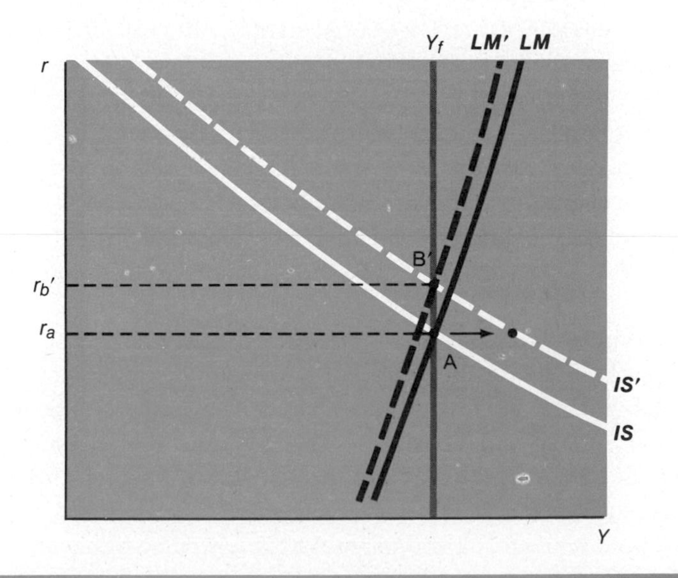

curve shifts to the right at full employment is smaller as the interest sensitivity of expenditures is greater. The required leftward shift in the *LM* curve, and therefore the increase in prices, is smaller in the lower portion of the figure, where the *IS* curve is flatter.

This factor is less important than it once was, if it remains important at all. Neo-Keynesians such as Franco Modigliani see substantial interest rate effects on consumption expenditures operating through both MEI effects on consumer durable goods purchases and interest-induced wealth effects on consumption expenditures at large. This book has recognized that position by including interest rate effects on consumption expenditures in the theoretical models of earlier chapters.

Price Flexibility as a Factor in Monetarism

Still another factor in the neo-Keynesian–monetarist split on the monetarist propositions is that some monetarists see a greater short-term downward flexibility in prices and money wages, and they see the effects of these price and money wage adjustments on expenditures and output as occurring more quickly. This does not affect the stability of velocity, but it does mean that price and money wage deflation tends to be substituted for reductions in output more promptly when the *IS* curve declines. If deflation is preferable to unemployment, stable money supply growth performs more acceptably.

Figure 14–11 illustrates the point. With the decline in the *IS* curve to *IS*′, output falls to Y_b if prices are constant at P_x. After a given period of time, neo-Keynesians might see prices declining to P_x' under pressure from excess labor and output supplies, in which case output would be restored to Y_c through the influence of the increased real money supply producing interest rate effects on aggregate expenditures. This is shown in the graph by the *LM* curve shift rightward to the position labeled m_0/P_x'. Monetarists, however, might see prices as declining by more within the same period, to P_x'', shifting the *LM* curve further to the right and restoring output further, to Y_d.

In the long term, prices and money wages will fall to the point where the *LM* curve has shifted far enough to the right to intersect *IS*′ at the full-employment line, as in Figure 14–12. This is the classical world of price and money-wage flexibility. The result is symmetrical with the demand-pull inflation case. Until the *LM* curve reaches this point, an excess supply of labor and output will exist, so that prices and money wages will continue to fall and will move the *LM* curve rightward. The long

Figure 14–11 **Price Flexibility as a Factor in Monetarism**

The decline in output caused by a real disturbance becomes smaller as the decline in prices becomes larger.

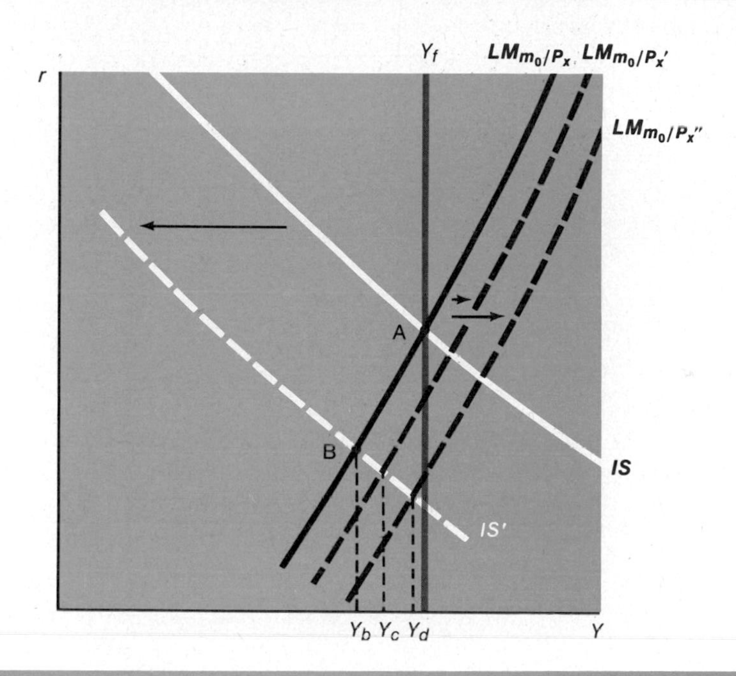

term may be a very long time, however, perhaps a decade or more—hence, the assumption of short-term price and money-wage inflexibility and the short-term result of unemployment.

Rational Expectations and Monetarism

Recently, some monetarists have begun to apply the *theory of rational expectations* to suggest that this long-term result—full employment restored—can be obtained much more quickly than Keynesians and neo-Keynesians have believed. As noted in Chapter 11, the theory of rational expectations holds that economic units fully utilize their forecasts of future macroeconomic activity in making their economic decisions. While this is a plausible enough idea, it is one which has been neglected in

Figure 14–12 **Rational Expectations and Monetarism**

The rational expectations view suggests that the price and money-wage adjustments required for restoring full employment in the face of a decline in aggregate demand may come fairly quickly.

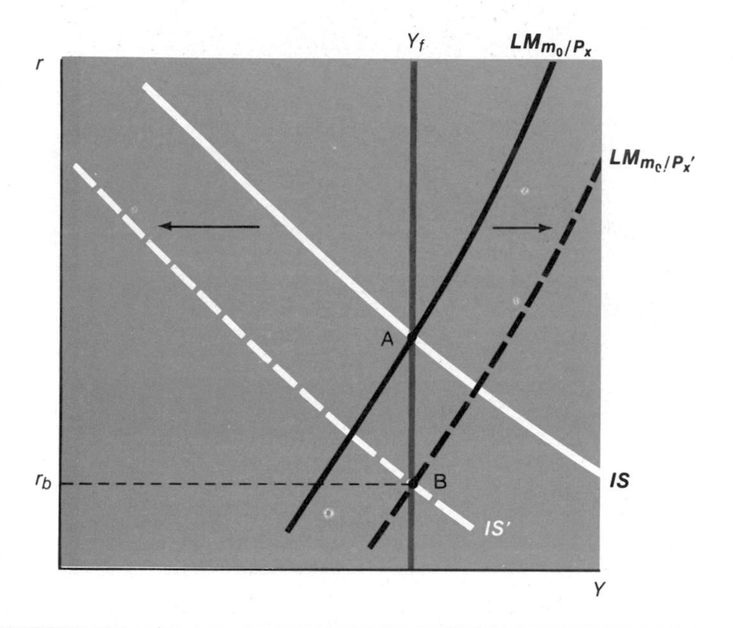

macroeconomics until recently, especially in the large statistical models which are used to predict and simulate economic activity.

According to the rational expectations view, price and money-wage reductions come very quickly when demand declines at full employment, because workers, by applying their forecast that in the eventual equilibrium prices will have declined proportionately to money wages, know that wage cuts will not reduce their real wages. The interest rate moves quickly to r_b in Figure 14–12, since lenders and borrowers, knowing that such a rate eventually will prevail, immediately agree to it. Interest-sensitive expenditures move quickly to the level appropriate to the full-employment expenditure, since the full-employment interest rate is promptly anticipated. Obviously, immediate return to full employment through this process is an exaggeration. Still, there is something in spelling out the effects of forecasts on economic decisions and incorporating the speedier adjustments they imply into the models.

Summation of Neo-Keynesian and Monetarist Differences

In sum, differences as to the interest and income sensitivity of money demand and expenditures and the extent of price and money-wage flexibility during recession appear to contribute something to the neo-Keynesian–monetarist split on the monetarist propositions. But theoretical and empirical research has greatly reduced the differences which once existed on these matters between Milton Friedman and prominent neo-Keynesians such as Franco Modigliani. Friedman and Modigliani agree that monetary influences are extremely important; and, in that agreement, both differ from the early Keynesians more than they differ from each other.

The difference between Friedman and Modigliani on the most interesting monetarist proposition, Friedman's recommendation of stable money supply growth for ordinary circumstances, may arise less from a difference as to how well stable money supply growth will work than from a difference as to the prospects for improving the stabilization result with discretionary policies. Friedman's point that, because of uncertainty and lags, discretionary monetary policies very likely destabilize the economy rather than stabilize it, is an important element in his position. He argues that, more often than not, the monetary authority moves too late and too much, since the ultimate impact of its action is uncertain and cannot be observed immediately. Modigliani has more confidence in the ability of the monetary authority to fine-tune the economy with discretionary monetary policies.

Moreover, there is the matter of the interpretation of the extraordinary circumstances in which Friedman would advise the use of discretionary monetary policies. A broad view of what qualifies as an extraordinary circumstance narrows the difference between Friedman and the neo-Keynesians. For example, many monetarists might agree that it would have been advisable to accelerate the growth of the money supply temporarily during 1973 and 1974 in the face of the cost-push inflationary pressures arising from the sharp increase in the price of imported oil. The danger to the full-employment goal was clear and present, and prices would have risen in any event, assuming that prices in other areas of the economy are somewhat inflexible downward in the short term. Accommodating the price increase with monetary expansion would have avoided the effect on real money balances and unemployment.

Finally, there is Friedman's admonition that, short of adopting a policy of stable money supply growth, adopting a policy of avoiding the wide swings in the rate of money supply growth of the past would constitute a major improvement in the conduct of monetary policies. Few neo-Keynesians would reject this point or debate the importance of Friedman's contribution in making it.

Summary

1. While economists agree on much of the subject matter of macroeconomics, differences have existed and continue to exist over such matters as the relative importance of real and money supply disturbances as sources of unemployment and inflation problems, the extent to which discretionary stabilization policies should be used, and whether monetary or fiscal policies should be emphasized.

2. It is possible to distinguish an early Keynesian position from a modern position on these matters and, within the latter, to contrast a neo-Keynesian position with the monetarist propositions associated with Milton Friedman.

3. Modern economists tend to agree that monetary influences are important and, as a result, differ more from the early Keynesians than from each other.

4. Neo-Keynesians retain the early Keynesian views that real disturbances are important sources of economic instability and that activist discretionary stabilization policies by government are desirable. They differ from the early Keynesians in that they regard money supply disturbances as important sources of economic instability and view discretionary monetary policies as useful elements in the government stabilization policy program.

5. The monetarist propositions are (1) that money supply disturbances have been the source of severe unemployment and inflation problems, (2) that discretionary stabilization policies of the sort recommended by Keynes and the neo-Keynesians should not be used in ordinary circumstances, and (3) that monetary policies should be emphasized when activist discretionary policies are used.

6. Differing views on the size of money demand and expenditure interest sensitivity are the important factors in the differences between early Keynesian and modern economists and may have some role in the neo-Keynesian–monetarist split within modern macroeconomics. Dif-

ferences over the extent of price and money-wage flexibility during recession also may contribute to the modern differences. However, an important element in the modern difference on the extent to which discretionary stabilization policies should be used appears to rest in a difference of opinion as to whether uncertainty and lags are such that fine tuning with discretionary policies is more likely to worsen or improve the stabilization result.

Concepts for Identification

negative interest rate case
monetarist propositions
classical money demand function
income velocity of money supply circulation
quantity theory of money model
money demand interest sensitivity
expenditure interest sensitivity
price and money-wage flexibility

Questions and Problems for Review

1. Explain why the *LM* curve becomes flatter as real money balances demanded become more sensitive to the interest rate.

2. Explain why the *IS* curve becomes flatter as expenditures become more sensitive to the interest rate.

3. Using the *IS-LM* model, show how the early Keynesian attitudes regarding the interest sensitivity of money demand and expenditures contributed to their positions on: (1) real as opposed to monetary disturbances as sources of severe recessions; (2) the need for discretionary policies by government; and (3) whether fiscal or monetary policies should be emphasized.

4. Illustrate graphically how the monetarist propositions hold completely when the *IS-LM* model is modified to include the classical money demand function (barring aggregate supply disturbances and the negative interest rate case).

5. Demonstrate graphically that the negative interest rate case renders monetary policies totally ineffective under both neo-Keynesian and monetarist assumptions, given the model as constituted in this chapter.

6. Explain the similarity between the negative interest rate case and the Keynesian liquidity trap case.

7. Define *income velocity of money supply circulation.* Using the *IS-LM* model, show that income velocity remains constant when the investment expenditure function fluctuates if the classical money demand function is employed. Show that, if real money balances demanded are inversely related to the interest rate, income velocity declines when the investment expenditure function declines and increases when the investment expenditure function increases.

8. Illustrate graphically that a high interest sensitivity of expenditures contributes to the monetarist propositions.

9. Demonstrate that the extent to which the crowding out effect limits the strength of fiscal ease applications depends on the interest sensitivity of money demand and expenditures.

10. Evaluate Milton Friedman's suggestion that the government confine itself to stabilizing the rate of money supply growth except under extraordinary circumstances. What determines whether this rule will provide an acceptable stabilization result? What is the basis for Friedman's view that attempts to fine-tune the economy with discretionary monetary policies may worsen rather than improve the stabilization result?

References

Friedman, Milton. "Comments on the Critics." *Journal of Political Economy* 80 (September–October 1972): 912–923.

———. "The Role of Monetary Policies." *American Economic Review* 58 (March 1968): 1–17.

Modigliani, Franco. "The Monetarist Controversy or, Should We Forsake Stabilization Policies." *American Economic Review* 67 (March 1977): 1–19.

Tobin, James. "Friedman's Theoretical Framework." *Journal of Political Economy* 80 (September–October 1972): 852–863.

Appendix to Chapter 14

Mathematical Demonstrations

Many of the points made in this chapter can be demonstrated more efficiently with techniques of rudimentary calculus than with graphs. This appendix presents such demonstrations, utilizing the algebraic *IS-LM* model presented in Chapter 10 for the purpose.

A major concern of this chapter has been how differences in the interest sensitivity of money demand and expenditures affect the impacts on price and output equilibriums made by real and monetary disturbances. Investigating this problem mathematically involves obtaining the total derivatives for prices and output with respect to the real and monetary parameters and observing the role of money demand and expenditure interest sensitivity in these derivatives.

As a first step, rewrite Equation 10–35, the *IS* curve, and Equation 10–36, the *LM* curve, as:

$$[1 - b(1 - t)]Y + (i + s)r = E_0 \tag{14–6}$$

and

$$kY - qr = m_0/P - L_0. \tag{14–7}$$

Recall from Equation 10–34 that:

$$E_0 = a_0 - bTx_0 + bTr_0 + I_0 + G_0. \qquad \text{14–8}$$

Recall also, from Equations 10–25, 10–26, and 10–28, that a larger $(i + s)$ reflects a more interest-sensitive aggregate expenditure in the model, while a larger q reflects a more interest-sensitive money demand.

The next step is to differentiate Equations 14–6 and 14–7 to obtain:

$$[1 - b(1 - t)]dY - (i + s)dr = dE_0 \qquad \text{14–9}$$

and

$$kdY - qdr = dm_0/P_x - \; m_0/P_x^2)dP - dL_0, \qquad \text{14–10}$$

the differentiated forms of the IS and LM curves, where P_x is the existing price level. Because of the clean-break assumption regarding responses of Y and P to fluctuations in demand relative to full-employment output, it is possible to let dP equal zero for fluctuations in aggregate demand within the unemployment range and to obtain by substitution (or by matrices and Cramer's Rule) from Equations 14–9 and 14–10 the statement:

$$dY = \frac{qdE_0 + (i + s)[dm_0/P_x - dL_0]}{k(i + s) + q[1 - b(1 - t)]}. \qquad \text{14–11}$$

Similarly, for situations in which aggregate demand increases at full-employment output, let dY equal zero and obtain by substitutions from Equations 14–9 and 14–10 the statement:

$$dP = \frac{dm_0/P - dL_0 + q[dE_0/(i + s)]}{m_0/P_x^2}. \qquad \text{14–12}$$

The appropriate total derivatives in Y and P can be obtained very efficiently from these statements as needed.

Earlier in the chapter, Figure 14–1 and the text explaining it illustrated the Keynesian point that real disturbances rather than monetary disturbances cause severe unemployment problems and that fiscal rather than monetary policies are the effectual devices for dealing with such problems. These views were said to result from the Keynesian ideas that money demand is quite sensitive to interest rate, even infinitely interest sensitive at low but positive interest rates, and that expenditures are relatively insensitive to interest rate. These points are demonstrated mathematically by obtaining the derivatives:

$$dY/dE_0 = \frac{1}{k(i + s)/q + 1 - b(1 - t)}, \tag{14–13}$$

$$dY/dm_0 = \frac{1}{(k + q/(i + s)[1 - b(1 - t)])P_x}, \tag{14–14}$$

and

$$dY/dL_0 = \frac{-1}{k + q/(i + s)[1 - b(1 - t)]}. \tag{14–15}$$

from Equations 14–11 and 14–12 and noting that dY/dE_0 is large, dY/dm_0 is small, and dY/dL_0 is small (ignoring sign) under the Keynesian view that q is large and $(i + s)$ is small. The derivative dY/dE_0 reflects both the severity of the recession with the real disturbances and the strength of fiscal policies in combating the recession. The derivative dY/dm_0 reflects both the weak impact on Y of a money supply reduction (barring expectational effects on E_0) and the weakness of monetary policies in eliminating recession. Indeed, in the liquidity trap situation, q is infinite, so that dY/dm_0 approaches zero, indicating that monetary policies are completely powerless to raise Y. The derivative dY/dL_0 reflects that money demand disturbances have very little effect on Y under Keynesian assumptions.

It is also true that a real disturbance which increases aggregate demand at full employment tends to cause severe inflationary problems under the Keynesian assumptions, to the extent that the inflation rate is related to the change in price equilibrium provoked. From Equation 14–12, the derivative:

$$dP/dE_0 = \frac{P_x^2}{m_0}\left(\frac{q}{(i + s)}\right) \tag{14–16}$$

indicates that the change in price equilibrium for a given increase in the expenditure constant is large, based on the Keynesian view that q is large and $(i + s)$ is small.

It does not follow that the Keynesian position on interest sensitivity implies moderate inflationary pressures with monetary disturbances, however. The derivatives:

$$dP/dm_0 = P_x/m_0 \qquad \text{14–17}$$

and

$$dP/dL_0 = -(P_x^2/m_0), \qquad \text{14–18}$$

from Equation 14–12, are independent of q and $(i + s)$, given the initial price level and money supply.

Figure 14–4 illustrated that the monetarist propositions hold completely, barring aggregate supply disturbances and the negative interest rate case, if the classical money demand function, presuming $q = 0$ and $dL_0 = 0$, is incorporated into the model. The mathematical demonstration of this point involves Equations 14–13 and 14–16, where dY/dE_0 and dP/dE_0 are zero when q is zero, ignoring any zero constraint on interest rate. Therefore, real disturbances, including fiscal policies, have no effect on price and output equilibriums. Since money demand disturbances do not occur, money supply disturbances are the only source of unemployment and inflation problems. A constant m_0 produces a perfect stabilization result in P and Y, and fiscal policies have no effect on P or Y. Of course, setting aggregate supply disturbances aside ignores growth in full-employment output over time.

The point that the monetarist propositions perform better as q is smaller and as $(i + s)$ is larger is supported by Equations 14–13 and 14–16. The derivatives dY/dE_0 and dP/dE_0 are smaller as q is smaller and as $(i + s)$ is larger.

Part 5

Classical Economics and Real Balances

15

Classical Economics: Origins of Monetarism

In the simple classical model, real money balances demanded bear a stable relationship to real income, and prices and money wages are flexible in both directions. The money demand function contributes to the monetarist propositions. Adding flexible prices and wages produces the propositions that full employment is assured and that money is neutral.

While monetarism is a criticism of Keynesian economics, it is more counterrevolution than revolution. The origins of monetarism are in the pre-Keynesian, or classical, economics Keynes challenged. There is some justification in terming monetarism modern classical economics.

Classical economics refers to the economics orthodoxy which took form during the early 1800s, primarily in the writings of David Ricardo (1772–1823), and prevailed until the 1930s, when the Keynesian break with tradition occurred.

Keynes used the term classical economists to refer to both the predecessors of Ricardo and to those who followed him and elaborated the basic Ricardian economics.[1] The most prominent predecessor presumably was Adam Smith (1723–1790), author of *Wealth of Nations,* which was published in 1776. Keynes lists James Mill (1773–1836) as a contemporary of Ricardo and as followers mentions specifically John Stuart Mill

[1] John Maynard Keynes, *The General Theory of Employment, Interest, and Money* (New York: Harcourt, Brace, 1936), p. 3.

(1806–1873), Alfred Marshall (1842–1924), Francis Edgeworth (1845–1926), and A. C. Pigou (1877–1959). Professor Pigou was still active when Keynes's book appeared in 1936, and, as Chapter 16 will show, made an important response to it. Many present-day economists would include the American economist Irving Fisher (1867–1947) as an important classical economist, although Fisher's views, in many respects, were too modern to be labeled classical.

While no classical economist presented a systematic macroeconomic model with explicit assumptions set out in a single place, Keynes and others constructed such a model from their writings, creating a composite classical "straw man" for criticism. This classical model differs from the model in earlier chapters of this book in the two important respects noted in Chapter 14.

First, it employs a money demand function in which the quantity of real money balances demanded bears a constant relation to real income. It is true, of course, that one can find in the writings of pre-Keynesian economists such as Irving Fisher passages which put forth factors such as interest rate and the expected change in prices as influences on money demand, but the money demand function which has become the frame of reference for classical opinion ordinarily neglects these factors entirely.

Second, the classical model treats prices and money wages as being flexible in both directions. Unlike the model in Chapters 10–14, the classical model presents prices and money wages as declining when excess supplies of output and labor are present.

Modern economists, particularly the monetarists, have returned partially to both of these classical assumptions, with the return to the first being much greater than the return to the second.

The classical money demand function arose from the classical emphasis on the transaction motive for holding money balances, including the neglect of the interest rate as a factor influencing the amount of transaction money balances held. It produces a feature in which spending disturbances do not affect price and output equilibriums, barring the case where a negative interest rate is required for a full-employment expenditure.

The result is an exaggerated monetarism, where the monetarist propositions discussed in Chapter 14 hold completely, barring aggregate supply disturbances and the negative interest rate case. Changes in money supply become the only source of inflation and unemployment problems, a constant money supply produces price and output stability, and fiscal policies have no effect on prices and output. This first feature of the classical model does not require price and money-wage flexibility, though, in the situation where money demand is somewhat sensitive to the interest rate, flexible prices and money wages may make the monetarist propositions more acceptable by substituting price and money-wage deflation for unemployment when aggregate demand declines.

In any event, since Chapter 14 has demonstrated these implications of the classical money demand function in detail, they will not be explored further here. This chapter will concentrate on two additional features of the classical model which obtain when the price and money-wage flexibility assumption is included. These classical propositions are (1) that a full-employment equilibrium is assured, barring the negative interest rate case, and (2) that the money supply is neutral in the sense that changes in it do not affect the equilibrium values of the real variables of the model. Chapter 14 did not explore these results, though it brushed on the first in noting that monetarists point to price and money-wage reductions as factors dampening the reduction in output which occurs when real disturbances diminish aggregate demand.

Why is it necessary to observe what happens when prices and money wages are flexible? The purpose is twofold. First, this observation clarifies the importance of the price and money-wage inflexibility assumption of the models examined heretofore. But its importance extends beyond that. The results obtained in a price and money-wage flexibility model are appropriate to situations in which prices and money wages can be treated as flexible. This means that they are appropriate, at least as a first approximation, for situations in which aggregate demand increases at full employment. Prices and money wages are flexible upward at full employment under Keynesian, neo-Keynesian, and monetarist assumptions alike. Moreover, price and money-wage flexibility is the appropriate assumption even for situations involving reductions in aggregate demand where attention focuses on the longer-term properties of the economy. Prices and money wages are reasonably flexible downward in the longer term. Recall that consumer prices declined by about 25 percent in the United States during 1929–1933 under the pressure of the severe aggregate demand deficiency of the Great Depression.

The Classical Model

Figure 15–1 presents the classical model that will be used here to demonstrate the two classical propositions. The *LM* curve, reflecting the classical money demand function, is a vertical line which does not shift except with changes in money supply or prices. The other source of *LM* curve

Figure 15–1 **The Classical Model**

When the classical model is in equilibrium, the *LM* curve is a vertical line at the full-employment output.

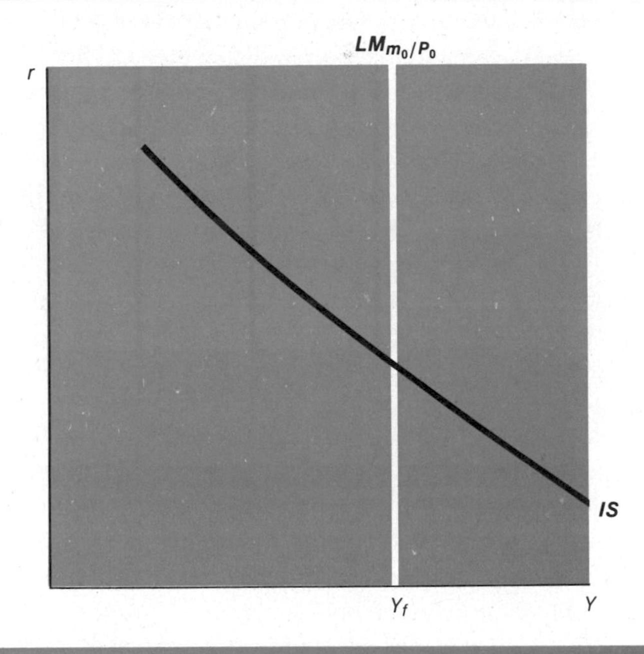

shifts—money demand disturbances—do not occur, since real money balances demanded are a constant function of real income. Prices and money wages are flexible.

Aside from these matters, the model is the same as that developed in Chapter 10. Investment expenditures vary inversely with interest rate. Consumption expenditures vary inversely with interest rate and directly with private disposable income. Government purchases are a constant. Taxes vary directly with income. Transfer payments are a constant. All of these relationships are defined in real terms. The benchmark for full employment is given by labor market equilibrium and the aggregate production function.

Full Employment Assured

Price and money-wage flexibility assures full employment, barring the situation where a negative interest rate is required for full-employment expenditure. This is true because, with that exception, price and money-wage adjustments will always move the *LM* curve to the point where it intersects the *IS* curve at full-employment output.

Consider Figure 15–2, for example, which illustrates the impact of money supply disturbances. Beginning with an initial full-employment and price stability situation at Point A, a reduction in money supply shifts the *LM* curve to the left, as to LM_2. With prices and money wages flexible, the excess supplies of labor and output which exist at Point B bid money wages and prices lower. Falling prices and money wages increase the real money supply, force interest rates lower, expand interest-sensitive expenditure, and support a higher output. This process continues until output is restored to Y_f, at which point the excess supplies of labor and output are eliminated. In terms of the figure, prices and money wages fall until the *LM* curve is again at LM_1.

An increase in money supply, coming in an initial full-employment situation, is no problem insofar as full-employment output is concerned. It shifts the *LM* curve for existing prices to the right, as from LM_1 to LM_3 in

Figure 15–2 **Money Supply Disturbances with Prices and Money Wages Flexible**

Money supply disturbances do not disturb the full-employment equilibrium of the classical model. The *LM* curve shifts in response to such disturbances, but price and money-wage adjustments return it to its original position.

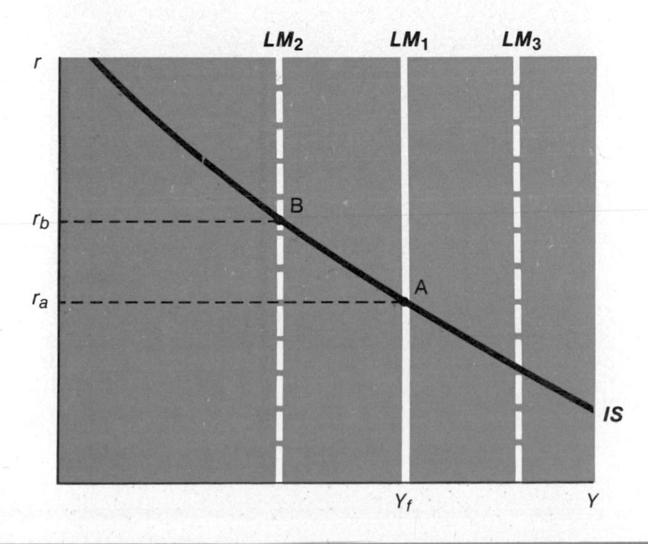

Figure 15–2. Prices and money wages merely rise in response to the resulting expenditure gap. Equilibrium is restored when the price increase has restored the *LM* curve to LM_1. Output remains at the full-employment level throughout the inflationary process.

Similarly, real disturbances do not result in less than full employment equilibriums in the classical model, except in the negative interest rate case. The vertical *LM* curve is sufficient to produce this result, but price and money-wage flexibility would produce full employment even if money demand were somewhat interest sensitive. Figure 14–13 of Chapter 14 illustrated this last point.

The exception, the negative interest rate case, is illustrated in Figure 15–3. Here, the real disturbance has moved the *IS* curve from IS_1 to IS_2,

Figure 15–3 **The Negative Interest Rate Case**

The negative interest rate case presents an exception to the classical proposition that price and money-wage flexibility assures a full-employment equilibrium.

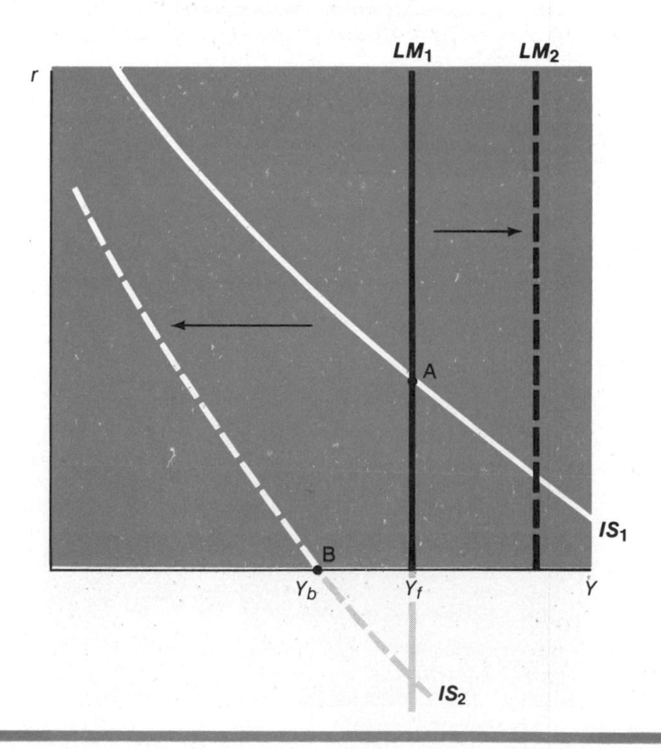

where it intersects the Y_f line at a negative interest rate. In this situation, price and money-wage reductions occur, moving the *LM* curve from LM_1 to LM_2, since aggregate demand at Point B falls short of full-employment output, but output will not expand beyond Y_b. Since no one will hold assets with a negative yield in preference to money, price-induced increases in the real money supply are simply held as money once the zero interest rate is reached. The demand for real money balances becomes infinite at a zero rate of interest, posing a liquidity trap block to the interest rate effect on expenditures, even if money demand is otherwise interest insensitive. Prices and money wages can fall to zero, but aggregate demand and output will not increase beyond Y_b.

Price and money-wage flexibility also insures full employment in the face of aggregate supply disturbances, excluding cost-push inflationary pressures such as wage-push inflation, which are ruled out because they involve wage and price inflexibility. An aggregate supply disturbance —such as a technological advance or an increase in the natural rate of unemployment—which simply shifts the full-employment output benchmark will be met by price and money-wage adjustments which move the *LM* curve to the new full-employment line.

Money Supply Neutrality

Money supply neutrality means that changes in money supply do not affect the equilibrium values of any of the real variables of the model. The real variables include Y, N, W/P, r, I, S, C, and m_0/P, where, as in earlier chapters, Y refers to real income and output, N to employment, W/P to the real wage, r to the rate of interest, I to real investment expenditures, S to real saving, C to real consumption expenditures, and m_0/P to the real money supply.

In demonstrating that full employment is assured, the preceding section showed that equilibrium Y is invariant at Y_f in the face of money supply disturbances. Since the labor market then remains in the same equilibrium as before, N and W/P are also unaffected.

Figure 15–4 illustrates the invariance of the rate of interest with respect to money supply disturbances. The key to this behavior is that changes in the money supply simply involve *LM* curve shifts in the model, which wash out in price and money-wage adjustments and leave the *IS* curve unchanged. In the figure, the *LM* curve moves from LM_1 to LM_2 with a reduction in m_0 or from LM_1 to LM_3 with an increase in m_0, expressing LM_2

Figure 15–4 **Money Supply Disturbances and the Rate of Interest**

Once and for all money supply changes leave the equilibrium interest rate unchanged in the classical model, since price and money-wage adjustments return the *LM* curve to its original position.

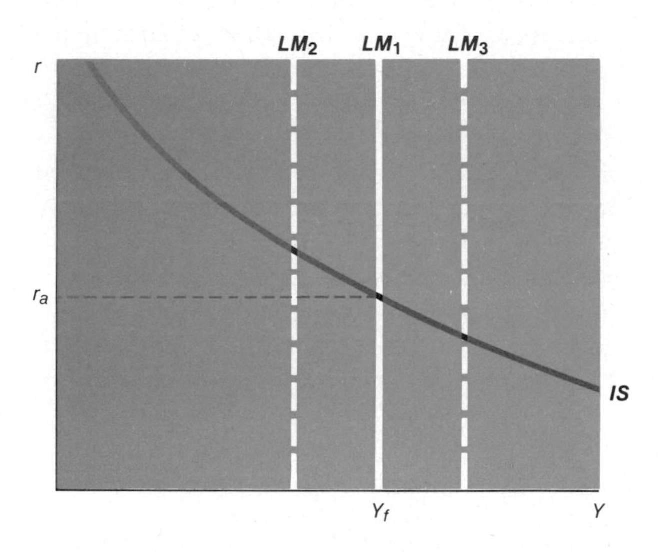

and LM_3 before prices change. The *LM* curve always returns to LM_1 through responses of prices and money wages to deflationary and inflationary gaps, however. Equilibrium r remains unchanged at r_a.

This invariance of the rate of interest in the face of money supply disturbances led the classical economists to describe it as a nonmonetary phenomenon. It did not vary with money supply disturbances and would not vary with money demand disturbances (though this last point is moot, since, given the classical money demand function, money demand disturbances do not occur). The equilibrium rate of interest responded only to nonmonetary disturbances. It would vary with shifts in the saving and investment expenditure functions, since these shifts would move the *IS* curve and cause it to intersect the full-employment line at a different rate of interest. Also, the equilibrium interest rate would vary with aggregate supply disturbances such as shifts in the supply of labor and technological advances, since these would move the full-employment line and cause it to intersect the *IS* curve at new points.

Keynes, by contrast, offered a monetary theory of the rate of interest in which the equilibrium interest rate depends also on the money supply and the money demand function. Note, however, that Keynes's monetary theory of the rate of interest depends on his assumption that prices and money wages are rigid rather than on his assumption that money demand is a function of interest rate and is otherwise volatile.

For example, in the top portion of Figure 15–5, where prices and money wages are considered flexible, the interest rate always returns to r_a following a monetary disturbance even though the *LM* curve slopes positively, reflecting an interest-sensitive money demand. But in the lower portion of the figure, where prices and money wages are assumed to be held rigidly downward, a reduction in money supply shifting the *LM* curve from LM_1 to LM_2 raises the equilibrium interest rate from r_a to r_b even though money demand is not interest sensitive. Similarly, with prices and money wages inflexible upward until full employment is reached, an increase in money supply or a decrease in the money demand function coming in the initial unemployment situation at Point B in the lower portion of Figure 15–5 shifts the *LM* curve to the right and reduces the equilibrium interest rate. Monetary disturbances affect the equilibrium rate of interest when prices and money wages do not change.

Since money supply is neutral with respect to *Y* and *r* in the classical model, it also is neutral with respect to *I*, *S*, and *C*, since *I*, *S*, and *C* depend only on *Y* and *r* in the model. The same is true for real money balances, m_0/P, the remaining real variable. If a disturbance in m_0 leaves *Y* unchanged, it must also leave *Md* unchanged, because *Md* depends only on *Y* in the classical model. Since m_0/P must equal *Md* in equilibrium, it also must be unchanged.

A more familiar way to put this last point is that changes in money supply provoke proportionate changes in prices in the classical model.[2] This must be true if changes in m_0 leave m_0/P unchanged. For example, if m_0 is initially 200 and *P* is initially 1.0, a 10 percent increase in m_0 to 220 must be accompanied by a 10 percent increase in *P* to 1.1 if m_0/P is to remain unchanged. That is, $200/1.0 = 220/1.1 = 200$. Since, as pointed out earlier, changes in m_0 leave W/P unchanged, it is possible to further note that changes in money supply provoke proportionate changes in both prices and money wages in the classical model.

To the classical economists, money was but a lubricant which made the economic machine work. It affected nothing real in the economy.

---

[2] The mathematical expression of this relationship is Equation 14–17 of the appendix to Chapter 14, which reduces to $dP/P_x = dm_0/m_0$ (whether or not q equals zero).

Figure 15–5 **Keynes's Monetary Theory of Interest**

Keynes's assumption that money wages are inflexible downward produced a monetary theory of the rate of interest. If money wages are inflexible downward, monetary disturbances affect the equilibrium interest rate, except when they expand aggregate demand in an initial full-employment equilibrium.

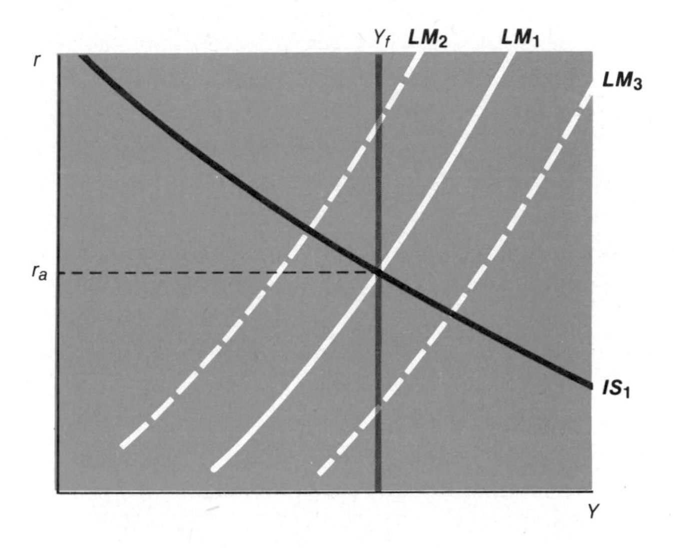

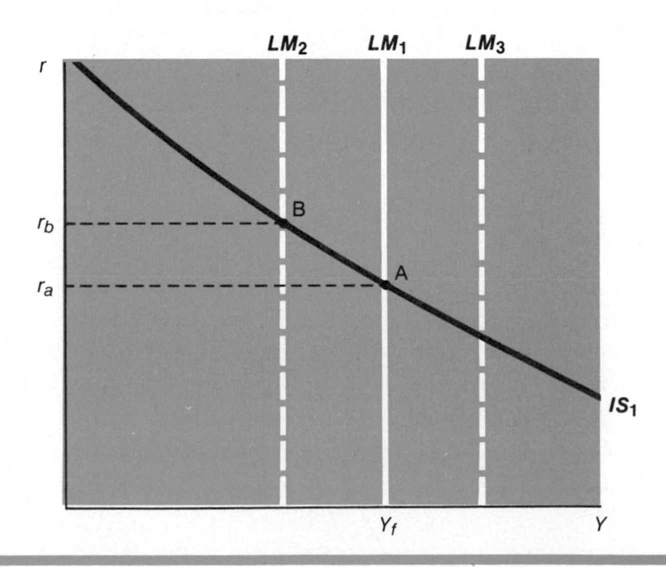

Changes in the money supply were offset by proportionate changes in prices and money wages and left the real variables of the economy unchanged.

Dynamic Money Supply Disturbances and Money Neutrality

To this point, only once and for all changes in the money supply have been dealt with in demonstrating money supply neutrality. In Chapter 11, Figure 11–15 showed that a dynamic money supply disturbance involving an increase in the rate at which the money supply is being increased per period in a full-employment situation will affect the steady-state equilibrium values for market interest rate and real money balances, raising the former and reducing the latter. Does this mean that money is not neutral in the classical model for cases involving dynamic money supply disturbances? Is money supply neutrality restricted to once and for all money supply changes?

The answer to these questions is no, so far as the simple classical model used here is concerned. While it is true that the expected increase or decrease in prices such a disturbance provokes will raise or lower the market rate of interest by the expected change in prices, it leaves the real rate of interest unaffected in the steady-state equilibriums. The real interest rate variable is unaffected. Moreover, while real money balances were affected by the dynamic money supply disturbance in the Chapter 11 illustration, they are not affected in the simple classical model because expected inflation does not affect the demand for real money balances. Real money balances demanded bear a constant relation to real income. Dynamic money supply disturbances leave the steady-state equilibrium value of real money balances unchanged in the simple classical model.

If the classical model is to be used to examine the long-term equilibrium properties of the economy, it is best to relax the classical money demand function assumption and permit expected changes in prices to influence the demand for real money balances, as in Chapter 11. As expressed there, shifts in the expected change in prices, by affecting market interest rates, influence the demand for real money balances, since interest yields on money are inflexible relative to the general structure of interest rates. With this modification, dynamic money supply disturbances affect equilibrium real money balances, though the once and for all variety still leave them unchanged.

Price and Money-Wage Flexibility and Macroeconomic Policy

What messages does the price and money-wage flexibility aspect of the classical model have for macroeconomic policy? Insofar as the assurance of full employment is concerned, it does seem clear that deflation does not act promptly enough in the actual world to provide satisfactory employment results in the face of severe real disturbances or aggregate supply disturbances which increase full-employment output. Still, it is useful to recognize that price and money-wage reductions do occur during extended recessions and do work to restore employment and output. Moreover, while price and money-wage flexibility does not assure full employment in the short term in the actual world, the long term is another matter. The next chapter demonstrates that in a slightly modified flexible price model, even the barrier posed by the negative interest rate case of Figure 15–3 disappears in the long term.

The neutrality of money also is a useful concept. This proposition is the source of the view, taken very seriously by most economists, that monetary policies cannot depress the unemployment rate and the real rate of interest, which are real variables, below their natural levels for extended periods of time. The natural rate of unemployment, as defined earlier, is the rate consistent with equilibrium in the labor market when price and money-wage inflation is being anticipated correctly, as occurs beyond the short term. The *natural real rate of interest* is the real rate of interest consistent with full-employment equilibrium and correctly anticipated inflation. To attempt to hold either the unemployment rate or the real interest rate permanently below these levels with monetary policies is inflationary and will be unsuccessful beyond the short term. Indeed, in the very long term, when prices and money wages are flexible downward as well as upward, monetary policies can neither raise nor lower the unemployment and real interest rates from their natural levels. These are applications of the neutral money concept.

Summary

1. The classical model differs from the model used in earlier chapters in two important respects. These are (1) that real money balances demanded bear a constant relation to real income, and (2) that prices and money wages are treated as flexible in both directions.

2. The first of these differences produces a situation where the

monetarist propositions hold completely, barring aggregate supply disturbances and the negative interest rate case.

3. Adding price and money-wage flexibility produces two additional features. First, full employment is assured, barring the negative interest rate case. Second, the money supply is neutral in the sense that disturbances involving it do not affect any of the real variables of the economy. This extends even to dynamic money supply disturbances, as long as the simple classical money demand function is retalned.

4. The feature of the classical model which states that full employment is assured, barring the negative interest rate case, has an important policy implication in that it points out that price and money-wage adjustments do help to restore output when demand is weak.

5. The neutrality of money concept has an important policy implication in that it is the forerunner of the modern view that monetary policies cannot permanently depress the unemployment rate and the real rate of interest below their natural levels. To attempt to use them for this purpose is merely to produce inflation in the long term.

Concepts for Identification

classical economists
classical model
classical propositions
neutral money
monetary theory of interest
real theory of interest
dynamic money supply disturbance
natural real rate of interest

Questions and Problems for Review

1. Present an *IS-LM* representation of the classical model in equilibrium.

2. Using the *IS-LM* representations of the classical model, demonstrate the proposition that price and money-wage flexibility assures a full-employment equilibrium, barring the negative interest rate case. Demonstrate the proposition for real, monetary, and aggregate supply disturbances, except supply disturbances such as wage-push inflation which conflict with the price and money-wage flexibility assumption. Show the negative interest rate case exception and explain it.

3. Use the *IS-LM* representation of the classical model to demonstrate the neutral money proposition.

4. Money is not neutral with respect to dynamic money supply disturbances in a modified classical model in which the demand for real money balances is sensitive to the expected change in prices. Explain.

5. Explain the classical view that the *real* rate of interest is a real phenomenon affected by real disturbances but not by monetary (including money demand) disturbances.

6. The Keynesian proposition that the real rate of interest is affected by monetary disturbances (and that it is therefore partially a monetary phenomenon) arises from the assumption that money wages are rigid rather than from the assumption that money demand is sensitive to the interest rate. Explain.

7. A once and for all change in the money supply provokes a proportionate change in prices in the classical model. Explain why this must be true.

8. Verify the entries in the table listed below, using *IS* and *LM* curves and the assumptions of the classical model. The changes are changes in equilibrium values resulting from the disturbances listed in the left-hand column. The disturbances are of the once and for all variety. A plus is an increase, a minus a decrease, and a zero no change.

Disturbance	ΔY	ΔP	Δr	ΔI
Increase in the consumption function	0	0	+	−
Decrease in the money supply	0	−	0	0
Increase in the tax function	0	0	−	+
Increase in the private saving function	0	0	−	+
Increase in the money supply	0	+	0	0
Increase in the investment function	0	0	+	+

References

Ackley, Gardner. *Macroeconomics: Theory and Policy.* New York: Macmillan, 1978, chaps. 4 and 5.

Fisher, Irving. *The Purchasing Power of Money.* 2d ed. New York: Macmillan, 1926.

———. *The Theory of Interest.* New York: Macmillan, 1930.

Friedman, Milton. "The Role of Monetary Policies." *American Economic Review* 58 (March 1968): 1–17.

Keynes, John Maynard. *The General Theory of Employment, Interest, and Money.* New York: Harcourt, Brace, 1936, chaps. 1, 2, 13, and 14.

Wicksell, K. *Money.* Lectures on Political Economy. Translated by E. Classen. Vol. 2. New York: Macmillan, 1934–1935.

16

Consumption Expenditures, Money Balances, and Government Debt

Making consumption expenditures directly sensitive to real money balances and real government debt removes the Keynesian liquidity trap and the negative full-employment interest rate exceptions to the classical proposition that price and money-wage flexibility assures full employment. It has implications for the neutral money proposition and the monetarist propositions as well.

As indicated earlier, consumption expenditures sometimes are regarded as depending not just on real income and interest rate but also on real money balances and real government debt. The models in Chapters 4 through 14 neglected these relationships in order to keep the analysis simple. For the most part, realism did not suffer. Economists have regarded the relationships as matters of considerable theoretical interest, and perhaps of empirical importance for long-term analysis, but have tended to omit them from short-term analyses on the grounds that they are weak. Still, there has been an increase in interest in even the short-term implications of the effects during the past decade or so, particularly in relation to their role in fiscal policy strength. This chapter will consider them in some detail.

The influences in question are often termed Pigou effects, after A. C. Pigou, the prominent English classical economist, whose career was roughly coterminous with that of Keynes. The rationale for them is that if the real money supply or real government debt increases—either because prices decline or because the nominal supplies of money or government debt increase—consumers feel wealthier and as a result increase their consumption expenditures. Real wealth having increased, goals for wealth accumulation can be met with less saving than before, so that consumption expenditures increase.

Opinion varies somewhat as to whether Pigou effects should involve real government debt as well as real money balances and whether both items should be involved in their entirety. In general, since the issue is the determination of aggregate consumption expenditures, only the elements of these measures which constitute net wealth for the community as a whole should be involved. Some economists include only cash plus member bank reserves in Pigou effects, arguing that checkable deposits, commercial bank savings deposits, and government interest-bearing debt should be excluded because they involve cancelling effects as debts of financial institutions and taxpayers. Others include government debt, or a portion of it, on the grounds that taxpayers are insensitive, or relatively insensitive, to government debt as personal debt. Still others include demand deposits, with or without real government debt, arguing that most demand deposits do not pay interest and hence are not effective liabilities of bankers. Here, Pigou effects involving real money balances or components of real money balances will be referred to as *simple Pigou effects.* If real government debt is included, they will be termed *broader Pigou effects.*

Pigou Effects and the Classical Proposition That Full Employment Is Assured

The role of real money balances and real government debt in the consumption function entered the literature in responses by A. C. Pigou and G. Haberler to the Keynesian attack on the classical proposition that price and wage flexibility assures a full-employment equilibrium for the economy.[1] Recall the process by which this operated in the simple classical model of Chapter 15. If aggregate demand were to decline in an initial situation of full employment, prices and money wages would fall under

---

[1] Gottfried Haberler, *Prosperity and Depression,* 3rd ed. (Geneva, Switzerland: League of Nations, 1941), pp. 388–389; A. C. Pigou, "The Classical Stationary State," *Economic Journal* 53 (December 1943): 349.

pressure from excess supplies of labor and output, assuming that prices and money wages were flexible downward. With prices declining, the real money supply would increase, the interest rate would decline, and interest-sensitive expenditures would increase. Ultimately, expenditures again would support full-employment output, and full employment would be restored.

The Keynesians did not believe prices and money wages were flexible enough downward in the short term to be relied upon to produce full employment in such a situation, but they saw the process as faulty in any event. What if the rate of interest required for full-employment demand is below the floor on interest posed by the liquidity trap? The same liquidity trap which blocks the functioning of monetary policies during serious recessions can block the effects of declining prices and money wages, since both work through impacts of increases in real money balances on the interest rate and interest-sensitive expenditures. Or what if even a zero interest rate is not sufficient to provide a full-employment level of demand? This is the negative interest rate case exception to the classical full-employment result noted in Chapter 15. Even if a liquidity trap does not exist at a positive rate of interest, one certainly exists at a zero interest rate. Neglecting storage costs for safe holding of money, the demand for money must become completely elastic when interest reaches zero. No one would hold a security promising to repay a smaller number of nominal dollars than it costs in preference to money, since money maintains its nominal value.

Figure 16–1 presents these two exceptions to the classical full-employment result. At the top is the Keynesian liquidity trap case, where a rate of interest below the liquidity trap is required for full-employment expenditure and output. At the bottom is the negative interest rate case of Figure 15–3, Chapter 15. The two cases actually are the same in the sense that they impose a floor on interest rates which is above the interest rate required for full-employment output. Without Pigou effects, prices and money wages can fall to zero without restoring full employment. Real money balances increase, the *LM* curve shifts to the right (as from LM_1 to LM_2 and LM_3), but the *LM* curve will never intersect the *IS* curve at full-employment output. Price and money-wage flexibility thus does not assure full employment in all situations.

Haberler and Pigou argued that these representations are faulty in that they neglect the direct effects of price-induced increases in real money balances on consumption expenditures. If consumption expenditures increase when real money balances increase, declining prices and money wages will stimulate additional expenditures even if reductions in interest

Figure 16–1 **The Interest Rate Floor Cases**

The Keynesian liquidity trap case and the negative interest rate case are exceptions to the classical proposition that price and money-wage flexibility assures full employment.

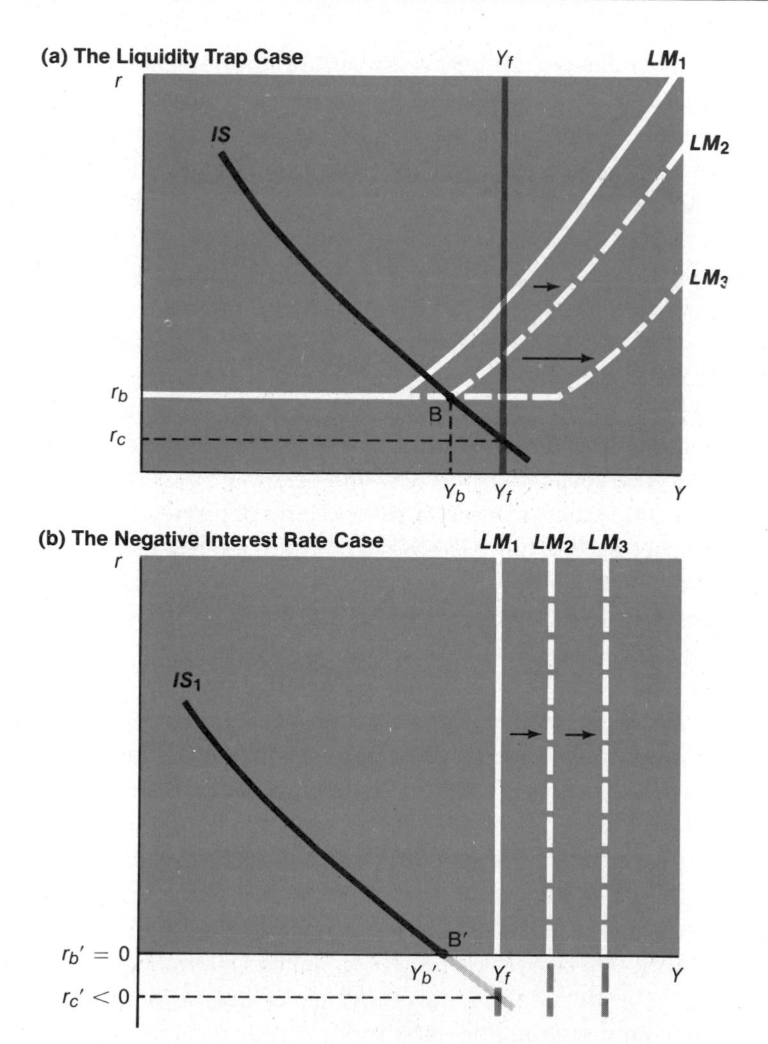

rates are blocked. That is, if the consumption expenditure function of the classical model of Chapter 5 is modified from:

$$C = f(Yd, r) \qquad \text{16–1}$$

to:

$$C = f(Yd, r, m_0/P), \qquad \text{16–2}$$

where C varies directly with m_0/P, then flexibility in prices and money wages does assure full employment.[2] The classical result that price and money-wage flexibility assures full employment is restored. This is an important point because it means that the Keynesian equilibrium involving shortfall unemployment must rest on price and money-wage adjustments which are absent, slow working, or weak rather than on a liquidity trap.

Figure 16–2 illustrates how the Pigou effect extracts the model from the liquidity trap and negative interest rate situations of Figure 16–1. Placing real money balances into the consumption expenditure function, as in Equation 16–2, makes the *IS* curve as well as the *LM* curve shift with changes in real money balances. As prices decline and real money balances increase, households feel wealthier, consumption expenditures increase, and the *IS* curves, which present the total expenditures forthcoming at each rate of interest, shift to the right. Beginning with the initial unemployment situations at Points B and B′, respectively, with *IS* and *LM* curves relating to P_x, price reductions shift both the *IS* and the *LM* curves to the right. Full employment is restored at price level P_x', the price level at which the *IS* and *LM* curves intersect at the full-employment line. Price and money-wage reductions have restored full employment.

While Equation 16–2 incorporates only the simple Pigou effect, the inclusion of real government debt in the consumption function only reinforces these results. The *IS* curve then shifts further to the right for a given decline in prices. Real government debt and real money balances both increase as prices decline and both increases stimulate consumption expenditures. The price decline required for restoring full employment is smaller with the broader Pigou effect.

[2] Haberler and Pigou spoke of real money balances in their presentations of the Pigou effect. Don Patinkin has suggested that real government debt, or a portion of it, should be included. See Don Patinkin, "Price Flexibility and Full Employment," *American Economic Review* 38 (September 1948): 543–564; and Don Patinkin, *Money, Interest, and Prices*, 2d ed. (New York: Harper & Row, 1965), pp. 288–294.

Figure 16–2 **The Pigou Effect and Full Employment Assured**

Pigou effects remove the Keynesian liquidity trap case and the negative interest rate case exceptions to the classical proposition that price and money-wage flexibility assures full employment.

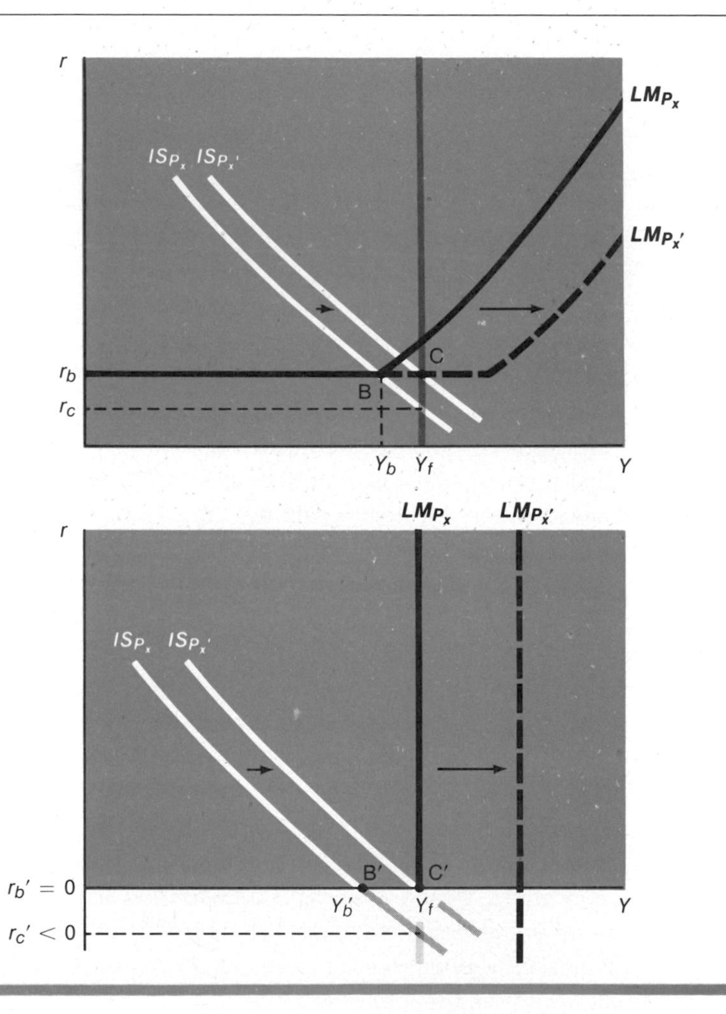

Pigou Effects and the Classical Proposition of Neutral Money

The Pigou effect, then, restores the classical result that price and money-wage flexibility assures full employment in the face of the special cases involving interest rate floors. What does it imply for the neutrality of money? Is money supply still neutral in the sense that changes in it do not disturb the real variables of the economy when the Pigou effect is added to the classical model?

The answer to these questions is that the money supply still is neutral if the Pigou effect involves only real money balances or real member bank reserves plus real cash in the consumption expenditure equation, provided that the classical demand function for money is retained.[3] If the Pigou effect involves real government bonds as well, the money supply no longer is neutral.

Figure 16–3 illustrates these results. In the upper portion, the Pigou effect involves only real money balances. The consumption expenditure function is as in Equation 16–2. When the money supply is increased from m_0 to m_0', both the *IS* and *LM* curves shift to the right and prices rise. In the new equilibrium, however, prices will have increased in proportion to the increase in the money supply, real money balances will be unchanged, the *IS* and *LM* curves will be in the same positions as before, and all the real variables will be unchanged.[4]

The lower portion of the figure illustrates the situation when the Pigou effect involves both real money balances and real government debt. The consumption expenditure equation is:

$$C = f(Yd, r, m_0/P, Bg/rP), \qquad 16\text{–}3$$

where C varies directly with (Bg/rP), the real value of the government debt—assuming, for simplicity, that all government debt is in bonds, that the number of government bonds is Bg, and that each pays one dollar per

[3] Strictly speaking, the ratio of member bank reserves to M-1+ deposits must remain constant in order for money to remain neutral when the Pigou effect involves member bank reserves plus cash.

[4] This is easy to see when the *LM* curve is vertical, since it must end up in its original position to close the expenditure gap. For the *LM* curve to be in its original position, real money balances must be unchanged, so that the *IS* curve also must be in its original position. In fact, the results hold for the simple Pigou effect even if money demand is sensitive to interest rate. This can be verified by replacing Equation 10–16 of Chapter 10 with the new consumption expenditure equation:

$$C = a_0 + bYd - sr + em_0/P,$$

which differs by incorporating em_0/P to represent the Pigou effect. The new differentiated *IS* curve, when combined with Equation 14–10, the unchanged differentiated *LM* curve from the appendix to Chapter 14, produces the solutions $dr = 0$ and $dP/P_x = dm_0/m_0$ when dY, dL_0 and dE_0 are set to zero. The equilibrium values for real money balances and the interest rate (and the other real variables) are unaffected by a change in m_0 whether or not q equals zero.

Figure 16–3 **Money Supply Disturbances with Pigou Effects**

The real variables of the economy remain unchanged in the face of once and for all money supply disturbances if only the simple Pigou effect is added to the classical model. However, that is not the case when the broader Pigou effect is added.

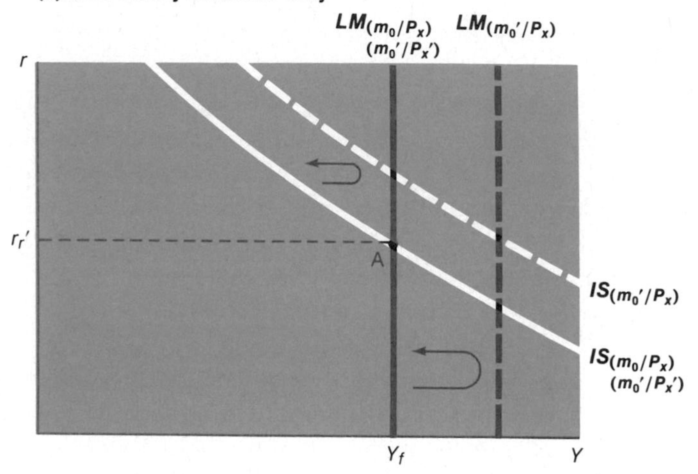

(b) Real Money Balances and Real Government Debt

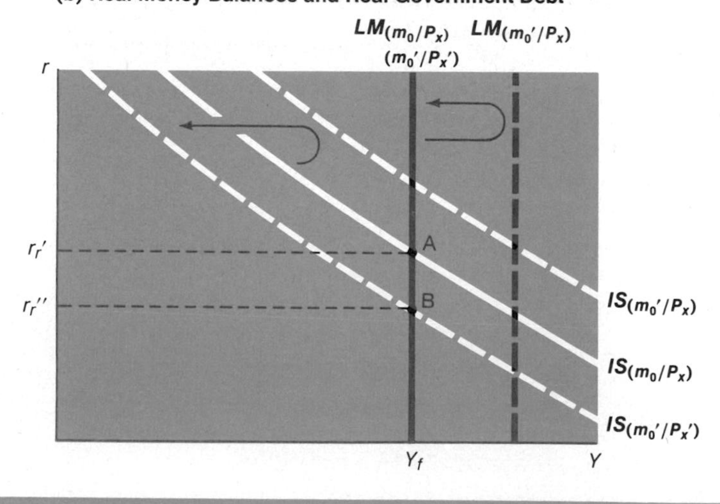

year in perpetuity to the holder. Each government bond, therefore, is worth \$1/r on the market or \$1/rP in real terms, so that the aggregate real value of government bonds is (Bg/rP).

The increase in money supply from m_0 to m_0' again shifts both the *IS* curve and the *LM* curve to the right, opening up an expenditure gap. Prices again rise proportionately to the increase in m_0, returning the *LM* curve to its original position and closing the expenditure gap. The *IS* curve cannot be in the same position as before in the new equilibrium, however, since, while real money balances are the same, real government bonds are lower, dampening consumption expenditures and placing the *IS* curve to the left of its original position. For the same interest rate, total expenditures must be lower. The number of government bonds is unchanged at *Bg,* but *P* has risen. With the *IS* curve to the left of its original position, the new equilibrium must be at a point such as Point B, involving a lower rate of interest, higher real investment expenditures, higher real saving, and lower real consumption expenditures. The money supply therefore is not neutral, since real variables are affected.[5]

If the increase in the money supply is accompanied by an equal percent increase in the the number of government bonds outstanding, none of the real variables of the economy will be affected. In this case, the proportionate increase in prices required for returning the *LM* curve to its initial position also leaves the *IS* curve in its initial position, since real government bonds as well as real money balances are unchanged. The same real consumption expenditures as before are forthcoming at each r and Y. This is not neutral money, since bonds also are being varied.

In any event, the money supply ordinarily is increased in a way that leaves the *IS* curve even farther to the left of its initial position in equilibrium. Usually, in the United States, the money supply is increased by open-market operations involving the creation of member bank reserves in exchange for government securities. The number of government securities outstanding diminishes as the money supply increases. Therefore, the real value of government securities diminishes not only because prices have increased but also because the number of government bonds is smaller. The *IS* curve is pushed even farther to the left in the new equilibrium. The interest rate falls by more and prices increase by less.

[5] If real money balances demanded are sensitive to interest rate, equilibrium real money balances also will be affected. They will be higher, since the interest rate is lower—which is to say, prices will increase less than in proportion to the money supply.

Dynamic Money Supply Disturbances and Money Neutrality

Dynamic money supply disturbances, like once and for all changes in the money supply, do not disturb the neutrality of money concept, even with simple Pigou effects included, as long as the classical demand function for money is retained. What if the classical money demand function is relaxed and real money balances demanded are made an inverse function of the expected change in prices? Chapter 15 explained that this situation disturbs neutral money for dynamic money supply changes, even without Pigou effects, since variations in the expected change in prices will, in this case, affect the demand for real money balances and hence the equilibrium value for real money balances. Even a simple Pigou effect produces a further qualification to neutral money for dynamic money supply disturbances, because this change in equilibrium real money balances will influence real consumption expenditures and saving and thereby the *IS* curve and the steady-state equilibrium values for real interest rate, real saving, real consumption expenditures, and real investment expenditures. For example, if the rate of change in m_0 per period is raised from zero to 10 percent and maintained at the new level, an expected inflation rate of 10 percent will be provoked, and equilibrium real money balances will decline. Real consumption expenditures then will be dampened via the simple Pigou effect, the steady-state equilibrium values for the real interest rate and real consumption expenditures will decline, and the steady-state equilibriums for real saving and real investment expenditures will increase.

The dynamics of the disturbance can be described exactly as in Figure 11–15 of Chapter 11 and its accompanying discussion, except that now, with the simple Pigou effect present, the decline in steady-state equilibrium real money balances in the lower portion of Figure 11–15 leaves both the real and market rates of interest lower in the new steady-state equilibrium than those represented in the middle portion of the figure. The market rate of interest still ends up higher than the real rate of interest by the actual and expected inflation rates of 10 percent, but the real rate of interest is below its predisturbance value because of the simple Pigou effect. The impact of the disturbance is represented in Figure 16–4.

The Pigou Effect and the Monetarist Propositions

Inquiring into the implications of the Pigou effect for the monetarist propositions necessitates a return to the world described in Chapter 14, where real money balances demanded are sensitive to the real rate of interest, as well as to the expected change in prices, and where price and

Figure 16–4 **A Dynamic Money Supply Disturbance with a Pigou Effect and a Money Demand Sensitive to the Expected Change in Prices**

When the classical model is modified to allow the expected change in prices to influence real money balances demanded, adding even a simple Pigou effect has the result that dynamic money supply disturbances affect the steady-state equilibrium value for the real rate of interest.

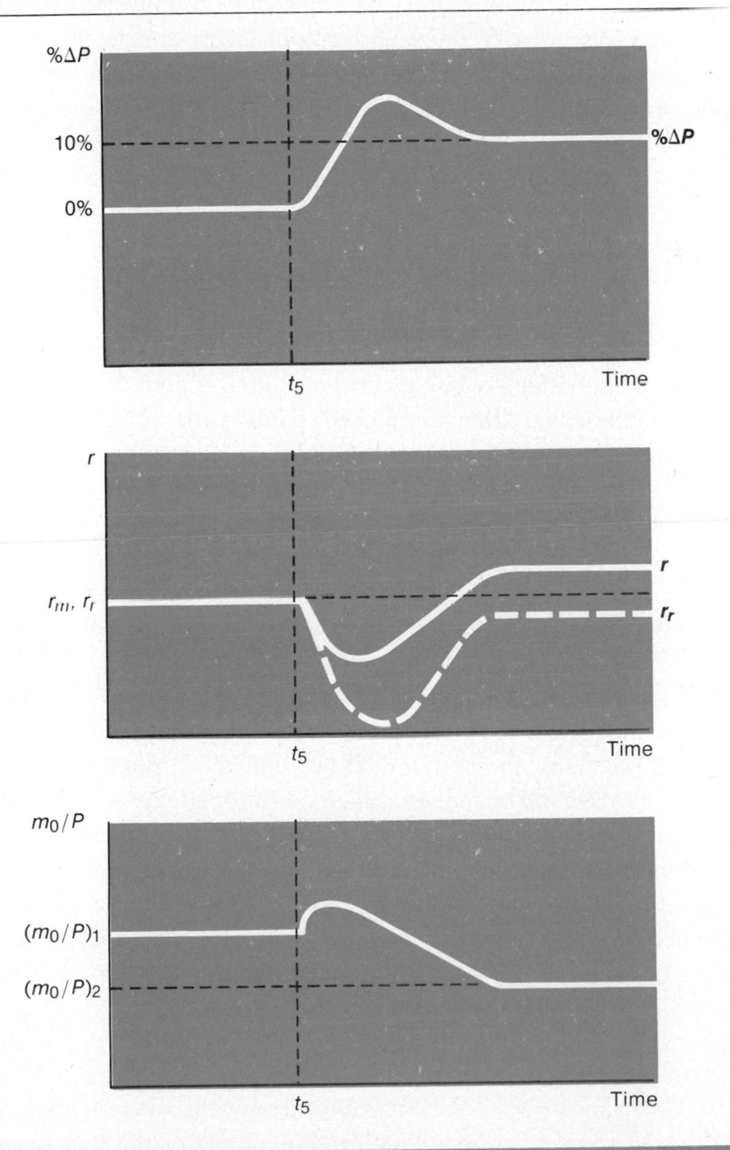

money-wage adjustments restore output and employment rather slowly when aggregate demand is deficient. Recall that the monetarist propositions involve Milton Friedman's view that money supply disturbances are the principal source of severe unemployment and inflation problems and his recommendation that governments should confine themselves to stabilizing money supply growth, except in extraordinary circumstances, when monetary rather than fiscal policies should be used.

Pigou effects contribute to the view that money supply disturbances are the principal disrupter of price and output levels and to the view that money supply growth should be stabilized, since these effects diminish the price and output impacts of real disturbances. That is, they add built-in stability to the economy in the face of real disturbances. This characteristic is demonstrated in the following section. However, the subsequent section shows that the implications of Pigou effects for the monetary versus fiscal policy issue are not so clear.

Pigou Effects and Real Disturbances

Insofar as built-in stability is concerned, Pigou effects reduce both the inflation which occurs when the *IS* curve shifts to the right at full employment and the unemployment and deflation which occur when it shifts to the left. For example, when the investment function, the consumption function, or government purchases increase at full employment, an expenditure gap opens up and prices rise. With no Pigou effect present, the price rise closes the expenditure gap by reducing real money balances, forcing interest rates higher and diminishing interest-sensitive expenditures.

The Pigou effect supplements these ordinary interest rate effects in two ways. First, the increase in prices reduces real government debt as well as real money balances, and both reductions directly dampen consumption expenditures. Second, interest-induced wealth effects which dampen consumption expenditures work through impacts on real government debt as well as on real capital stock, so that the interest rate effects are stronger. (Recall from Equation 16–3 that the real value of government debt varies inversely with the interest rate.) In sum, prices do not have to increase by as much to eliminate a given expenditure gap. Real disturbances provoke smaller increases in prices.

Pigou effects add built-in stability in a slightly different way when real disturbances provoke a decline in aggregate demand, since, with prices and money wages somewhat inflexible downward, short-term impacts affect output more than prices. Of course, to the extent that prices do decline, price-induced wealth effects operating through real money balances and real government debt provide an offsetting stimulation of consumption expenditures. Moreover, since interest rates decline whether prices decline or not, interest-induced wealth effects on consumption expenditures operating through increases in the real value of government debt are added. In addition to these effects, the decline in output and real income increases the government deficit as tax receipts fall and transfer payments rise. With the money supply fixed, the financing of the increased deficit increases real government debt outstanding, so that consumption expenditures are further stimulated. The sum of these effects supplements ordinary interest rate effects in partially offsetting the decline in output and prices.

Pigou Effects and Monetary versus Fiscal Policies

The Pigou effect strengthens the impacts of monetary policies on aggregate demand when only real money balances or real member bank reserves plus real cash are included in the consumption expenditure function. Monetary policies are stronger because they have another channel through which to work. Figure 16–5 illustrates the effect.

The top portion of the figure shows an initial equilibrium at Point A involving initial money supply m_0 and initial price level P_x. Without the simple Pigou effect, achieving full employment with monetary policies would involve increasing the money supply to m_0'', so that the equilibrium would be shifted to Point B. With the simple Pigou effect present, however, the *IS* curve shifts to the right as the money supply increases, since more consumption expenditures are forthcoming at each *r* and *Y* combination, and full employment results when the money supply is increased only to m_0'.

The same effect occurs when monetary policies are employed to close an expenditure gap. As the money supply is reduced, the *IS* curve shifts to the left because of the direct effect of diminished real money balances in dampening consumption expenditures. The money supply does not have to decline by so much to eliminate a given expenditure gap.

Increased strength may not mean much for monetary policy effectiveness, of course. For example, to exaggerate the case, if U.S. monetary policies were twice as strong, it would mean essentially that the Federal Reserve would need to conduct only half the volume of open-market operations in U.S. government securities to remove a particular aggregate expenditure deficiency or gap. But buying \$10 million in securities may not be appreciably easier than buying \$20 million.

Figure 16–5 **Monetary Policy and the Simple Pigou Effect**

The simple Pigou effect adds a channel for monetary policies; it increases their strength and allows them to avoid the block to their effectiveness posed by floors on the interest rate.

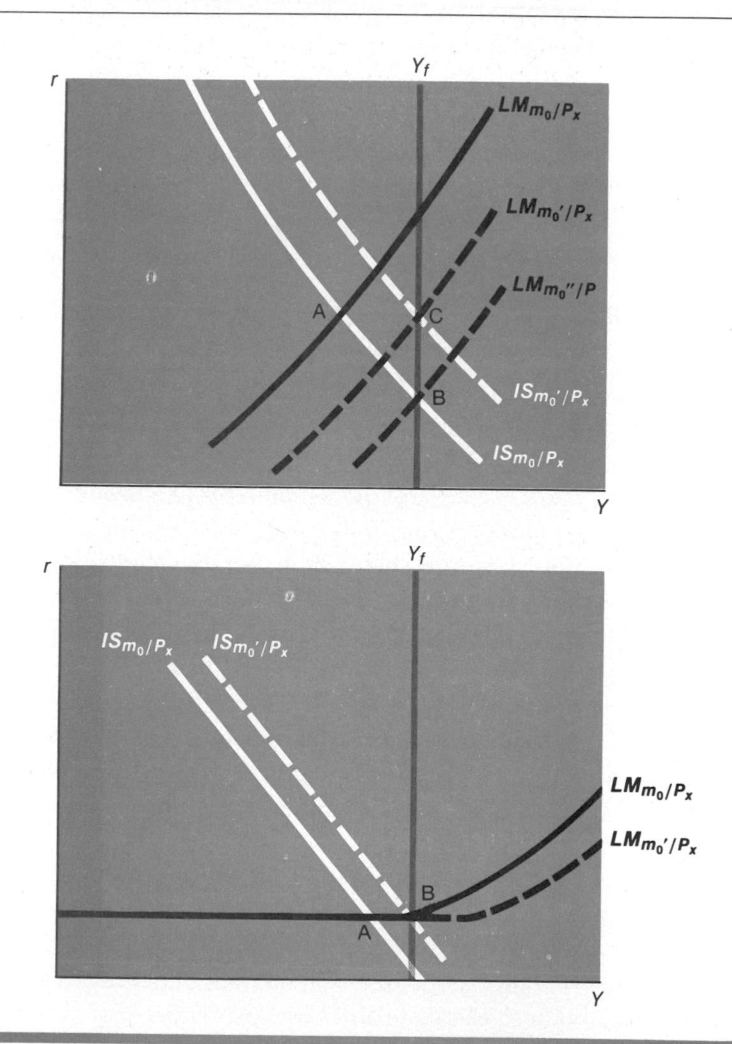

The contribution of the simple Pigou effect to monetary policy effectiveness may occur mainly in the liquidity trap case and the negative interest rate case. Here, the difference is between some strength and no strength, which obviously is important. The liquidity trap case is illustrated in the bottom portion of Figure 16–5. In the initial equilibrium at Point A, monetary policies do not stimulate output at all without a Pigou effect. The *LM* curve simply shifts outward on itself in the relevant range and leaves output unaffected. With the simple Pigou effect present, however, increases in money supply move the *IS* curve to the right as consumption expenditures respond directly to the increase in real money balances. With an increase in money supply from m_0 to m_0', full-employment equilibrium is achieved at Point B.

The simple Pigou effect does not influence the strength of fiscal policies if money supply and prices do not change during the fiscal operation. Of course, if the money supply tends to increase as the interest rate increases and the monetary authority does not offset this effect, or if increased deficits associated with fiscal ease are financed with money creation, fiscal ease becomes stronger with a simple Pigou effect present.[6]

If the Pigou effect involves real government debt as well as real money balances in the consumption expenditure function, its implications for the strength of monetary policies relative to that of fiscal policies are less clear. With monetary policies, the point often is made that, if the Pigou effect operates only through real member bank reserves plus real cash insofar as the money supply component is concerned, increases in the money supply which proceed through open-market operations reduce government debt outstanding dollar for dollar with the increase in member bank reserves, so that no net wealth effect is produced on that score. Therefore, in this version, the Pigou effect may leave the strength of monetary policies unchanged.

The Pigou effect with real government debt included may strengthen fiscal policies, however. For example, an application of fiscal ease ordinarily involves an increase in the government deficit and an increase in the number of government securities outstanding. The broader Pigou effect therefore adds to the fiscal ease impact a wealth effect on consumption expenditures.

Putting these two considerations together implies that the broader Pigou effect makes fiscal policies stronger relative to monetary policies when only member bank reserves are included in the money supply component. There is a further consideration working in the other direction, however. Recalling Equation 16–3 again, real government debt depends on the interest rate as well as the number of government securities outstanding. Since the interest rate ordinarily rises during fiscal ease applications and declines during monetary ease applications, there is an

[6] Strictly speaking, this last instance is no longer a pure fiscal policy operation. Both monetary and fiscal policies are involved.

interest rate effect which tends to diminish real government debt with fiscal ease operations and increase real government debt with monetary ease applications. It may be either stronger or weaker than the effect on the relative strength of the two policies noted earlier, so that it becomes unclear, without precise knowledge of all the magnitudes involved in the model, whether the broader Pigou effect makes monetary policies stronger or weaker than fiscal policies.[7]

It is not clear that the implications of the broader Pigou effect for the strength of fiscal relative to monetary policy is a very important consideration in the monetary versus fiscal policy debate. As indicated earlier, monetary policy strength may not have much to do with monetary policy effectiveness, barring the liquidity trap or negative interest rate cases. Implications for the absolute strength of fiscal policies may be more important. If fiscal ease is stronger as a result of including real government debt in the consumption function, a smaller increase in the federal deficit is required for achieving full employment with a fiscal ease application. However, the amount of crowding out of investment expenditures involved is the more important consideration, and it is independent even of implications for fiscal policy strength. The *IS* curve will move farther to the right with a given fiscal ease application if real government debt is in the consumption expenditure function, but it will intersect the full-employment line at the same rate of interest and hence will involve the same crowding out of investment expenditures.

Pigou Effects: Concluding Observations

Whether Pigou effects should be included in models employed for explaining, analyzing, and forecasting macroeconomic activity depends on whether they are empirically important. Fairly persuasive evidence exists to support the view that they are statistically significant.[8] Still, most of the

---

[7] Equation 16–3 exaggerates the size of the interest-induced effect on real government debt insofar as the U.S. federal government debt is concerned, however. About one-half of the U.S. debt during recent years has been in securities which mature in less than one year, where effects of interest rate changes on market values are relatively weak. The market value today of a U.S. bill maturing tomorrow for a redemption value of $10,000 changes very little if interest rates vary today, since the bill will be worth $10,000 tomorrow in any event.

[8] See, for example, the survey by Don Patinkin in *Money, Interest, and Prices,* note M, pp. 651–664.

large statistical macroeconomic models include them only in a very limited way, if at all.

Summary

1. Pigou effects are wealth effects which make real consumption expenditures vary directly with real money balances and perhaps with real government debt as well.

2. Pigou effects restore the classical result that price and money-wage flexibility assures full employment in the face of the Keynesian liquidity trap and negative interest rate case exceptions.

3. The classical concept of the neutrality of money is not disturbed by simple Pigou effects as long as the classical money demand function is retained, but it is invalidated by Pigou effects that incorporate real government debt.

4. Chapter 15 concluded that, if real money balances demanded vary inversely with the expected change in prices, neutrality of money is lost even without Pigou effects, since dynamic money supply disturbances will then affect equilibrium real money balances. Including even simple Pigou effects involves further qualifications. Dynamic money supply disturbances then affect equilibriums for real interest rate, real saving, real investment expenditures and real consumption expenditures.

5. Insofar as the monetarist propositions are concerned, Pigou effects contribute to the view of money supply disturbances as the principal source of price and employment problems and also to the performance of stable money supply growth. The implications of Pigou effects for the monetary versus fiscal policy issue are less clear. The simple Pigou effect makes monetary policies stronger relative to fiscal policies. However, with a Pigou effect including real government debt, the effect on the relative strength of monetary and fiscal policies depends on the strength of the various relationships involved in the model at large.

6. Whether Pigou effects should be included in models used for macroeconomic analyses and forecasting depends on their empirical strength. Economists often omit them from short-term analyses on the grounds that they are weak.

Concepts for Identification

simple Pigou effect
broader Pigou effect
real government debt

Questions and Problems for Review

1. Identify the various wealth items through which Pigou effects may operate. Indicate why each should or should not be included in the basis for the effects.

2. Demonstrate graphically how Pigou effects remove the Keynesian liquidity trap case and the negative interest rate case exceptions to the classical proposition that price and money-wage flexibility assures full employment.

3. Using a once and for all money supply disturbance, show that adding a simple Pigou effect to the classical model does not disturb the neutral money proposition. Explain why neutral money also holds for dynamic money supply disturbances when only simple Pigou effects are added.

4. Show that the broader Pigou effect does invalidate the classical neutral money proposition.

5. Explain how Pigou effects reduce the price increase which occurs when the investment expenditure function increases in a fully employed economy.

6. Pigou effects may reduce the decline in output which occurs when the investment expenditure function declines in an economy characterized by downward wage rigidity. Explain.

7. The simple Pigou effect increases the strength of monetary ease relative to that of fiscal ease in effecting increases in output and employment. Explain.

8. Discuss the implications of broader Pigou effects for the strength of monetary and fiscal ease.

9. While broader Pigou effects may reduce the size of the increase in government purchases of goods and services needed to move the economy to full employment in a given situation, they do not affect the amount of crowding out of investment expenditures. Explain.

References

Haberler, Gottfried. *Prosperity and Depression.* 3rd ed. Geneva, Switzerland: League of Nations, 1941, pp. 388–389

Patinkin, Don. *Money, Interest, and Prices.* 2d ed. New York: Harper & Row, 1965, especially chaps. 10–12 and note M, pp. 651–664.

———. "Price Flexibility and Full Employment." *American Economic Review* 38 (September 1948): 543-564. Reprinted in *Readings in Monetary Theory.* Edited by F. A. Lutz and L. W. Mints. Homewood, Ill.: Richard D. Irwin, 1951, pp. 252–283.

Pigou, A. C. "The Classical Stationary State." *Economic Journal* 53 (December 1943): 343–351.

Part 6

Extensions and a Policy Summary

17

Investment Expenditures and Income

Making investment expenditures vary directly with aggregate output and real income or with changes in the level of aggregate output and real income gives rise to a number of interesting implications. Most importantly, perhaps, the built-in stability of the economy is reduced.

Economists sometimes regard investment expenditures as varying directly with the level of output and real income or with changes in the level of output and real income. Parts 3, 4, and 5 neglected these relationships, however—investment expenditures were considered a function of the interest rate but not of Y or changes in Y.

This chapter considers these relationships. The following section examines investment expenditures as a function of the level of output and real income; then, the subsequent section considers investment expenditures as a function of changes in the level of output and real income. Both sections proceed by first examining the theoretical rationales for the relationships and then considering their implications for macroeconomic theory and policy.

Investment Expenditures and the Level of Output and Income

Why might investment expenditures vary directly with the level of output and real income?

1. One rationale suggests that yields expected on new acquisitions of capital goods—which is to say, the marginal efficiency of investment estimates—may be related to the level of Y, either because Y is related to realized profits, which may influence expected profits, or because a Y which is high relative to full employment Y generates optimism.

2. It is possible that Y, being related to realized profits and more specifically to retained earnings of producers, influences investment expenditures by affecting the volume of internal funds available to finance investment expenditures. On the face of it, this argument seems weak, since profit maximization does not dictate that investment expenditures should be made merely because internal funds are available. If investment opportunities meeting the MEI $>r$ test are not available, internal funds should be used to retire debt or be placed temporarily in securities.

Still, internal funds may be cheaper than external funds or may be regarded as cheaper when costs of external financing are adjusted upward to reflect disadvantages associated with external financing. Chapter 7 made several points concerning this matter. Equity financing via new stock issues dilutes existing stockholders' control of the firm, unless they purchase the new stock. Debt financing increases the chance that the firm will fail, since it involves fixed interest charges and debt repayment amounts which must be met whether or not the firm prospers.

3. Another possibility for a relationship between positive investment expenditures and Y is that a higher output requires a larger capital stock to produce it and therefore involves a greater demand for capital goods to replace those used up in the process of production. This probably does not provide a significant short-term relationship between investment expenditures and Y, however, since considerable lags are involved before capital goods which are newly acquired to service higher income levels influence the demand for replacement capital goods.

Implications of a Positive Relationship between Investment Expenditures and Y

If investment expenditures do vary directly with Y, a number of interesting implications arise.

First, the relationship aggravates the reductions in equilibrium output and real income which attend declines in aggregate demand. The rationale is the same as for the C and Y relationship. As Y begins to decline in response to real or monetary disturbances, induced effects are produced on investment expenditures. These add to the decline in total demand and thereby to the decline in aggregate output.[1]

Second, the relationship between investment expenditures and Y augments the impact on Y of monetary and fiscal policies initiated to stimulate the economy in a recession. As monetary or fiscal ease stimulates expenditures and as output and real income respond, induced effects on investment expenditures now occur which add to the increase in overall demand and bring forth additional responses in output and real income.[2] Moreover, the crowding out of investment expenditures which attends the use of fiscal ease because of the increase in interest rates is not as great when the investment expenditure and Y relationship is present, since the expansion of Y now produces an offsetting increase in investment expen-

---

[1] This is demonstrated mathematically by substituting the equation $I = I_0 - ir + hY$ for Equation 10–21 in the linear model of Chapter 10, where $0 < h < 1$ represents the marginal propensity to investment from Y. The IS curve now is:

$$r = \frac{E_0 - [1 - b(1 - t) - h]Y}{i + s}$$

and the trial equilibrium for Y is:

$$Y = \frac{qE_0 + (i + s)(m_0/P_x - L_0)}{(i + s)k + [1 - b(1 - t) - h]},$$

where $E_0 = a - bTx_0 + bTr_0 + G_0 + I_0$, as before.

The relevant multipliers emerge from this as:

$$\Delta Y/\Delta E_0 = \frac{1}{(i + s)k/q + 1 - b(1 - t) - h},$$

$$\Delta Y/\Delta m_0 = \frac{1}{(k + q/(i + s)[1 - b(1 - t) - h])P_x},$$

and

$$\Delta Y/\Delta L_0 = \frac{-1}{k + q/(i + s)[1 - b(1 - t) - h]},$$

each of which is larger (neglecting the sign for $\Delta Y/\Delta L_0$) as a result of the inclusion of h. These multipliers take prices as fixed at P_x, for convenience.

[2] Notice from the preceding footnote that $\Delta Y/\Delta m_0$ and $\Delta Y/\Delta E_0$ (hence, $\Delta Y/\Delta G_0$, $\Delta Y/\Delta Tr_0$, and $-\Delta Y/\Delta Tx_0$) are larger with $0 < h < 1$ present.

ditures. Indeed, investment expenditures may even increase with a fiscal ease application. Consumption expenditures bear more, and investment expenditures less, of the crowding out effect.

Furthermore, if investment expenditures do increase, and increase by more than private saving increases, the government deficit declines instead of increasing as fiscal ease is applied.[3] The increase in the government deficit required for bringing the economy to full employment with fiscal policies is smaller, in any event, with the investment expenditure and Y relationship present, since fiscal policies become stronger. But it also becomes possible (though empirically unlikely) that the government deficit will actually decline.

An Upward Sloping *IS* Curve?

Other implications arise from the fact that the *IS* curve now can slope upward. Before, it had to slope downward. An increase in Y had to be accompanied by a reduction in r, which stimulated I, in order for E to remain equal to Y, since C would increase by less than Y. Now, however, an increase in Y provokes an increase in both C and I. If $\Delta C/\Delta Y$ and $\Delta I/\Delta Y$ sum to more than 1, the *IS* curve slopes upward. An increase in Y provokes a larger increase in E, so that r must increase, to diminish E, if E is to remain equal to Y.[4] Of course, if $(\Delta C/\Delta Y + \Delta I/\Delta Y)$ is less than 1, the *IS* curve still slopes downward.

If the *IS* curve does slope upward, but less steeply than the *LM* curve, reductions in the money supply and increases in the money demand function provoke reductions in the equilibrium interest rate, rather than causing increases as they do when the *IS* curve slopes downward. For example, in Figure 17–1, where the *IS* curve slopes upward, but less steeply than the *LM* curves, a shift in the *LM* curve from LM_1 to LM_2, reflecting the monetary disturbances, causes the equilibrium interest rate to decline from r_a to r_b. Prices are taken as fixed at P_x, for convenience. By

---

[3] Since $I = Sp + Sg$ will prevail in equilibrium, where Sp is private saving and Sg is government saving, Sg will increase—that is, the government deficit will diminish—if I increases by more than Sp increases. Sp will increase since it varies directly with both r and Y.

[4] Recall that the *IS* curve becomes:

$$r = \frac{E_0 - [1 - b(1 - t) - h]Y}{i + s}$$

when $I = I_0 - ir + hY$ is substituted for Equation 10–21 of Chapter 10. Its slope, $\Delta r/\Delta Y = -[1 - b(1 - t) - h]/(i + s)$, is positive if $[h + b(1 - t)] > 1$.

Figure 17–1 **Monetary Disturbances When the *IS* Curve Slopes Upward (Though Less Steeply than the *LM* Curve)**

If tho *IS* curve slopes upward but is less steeply sloped than the *LM* curve, reductions in the money supply and increases in the money demand function cause the equilibrium interest rate to fall.

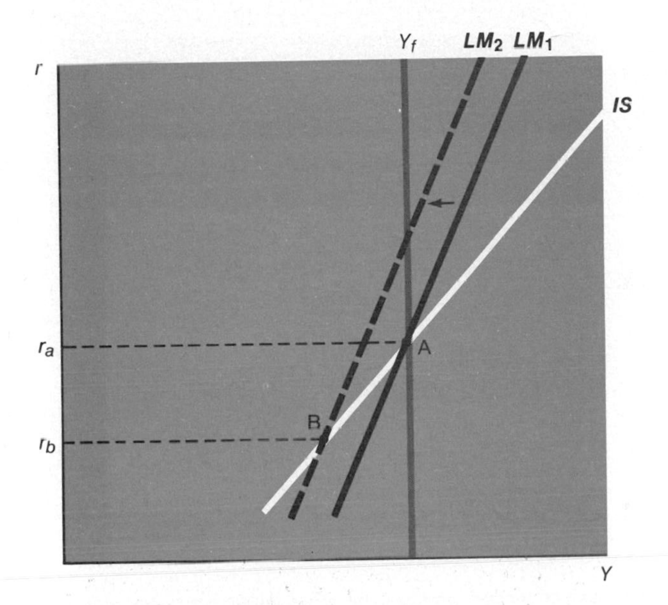

contrast, in Figure 17–2, where the *IS* curve slopes downward, the leftward shift in the *LM* curve, again from LM_1 to LM_2, causes the equilibrium interest rate to rise from r_a to r_b'. Similarly, curing a recession with monetary ease, as in Figure 17–3, involves an increase, rather than a decrease, in the equilibrium interest rate, which rises from r_a to r_b'' in the figure when the *LM* curve shifts from LM_1 to LM_2.

If the *IS* curve slopes upward more steeply than the *LM* curve, the model becomes unstable in the sense that it will not return to equilibrium on the normal dynamic assumptions when equilibriums falling within the unemployment range are disturbed. For example, in the upper portion of Figure 17–4, if the initial equilibrium at Point A is disturbed with an increase in the money supply which shifts the *LM* curve to LM_2, equilibrium *Y* declines from Y_a to Y_b. But an increase in the money supply opens up an excess supply of money, causing the interest rate to fall and

Figure 17–2 Monetary Disturbances When the *IS* Curve Slopes Downward

If the *IS* curve slopes downward, reductions in the money supply and increases in the money demand function cause the equilibrium interest rate to rise.

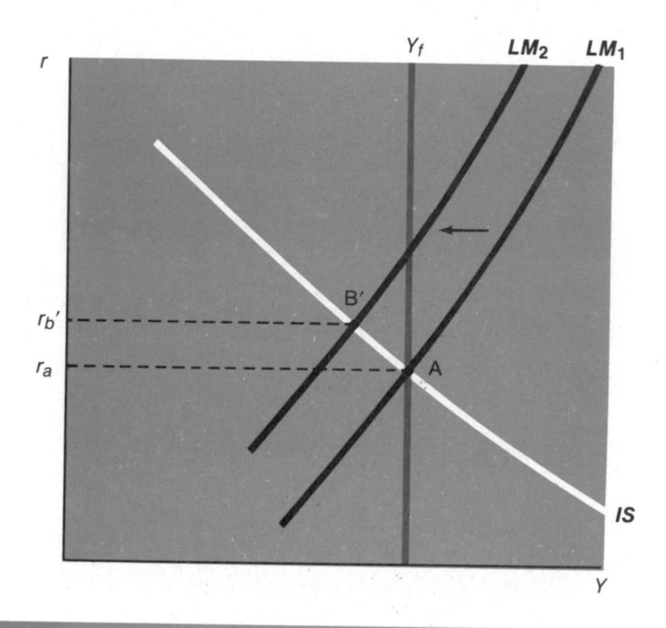

expenditures and output to rise. Therefore, Y moves away from its new equilibrium value rather than toward it.

The model also is unstable for real disturbances within the unemployment range when the *IS* curve slopes upward more steeply than the *LM* curve, though this is more difficult to demonstrate graphically. The key is that an increase in E_0 shifts the *IS* curve to the left, rather than to the right, when the *IS* curve slopes positively. This happens because adding the income effect on investment expenditures, which produces the positive slope, rotates the *IS* curve counterclockwise.

Therefore, an increase in the investment demand function, which shifts the *IS* curve from IS_1 to IS_2 in the lower portion of Figure 17–4, determines a lower equilibrium for Y when the *IS* curve slopes upward more steeply than the *LM* curve. But output responds with an increase when the investment expenditure function increases, on the usual assumptions,

Figure 17–3 **Monetary Ease When the *IS* Curve Slopes Upward (Though Less Steeply than the *LM* Curve)**

When the *IS* curve slopes upward and is less steeply sloped than the *LM* curve, an increase in the money supply applied in a less than full employment situation causes the equilibrium interest rate to rise rather than fall.

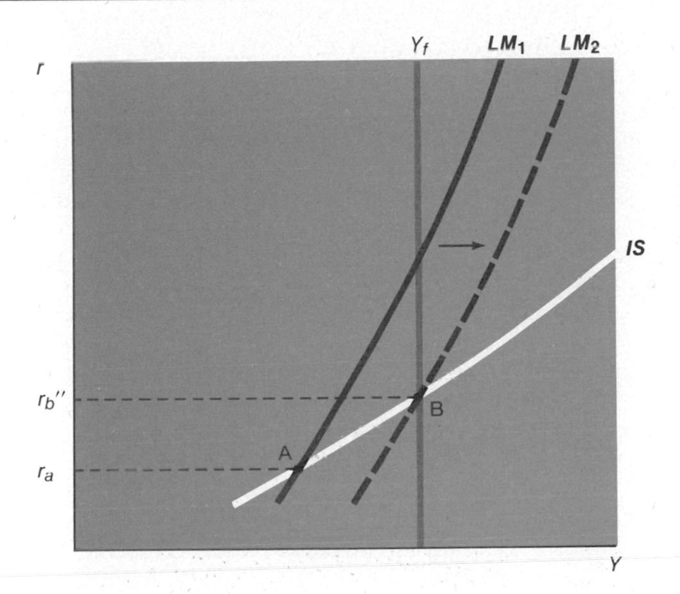

since the demand for goods and services has increased. Consequently, Y moves away from its new equilibrium value rather than toward it.

W. H. Branson has inferred from the Duesenberry, Friedman, and Modigliani, Ando, and Brumberg works on the consumption function and from C. W. Bischoff's work on the investment expenditure function that the marginal propensity to consume and invest from income is less than 1.[5] If this is the case, the *IS* curve slopes downward, and the complications of upward sloping *IS* curves are avoided.

Still, the question is not completely settled. Bischoff's work indicates

[5] W. H. Branson, *Macroeconomic Theory and Policy,* 2d ed. (New York: Harper & Row, 1979), pp. 235–236, 239. The Bischoff work referred to is C. W. Bischoff, "Business Investment in the 1970s: A Comparison of Models," *Brookings Papers on Economic Activity* 1 (1971): 28.

Figure 17–4 **Unstable Equilibrium: The *IS* Curve Slopes Upward More Steeply than the *LM* Curve**

If the *IS* curve slopes upward and is more steeply sloped than the *LM* curve, monetary or real disturbances occurring in the less than full employment situation cause *Y* to move away from its new equilibrium rather than toward it.

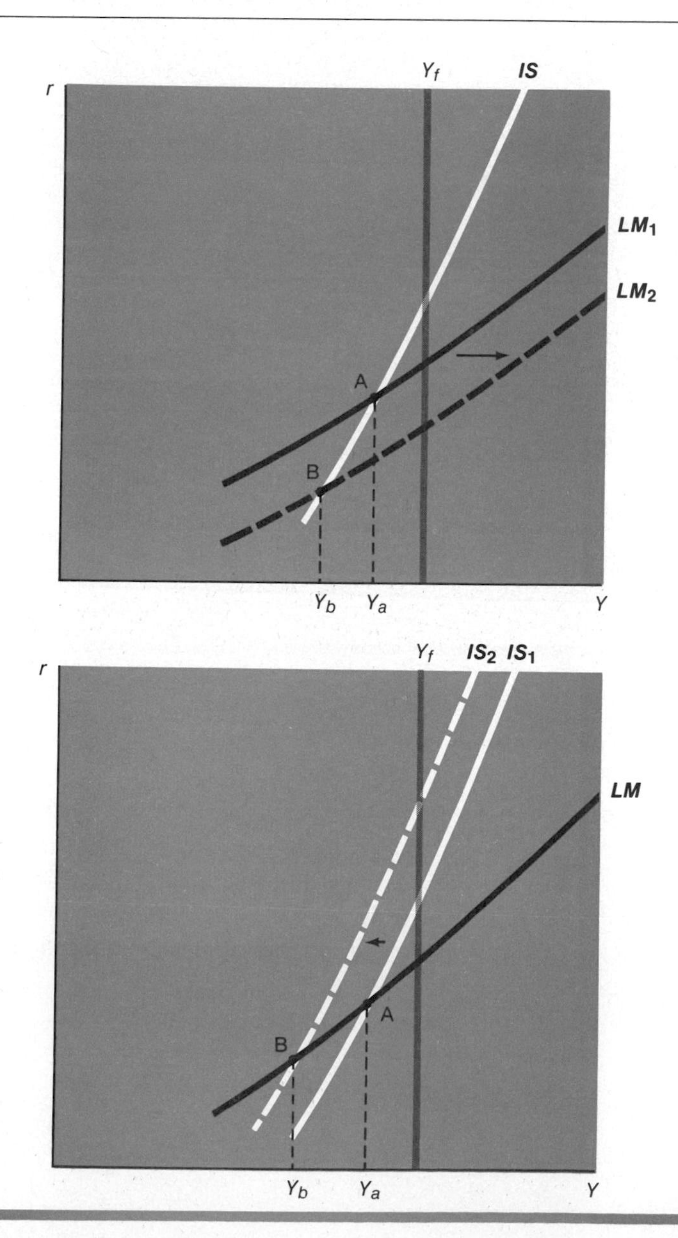

that income-induced effects on investment expenditures are much larger in the short term, which is several years, than in the long term. This may be a problem. Moreover, his investment expenditures consist of plant and equipment expenditures only. They exclude residential construction expenditures, where long-term income-induced effects may be large.

Whatever the importance of these qualifications, it does seem clear that the *IS* curve is not steeper than the *LM* curve, given the money demand interest elasticity estimates reviewed in Chapter 9. It seems very unlikely that the relationship between investment expenditures and the level of Y is strong enough to produce the unstable cases discussed in connection with Figure 17–4.

Investment Expenditures and the Change in Output and Real Income

The aggregate production function:

$$Y = F(N, K) \tag{17-1}$$

implies that an optimum amount of capital exists for each level of output if matters such as the qualities of labor and capital, their relative costs, and production technology are given. If this relationship is such that β of capital is needed for producing one unit of output, and if actual capital is adjusted to optimum capital with a lag of one period, the capital stock for Period t will be:

$$K_t = \beta Y_{t-1}. \tag{17-2}$$

Similarly, for period $t - 1$, capital will be:

$$K_{t-1} = \beta Y_{t-2}. \tag{17-3}$$

Since net investment expenditures represent capital accumulation, net investment expenditures for Period t must be:

$$I_{nt} = K_t - K_{t-1} = \beta(Y_{t-1} - Y_{t-2}). \tag{17-4}$$

These calculations represent a formulation in which net investment expenditures for the current period depend on the change in output and real income recorded in the preceding period.

This relationship, often termed an *accelerator effect,* has been of great interest to business cycle theorists because it is capable of considerably complicating the adjustment path that aggregate output follows when equilibrium is disturbed. Consider, for example, Figures 17–5 and 17–6, which illustrate the implications of including an accelerator effect of varying strengths in a simple period model containing the equations:

$$C_t = a_0 + bY_{t-1} = 50 + 0.6Y_{t-1}, \quad \text{17–5}$$

$$I_t = I_0 + v(Y_{t-1} - Y_{t-2}), \quad \text{17–6}$$

and

$$Y_t = C_t + I_t. \quad \text{17–7}$$

Figure 17–5 **Adjustment Paths for Y Following an Increase in Autonomous Investment Expenditures, for v = 0, v = 0.12, and v = 0.8**

With a weak accelerator effect ($v = 0.12$), the period model approaches its new equilibrium Y value smoothly when disturbed but more rapidly than when no accelerator effect is present ($v = 0.0$). With a moderate accelerator effect ($v = 0.8$), the adjustment path is oscillatory but converges toward the new equilibrium.

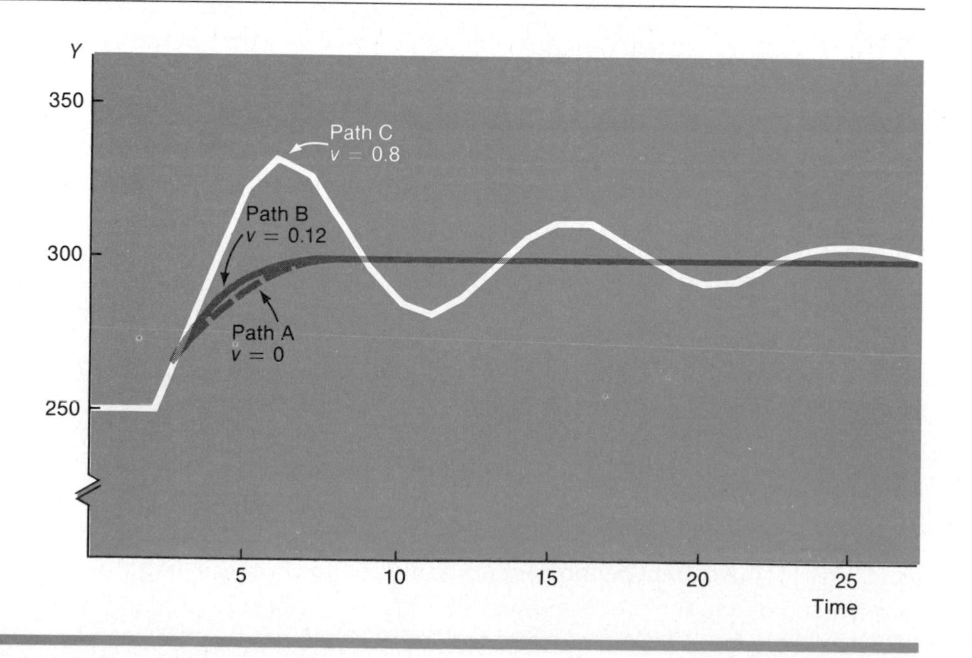

Figure 17–6 **Adjustment Paths for Y Following an Increase in Autonomous Investment Expenditures, for $v = 1.1$ and $v = 2.8$**

With strong accelerator effects, the period model does not settle to its new Y equilibrium when disturbed. For $v = 1.1$, the adjustment path is oscillatory, and the oscillations are successively larger. For $v = 2.8$, the model moves through the new equilibrium and away from it in a smooth adjustment path.

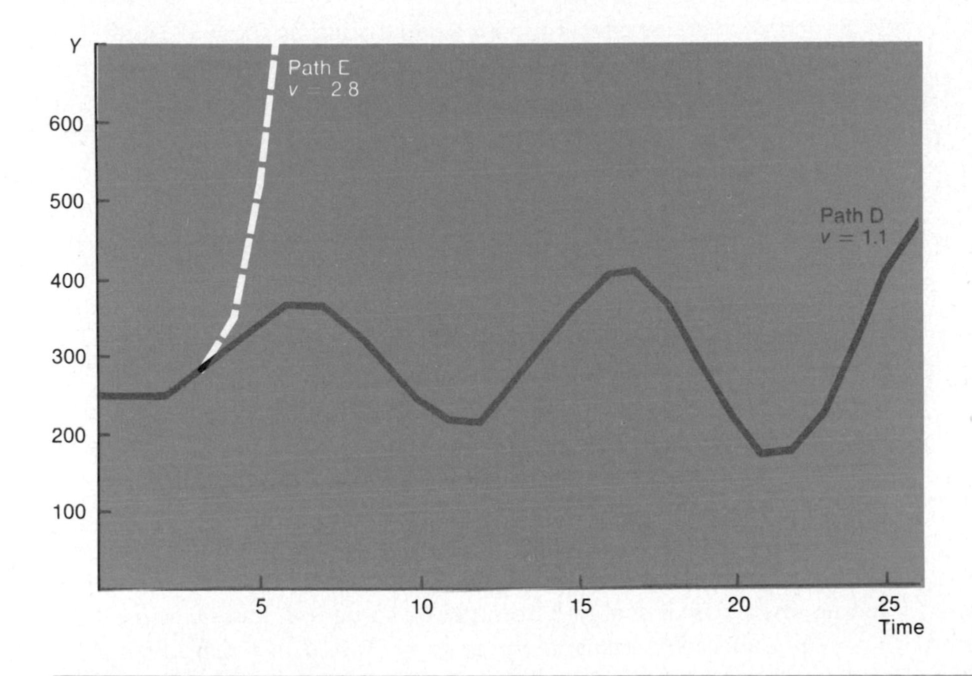

Consumption expenditures, in Equation 17–5, depend upon the output and real income levels of the preceding period. Investment expenditures, in Equation 17–6, contain the autonomous component I_0 and depend in addition on an accelerator effect relating them to the change in real income recorded during the preceding period. The accelerator effect grows stronger as v, the accelerator coefficient, becomes larger. The model, therefore, contains a multiplier effect and an accelerator effect but no monetary influences.

Figure 17–5 compares the adjustment paths for situations with no accelerator effect ($v = 0$), a weak accelerator effect ($v = 0.12$), and a moderate-sized accelerator effect ($v = 0.8$) generated by the model when an initial equilibrium for $I_0 = 50$ is disturbed by increasing I_0 to 70 in Period 3. With no accelerator effect, output adjusts smoothly to the new equilibrium along Path A following the disturbance. With the weak accelerator effect present, the adjustment occurs along Path B. The adjustment path is still smooth but the movement toward equilibrium is more rapid in the initial periods. The moderate-sized accelerator effect produces adjustment Path C. Y overshoots its new equilibrium initially and then fluctuates about it during the approach.

Strong accelerator effects produce paths such as those illustrated in Figure 17–6. For $v > 1.0$, the model becomes unstable in the sense that once equilibrium is disturbed, Y does not adjust to the new equilibrium. In Path D ($v = 1.1$), for example, Y begins an oscillatory movement about the new equilibrium after overshooting it initially, but the oscillations get larger instead of smaller. With a still stronger accelerator effect, paths like Path E ($v = 2.8$) are possible. When disturbed, Y simply explodes through the new equilibrium in a smooth expansion path.

These unstable paths would be constrained in a more complete model by the full-employment constraint on Y acting as a ceiling and by a minimum for investment expenditures existing on the downside, together imposing limits on the movements of Y. Still, Y would not settle to equilibrium but, under the usual assumptions, would fluctuate between the full-employment ceiling and the floor posed by the minimum on investment expenditures.[6]

Table 17–1 illustrates the generation of adjustment Path C in Figure 17–5, the dampened oscillatory path. Since equilibrium occurs in the model when Y is unchanged from period to period, that is, where $Y_t = Y_{t-1} = Y_{t-2}$, the initial equilibrium for $I_0 = 50$ and $v = 0.8$ obtains as:

$$Y_t = C_t + I_t$$

$$Y_t = a_0 + bY_{t-1} + I_0 + v(Y_{t-1} - Y_{t-2})$$

[6] The accelerator model presented here closely follows the accelerator mechanism incorporated into a more elaborate model introduced by J. R. Hicks in *A Contribution to the Theory of the Trade Cycle* (London: Oxford University Press, 1950). For a concise treatment of the Hicks model, see T. F. Dernburg and J. D. Dernburg, *Macroeconomic Analysis* (Reading, Mass.: Addison-Wesley, 1969), pp. 134–173. The conditions involving v and b which produce the adjustment path types illustrated in Figures 17–5 and 17–6 are developed there. If $v < 1.0$ is the case, the stable paths of Figure 17–5 occur. The smooth-stable path occurs if $v < (1 - \sqrt{1 - b})^2$, but the oscillatory-stable path occurs if $1 > v > (1 - \sqrt{1 - b})^2$. The unstable paths of Figure 17–6 occur where $v > 1.0$. The explosive path requires that $v > (1 + \sqrt{1 - b})^2$, while $1 < v < (1 + \sqrt{1 - b})^2$ produces the unstable-oscillatory path.

Table 17–1

Path C, the Stable-Oscillatory Path (b = 0.6, v = 0.8)

t	C	I	Y	ΔY
1	200.0	50.0	250.0	0.0
2	200.0	50.0	250.0	0.0
3	200.0	70.0	270.0	20.0
4	212.0	86.0	298.0	28.0
5	228.8	92.4	321.2	23.2
6	242.7	88.6	331.3	10.1
7	248.8	78.1	326.8	−4.4
8	246.1	66.4	312.5	−14.3
9	237.5	58.6	296.1	−16.5
10	227.7	56.8	284.5	−11.6
11	220.7	60.7	281.4	−3.1
12	218.9	67.5	286.4	5.0
13	221.8	74.0	295.8	9.4
14	227.5	77.5	305.0	9.2
15	233.0	77.4	310.4	5.4
16	236.2	74.3	310.5	0.1
17	236.3	70.1	306.4	−4.1

$$Y_t = a_0 + bY_t + I_0 + vY_t - vY_t$$

$$Y_t = \frac{a_0 + I_0}{1 - b} = \frac{50 + 50}{1 - 0.6} = 100/0.4 = 250.$$

Similarly, the new equilibrium for the I_0 of 70 is $Y_t = 120/0.4 = 300$.[7]

Y does not adjust immediately to the new equilibrium, however. In Period 3, it rises to 270, reflecting the increase of 20 in I_0 introduced in the period. In Period 4, Y rises further to 298, reflecting the increase in C resulting from the higher level of Y in Period 3 and the accelerator-induced increase in I caused by the change in Y recorded in Period 3. Y continues to rise during Periods 5 and 6, but the increases in Y are successively smaller, so that by Period 7 the accelerator-induced element in investment has diminished to the point where total expenditures and output begin to decline. With Y declining in Period 7, the accelerator-induced element in investment expenditures becomes negative in Period 8, causing invest-

[7] Indeed, these are the initial and new equilibrium values for all five adjustment paths presented in Figures 17–5 and 17–6, since v does not affect the equilibrium values. For Paths E and D, the adjustment paths do not lead to the new equilibrium for Y_t of course.

ment expenditures to fall temporarily below I_0. By Period 9, investment expenditures have fallen enough below I_0 that the multiplier effect on C is overcome and Y moves below its eventual equilibrium level of 300, beginning its oscillatory movement toward equilibrium.

Qualifications of the Accelerator Effect

The operation of accelerator effects in the real world is subject to a number of qualifications which appear to rule out adjustment paths such as those associated with the large values of v in the foregoing illustrations, even granting that the optimum aggregate capital to output ratio may substantially exceed unity. The illustrations ignore monetary influences entirely. Monetary influences dampen fluctuations in output and real income by producing offsetting impacts on interest-sensitive and wealth-sensitive expenditures, including impacts which affect the optimum capital to output ratio itself by inducing substitutions between capital and labor. Moreover, even putting monetary influences aside, lags attend the operation of the accelerator mechanism. In most industries, actual capital is not adjusted to optimum capital within a year because of lags in planning, ordering, and producing capital goods. Also, producers' estimates as to optimum capital are not fully adjusted to changes in output levels until the changes are perceived to be permanent. The same permanent income hypothesis which explains lagged responses in consumption expenditures suggests lagged responses of investment expenditures to changes in output.

Most important, perhaps, the rigid accelerator mechanism underlying the expansion paths of Figures 17–5 and 17–6 completely ignores the role of excess capacity. In an economic recovery, unless the recession has been of extended duration, substantial excess capacity exists when the recovery begins. This blunts the operation of the accelerator mechanism, since increases in output levels must first employ the excess capital already on hand. Substantial accelerator effects on net investment expenditures may not appear until full employment is approached; and, of course, once full employment is achieved the mechanism is severely constrained, since output no longer increases freely.

The situation differs as the economy moves into recession, but the accelerator mechanism still does not work precisely as the rigid accelerator model indicates. As soon as output declines, excess capacity appears, so that investment expenditures fall immediately to the level of autonomous investment expenditures regardless of the size of the decline in output, at least until the excess capacity is used up.

The area in which accelerator effects can operate fully may be quite limited. The rigid accelerator mechanism probably has its greatest applicability in explaining inventory investment, where adjustment of actual levels to optimum levels can proceed relatively quickly.

Empirical Studies and the Accelerator Effect

In light of these qualifications, it is not surprising that empirical research has failed to document accelerator effects of the strength reflected in the adjustment paths associated with the higher v values in the foregoing illustrations. Still, empirical research does not suggest that accelerator effects are inconsequential. Jorgenson and Seibert, Bischoff, and others have found flexible versions of the accelerator model, which take into account various qualifications of the rigid accelerator mechanism, to be useful predictors of investment behavior.[8]

Summary

1. Investment expenditures sometimes are regarded as varying directly with the level of output and real income and directly with changes in the level of output and real income as well as inversely with the interest rate.

2. Making investment expenditures a positive function of Y produces a number of interesting implications. It aggravates the fluctuations in Y which attend real and monetary disturbances, and it increases the strength of both monetary and fiscal ease. If the income-induced effect on investment expenditures is very strong, the *IS* curve can slope positively, possibly by enough to produce unstable equilbriums in the *IS-LM* model. Empirical results seem to rule out the investment expenditures and Y relationship as a source of unstable equilibriums, however.

3. Making investment expenditures a positive function of ΔY—that is, introducing an accelerator effect—can, when equilibrium is disturbed, produce complicated adjustment paths, oscillatory as well as smooth, and unstable as well as stable. The rigid accelerator mechanism is subject to a number of qualifications, but economic researchers have found models with flexible versions of the accelerator effect to be useful predictors of investment expenditures.

---

[8] D. W. Jorgenson and C. D. Seibert, "A Comparison of Alternative Theories of Corporate Investment Behavior," *American Economic Review* 58 (September 1968): 681–712; and Bischoff, "Business Investment."

Concepts for Identification

replacement capital goods	period model
unstable equilibrium	adjustment paths
marginal propensity to invest from income	oscillatory movement about equilibrium
optimum capital stock	rigid accelerator mechanism
accelerator effect	flexible accelerator

Questions and Problems for Review

1. Present and explain three reasons why investment expenditures might vary directly with aggregate output and real income.

2. Explain why a positive relationship between investment expenditures and Y aggravates the decline in equilibrium Y which occurs when the investment or consumption expenditure functions decline.

3. Does a positive relationship between investment expenditures and Y make monetary ease stronger when applied in recessions to expand aggregate output and employment? Explain. Does it make fiscal ease stronger in such situations? Explain.

4. Explain why the crowding out of investment expenditures which accompanies fiscal ease applications is smaller if investment expenditures vary directly with aggregate output and real income.

5. Given that investment expenditures vary directly with Y, present and explain the condition which causes the IS curve to slope upward.

6. Assume that the IS curve slopes upward but is less steeply sloped than the LM curve. Show that the equilibrium rate of interest increases in response to both monetary ease and fiscal ease when these policies are applied in a less than full employment situation.

7. Show that equilibriums for r and Y are unstable within the less than full employment range for both monetary and real disturbances if the IS curve slopes positively and more steeply than the LM curve.

8. Using the model set out in Equations 17–5, 17–6, and 17–7 of this chapter, generate the numerical values for the adjustment Paths A and B of Figure 17–5 and D and E of Figure 17–6. Generate values for ten periods for Path E and for twenty-five periods for Paths A, B, and D. The disturbance is an increase in I_0 from 50 for Periods 1 and 2 to 70 for Periods 3 and beyond.

9. Evaluate the accelerator effect as a mechanism for explaining actual behavior. Indicate some of the modifications a more flexible accelerator mechanism might incorporate to improve the accuracy of the explanation.

References

Bischoff, C. W. "Business Investment in the 1970s: A Comparison of Models." *Brookings Papers on Economic Activity* 1 (1971): 13–63.

———."The Effect of Alternative Lag Distributions." In *Tax Incentives and Capital Spending.* Edited by G. Fromm. Washington, D.C.: Brookings Institution, 1971.

Dernburg, T. F., and Dernburg, J. D. *Macroeconomic Analysis.* Reading, Mass.: Addison-Wesley, 1969, chap. 8.

Eisner, Robert. "A Permanent Income Theory for Investment." *American Economic Review* 57 (June 1967): 363–390.

Hicks, J. R. *A Contribution to the Theory of the Trade Cycle.* London: Oxford University Press, 1950.

Jorgenson, D. "The Theory of Investment Behavior." In *Determinants of Investment Behavior.* Edited by R. Ferber. New York: National Bureau of Economic Research, 1967, pp. 129–155.

———. "Econometric Studies of Investment Behavior: A Survey." *Journal of Economic Literature* 9 (December 1971): 1,111–1,118.

Jorgenson, D., and Seibert, C. D. "A Comparison of Alternative Theories of Corporate Investment Behavior." *American Economic Review* 58 (September 1968): 681–712.

Kuznets, Simon. "Relation between Capital Goods and Finished Products in the Business Cycle." In *Economic Essays in Honor of Wesley Clair Mitchell.* New York: Columbia University Press, 1935, pp. 209–267.

Meyer, J. R., and Kuh, E. *The Investment Decision.* Cambridge, Mass.: Harvard University Press, 1957.

Samuelson, Paul A. "Interactions between the Multiplier Analysis and the Principle of Acceleration." *Review of Economics and Statistics* 21 (May 1939): 75–78.

18

Economic Growth

Increases in the capital to labor ratio and technological advance have been the most important sources of growth in U.S. per capita output. Government growth policy has centered on increasing the capital accumulation rate. The natural resources constraint may be growing in importance as a retardant to future growth in per capita output.

Economic growth means the increase in an economy's aggregate output and real income over time—either the simple increase or the increase in per capita terms. *Economic growth rates* refer to the percent changes per unit of time.

In discussing growth and growth targets, it is often useful to define growth more narrowly, speaking of increases in full-employment output instead of increases in actual output. Defining growth in this way abstracts from the problem of maintaining full employment, separating increases in output which merely move the economy to full employment from those which represent increases in the economy's potential output.

This approach is a useful one. Maintaining full-employment output and influencing the growth of full-employment output over time are separate macroeconomic goals. Policies which produce one sometimes are detrimental to the other. For example, cuts in personal income tax rates will stimulate output in an unemployment situation by raising aggregate demand and employing existing resources more fully. But they ordinarily lower the growth of full-employment output, since they increase interest rates, which tends to diminish investment expenditures and retard capital accumulation. Moreover, separate mixes of gains and sacrifices often are involved in seeking the two goals. Policies to produce full employment in an initial unemployment situation ordinarily can increase consumption for everyone if distribution effects are neutralized, since aggregate consumption expenditures increase as output and real income increase. But policies to raise full-employment output growth over time may require sacrifices in consumption by the present generation. This is usually the case when they are applied in full-employment situations, for example, since stimulating growth in such situations ordinarily involves shifting current full-employment output from consumption to capital accumulation, that is, to investment expenditures.

Figure 18–1 illustrates the distinction between full-employment output growth and output growth which merely reflects recovery from economic recession. The broken line plots the increase in full-employment output for the United States for the years 1952–1977. These plottings are estimates by the President's Council of Economic Advisers of what aggregate output and real income would have been if unemployment rates consistent with full employment had been maintained. The solid line plots actual output during the period. It reflects both a growth trend and cyclical movements of output about the full-employment estimates. For example, during 1971 to 1972, which was a period of recovery from recession, actual output grew by 5.7 percent, but estimated full-employment output grew by only 3.5 percent. Therefore, only about 60 percent of the growth in actual output was growth in full-employment output. The remainder reflected the movement toward full employment as the economy recovered from recession.

This chapter will chiefly concern itself with matters relating to growth of full-employment output, discussing such questions as the following: What are the sources of growth in full-employment output and full-employment output per capita? What can the government do to influence these items? Should the government seek to influence growth? If so, what is the proper growth target?

This concentration on full-employment output growth does not mean that the trend of full-employment output over time is independent of whether full employment is maintained. Severe recessions dampen the trend of full-employment output by retarding the rate of capital accumulation, so that full-employment output per capita is smaller even when the demand deficiency is removed. The real incomes of U.S. residents were

Figure 18–1 **U.S. Actual GNP and Full-Employment GNP, 1952–1977**

Full-employment GNP, estimated by the President's Council of Economic Advisers, is the GNP that would have been produced during the year in question if the full-employment unemployment rate (the natural rate of unemployment) had been maintained.

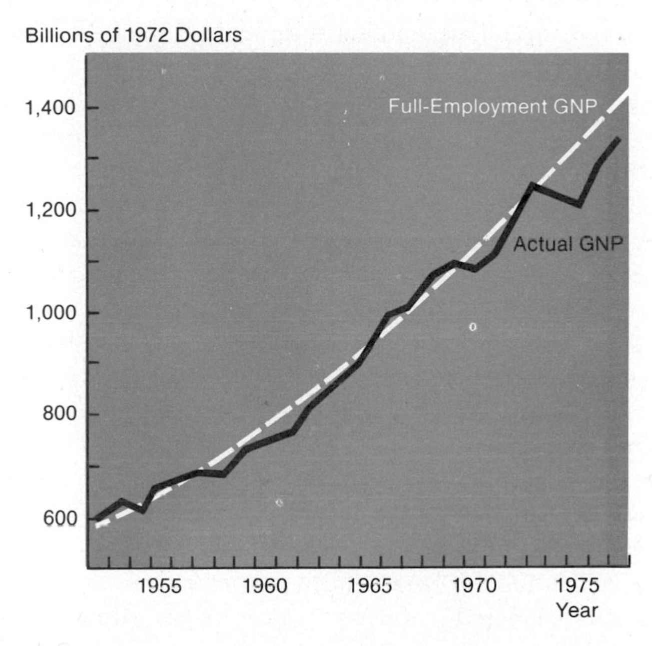

Source: President's Council of Economic Advisers, *Economic Report of the President* (Washington, D.C.: Government Printing Office, 1978), p. 84.

lower during the 1940s and 1950s, and perhaps even beyond that, even at full employment, because of the low rates of investment expenditures recorded during the Depression of the 1930s. Labor had less capital to work with during the later decades because of the capital accumulation which was lost during the 1930s.

The Sources of Economic Growth

Real U.S. GNP has multiplied by about ten times since 1900. This growth reflects increases in actual rather than full-employment output, but the difference between the two is not great when such long periods of time are being considered. Real GNP per capita has multiplied by about four times.

The tenfold increase in aggregate output has resulted from increased labor employment, capital accumulation, and technological advance. Technological advance actually is a catchall and includes all things which have increased the output producible with given levels of labor and capital inputs. It reflects such things as improvements in the quality of labor through increased educational levels, improvements in the quality of capital through inventions, and improvements in the techniques of production, including those arising from increased sizes of firms.

Labor employment means labor input in hours, so that the increase in labor employment reflects (1) growth in the labor force, which is the result of growth in the working-age population and trends in labor force participation rates, and (2) trends in average hours worked per week. For the United States, the most important factors in increased labor employment during recent decades have been the birth rate fluctuations during the 1930s and World War II, the increase in labor force participation rates produced by the influx of women into the labor force, and the steady reduction in average hours worked per week. Average hours worked per week have declined because workers have chosen to consume a portion of the increased real income potential resulting from increasing real wages in the form of increased leisure. Another possible reason for the decline is that employers have regarded worker productivity as being greater with shorter work weeks.

Capital accumulation is produced by net investment expenditures. Earlier chapters ignored this effect of positive net investment expenditures, treating full-employment output as fixed in order to highlight the stabilization problem. Not only has the U.S. capital stock grown since 1900, it has grown faster than labor employment, so that the capital to labor ratio has increased.

Of the three factors listed for technological advance, the first, improved labor quality, is reflected in the sharp increase in the median number of school years completed by persons twenty-five years old and older in the United States. While data for the earlier years of the century are not available, the number rose from 8.5 years to 12.4 years just from 1940 to 1976.

Obvious examples of the second factor in technological advance, improvements in the quality of capital through invention, include the steam engine, the gasoline engine, nuclear power, the telephone, the electronic computer, and synthetic fibers.

Improvements in the techniques of production, the third factor in technological advance, include such things as the introduction of interchangeable parts, self-service stores, more efficient factory designs, improvements in work scheduling, improvements in inventory planning, and the like. Improved techniques also include economies of scale, the most important source of which is the greater specialization of labor permitted by larger firm sizes. Workers who specialize in a single task do not spend time moving from task to task. They utilize capital more efficiently, since each worker need not be equipped with the whole range of tools and machines necessary to the production of specific products. Most important, workers who specialize in a single task are more skilled. They gain skills faster, from constant and uninterrupted repetition, and they can confine themselves to the tasks best suited to their interests and natural abilities.

Denison's Estimates of the Sources of Economic Growth

Edward F. Denison has provided estimates of the importance of these several sources of U.S. real output growth. In a study published by the Brookings Institution in 1974, he presents the average of the annual growth rates of national income for 1929–1969 as 3.41 percent and allocates this among sources as indicated in Table 18–1. This work updates his earlier, well known study performing a similar task for the periods 1909–1929 and 1929–1957.

Capital input—that is, capital accumulation—accounts for 0.50 percent

Denison's Sources of Economic Growth: Allocation of Average Annual Growth Rates for U.S. Output, 1929–1969

Table 18–1

	Percent
National income	3.41
Capital input	0.50
Labor input	1.32
Increase in labor input (hours)	0.87
Increase in labor quality	0.36
Unallocated	0.09
Advances in knowledge	0.92
Improved resource allocation	0.30
Economies of scale	0.36
Other	0.01

Source: Edward F. Denison, *Accounting for United States Economic Growth, 1929–1969* (Washington, D.C.: Brookings Institution, 1974), p. 127. Reprinted by permission.

of the 3.41 percent average growth rate. Labor input, which is subcategorized into growth in labor employment in hours, increase in labor quality (mostly from higher educational levels), and "unallocated," accounts for 1.32 percent. Advances in knowledge, which is Denison's term for new inventions plus new technology, excluding economies of scale, contribute 0.92 percent. If the increase in labor quality is grouped with advances in knowledge, improved resource allocation, and economies of scale as technological advance, technological advance accounts for 1.94 percent, more than half of the estimated average annual growth rate in output.

Denison's allocations are estimates, of course, and must be accepted as such. Their accuracy depends on the procedures he applies in obtaining them. Still, they give an indication of the relative importance of the several sources of growth in an area where estimates are needed.

Growth in Output Per Capita

Increases in the capital to labor ratio and technological advance have been the major contributory factors in the fourfold increase in U.S. output per capita evidenced since 1900. Increases in labor employment and increases in capital which merely match increases in labor employment drop out as factors in per capita output growth. Trends in labor force participation rates and average hours worked per week, which affect the labor employment to population ratio, also have influenced per capita output growth. And the population growth rate affects per capita output growth independently of its effect on the capital to labor ratio, since it influences the pressure of population on natural resources.

Government Policy and Growth

The discussion of the sources of growth in the preceding section suggests the types of government policies which can influence growth in full-employment output per capita. Interest focuses on policies to influence the rate of capital accumulation, since such policies seem capable of bringing about fairly significant changes in the capital to labor ratio, and hence in the level of per capita output, within reasonable periods of time. Policies to affect the rate of population growth—tax exemptions for dependents, immigration policies, and the like—can have some effect, however, since they also can influence the capital to labor ratio and since they can affect the pressure of population on natural resources. But population policies work more slowly, especially if they work via the birth rate rather than upon immigration.

The government also influences growth through policies designed to affect the rate of technological advance. Policies to reduce the private costs of education and increase its availability have improved the quality of the labor force. The job training programs of the 1960s and 1970s and the revision in immigration policies of the mid-1960s which established skills rather than national origins as a criterion presumably had a similar effect. Tax incentives for research and development expenditures and direct government grants to support research in universities, nonprofit institutions, and private firms stimulate growth by producing new inventions and new technologies. More direct government involvements, such as the Manhattan Project of World War II and the space program, have produced technology with applications well beyond bombs and men on the moon.

Policies to increase labor force participation rates or to remove barriers to growth also can augment per capita output growth. Equal opportunity activities by government may have raised labor force participation rates in the United States by increasing the influx of women into the labor force during recent years. Antimonopoly laws and vigilance can remove market imperfections which impede the application of new inventions and techniques.

Policies to Stimulate Capital Accumulation

Since influencing capital accumulation is the major focus of attention in growth policy, it is useful to look more closely at the mechanics of this process. The government affects the rate of capital accumulation by influencing the proportion of full-employment output going to investment expenditures. There are two primary techniques for this.

First, the government can apply fiscal restraint to raise full-employment government saving. This increases the aggregate saving function, lowers the interest rate, and stimulates investment expenditures. The fiscal restraint must be combined with monetary ease if full employment is to be maintained. The lower rate of interest increases the demand for money balances, so that a once-over acceleration of money supply growth must occur to provide the money balances necessary to full-employment aggregate demand.

Second, government can use the investment tax credit. If an investment tax credit of 10 percent is introduced, producers are permitted to deduct 10 percent of the amount of their current investment expenditures from taxes. This raises the after-tax expected marginal efficiency of investment on investment opportunities and produces a larger flow of investment expenditures at each interest rate—that is, it shifts the investment demand schedule to the right. This will increase interest rates, since it produces a rightward shift in the *IS* curve, but investment expenditures still will increase, since consumption expenditures and government purchases are sensitive to interest rates. Prices will rise unless the investment tax credit is combined with a temporary monetary restraint, since money demand declines as interest rates rise.

Figures 18–2 and 18–3 illustrate these effects with the *IS-LM* model, neglecting the growth in full-employment output itself, for convenience, as in earlier chapters.

Figure 18–2 presents the fiscal restraint case. Beginning in an initial full-employment equilibrium at Point A, an increase in tax rates, a reduction in government purchases, or a reduction in transfer payments shifts

Figure 18–2 **Stimulating Growth by Increasing Government Saving**

An application of fiscal restraint, combined with the proper amount of monetary ease, can raise the aggregate saving and investment rates, and therefore the rate of capital accumulation, without sacrificing either price or employment goals.

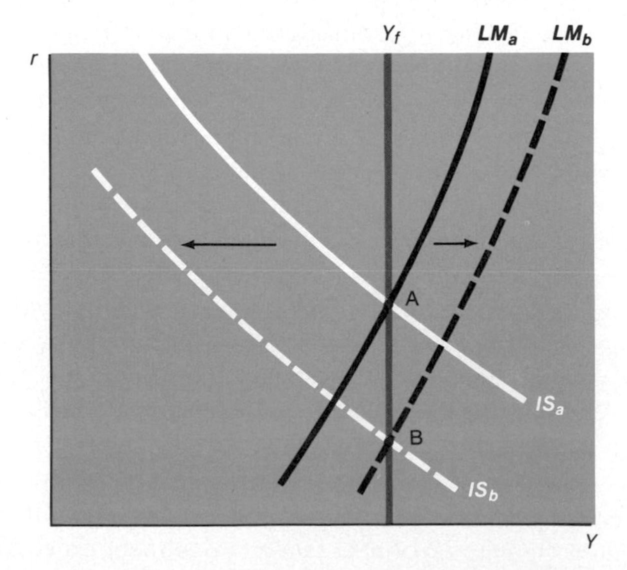

Figure 18–3 **Stimulating Growth with an Investment Tax Credit**

An investment tax credit can raise the full-employment aggregate saving and investment rates, and therefore the full-employment capital accumulation rate, provided that expenditures other than investment expenditures vary inversely with the interest rate. If combined with the proper amount of monetary restraint, it can do this without sacrificing the price stability goal.

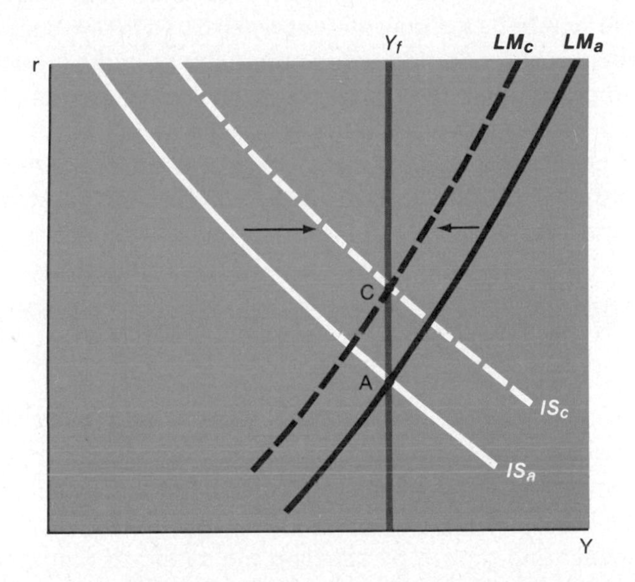

the *IS* curve to the left. Full-employment equilibrium is restored at Point B, assuming that compensatory expansive monetary policies to shift the *LM* curve to LM_b are applied. Investment expenditures must be higher at Point B since the interest rate is lower. Full-employment output is shifted to investment expenditures from consumption expenditures, government purchases, or both, depending on the combination of tax, transfer payment, and government purchase policies employed.

Figure 18–3 illustrates how the investment tax credit raises investment expenditures at full-employment output. Beginning again at an initial equilibrium at Point A, the introduction of the investment tax credit shifts the investment demand schedule and hence the *IS* curve to the right. The *IS* curve moves from IS_a to IS_c. If inflation is to be avoided, the *LM* curve must be shifted to the left, from LM_a to LM_c, with monetary restraint. In any event, the new equilibrium will be at Point C, where IS_c intersects the full-employment line. Investment expenditures will be higher, provided that consumption expenditures plus government purchases are somewhat sensitive to the interest rate, even neglecting the possibility for higher investment expenditures posed by growth in full-employment output.

The government also can stimulate capital accumulation and full-employment output growth per capita simply by increasing government investment expenditures, which involve expenditures for highways, educational facilities, public buildings, and the like—even railroads and automobile factories if the government is permitted to own such facilities. Graphically, this shifts the *IS* curve to the right, as in the investment tax credit example in Figure 18–3, and moves the equilibrium from Point A to Point C. As before, monetary restraint is necessary if inflation is to be avoided. The increased government investment expenditures would be offset to some extent by an interest-induced reduction in private investment expenditures, but total public and private investment expenditures will increase if private consumption expenditures are interest-sensitive.

The Neoclassical Growth Model

The neoclassical growth model, introduced by Robert Solow, formalizes the relationships among growth in full-employment output and growth in full-employment output per capita and their determinants.[1] It presents a useful vehicle for posing the question of the appropriate role for government in influencing growth by affecting the saving to output ratio with fiscal policies.

The model employs the aggregate production function:

$$Y = F(N, K), \qquad \text{18–1}$$

where Y, N, and K are aggregate output, labor input, and the capital stock, as before. It assumes constant returns to scale in N and K and positive but diminishing marginal products in the two factors of production. Technological advance proceeds at a constant rate over time and is neutral in the sense that it increases the marginal products of capital and labor by the same percentages. The saving to output ratio, $s = S/Y$, and the rate of growth of labor input over time are constants in the model. Full employ-

[1] See R. M. Solow, "A Contribution to the Theory of Economic Growth," *Quarterly Journal of Economics* 70 (February 1956): 65–94.

ment is assured by price and money-wage flexibility. The special, interest rate floor cases are neglected.

An interesting feature of the model is that the growth rates for full-employment output and full-employment output per capita are independent of the saving to output ratio in the long term. The rate of growth of full-employment output settles to the growth rate for labor input plus the rate of technological advance. The growth rate for full-employment output per unit of labor input settles simply to the rate of technological advance, and the growth rate for full-employment output per capita is the same, if trends in labor force participation rates and the average work week are neglected.

These results do not negate a role for government fiscal policy in influencing economic growth, however. It is true that the growth of output per unit of labor input from period to period will settle down again to the rate of technological advance following an increase in the aggregate saving ratio induced by fiscal policy. But the period to period growth will accelerate temporarily during the period of adjustment, and the period of adjustment may be several decades. More important, output per unit of labor input will be higher as a result of the increase in the saving ratio, even in the long-term equilibrium, so that a comparison of points along the old and new long-term growth paths will show that growth has occurred.

Figure 18–4 illustrates these points. With s_1, an initial saving ratio, output per unit of labor input expands along the path labeled s_1 when the model is in long-term equilibrium. Since the logarithm of Y/N is plotted on the vertical axis, the slope of s_1 reflects the rate of growth of Y/N over time; the slope equals the rate of technological advance per unit of time. The line is straight because the rate of technological advance is constant by assumption.

If government saving is increased at time t_1 through fiscal policies so that the community's aggregate saving ratio rises to s_2, the rate of capital accumulation increases, and the economy moves along the broken line path toward the new long-term equilibrium growth path labeled s_2. The rate of growth accelerates temporarily, as evidenced by the steeper slope of the broken line adjustment path, but eventually it settles down again to the rate of technological advance. But notice that output per unit of labor input is higher at all points in time, even in long-term equilibrium, than it would have been if the saving ratio had not been increased. For time t_2, for example, Point B is higher than Point C, which would have prevailed had s not been increased from s_1 to s_2. The increase in the saving ratio has produced economic growth, even comparing only points in long-term

Figure 18–4 **The Effect of a Fiscal Policy Induced Increase in the Aggregate Saving Ratio on the Rate of Growth of Output per Unit of Labor Input**

A fiscal policy induced increase in the ratio of aggregate saving and investment to full-employment output will temporarily raise the growth rate of full-employment output per unit of labor input and will permanently raise the level of full-employment output per unit of labor input.

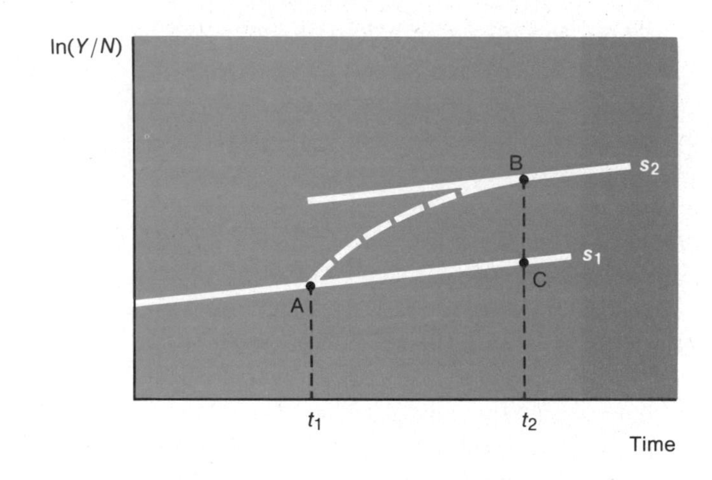

equilibrium. It does this because the higher saving ratio sustains a higher capital to labor ratio.

The Golden Rule of Accumulation

Granting that government can affect output per unit of labor input—a measure used here as a proxy for per capita output and real income—by influencing the aggregate saving ratio, the question arises as to the saving ratio the government should target. E. S. Phelps has provided one answer with his *Golden Rule of Accumulation,* which holds that the optimum saving ratio is the one which maximizes consumption per unit of labor input at all points in time, once the growth path relating to it is achieved.[2]

[2] The s which produces the maximum C/N at one point in time along the path produces it for all points in time, since the slopes of the lines, being simply the rate of technological advance, are independent of s.

This is the same as maximizing consumption per capita if the difference between the growth trends of labor employment and population is neglected.

Figure 18–5 illustrates Phelps's rule. The top portion of the figure

Figure 18–5 **Increases in the Aggregate Saving Ratio and the Long-Term Growth Paths for Output per Unit of Labor Input (Y/N) and Consumption per Unit of Labor Input (C/N)**

The Golden Rule of Accumulation would suggest targeting an aggregate saving ratio somewhere between s_2 and s_3 in this example, since the ratio yielding the long-term growth path which maximizes consumption per unit of labor input occurs within this range.

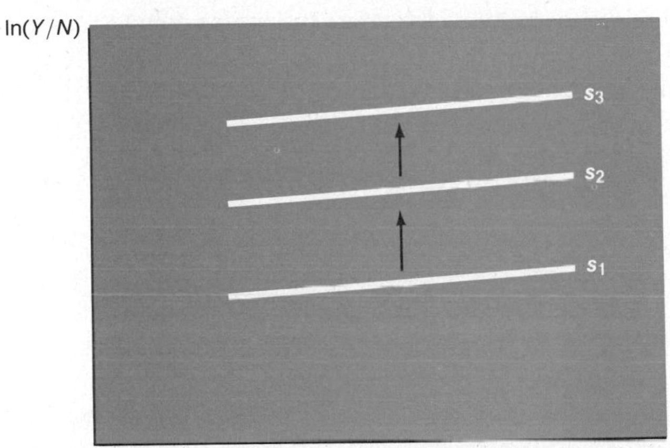

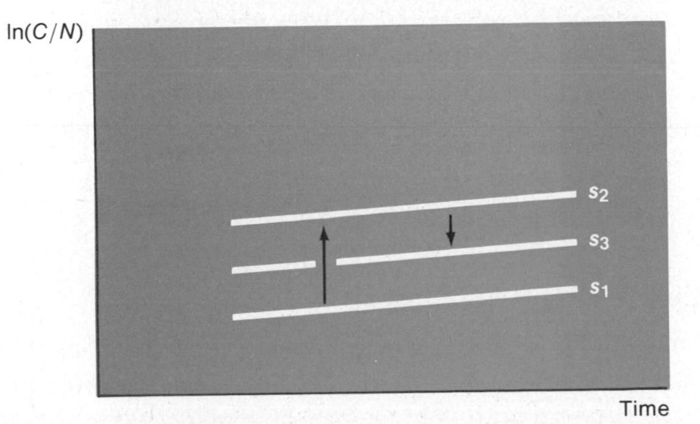

presents the growth path for Y/N for the successively higher saving ratios s_1, s_2, and s_3. The equilibrium capital to labor ratio is higher as the saving ratio rises; so, since the marginal product of capital is positive, Y/N is higher at each point in time.

The lower portion of the figure presents the growth path for consumption per unit of labor input for the three saving ratios. It is higher for s_2 than for s_1 but lower for s_3 than for s_2. Phelps's Golden Rule path obviously occurs for a saving ratio between s_2 and s_3, or for s_2 itself.

Why does the movement from s_2 to s_3 increase Y/N but diminish C/N? The reason is that the increase to s_3 increases required investment expenditures by more than it increases output. Higher levels for s produce higher capital to labor ratios and consequently higher output to labor ratios, but higher capital to labor ratios require higher investment expenditures for their maintenance. Eventually, as s increases, the marginal product of capital diminishes to the point where the increase in required investment expenditures is greater than the increase in output.

A nation which chooses the Golden Rule path but is presently below it—as most observers believe is the case with the United States—faces the further problem, in deciding upon the target s, of choosing the pace at which the Golden Rule path is to be approached. It can target the s appropriate to the Golden Rule path and approach the path at the pace this s produces. But it also can choose a more rapid or a more leisurely approach, temporarily effecting a higher or lower s than the Golden Rule s, accumulating the capital stock necessary to the path more rapidly or more slowly.

In general, the more rapidly the Golden Rule path is approached, the greater must be the sacrifice of consumption by present generations. This sacrifice provokes one major criticism of the Golden Rule of Accumulation as a criterion for growth policy. Why, it is argued, should the present generation sacrifice consumption to approach the Golden Rule path rapidly, or even to approach it at all, when the evidence of history has been that later generations are richer in any event because of technological advance?

The Laissez Faire Position

Economists with a strong laissez faire orientation, including most monetarists, reject Phelps's Golden Rule as a prescription for government growth policy on a more fundamental philosophical basis. They argue that the government should avoid influencing the aggregate saving ratio insofar as possible, letting it, as well as the aggregate investment function, simply reflect private attitudes with respect to saving and investment. They suggest that government balance its full-employment budget or, alternatively, if government investment expenditures are recognized, that government set its full-employment saving at zero, letting its investment expenditures be financed in capital markets in competition with private investment expenditures. The objective of laissez faire, noninterference by government in economic matters, thus is served.

The zero government saving prescription may produce a lower aggregate saving ratio than is desirable, however. There are several reasons for this.

1. Zero government saving is not neutral if taxes levied to finance government consumption purchases come partly from what would have been private saving. In that case, aggregate saving is diminished by the presence of government, even with government saving at zero.

2. In the actual world, private corporations do not pursue investment expenditures to the point where expected marginal efficiencies of investment equal costs of funds for financing. The corporations require a cushion of expected yields over costs of funds, and the cushion does not entirely reflect premiums to cover risks which apply to the community at large. It may reflect a restriction of output and investment levels which results from monopoly control. It may reflect premiums charged by existing equity holders for new equity issues as compensation for the dilution of existing ownership percentages.

3. Even if zero saving were neutral, and markets perfect, it is not clear that the interests of future generations would be adequately provided for by the laissez faire approach to growth policy. Future generations are not able to place their votes in current capital markets. They are represented only in the estate motive for saving, which probably is insufficient for their needs. People are concerned for their children and grandchildren, but not much beyond that. Moreover, estate taxes blunt the effect of the estate motive on the saving ratio.

4. Finally, investment expenditures which do not appear profitable to an individual firm often provide externalities which make them profitable for the community as a whole. Investment expenditures of this sort must be undertaken as government investment expenditures or be subsidized by government if they are to take place. The best examples of these expenditures are space ventures, the early nuclear projects, and the like, which have provided technological spin-offs which have benefited the community at large but would not have benefited individual firms sufficiently to justify the private investment expenditures necessary to the projects.[3]

Many economists, reviewing these arguments and considering the merits of the Phelps recommendation, end up somewhere in the middle. They accept the argument that government full-employment saving maintained at zero, with no tax incentives to investment, might result in too little provision for future incomes and consumption. But they see the Golden Rule as requiring too much sacrifice of consumption by present generations. While the Phelps rule seems fair at first glance, since it counts consumption in the future equally with present consumption, in fact it may not be fair. Under the rule, future generations would enjoy higher per capita consumption than the current generation because of the increase in per capita income which would occur as the Golden Rule path was approached and because technological advance might continue to produce growth in per capita income even after the path was reached.

The Future

Perhaps future generations will not be so rich as past trends suggest, however. The sharp increases in energy prices of the 1970s have reawakened speculation that the earth's fixed supply of land and its exhaustible supplies of fossil fuel and other mineral resources will dictate that the per capita output growth rates of the future will not match those of the past. Ultimately, the pressure of population on natural resources will become a problem unless zero population growth can be achieved or space colonies become a reality. Problems of space for living and producing food will afflict even the industrialized nations.

There is the further problem of environmental pollution. The economic growth of the past has been artificially high in the sense that adequate provision has not always been made for allocating resources to maintain the environment. If conditions have now reached the state where such expenditures will have to be made in the future, output growth in the kinds of goods and services which have been consumed in the past will suffer.

Whether per capita output growth will continue for the United States in the future as in the past probably depends on whether technological

[3] For a more complete treatment of the case against the laissez faire position on growth, see James Tobin, "Economic Growth as an Objective of Government Policy," *American Economic Review* 54 (May 1964): 1–20.

advance proceeds at a pace sufficient to offset the natural resources constraint, including the need to maintain the environment. (Increases in the capital to labor ratio could contribute to increases in per capita output, of course.)

The most pressing need for the next few decades appears to be for technological advance in the area of energy resources. New energy sources are needed to replace oil and natural gas. New technology is needed for meeting current objections to nuclear energy and for utilizing coal resources more effectively. Gloomy past forecasts as to economic growth based on the obvious truth that fossil fuels are exhaustible have proved to be wrong, because discoveries of new reserves have outpaced consumption of known reserves. But perhaps that avenue is closing. In that event, technological advance in the energy area is needed if past growth rates of per capita output are to be maintained, or, indeed, if declining per capita output is to be avoided. Government activities to stimulate such advances should be a priority item in government growth policy.

The neoclassical growth model ignores the constraint posed by natural resources simply by treating such resources as free goods, available in any necessary supply. It yields positive per capita output growth rates with technological advance and constant per capita output without it, assuming the saving ratio is constant.

The natural resources constraint could be introduced into the model as requiring diminishing returns to scale in capital and labor. That is, equal percentage increases in capital and labor inputs would provoke less than proportionate increases in output, with natural resources fixed and exhaustible. Per capita output then would decline over time, in the absence of continuous increases in the capital to labor ratio, unless technological advances offset the negative influence of natural resources.

Summary

1. Economists usually define economic growth as the increase in an economy's full-employment output over time when they are speaking of the growth goal, either the simple increase or the increase in per capita terms.

2. The chief sources of growth in full-employment output are growth in labor employment, capital accumulation, and technological advance. Technological advance reflects such things as improvements in the

quality of labor through increased educational levels, improvements in the quality of capital through inventions, and improvements in the techniques of production, including those which arise from increased sizes of firms.

3. Increases in the capital to labor ratio and technological advance have been the chief contributory factors to growth in U.S. output per capita. Changes in the labor employment to population ratio, reflecting trends in labor force participation rates and the average work week, also affect growth in per capita output. And the population growth rate influences growth in per capita output independently of its effect on the capital to labor ratio, since it affects the pressure of population on natural resources.

4. The government influences growth in output per capita through policies affecting the sources of growth. The primary focus of government growth policy has been on increasing capital accumulation rates, and the primary means for accomplishing this has involved using fiscal policies to increase the aggregate saving function and imposing investment tax credits. Other possibilities include policies to affect population growth rates, labor force participation rates, the average work week, education and training levels, and research leading to technological advance.

5. The Golden Rule of Accumulation suggests that the long-term target of government growth policy should be the aggregate saving ratio corresponding to the growth path which maximizes consumption per unit of labor input, a proxy for per capita consumption. The intermediate term target for the aggregate saving ratio might be higher or lower, depending on how quickly the community wishes to approach the Golden Rule path.

6. An alternative view, the laissez faire position, is that the government should adopt a neutral policy toward the aggregate saving function and the investment demand schedule, insofar as possible, and let the private market determine both the rate of economic growth and the level of the equilibrium growth path.

7. Whether the growth of output per capita in the future will match that of the past, or even be positive, probably depends on whether technological advance, particularly in the area of energy resources, can offset the constraint posed by fixed and exhaustible natural resources.

Concepts for Identification

economic growth
economic growth rates
growth in full-employment output
capital accumulation
technological advance
economies of scale
investment tax credit
neoclassical growth model
neutral technological advance
saving ratio
long-term growth path
Golden Rule of Accumulation
laissez faire
diminishing returns to scale

Questions and Problems for Review

1. Distinguish between growth in actual output and growth in full-employment output.

2. Technological advance encompasses improvements in the quality of labor, the quality of capital, and the techniques of production. Give eight examples of technological advance from U.S. economic experience, including at least one from each of those categories.

3. Population growth is one factor in the growth of labor employment (hours) in the United States since 1929. Identify two other factors and explain their roles.

4. Discuss various policies the government can employ to cause the output per capita of future generations to be higher than it otherwise would be.

5. Illustrate graphically how the government can utilize general monetary and fiscal policies to raise the amount of full-employment output allocated to saving and investment without sacrificing price or employment goals.

6. Beginning in a situation with initial price stability and full employment, illustrate how imposing an investment tax credit can raise full-employment saving and investment expenditures without disturbing prices. What monetary policy adjustment is required for this result? Explain why expenditures other than investment expenditures must vary inversely with the interest rate if saving and investment expenditures are to increase.

7. Explain how government policies which raise the full-employment saving ratio can raise the long-term equilibrium level of output per unit of labor input but lower the long-term equilibrium level of consumption per unit of labor input.

8. Evaluate Phelps's Golden Rule of Accumulation as a rule for growth policy. Is it fair to the current generation?

9. What is the laissez faire rule for government growth policy? Evaluate the rule.

References

Denison, E. F. *The Sources of Economic Growth in the United States and the Alternative before Us.* New York: Committee for Economic Development, 1962.

———. *Accounting for United States Economic Growth, 1929–1969.* Washington, D.C.: Brookings Institution, 1974.

Phelps, E. S. "The Golden Rule of Accumulation: A Fable for Growth Men." *American Economic Review* 51 (September 1961): 638–643.

———. "Second Essay on the Golden Rule of Accumulation." *American Economic Review* 55 (September 1965): 793–814.

Solow, R. M. "A Contribution to the Theory of Economic Growth." *Quarterly Journal of Economics* 70 (February 1956): 65–94.

Tobin, James. "Economic Growth as an Objective of Government Policy." *American Economic Review* 54 (May 1964): 1–20.

19

The Foreign Sector

Nations can operate the foreign exchange market with fixed, flexible, or managed float rates. Managed float, the present U.S. system, is a compromise between fixed and flexible systems. It seeks to provide the adjustments in exchange rates needed to accommodate fundamental balance of payments disturbances while avoiding the wide short-term fluctuations in rates which can occur under completely flexible systems.

The discussion to this point has related to closed rather than open economies in the sense that it has not dealt for the most part with transactions between domestic residents and residents of foreign countries. This chapter relaxes that restriction and moves to the case of the open economy. It is important to do so. Transactions with foreign countries are significant for almost all of the world's economies, and they have important implications for the stability and stabilization of domestic economies. This is true even for the United States, where the foreign sector is small relative to the total economy, in comparison with "trading" nations such as Denmark and the Netherlands. As noted earlier, the sharp increase in the price of imported oil in the mid-1970s had a significant effect on the cost of living of U.S. citizens, centering in prices of imported goods and services. Moreover, the chronic balance of international payments problem the United States was experiencing even prior to the increase in oil prices has posed an important constraint on the ability of the U.S. stabilization authorities to achieve employment, price, economic growth, and free trade goals simultaneously.

This chapter begins with a discussion of the foreign exchange market arising from transactions between domestic residents and residents of foreign countries, then examines the operation of this market under both fixed and flexible foreign exchange rate systems and interprets the present U.S. system of managed float as something between the two. Subsequent sections incorporate the foreign sector into the *IS-LM* model presented in earlier chapters, analyze the effects of macroeconomic disturbances with an international sector present, and note the problems that sector poses for pursuing domestic price, employment, and growth goals.

The Foreign Exchange Market

Transactions involving foreign countries fall into the same categories as domestic transactions. They include purchases and sales of goods and services (including factor services and intermediate goods), purchases and sales of securities, and purchases and sales of existing physical production facilities. Also, they include simple transfers of income, as when governments make grants to foreign governments or when private corporations or governments pay pension benefits to persons who have retired abroad.

Transactions between parties who are not residents of the same country differ from transactions between parties who are residents of the same country, however, in that they involve, at some point, an exchange of domestic for foreign currency. That is, they involve demands and supplies for foreign exchange. This occurs because both parties ordinarily want to pay and be paid in their own currencies.

For example, a U.S. auto dealer who imports an automobile from a West German manufacturer will want to pay in dollars, which is what the dealer receives when the autos are sold to U.S. consumers, while the German exporter will want to be paid in deutsche marks, in which production costs are incurred. The German exporter may accept a check drawn in dollars on a U.S. bank in payment, especially if the German maintains a dollar deposit in a New York bank for conducting export business. But ultimately the German will exchange these dollars for marks, perhaps by cabling the New York bank to transfer the funds to the account of the German's Hamburg bank, which then pays marks to the German at the going dollar price of marks.

Alternatively, the German exporter can ask for payment in marks. In this case, the U.S. importer may purchase a *foreign exchange draft* written in marks for dollars at a U.S. bank and send it to the German exporter in payment. The foreign exchange draft is a check drawn by the bank or its correspondent on a mark balance in a German bank. More likely, the U.S. bank simply accepts dollars from the U.S. importer and cables its branch or correspondent bank abroad to pay the German exporter in marks. Or possibly the U.S. importer maintains a mark balance in a German bank and can pay simply by drawing a check on this balance. This still involves an exchange of dollars for marks—that is, a U.S. demand for foreign exchange—since the U.S. importer's mark balance must be replenished regularly with marks purchased with dollars.

Similarly, a U.S. demand for foreign exchange arises when U.S. residents purchase foreign securities, when U.S. corporations make interest and dividend payments to foreign holders of their securities, when U.S. individuals, firms, or governmental units make transfer payments to residents of other countries, when U.S. corporations purchase existing production facilities abroad, or simply when U.S. residents increase their transaction money balances of foreign currencies. The opposite type of transactions, that is, purchases of goods, services, or securities by foreign residents from U.S. residents, foreign purchases of existing production facilities in the U.S., transfer payments or interest and dividend payments from foreign residents to U.S. residents, or increases in foreign holdings of transaction money balances in dollars, gives rise to supplies of foreign exchange.

Figure 19–1 presents the market for foreign exchange arising from such transactions. The market determines the price of foreign exchange. For convenience, the figure treats foreign currency as if it were composed only of marks, so that the demands and supplies for foreign exchange are demands and supplies for marks, and the price of foreign exchange, or *foreign exchange rate,* on the vertical axis, is the dollar price of marks. Also neglected are transactions involving transfer payments, purchases and sales of existing physical assets, and net changes in "other country" transaction money balances (U.S. holdings of foreign money and foreign holdings of U.S. money), so that the demand for foreign exchange is simply the sum of U.S. demands for imports of newly produced goods and services from abroad (Zg) and imports of foreign securities (Zs). Similarly, the supply of foreign exchange to the United States is the foreign demand for U.S. exports of newly produced goods and services (Xg) and exports of dollar denomination securities to foreign countries (Xs). Both the imports and exports of goods and services and the imports and exports of securities are flows, defined as quantities per unit of time. Zs and Xs are net

Figure 19–1 **The Foreign Exchange Market**

The equilibrium foreign exchange rate in the figure is f_a, where the quantities of foreign exchange demanded and supplied are equal. In the absence of intervention by governments, the foreign exchange rate will tend to stay around this level.

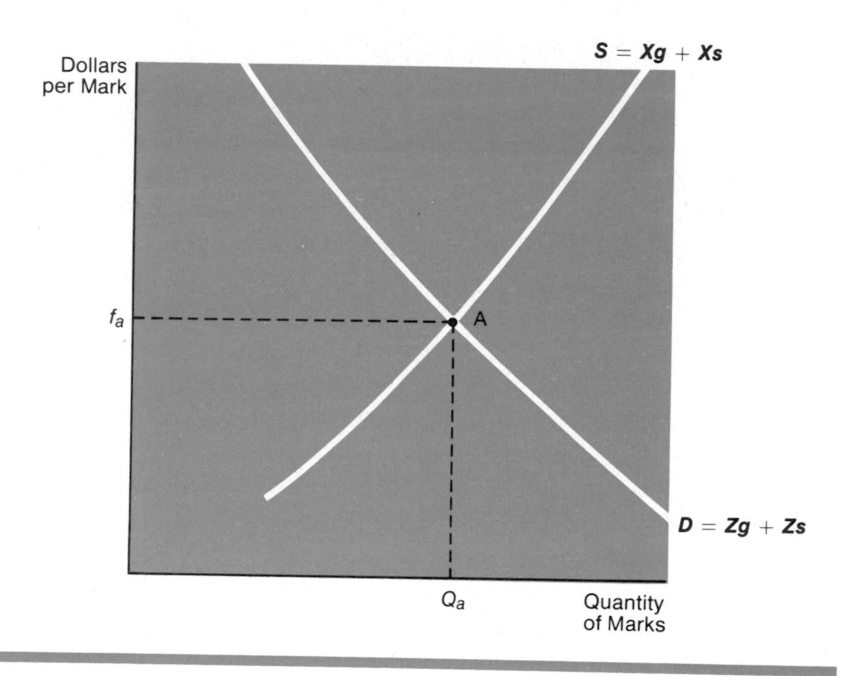

increases in foreign securities held by U.S. residents and U.S. securities held by foreign residents respectively. They are securities purchased less receipts from securities sold or repaid.

Since foreign and domestic prices, interest rates, and real incomes are held constant in these representations, the demand curve for foreign exchange slopes negatively. As the dollar price of marks increases, foreign goods and services become more expensive to U.S. residents. For example, a foreign auto costing 12,000 marks is priced at $3,000 to U.S. residents when a mark costs 25 cents, but at $6,000 when the price of the mark rises to 50 cents. The quantity of foreign autos demanded, and the quantity of marks demanded, therefore diminishes as the dollar price of marks increases, assuming the normal inverse demand and price relationship.

The supply of foreign exchange curve is presented here as sloping positively. U.S. goods and services become cheaper to foreigners as the dollar price of marks increases, since more dollars can be obtained per mark. The quantity of U.S. exports of goods and services therefore should increase as the dollar price of marks increases, and Figure 19–1 indicates that the number of marks supplied increases also.[1]

If the market were allowed to operate as a free market, without intervention by governments, central banks, or international monetary institutions, the dollar price of marks would be determined at f_u, where the market clears.[2] Otherwise, excess supplies or demands for marks would exist and bid the foreign exchange rate to that level. In such an equilibrium, international payments are balanced. The balance of international payments, defined as foreign exchange supplied less foreign exchange demanded, or:

$$BP = (Xg + Xs) - (Zg + Zs),$$

is zero. Alternatively:

$$BP = (Xg - Zg) + (Xs - Zs) = 0,$$

which is to say, the balance on current account, which has been reduced to net exports of newly produced goods and services by neglecting transfer payments, just offsets the balance on the capital account, which is net exports of securities (purchases and sales of existing real capital goods and changes in desired holdings of money balances having been neglected).

Fixed, Flexible, and Managed Float Foreign Exchange Rate Systems

Nations may operate either fixed or flexible foreign exchange rate systems or they may adopt something in between, often called managed float systems. Under fixed foreign exchange rate systems, nations announce

[1] In fact, the number of marks supplied will increase, and the supply curve of foreign exchange will slope positively, only if the foreign demand for U.S. exports of goods and services is price elastic in marks. In this case, the quantity of U.S. goods and services demanded by foreign countries rises more than in proportion to the rise in the dollar price of marks, so that total expenditures in marks increase.

[2] It is this price, plus a broker-dealer fee, which a U.S. importer would pay to a bank in purchasing a foreign exchange draft written in marks.

that they will maintain foreign exchange rates at specified levels, barring fundamental disturbances in their balance of international payments positions, and accomplish this via a variety of means, including intervening with purchases and sales of gold or foreign exchange as necessary and inducing such intervention by other nations. For example, in Figure 19–2, which again aggregates the U.S. foreign exchange markets into a single market, the United States, to maintain foreign exchange rate f_a in the face of a shift in the demand curve from D_1 to D_2, must eliminate the excess U.S. demand for foreign exchange which exists at f_a with D_2, or $(Q_2 - Q_a)$.

One means of doing this is to purchase dollars with gold in the foreign exchange market, in effect reducing the U.S. demand for foreign exchange below Q_2. Another method involves increasing the supply of foreign exchange beyond Q_a by purchasing dollars with foreign exchange from the Federal Reserve's foreign exchange reserves. A third possibility is to induce foreign central banks to add to the supply of foreign exchange,

Figure 19–2 **An Increase in the U.S. Demand for Imports**

A shift in the demand curve for foreign exchange from D_1 to D_2 causes the equilibrium foreign exchange rate to rise from f_a to f_b. Maintaining f_a requires eliminating $(Q_2 - Q_a)$, the excess demand for foreign exchange the shift produces at f_a.

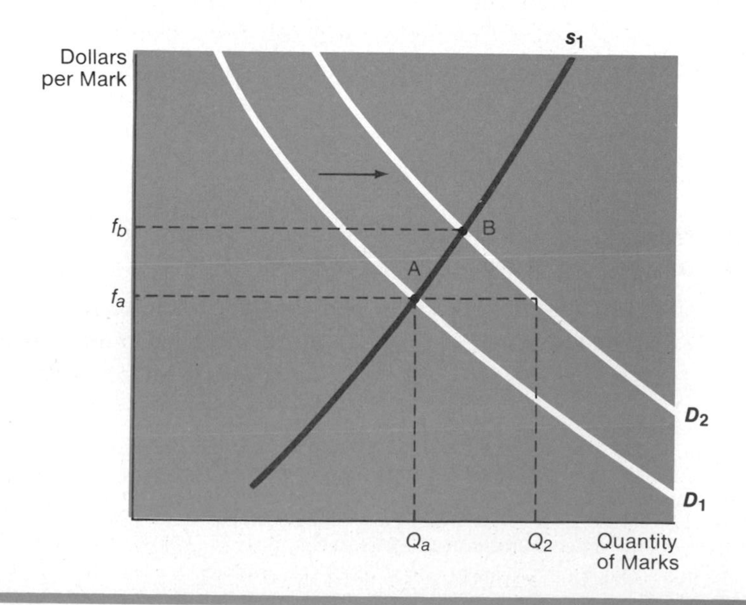

trading their currencies for dollars which they add to their own official foreign exchange reserves.

Long-lasting, or *fundamental,* disturbances cannot be accommodated in this way, since nations in chronic deficit in international payments eventually exhaust their foreign exchange and gold reserves and other nations become unwilling to make further additions of the weak currency to their own foreign exchange reserves. Fundamental disturbances arise from differing inflation rates or real productivity trends over time among nations or simply from permanent shifts in tastes and preferences.

Ideally, such disturbances are accommodated under fixed foreign exchange rate systems by occasional adjustments in foreign exchange rates. For example, if the shift in the demand curve in Figure 19–2 were deemed to be fundamental rather than short-term, the United States, if it were operating a fixed foreign exchange rate system, should adjust the rate at which it fixed the price of foreign exchange from f_a to f_b. Of course, there are the problems of distinguishing between fundamental and short-term disturbances and of ascertaining the precise level at which the rate should be fixed.

Flexible Foreign Exchange Rates

Under a completely flexible foreign exchange rate system, foreign exchange rates fluctuate freely in response to the forces of demand and supply in the market, balancing international payments automatically. A nation choosing such a system makes no attempt to fix foreign exchange rates. It simply ignores its balance of international payments. This means, in terms of Figure 19–2, that the foreign exchange rate is permitted to rise from f_a to f_b in response to market forces when the demand for foreign exchange curve shifts from D_1 to D_2.

A nation cannot by itself effect a completely flexible system in the sense that it cannot prevent intervention in the market by other nations, except by diplomacy. But it can operate a flexible rate system insofar as its own actions are concerned, simply ignoring its balance of international payments and relieving itself of any balance of payments problem in the process.

From Fixed to More Flexible Foreign Exchange Rates

From 1946 to early 1973, the world economy operated on a system of essentially fixed foreign exchange rates. This system collapsed in March of 1973 under pressure from chronic deficits in the U.S. balance of payments, and since that time the dollar has floated against other currencies in foreign exchange markets. It has been a managed float rather than the completely flexible system of foreign exchange rates described above, however, with central banks, including the U.S. Federal Reserve, intervening fairly often with purchases and sales of foreign exchange to smooth out (though not eliminate) fluctuations in foreign exchange rates.[3]

The system of fixed foreign exchange rates of the 1946 to 1973 period resulted from the International Monetary Conference at Bretton Woods, New Hampshire, held in 1944, at which the major trading nations of the world agreed to maintain a system of fixed rates, adjusting them only in cases of "fundamental" balance of payments disequilibriums. This Bretton Woods system, often termed an *adjustable peg system,* replaced the gold standard system of fixed rates which existed prior to World War II but which succumbed to the episode of competitive devaluations accompanying the worldwide depression of the 1930s. Under the gold standard, nations maintained fixed exchange rates by standing ready to exchange gold for currencies at set prices, in effect accommodating balance of payments deficits by giving up gold for currencies in excess supply.

Gold convertibility was continued under the Bretton Woods system until 1971, though gold purchases and sales had become limited to negotiated transactions between government central banks. The dollar balances accumulated by foreign private individuals, firms, and commercial banks as a result of the chronic U.S. balance of payments deficits were exchanged with foreign central banks, which in turn exchanged them with the U.S. government, either for gold or for U.S. foreign exchange reserves, or else the foreign central banks simply held the dollar balances as foreign exchange reserves.

By mid-1971, the Bretton Woods system was in considerable difficulty because of the chronic and continuing U.S. balance of payments deficits. U.S. gold reserves had declined from over $22 billion in the period immediately following World War II to just over $10 billion, dollar holdings of foreign central banks had accumulated to almost $50 billion, and the U.S. balance of payments deficit was running at an annual rate of well over $20 billion. Faced with this situation, the U.S. government ceased gold sales to foreign central banks and for a brief period permitted the dollar to float in foreign exchange markets in response to forces of demand and supply.

---

[3] The Federal Reserve reports regularly on its foreign exchange operations in the *Federal Reserve Bulletin*. See, for example, Board of Governors of the Federal Reserve System, "Treasury and Federal Reserve Foreign Exchange Operations," *Federal Reserve Bulletin* 64 (March 1978): 161–178, and 64 (September 1978): 717–735.

The system of fixed foreign exchange rates was restored promptly, however. In December 1971, as a result of a conference among the major trading nations at the Smithsonian Institution in Washington, D.C., it was agreed that the dollar would be maintained at a new level, below its former value, while the Japanese yen and the German mark, the currencies of the principal balance of payments surplus countries, would be maintained above their former values. But gold convertibility was not restored. The new levels were to be maintained by coordinated purchases and sales of foreign exchange by central banks.

The Bretton Woods system of fixed foreign exchange rates ended completely in early 1973. In February 1973, the United States announced its intention to devalue the dollar again. In March, under pressure from speculative capital fund flows from the dollar to the deutsche mark, the German central bank ceased its intervention to support the dollar and banded together with other nations from the European Economic Community in a joint float of their currencies relative to the dollar. This group of nations, which evolved into the European Monetary System in early 1979, has currencies which are fixed in relation to one another but fluctuate relative to the dollar.[4]

The Managed Float System

While, as stated earlier, the present system is not completely flexible, it differs sharply from the earlier fixed rate system. First, there is no attempt to keep foreign exchange rates rigidly fixed, and there is no commitment to maintain fluctuations within a specified range. Most important, the system is more flexible in the sense that there is more freedom for foreign exchange rates to move to new longer-term levels when fundamental balance of international payments disturbances occur. Optimally, the managed float system smooths out short-term fluctuations in foreign exchange rates but permits the rates to adjust to the longer-term levels.

Figure 19–3 illustrates how the managed float system might operate in response to the increase in the U.S. demand for foreign exchange curve considered earlier. Instead of permitting the dollar price of foreign exchange to rise to f_b, the new short-term market equilibrium rate, sufficient foreign currencies are provided to the market from Federal Reserve foreign exchange reserves or by foreign central banks to limit the foreign

[4] Seven of the nine members of the European Economic Community were fully participating members in the European Monetary System at its inception. They include Belgium, Denmark, France, West Germany, Ireland, Luxembourg, and the Netherlands. Italy elected to participate on a modified basis. The United Kingdom declined to join.

exchange rate adjustment to f_c, which is regarded as nearer the longer-term equilibrium rate. The amount of foreign exchange provided is $(Q_4 - Q_3)$. The foreign exchange rate adjusts, but the wider short-term fluctuation is avoided.

There is, of course, the problem of distinguishing short-term from longer-term movements in the equilibrium foreign exchange rate under managed float and of correctly gauging the latter, which are not observable. The nation which chronically errs in estimating longer-term movements in its foreign exchange rate will find itself accumulating or losing foreign exchange reserves over time.

Why Not Completely Flexible Foreign Exchange Rates?

Why are nations reluctant to move to the completely flexible foreign exchange rate systems? The principal reason is the belief that such

Figure 19–3 **A Managed Float Response to an Increase in the U.S. Demand for Foreign Exchange**

A managed float response to a shift in the demand curve for foreign exchange from D_1 to D_2 might involve providing the market with foreign exchange equal to $(Q_4 - Q_3)$, so that the foreign exchange rate would rise only to f_c.

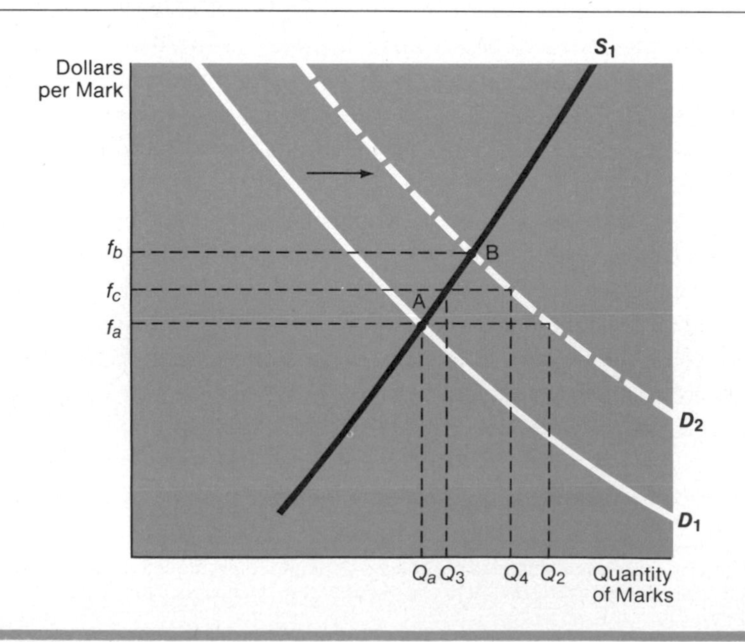

systems will result in extremely wide short-term fluctuations in foreign exchange rates. These wide fluctuations affect the price-competitiveness of firms engaged in export and import and firms whose products compete with imported products and subject them to the hardship of recurrent periods of feast and famine. If such hardships discourage firms from participating in export and import industries, the level of international trade declines, and nations lose a portion of the potential gains from international trade.

It is true that firms can hedge the foreign exchange rate risk of specific transactions by arranging prices in their own currency in advance or by buying or selling foreign exchange for future delivery in the futures market. But hedging techniques are much less effective at handling the risks that fluctuations in foreign exchange rates pose for long-term commitments of investment goods, labor, and entrepreneurial skills made by firms and individuals to export and import industries. Hence, wide fluctuations in foreign exchange rates may discourage firms and individuals from making such commitments, and the level of international trade may decline.

Why should foreign exchange rates fluctuate widely in the short term under completely flexible foreign exchange rate systems? Even though the foreign exchange rate which reflects a nation's fundamental international payments position may change only gradually over time, a freely floating rate may fluctuate very widely in the short term because of such things as speculative movements of capital funds, cyclical disturbances to interest rate levels occurring domestically or abroad which occasion sharp shifts in imports and exports of securities, and shifts in demands for exports and imports of goods and services which are themselves short term in nature. Moreover, the short-term responses of foreign exchange rates to these disturbances and to longer-term disturbances as well are aggravated by aggregate demand and supply curves for foreign exchange which are steeper (less price elastic) in the short term than in the long term. This last factor does not necessarily aggravate fluctuations in actual output levels for export, import, and import-competing firms in the aggregate, since it results from lags in output responses, but it disrupts and complicates planning, and it aggravates fluctuations in actual output levels for firms in industries where output responses take place more rapidly than the average.

During the period preceding the 1973 move to more flexible foreign exchange rates, the advocates of completely flexible foreign exchange rate systems argued persuasively that rates would not fluctuate widely in the short term under such systems. They anticipated that the activities of foreign exchange market speculators would smooth out fluctuations in foreign exchange rates. For example, if a currency depreciated beyond its longer-term level in response to a disturbance, speculators would enter the market and purchase the depreciated currency, anticipating the capital gain they would make by selling the currency on its return to its longer-term level. This would increase the demand for the depreciated currency and check its depreciation beyond its longer-term level. Of course, such speculation might not be a very efficient stabilizer, and might even be a destabilizing influence, if speculators instead believed that the depreciating currency would move even further beyond its longer-term level before returning to it. However, advocates of flexible foreign exchange rates pointed for support to the Canadian experience with flexible rates during 1952 through 1961. During this period, the price of the U.S. dollar in Canadian cents varied only from 95.97 cents to 99.91 cents.[5]

The experience with the U.S. dollar since the managed float commenced in March of 1973 is less supportive of the case for flexible foreign exchange rates, however. The dollar price of the currencies of the major U.S. trading partners has fluctuated substantially during this period despite regular intervention in foreign exchange markets by the Federal Reserve and foreign central banks to smooth out fluctuations. Figure 19–4, which presents the percentage deviations of the prices in dollars of the French, British, West German, and Japanese currencies from their March 1973 values for the period 1973 through 1978, reflects this.

It is true that the level of U.S. international trade has displayed no tendency to decline as yet. Both exports and imports of goods and services were higher for the U.S. in 1979 than in 1972. But effects on the level of trade take time, and other factors, such as the growing U.S. demand for oil imports and the stimulative effects on U.S. exports of a depreciated U.S. dollar, are involved. And foreign exchange rate fluctuations would have been greater under a completely flexible foreign exchange rate system. The question of whether completely flexible foreign exchange rates would reduce the level of U.S. international trade over time remains an open one.

Other Disadvantages of Flexible Foreign Exchange Rates

The disadvantages of wide short-term fluctuations in foreign exchange rates extend beyond disruption of activity levels in export, import, and import-competing industries. Sharp depreciations in a nation's currency

---

[5] Richard I. Leighton, *Economics of International Trade* (New York: McGraw-Hill, 1970), pp. 164–165. See also Egon Sohmen, *Flexible Exchange Rates* (Chicago: University of Chicago Press, 1961), p. 229.

Figure 19–4 **Price in U.S. Dollars of Major Foreign Currencies Compared with March 1973 Values, 1973–1978**

The dollar prices of the currencies of major U.S. trading partners have fluctuated significantly since the move to a more flexible foreign exchange rate system in 1973.

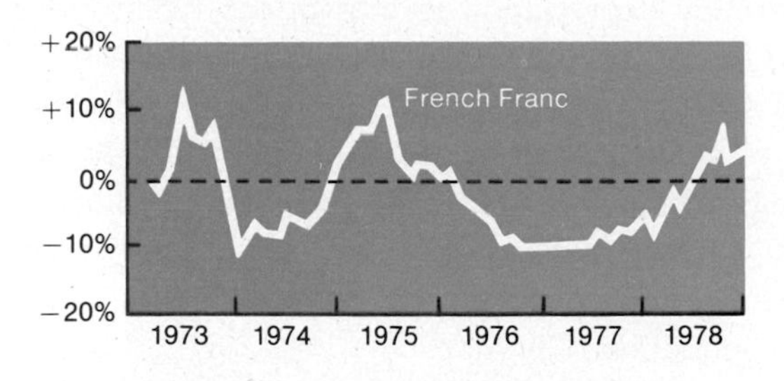

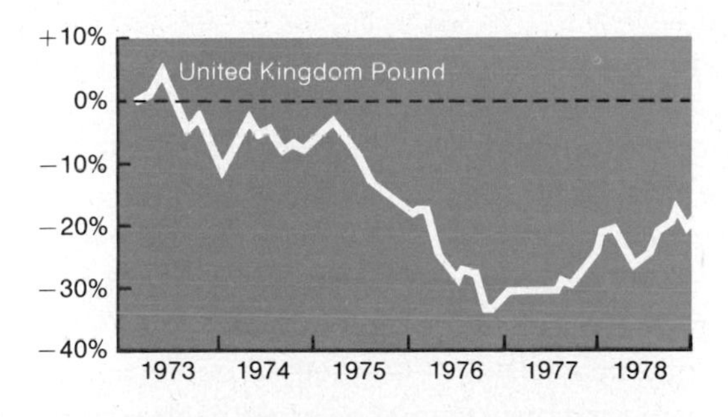

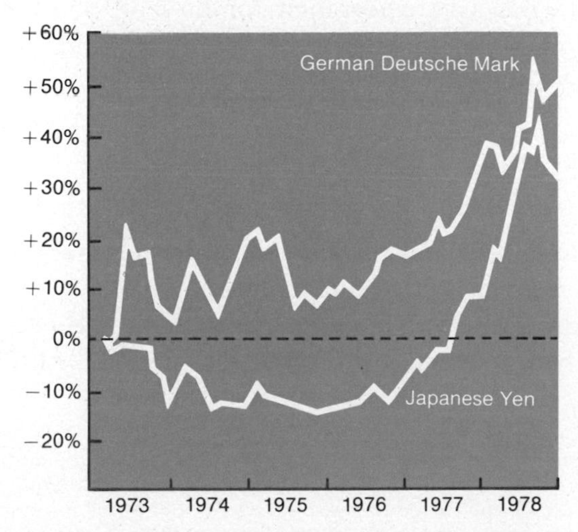

Source: Board of Governors of the Federal Reserve System, *Federal Reserve Bulletin* 65 (June 1979): A68, Table 3.29; and various earlier issues.

subject its residents to sharp reductions in the *terms of trade* for foreign transactions—that is, they increase the number of bushels of wheat which must be exported to pay for one imported automobile. This reduces the goods and services available domestically for consumption and capital accumulation.

Insofar as the nation's consumers are concerned, the most evident effect of currency depreciation is that prices of imported goods and services, and hence the consumer price index, increase.[6] This is a problem in itself for consumers, and it may create a further problem by inducing wage-push inflationary pressures within the domestic economy. The possibility of induced domestic wage-push inflation is especially important for a nation such as the United Kingdom, where labor unions are strong and food imports are an important item in relation to total consumer expenditures.

Sharp depreciations in a nation's currency may induce producer cost-push inflation as well. Since depreciation increases prices of imports, it weakens the foreign competition facing domestic producers and may permit them to raise prices sharply, especially in industries which are domestically highly concentrated. Prices of U.S.-made automobiles may have risen by more than they otherwise would have during the 1970s because the depreciation of the dollar had diminished the price-competitiveness of Japanese and German autos in the U.S. market.

A nation may have to bear these terms-of-trade and inflationary burdens of currency depreciation eventually if depreciation results from a fundamental deterioration in the nation's international payments position. But nations are reluctant to bear them for the sharp short-term depreciations in foreign exchange rates which may occur under flexible foreign exchange rate systems.

Why Not Fixed Foreign Exchange Rate Systems?

One reason for abandoning fixed foreign exchange rate systems is that such systems are not durable. The full gold standard succumbed to competitive devaluations during the 1930s, and the Bretton Woods system succumbed to speculative capital movements in 1973. The world

[6] Prices of imports rise less than in proportion to depreciations of the domestic currency if foreign producers reduce prices in terms of their currencies somewhat to preserve their markets. Moreover, for the United States, prices for imported oil have not been affected directly by dollar depreciation, since the cartel of foreign oil producers has fixed the price of oil in terms of U.S. dollars.

moved to a more flexible system for the dollar in 1973 because the fixed rate system could not be maintained.

The argument against fixed rate systems is broader than that, however. The basic difficulty is that the fixed rate systems do not seem to be able to provide the adjustments in foreign exchange rates needed to accommodate fundamental changes in international payments positions among major trading nations. The Bretton Woods system collapsed for that reason. It was an adjustable peg system which did not adjust. The U.S. dollar became overvalued relative to other major currencies, but devaluation of the dollar, as conceived at Bretton Woods, did not occur. The chief reason appears to have been a feeling on the part of U.S. authorities (probably a correct one) that devaluation would be met by competitive devaluations by other nations, who would seek to maintain the price-competitiveness of their export and import-competing industries. At best, it seemed to the U.S. authorities, devaluation would leave the relative position of the dollar unchanged. At worst, it might provoke a disruptive period of competitive devaluation similar to the one which caused the failure of the gold standard in the 1930s. In any event, the U.S. balance of payments deficit became chronic because the dollar became overvalued; it became evident that the dollar eventually would depreciate and would not recover; speculative movements of capital funds away from the dollar occurred; and the system collapsed.

But more important than the collapses of such systems are the means that nations in chronic deficit apply to improve their balances of international payments and conserve their foreign exchange and gold reserves before the collapses occur. They may impose tariffs or general taxes on imports to diminish the demand for foreign exchange. They may impose outright quotas on the foreign exchange that importers may purchase, to the same end. They may subsidize exports to increase the supply of foreign exchange. These devices interfere with the free flow of goods, services, and securities among nations and the gains which can be made from free trade.

Most important, nations with overvalued currencies may improve their international payments balance by sacrificing domestic objectives relating to full employment and economic growth. For example, a nation may tolerate an unemployment rate above the natural rate of unemployment so that the lower level of income will suppress imports of goods and services and reduce the demand for foreign exchange. It may tolerate a domestic rate of interest higher than that consistent with capital stock accumulation objectives in order to improve its international payments position by stimulating exports and diminishing imports of securities.

A later part of this chapter will look more carefully at the problem of sacrificing free trade, full employment, and economic growth to improve the international payments balance. In any event, an advantage of the more flexible foreign exchange rate systems over the fixed rate system is that they can produce the adjustments in foreign exchange rates needed to deal with fundamental disturbances and eliminate the need for sacrifice of free trade, full employment, and economic growth. To realize this advantage, direct restrictions on international trade must be avoided, and monetary and fiscal policies must be addressed to full employment and economic growth goals. A nation can still sacrifice these goals in order to avoid the decline in the terms of trade, the increases in import prices, and the possibility of induced domestic cost-push inflation a currency depreciation ordinarily involves. This trade-off can occur even under completely flexible foreign exchange rates. The important point is that the more flexible foreign exchange rate systems, by permitting currency depreciation, provide a choice.

The Gains from International Trade

Before concluding this section on fixed, flexible, and managed float foreign exchange rate systems, it is useful to consider more carefully the nature of the gains from trade which are sacrificed if nations impose tariffs or the like to improve their international payments position or if extremely wide fluctuations in foreign exchange rates discourage international trade under completely flexible systems. A simple example involving two countries (Countries A and B) and two commodities (Commodities X and Y) is helpful in illustrating how such gains arise.

Assume that Countries A and B have identical labor endowments but differing capital and natural resource endowments, so that production efficiencies differ. Country A can produce 150 units of X or 30 units of Y or any combination between these extremes, substituting 5 units of potential X for 1 unit of Y. Country B can produce 240 units of X or 60 units of Y or intermediate combinations gained via a substitution ratio of 4 of X for 1 of Y. Country B therefore has an absolute advantage in both X and Y but a greater advantage in Y. It can obtain a unit of Y domestically by giving up only 4 units of X, whereas Country A must give up 5 units of X to obtain 1 unit of Y domestically. Country B has a *comparative* advantage in producing Y.

Assume further that demand conditions in the two countries are such that without trade Country A would produce and consume 50 of X and 20 of Y, while Country B would produce and consume 80 of X and 40 of Y. Production possibilities therefore include, among others:

	Country A			Country B		
X	150	50	0	240	80	0
Y	0	20	30	0	40	60

With specialization and trade, both countries can increase their consumption patterns. If Country A specializes in X, producing 150 units, and Country B specializes in Y, producing 60 units, and A exchanges 90 of X for 20 of Y from B (an exchange ratio of 4.5 of X for 1 of Y, intermediate between the two production substitution ratios of 5 to 1 for A and 4 to 1 for B), the consumption possibilities for the two countries can improve as follows:

	Country A		Country B	
	X	Y	X	Y
Without trade	50	20	80	40
With trade	60	20	90	40

Both countries can have more of X with the same amount of Y. These are the gains from trade. They accrue whether or not one nation, as in the example, has an absolute advantage in producing both commodities.

The *IS-LM* Model with a Foreign Sector

The *IS-LM* model considered earlier extends readily to include a foreign sector. The major modification involves reinterpreting the *IS* curve to include the demand for domestic output from foreign countries and to exclude the portion of aggregate expenditures, both domestic and foreign, which is used to purchase output imported from abroad. Aggregate demand for domestic output is no longer just consumption expenditures plus investment expenditures plus government purchases, but that amount plus exports, less imports, of newly produced goods and services.

This section introduces that modification and explores the implications of disturbances to equilibrium with the international sector present. Disturbances to equilibrium now include those arising in the foreign sector as well as the domestic sector. Their impacts in both fixed and completely flexible foreign exchange rate cases are explored here, and the results which occur under managed float are inferred from these two extremes. In addition, this section illustrates the points made earlier concerning how nations with chronic deficits under fixed foreign exchange rate systems can improve their balance of international payments by compromising free trade, full employment, and economic growth and how flexible foreign exchange rate systems eliminate the need for these compromises.

The Foreign Sector and the *IS* Curve

Incorporating the international sector into the *IS-LM* model involves changing aggregate expenditure for output from:

$$E = C + I + G$$

to

$$E = C + I + G + Xg - Zg.$$

Xg and *Zg* are exports and imports of newly produced goods and services, respectively, now defined as current dollar expenditures deflated by the U.S. price index for aggregate output. *C, I,* and *G* are defined as in earlier chapters, *Xg* is included to reflect foreign demand for domestic output, and *Zg* is subtracted to remove the portion of *C, I, G,* and *Xg* which is for imported output of foreign factors of production. Even *Xg* includes an element of goods and services which are imported, processed, and reexported.

The equilibrium condition for obtaining the *IS* curve, which is $Y = E$, therefore changes from:

$$Y = C + I + G$$

to

$$Y = C + I + G + Xg - Zg.$$

The sense of the *IS* curve as a plotting of the aggregate expenditure for output forthcoming at each rate of interest remains. What has changed is that now it must be explicitly stated that the output in question is domestic output (the output of factors of production owned by domestic residents), that a portion of the demand for it comes from abroad, and that part of total domestic expenditures is for foreign rather than domestic output.

The determinants of consumption expenditures, investment expenditures, and government purchases are specified as earlier, except that Pigou effects are neglected. *C* therefore varies directly with *Yd* and inversely with r. I varies inversely with r. If I varies directly with Y, the influence is assumed to be weak enough to permit the IS curve to slope downward. G and Tr are constants, while Tx varies directly with real income. Yd is $Y - Tx + Tr$. Money demand varies inversely with r and directly with Y. The money supply is a constant. Responses of Y and P to aggregate demand break cleanly at Y_f, unless otherwise noted.

In the IS curve plotted in Figure 19–5, Xg is the constant:

$$Xg = Xg_0 \qquad 19\text{–}1$$

and Zg is:

$$Zg = f(Y), \qquad 19\text{–}2$$

Figure 19–5 The *IS-LM* Equilibrium with the Foreign Sector Included

When the foreign sector is included in the *IS-LM* model, the *IS* curve will shift with changes in U.S. and foreign price levels, the foreign exchange rate, and foreign income levels. Its slope and the amount by which it shifts are influenced by the size of the U.S. marginal propensity to import goods and services.

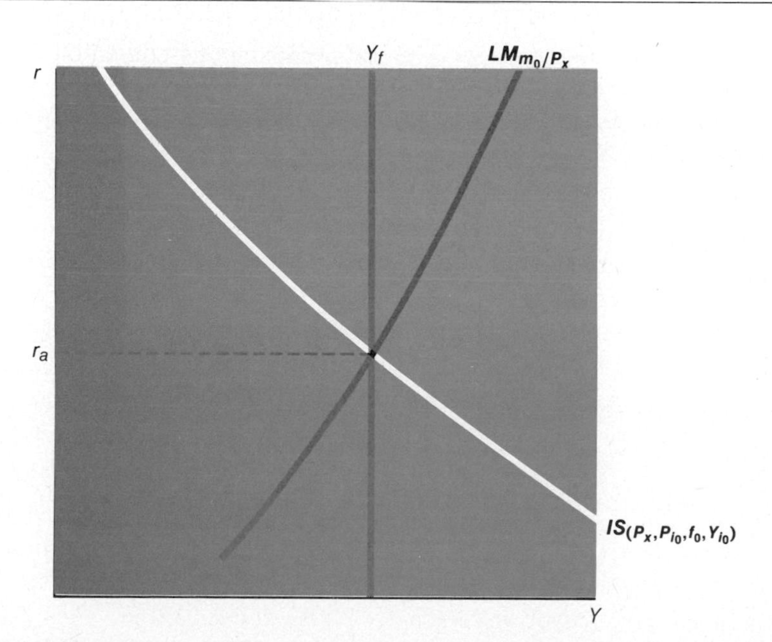

where Zg varies directly with Y. P, P_i, f, and Y_i are taken as fixed for this plotting, where:

P_i = the foreign price level,
f = the foreign exchange rate (the price in domestic currency of foreign currency), and
Y_i = foreign real income.

Zg varies directly with Y because consumption expenditures, including the portion which goes for imported output, rise as domestic real income rises.[7]

The *IS* curve is steeper with the international sector present, and it shifts horizontally by less when real disturbances occur. This is the case because a portion of the induced effect on consumption expenditures which takes place as real income changes now goes for foreign rather than domestically produced output.

The Foreign Sector as a Source of Domestic Price and Employment Problems

One implication of adding a foreign sector is that it presents an additional source of disturbances producing price and employment problems for domestic residents. For example, shifts in the foreign demand for domestic exports or shifts in domestic expenditures between imports and domestic output affect the *IS* curve and produce price and employment changes, provided that a flexible foreign exchange rate system is not in force. If export demand increases or if domestic expenditures shift from imports to domestically produced goods and services, aggregate demand for domestic output increases, and the *IS* curve shifts to the right. If this occurs in a fully employed economy, an expenditure gap appears and prices rise. Opposite disturbances produce leftward shifts in the *IS* curve and increase unemployment.

Disturbances involving Xg and the Zg function may arise merely from shifts in tastes and preferences between domestic and foreign goods and services. An example is the shift from domestic to European vacations by U.S. residents following World War II. They may arise partly from the supply side, as with the rapid growth of U.S. exports of commercial jet airplanes during the late 1950s as international airlines converted from propeller

[7] For convenience, this discussion neglects any dependence of Xg on Y which might be transmitted from Y to Zg to Y_i to Xg.

to jet aircraft and purchased many of the planes from U.S. manufacturers. During the late 1960s and into the 1970s, U.S. imports of oil grew rapidly relative to purchases of domestically produced oil as the U.S. demand for oil expanded relative to U.S. production capabilities.

Such disturbances also may arise from changes in foreign real income (Y_i), the foreign price level (P_i), or the foreign exchange rate (f). These changes can be induced by domestic disturbances, but they can be independent of domestic disturbances as well. The foreign exchange rate may fall because a foreign nation lowers the value of its currency with foreign exchange market intervention to stimulate exports and diminish imports, pursuing what often is called a beggar-thy-neighbor policy. Foreign real incomes and price levels may rise because of expansionist monetary and fiscal policies abroad.

Whatever the source of such disturbances, an increase in Y_i shifts the domestic *IS* curve to the right by increasing the foreign demand for domestic exports. A decline in Y_i reduces domestic exports and shifts the *IS* curve to the left. Similarly, the domestic *IS* curve shifts to the right as f rises and as P_i increases because these disturbances stimulate Xg and diminish Zg through price effects. Domestically produced goods and services become cheaper relative to foreign produced goods and services as the dollar price of foreign exchange rises and as foreign price levels rise. The domestic *IS* curve shifts to the left with decreases in f (currency depreciation by other nations) and reductions in P_i, since the price effects involved in these changes reduce Xg and induce a substitution of domestic expenditures from domestic output to Zg.[8]

Disturbances involving Xg and the Zg function occurring under fixed foreign exchange rate systems may produce accompanying money supply effects which aggravate their impacts, though ordinarily central banks act to neutralize the money supply effects. For example, a shift of expenditures in the United States from domestic output to imports not only shifts the *IS* curve to the left but also worsens the U.S. balance of payments, because imports of goods and services have increased and because the decline in U.S. interest rates produced by the leftward shift in the *IS* curve reduces U.S. exports of securities and stimulates U.S. security imports. To prevent the dollar price of foreign exchange from rising, or rising as far as it

[8] It is possible that $(Xg - Zg)$ would decrease as foreign prices increased, rather than as they decreased, and vice versa, if the domestic and foreign demands involved were extremely price inelastic. In this case, the *IS* curve would shift to the left as foreign prices increased, and to the right as they decreased. Experience does not support this possibility for changes in general price levels, however.

otherwise would, the Federal Reserve sells foreign exchange from its reserves.[9]

This sale has the same effect on reserves of U.S. commercial banks as do open market sales of U.S. government securities by the Federal Reserve. The Federal Reserve collects on the checks drawn on U.S. commercial banks to buy the foreign exchange it sells by reducing the reserve balances of the banks involved. The U.S. equilibrium money supply therefore declines, the *LM* curve shifts to the left, and the increase in the U.S. unemployment rate is aggravated. Again, the Federal Reserve ordinarily neutralizes these money supply effects of its foreign exchange operations as a matter of course, achieving preselected interest rate or money supply targets by providing compensating effects on bank reserves with open market purchases of U.S. securities.

Completely flexible foreign exchange rate systems wash out impacts of disturbances involving shifts in exports and imports of goods and services on domestic price and output equilibriums, but such systems permit disturbances involving exports and imports of securities to influence domestic output and prices. For example, if interest rates abroad increase for some reason, domestic exports of securities decline and security imports increase, raising the domestic price of foreign exchange. This stimulates domestic exports of goods and services and causes domestic expenditures to shift from imports to domestic output via a relative price effect. The *IS* curve shifts to the right, and prices increase, if the economy was initially fully employed.

In addition to problems based on aggregate demand originating in the foreign sector, anything that increases the domestic price of imported goods and services increases the cost of living to domestic consumers, whether or not domestic monetary and fiscal policies offset the aggregate demand effects on prices of domestically produced output described above. For example, increases in foreign price levels, with the dollar price of foreign exchange constant, or increases in the dollar price of foreign exchange, with foreign price levels constant, raise the U.S. consumer price index, since it incorporates prices of imported goods. This increase occurs even if monetary and fiscal restraint offsets the aggregate demand effects of the disturbances, that is, the effects working through impacts on $(Xg - Zg)$. Moreover, the direct contributions to increased U.S. consumer prices from increased prices of imports cannot be contained by monetary and fiscal restraint if domestic prices are rigid downward. Attempts to deal

---

[9] This sale occurs unless foreign central banks purchase the increased supplies of dollars in foreign exchange markets.

with them in this way merely produce domestic unemployment. In this sense, increases in import prices are cost-push inflationary pressures.

Built-in Stability from the Foreign Sector

The foreign sector adds built-in stability to the domestic economy in the face of autonomous demand disturbances of either domestic or foreign origin, assuming that the foreign exchange rate is fixed and that balance of payments effects on the money supply are neutralized by the central bank. This is true for both real and monetary disturbances. If aggregate demand for domestic output declines, the decline in equilibrium output and employment will be smaller when the foreign sector is present than when it is absent. This effect occurs because part of the induced reduction in consumption expenditures resulting from the decline in real income is a reduction in imported consumption goods and services. The income-induced reduction in consumption expenditures for domestic output therefore is smaller for a given marginal propensity to consume, and the total decline in aggregate demand for domestic output is smaller. The *import leakage* reduces the multiplier effect which aggravates the impact of autonomous disturbances on output and real income.

The foreign sector also dampens the increases in the domestic price level which occur when aggregate demand for domestic output increases in a fully employed economy, given fixed foreign exchange rates. The effect does not work through income-induced effects on imports, however, at least not in the simplified models that have been used here, since real income does not change. It works instead through price-induced effects on net exports of goods and services. As domestic prices increase relative to foreign prices, net exports of goods and services tend to decline. These effects remove a portion of the expenditure gap, so that prices do not have to increase by as much to close it compared with the case where the foreign sector is neglected.

The foreign sector dampens real disturbances of domestic origin under flexible foreign exchange rates. For example, since domestic interest rates decline when the investment function falls, net exports of securities must decline if foreign interest rates are fixed. Since the balance of international payments must be balanced in equilibrium under completely flexible foreign exchange rates, net exports of goods and services must increase. The foreign sector therefore contributes to aggregate demand for domestic output, cushioning its decline and reducing the decline in equilibrium output and employment.

Similar reasoning indicates that the foreign sector must dampen the price increase which occurs when real disturbances expand aggregate demand at full employment, even if foreign exchange rates are completely flexible. Since interest rates rise when such disturbances occur, net exports of securities will increase in the new equilibrium. With completely flexible foreign exchange rates assuring balanced international payments, net exports of goods and services must be smaller. This contributes to the closing of the expenditure gap and reduces the domestic price increases required for equilibrium.

When the foreign exchange rate is completely flexible, however, the foreign sector does not contribute built-in stability with monetary disturbances as it does when the foreign exchange rate is fixed. With reductions in the money supply or increases in the money demand function, domestic interest rates rise, so that net exports of securities increase. With international payments balancing under completely flexible foreign exchange rates, net exports of goods and services must decline, aggravating the decline in domestic output and employment as compared with the case where the foreign sector is neglected. When money supply increases or the money demand function declines at full employment, equilibrium domestic interest rates will be unchanged if foreign exchange rates are completely flexible. Net exports of securities and net exports of goods and services will be unchanged, so that the foreign sector neither dampens nor aggravates the price increase in this case.

The Foreign Sector and Stabilization Policies

Adding the foreign sector weakens both monetary and fiscal ease, as applied in recessions, if the foreign exchange rate is fixed, because imports of goods and services increase as real income expands. Monetary and fiscal ease produce smaller impacts on aggregate expenditures for domestic output, and therefore on domestic output, because net exports of goods and services decline as real income expands.

If foreign exchange rates are flexible, fiscal ease still is weaker for open as compared with closed economies, but monetary ease is stronger. As monetary ease is applied in a recession, domestic interest rates decline, and net exports of securities diminish. Since international payments must balance under flexible foreign exchange rates, net exports of goods and services must increase. Impacts of monetary ease on aggregate demand are augmented by increases in net exports of goods and services.

Fiscal ease still is weaker, however, since domestic interest rates increase as fiscal ease is applied. The increase in interest rates stimulates net exports of securities, so that net exports of goods and services must decline. Fiscal ease is weaker as a result of foreign sector effects, whether the foreign exchange rate is flexible or fixed.

Stabilizing the Open Economy

As noted earlier, an important disadvantage of fixed foreign exchange rate systems is that nations which develop chronic deficits under such systems because of long-term trends in relative inflation rates, productivity, and the like may find themselves compromising full employment, economic growth, and free trade to improve their balance of international payments positions. The basic problem is that fixed foreign exchange rate systems have not been able to provide the occasional adjustments in foreign exchange rates needed to accommodate such trends. This failure may be caused by nations feeling that devaluation will be met with competitive devaluations which will leave the relative price situation unchanged, by nations wanting to avoid the terms-of-trade and inflationary effects of devaluation, or even by nations regarding devaluations as detrimental to their prestige. Whatever the case, foreign exchange rates have not been adjusted adequately to handle fundamental disturbances under fixed foreign exchange rate systems in the past, causing nations with weakening currencies to strengthen their payments positions and conserve their foreign exchange reserves by compromising other goals.

An important advantage of flexible foreign exchange rate systems is that they can produce the necessary adjustments in foreign exchange rates automatically. They permit nations to simply ignore their balance of international payments positions. They free monetary and fiscal policies of balance of payments responsibilities and eliminate the need for sacrifices of full employment, economic growth and free trade objectives. Managed float systems provide the same advantage if they truly smooth out only the short-term fluctuations about foreign exchange rates reflecting fundamental balance of payments positions.

Figure 19–6 illustrates these points. Notice the addition of the balance of payments, or *BP*, curve, reflecting balanced international payments, to the *IS-LM* framework in the figure. The *BP* curve, like the *IS* curve, is plotted for a given foreign exchange rate, given foreign and domestic price levels, and a given level of foreign real income. The *BP* curve also reflects given foreign interest rates.

The *BP* curve must slope upward. An increase in *Y*, which increases imports of goods and services, must be compensated for by an increase in the domestic interest rate (*r*), which increases net exports of securities, if international payments are to remain balanced. Any point to the right of

Figure 19–6 **Adding the *BP Curve***

In the upper portion of the figure, price stability, full employment, growth, and balanced international payments are being achieved. In the lower portion, price stability, full employment, and growth are being achieved, but a deficit is occurring in the international payments balance.

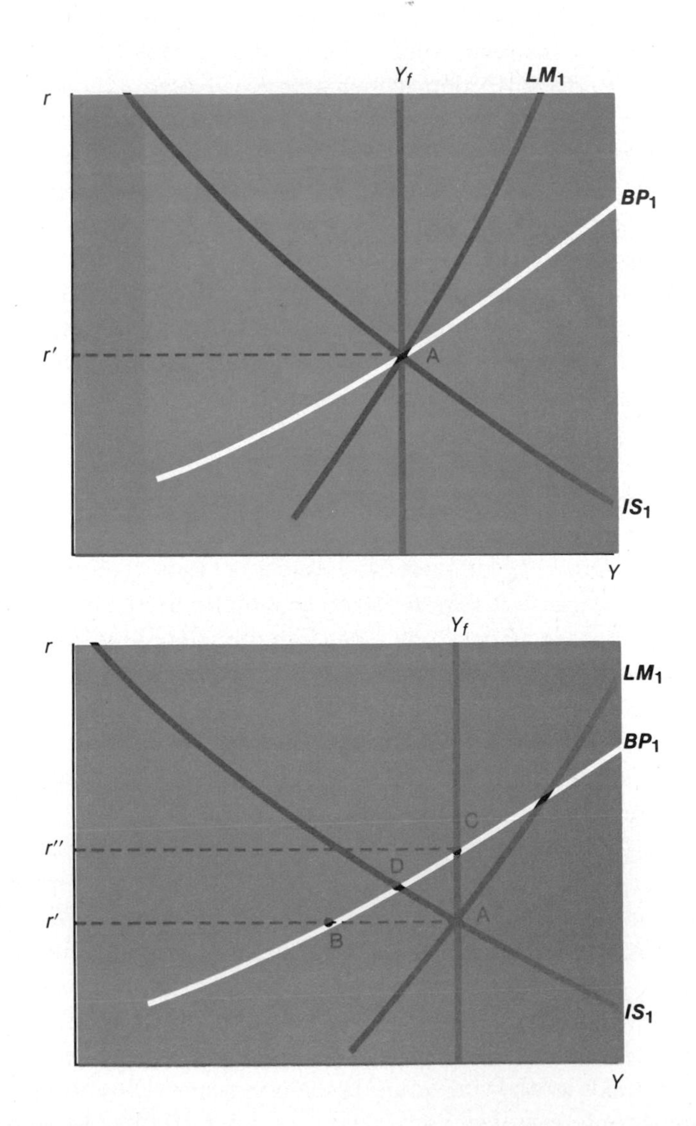

the *BP* curve reflects a balance of payments deficit, since Y is too large and r is too low for balance, while any point to the left of the curve reflects a balance of payments surplus.

The *BP* curve is shown as being less steeply sloped than the *LM* curve, though this is neither necessarily true nor necessary to the points being made. It seems the likely case, however, since empirical research has indicated that money demand is not highly interest elastic, while net exports of securities appear to be quite sensitive to interest rate differentials among countries.

Assume initially the situation illustrated in the top portion of the figure. Monetary and fiscal policies are such that the *LM* and *IS* curves intersect at the full-employment line at interest rate r', which is designated as the r consistent with the investment rate and growth rate targets, and the *BP* line also intersects the full-employment line at that point. This configuration represents full employment, price stability, the target economic growth rate, and balanced international payments.

Assume now that the situation has changed to that illustrated in the lower portion of the figure. A monetary and fiscal policy mix producing IS_1 and LM_1 yields price stability, full employment, and the target growth rate, but the balance of payments now is in deficit. A fundamental disturbance has occurred in the balance of international payments so that the *BP* curve for an unchanged foreign exchange rate is now to the left of a position which would pass through Point A and provide balanced international payments as well as the other three goals. Perhaps a period of relative inflation in the domestic economy has occurred. Perhaps real productivity has increased at a slower rate in the domestic economy than abroad. Whatever the case, the four goals now cannot be achieved simultaneously at the unchanged foreign exchange rate.

Since the disturbance to the balance of payments position is fundamental and long lasting, by assumption, the nation must take steps to improve its payments balance. Foreign exchange and gold reserves are exhaustible, and foreign nations will not forever add the excess of domestic currency in foreign exchange markets to their own official reserves.

One possibility is to apply monetary and fiscal restraint so as to move the *IS* and *LM* curve intersection to Point B. This maintains price stability and the target economic growth rate (provided that investment expenditures are not sensitive to Y) and balances international payments, since Point B is on the *BP* curve, but full employment is sacrificed. In effect, balanced international payments are achieved by suppressing domestic income and hence imports of goods and services below the levels consistent with full employment.

A second possibility is to mix monetary restraint with fiscal ease in order to achieve an *IS-LM* intersection at Point C. This produces price stability, full employment, and balanced international payments, since the *IS, LM,* and *BP* curves intersect at the full-employment line, but the target growth rate is sacrificed. At Point C, the interest rate is at r'', which is above r', the interest rate that produces the target investment and economic growth rates. Capital goods are accumulating too slowly. The higher interest rate has produced balanced international payments by stimulating net exports of securities, but it has crowded out domestic investment expenditures to the point where the growth target is not being met.

Of course, the monetary and fiscal mix can be adjusted so as to achieve an *IS-LM* intersection anywhere between Points B and C along the *BP* curve, trading off employment and growth goals in varying degrees to achieve balanced international payments. Since economic growth is generally secondary to full employment as a macroeconomic goal, the usual practice, under fixed foreign exchange rates, has been to sacrifice growth rather than full employment. There have been instances where full employment has been sacrificed for balanced international payments, however. The United Kingdom during the 1920s is a case in point. Moreover, during the late 1950s, critics of U.S. macroeconomic policies charged that full employment as well as the economic growth rate was being sacrificed to improve the international payments balance.

Where full employment is sacrificed, it is more likely to occur by default than by design. The monetary authority, finding itself with an *IS-LM* intersection at a point such as Point D in Figure 19–6, is inhibited from using monetary ease to achieve full employment, in effect shifting the *LM* curve to the right so that Point A would be achieved, because to do so would aggravate the balance of payments problem. Fiscal ease necessary to move the economy to Point C is not forthcoming promptly because of the administrative lag, because of a reluctance to unbalance the federal budget, or perhaps because of an unwillingness to further sacrifice the growth target by driving interest rates still further above r'.

During the Bretton Woods period of fixed foreign exchange rates, the United States regarded the conflict as being principally between growth and balanced international payments goals and applied a number of specific policies, mainly specific fiscal policies, to resolve the conflict.

One such effort was the *interest equalization tax,* which imposed a special tax on dividend and interest income from foreign securities. This tax was imposed in 1964 and eliminated in 1974 after the move to more flexible foreign exchange rates diminished the need for it. The purpose of the tax was to reduce the after-tax yield on foreign securities, thereby discouraging imports of such securities and reducing the interest rate at which U.S. international payments were balanced, given full-employment Y. In terms of the lower portion of Figure 19–6, the purpose was to shift the BP curve to the right so that it would intersect the full-employment line at an interest rate below r''.

The *foreign credit restraint program,* imposed in 1965 and also eliminated in 1974, was another policy designed to diminish foreign security imports and shift the BP curve to the right. This program placed direct restrictions on foreign lending by U.S. banks and financial institutions, and later on foreign lending by nonfinancial corporations.

The brief *import surcharge* of 1971 was still another U.S. attempt to shift the BP curve to the right, this time by diminishing U.S. imports of goods and services by increasing their tax-inclusive price to U.S. importers. Western European nations such as the United Kingdom and France went much further in the years immediately following World War II when, faced with balance of payments difficulties, they directly restricted the amounts of foreign exchange that importers, including tourists travelling abroad, could purchase.

All of these policies compromise free trade and the gains which can accrue from it. Less vulnerable on this count is the investment tax credit, discussed in the preceding chapter, which increases the flow of investment expenditures at each interest rate and output combination and thereby raises the interest rate at which growth objectives are met. That is, the same flow of investment expenditures is obtained at a higher interest rate, an interest rate more compatible with balance of payments objectives. In terms of the lower portion of Figure 19–6, beginning with the IS-LM intersection at Point A, an investment tax credit, which shifts the IS curve to the right, combined with monetary restraint, moves the IS-LM intersection upward vertically toward Point C and, at the same time, raises the interest rate consistent with growth objectives above r'.

The most obvious policy for resolving the conflict in goals is to adjust the level at which the foreign exchange rate is fixed. For example, Figure 19–7 shows that a nation can achieve full employment, stability in the price level for domestic output, the growth target, and balanced international payments, without using investment tax credits or policies which restrict free trade, by depreciating the domestic currency so that the BP curve shifts from BP' to BP'' and intersects with LM_1 and IS_1 at Point A. (Fiscal restraint keeps the IS curve at IS_1.) This does not provide a perfect stabilization result, since a once and for all increase in prices of imported

Figure 19–7 **Balancing International Payments by Depreciating the Domestic Currency**

If the existing foreign exchange rate produces a deficit in the international payments balance when monetary and fiscal policies are addressed to price stability, full employment, and economic growth goals, an adjustment in the foreign exchange rate can correct the problem.

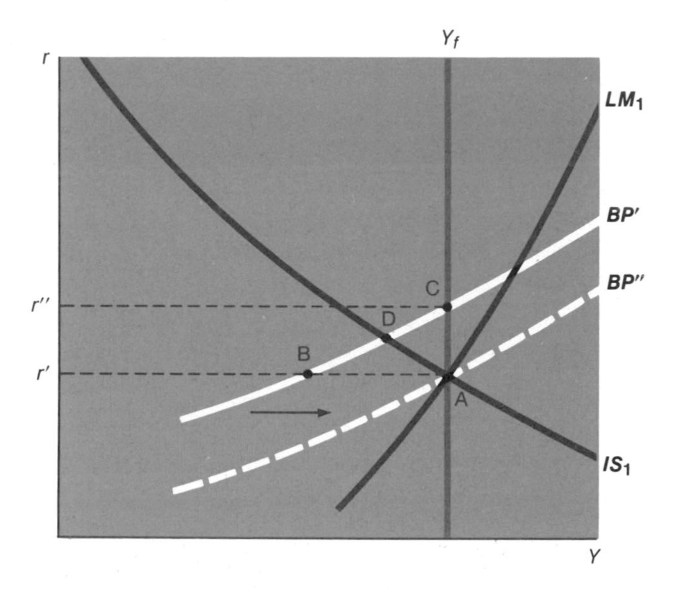

goods and services, which enter into the consumer price index, will occur. But prices of domestically produced output—which are the prices determined in the *IS-LM* graph—will not increase if the *IS-LM* intersection is maintained on the full-employment line, unless the increase in import prices induces domestic cost-push inflation pressures.[10]

Some dollar devaluation did occur during the Bretton Woods period;

[10] This statement is an exaggeration, though it is consistent with the previous assumption that responses of P and Y to aggregate demand break cleanly at Y_f. In fact, prices will increase somewhat in the export industries and import-competing industries as domestic resources are transferred to these areas in response to the increases in demand induced by currency depreciation. Prices will not fall correspondingly in the industries which are contracting, since prices and money wages are somewhat inflexible downward in the short term. The aggregate price level for domestic output therefore increases. This is a form of *demand shift inflation.*

the dollar was depreciated against other major currencies in 1971, and the German and Dutch currencies had been appreciated against the dollar on earlier occasions. But these adjustments were not sufficient to shift the U.S. *BP* curve to the Point A intersection position. This was the basic flaw in the Bretton Woods system and the cause of its eventual demise. It did not produce the foreign exchange rate adjustments required to accommodate the fundamental changes in balance of payments positions which occurred over time.

As stated earlier, the advantage of flexible foreign exchange rate systems is that they can produce these adjustments in foreign exchange rates automatically. Under such systems, the stabilization authorities can simply adjust the monetary and fiscal policy mix to achieve an *IS* and *LM* curve intersection such as Point A in the lower portion of Figure 19–6, and let the foreign exchange rate float freely, responding automatically to the demand and supply for foreign exchange to keep the *BP* curve in the Point A intersection position. A managed float system provides the same result if the managers are adept at distinguishing short-term from fundamental balance of payments disturbances. Even when this skill is absent, the managed float system does no great harm, providing that the domestic goals are not compromised. Foreign exchange reserves merely increase or decrease over time.

Summary

1. Transactions with foreign countries give rise to a market for foreign exchange, since both domestic and foreign parties want to pay and be paid in their own currency. The price of foreign exchange in terms of the domestic currency is called the foreign exchange rate.

2. Under fixed foreign exchange rate systems, governments announce levels at which they intend to maintain foreign exchange rates, and they maintain these rates by a variety of means, including intervention in the market with reserves of foreign exchange and gold. Foreign exchange rate adjustments are reserved for fundamental changes in balance of international payments positions.

3. Under completely flexible foreign exchange rate systems, the foreign exchange rate is left free to respond to the forces of demand and supply in the market and automatically balances international payments.

4. The Bretton Woods system of fixed foreign exchange rates, on which the world operated from 1946 to early 1973, developed the basic flaw of being unable to produce the adjustments in foreign exchange rates needed to accommodate fundamental changes in balance of payments positions among major trading nations. This meant, on the one hand, that the system was not durable, and it eventually collapsed. More important, it meant that nations which developed chronic deficits under the system, such as the United States and the United Kingdom, were led, before the collapse, to improve their payments positions by means which compromised full employment, economic growth, and free trade.

5. In 1973, the United States moved to a more flexible foreign exchange rate system, a system often termed managed float. This system is not completely flexible, since the Federal Reserve and foreign central banks regularly intervene in the market with supplies of foreign exchange to influence foreign exchange rates. However, there is no commitment to maintain fixed foreign exchange rates, as with the Bretton Woods type of system, or even to maintain fluctuations in rates within a specified range.

6. The great advantage of managed float and flexible foreign exchange rate systems is that they can produce the adjustments in foreign exchange rates needed to accommodate fundamental disturbances to international payments positions. This eliminates the need for compromises of full employment, economic growth, and free trade by nations whose currencies weaken over time. Nations in these circumstances can still compromise these goals in favor of an overvalued currency if they choose to do so in order to avoid the terms-of-trade and inflation effects of a depreciating currency.

7. Completely flexible foreign exchange rate systems have the disadvantage that they may produce very wide short-term fluctuations in foreign exchange rates. Such fluctuations are disruptive to activity levels in export, import, and import-competing industries, since they affect the price-competitiveness of the firms engaged in these industries. If participation in export and import industries is discouraged as a result, the level of international trade declines, and a portion of the gains nations can make from international trade is lost. In addition, sharp short-term currency depreciations produce terms-of-trade and inflation effects not required by the nation's fundamental international payments position. Managed float systems diminish these problems to the extent the managers are able to smooth out short-term fluctuations in foreign exchange rates.

Concepts for Identification

foreign exchange
foreign exchange market
foreign exchange rate
balance of international payments
fixed foreign exchange rates
flexible foreign exchange rates
managed float system
Bretton Woods adjustable peg system
currency depreciation
terms of trade
tariffs
gains from trade
BP curve
interest equalization tax
import surcharge

Questions and Problems for Review

1. Explain why the demand curve for foreign exchange in Figure 19–1 slopes negatively.

2. Present the case against a fixed foreign exchange rate system such as the Bretton Woods adjustable peg system.

3. A flexible foreign exchange rate system seems desirable on the face of it, since it balances international payments automatically and eliminates any need for foreign exchange reserves. Why are nations reluctant to employ a completely flexible foreign exchange rate system?

4. Evaluate the managed float system. Does it correct the major disadvantages of the fixed and flexible systems? Explain.

5. Create an example similar to the one presented in this chapter to illustrate the gains from trade. Use different numerical assumptions.

6. The demand for domestic output becomes:

$$C + I + G + Xg - Zg$$

when the foreign sector is included. Explain why it is necessary to subtract Zg.

7. The domestic *IS* curve will shift to the right when foreign price levels rise (with the domestic price level constant), or when the foreign exchange rate rises, or when foreign real income levels increase. Explain.

8. The *IS* curve is steeper when the foreign sector is included (with foreign exchange rates fixed), and it shifts by less with real disturbances. Explain.

9. With the foreign sector present, domestic prices increase by less when the investment expenditure function increases in an initial situation of full employment and price stability. This is true under both fixed and flexible foreign exchange rate systems. Explain.

10. If the United States operates under a flexible foreign exchange rate system, an increase in foreign demand for U.S. securities will shift the U.S. *IS* curve to the left. Explain.

11. Explain why the *BP* curve slopes upward.

12. Illustrate graphically the conflict which can occur between balance of international payments and economic growth goals for a nation committed to price stability, full employment, and fixed foreign exchange rates.

13. Illustrate graphically how an interest equalization tax can help to correct the problem posed in Question 12. Illustrate how an investment tax credit can help.

14. If the United States experiences a deficit in its international payments balance under a managed float foreign exchange rate system, and if the Federal Reserve supports the value of the U.S. dollar with sales from its foreign exchange reserves, the resultant money supply effect will complicate the domestic stabilization problem unless the Federal Reserve neutralizes the money supply effect with open-market operations. What is the money supply effect and why does it occur? What is the complication to the domestic stabilization problem arising from the money supply effect alone, assuming the economy otherwise would have price stability and full employment? Are open-market purchases or sales required for neutralizing the money supply effect?

References

Aliber, R. Z. "The Firm under Pegged and Floating Exchange Rates." *Scandinavian Journal of Economics* 78 (1976): 309–322.

Ellsworth, P. T., and Leith, J. Clark. *The International Economy.* 5th ed. New York: Macmillan, 1975.

Friedman, Milton. "The Case for Flexible Exchange Rates." In *Essays in Positive Economics.* Chicago: University of Chicago Press, 1953.

Friedman, Milton, and Roosa, R. *The Balance of Payments: Free versus Fixed Exchange Rates.* Washington, D.C.: American Enterprise Institute, 1967.

Kindleberger, C. P. "The Case for Fixed Exchange Rates, 1969." In *The International Adjustment Mechanism.* Boston: Federal Reserve Bank of Boston, 1970, pp. 93–108.

Lanyi, Anthony. "The Case for Floating Exchange Rates Reconsidered." *Essays in International Finance,* no. 72 (Princeton, N.J., International Finance Section, Princeton University, 1969).

Leighton, Richard I. *Economics of International Trade.* New York: McGraw-Hill, 1970.

Meade, J. E. "The International Monetary Mechanism." *Three Banks Review* 63 (September 1964): 3–25. Reprinted in *Readings in Macroeconomics,* edited by E. G. Mueller. New York: Holt, Rinehart and Winston, 1966, pp. 386–397.

Mundell, R. A. "The Appropriate Use of Monetary and Fiscal Policy for Internal and External Stability." *International Monetary Fund Staff Papers* 9 (March 1962): 70–79.

Smith, W. L. "Are There Enough Policy Tools?" *American Economic Review* 55 (May 1965): 298–320.

Sohmen, Egon. *Flexible Exchange Rates.* Chicago: University of Chicago Press, 1961.

Takayama, Akira. *International Trade.* New York: Holt, Rinehart and Winston, 1972.

20
Macroeconomic Policy

Lags attend applications of both monetary and fiscal policies and complicate their use as activist stabilization policy devices. Price and wage controls cannot effectively contain sustained demand-pull inflation but have potential usefulness as devices for checking wage-push inflation. The issue of an active or passive role for government in economic affairs is an enduring one.

Modern macroeconomics owes much to Keynes. There is little to quarrel with in Keynes's focus on aggregate demand for output relative to full-employment output as the key factor in unemployment and inflation problems. A shortfall of demand produces an unemployment problem. An excess of demand produces an inflation problem. Of course, cost-push pressures, if significant, can produce inflation even without excess demand. But cost-push inflation has not been a dominant factor in U.S. economic experience. Moreover, the strength of such pressures, to the extent that they do exist, often may depend on the proximity of the economy to full employment—that is, the message of the wage-push trade-off hypothesis. In that case, aggregate demand for output relative to full-employment output still is the key factor.

Despite agreement with Keynes on this important matter, modern macroeconomics differs from that of Keynes in a number of respects, especially in the policy area. Keynes recommended that governments conduct an activist program of discretionary stabilization policies, arguing that the economy would not produce an acceptable price and employment result if left to its own devices. He indicated that fiscal policies should be emphasized. Monetary policies were too weak to be helpful, at least during serious recessions. The early Keynesians extended the emphasis on fiscal policies to include near full-employment and inflation situations as well.

Today's macroeconomics displays more confidence in monetary policies and less satisfaction with fiscal policies, more confidence in the ability of the economy to right itself in the face of private sector disturbances and less confidence in the stabilizing capabilities of activist government programs of discretionary stabilization policies. Still, probably a majority of economists would choose the activist programs, even in ordinary circumstances, over Milton Friedman's suggestion of stable money supply growth plus a balanced full-employment federal budget.

Today's macroeconomists debate a number of other policy issues as well. The most important ones have been discussed in earlier chapters: Are monetary and fiscal policies enough for acceptable stabilization results? Must an activist stabilization policy program by government go beyond monetary and fiscal policies to be successful, occasionally or perhaps permanently adopting mandatory price and wage controls as well? What should be the government's role in economic growth? Should government set targets for future per capita real income and invoke activist policies to achieve them? Or should it pursue a more passive role, balancing its full-employment budget and letting the private sector dominate the determination of the investment expenditure rate and other matters affecting future per capita real incomes? What should be the government's role in the market for foreign exchange? Should the government actively manage foreign exchange rates, perhaps even maintaining fixed foreign exchange rates? Or should it simply ignore its balance of international payments, passively allowing the foreign exchange rate to fluctuate and balance international payments automatically?

This chapter brings the discussion of these matters together, touching on most of them again, expanding some of them, and offering some conclusions. It begins by looking again at monetary and fiscal policies, this time paying special attention to the problem of lags. Next, it expands the earlier discussion of price and wage controls and examines the record of macroeconomic policy performance since 1960. Finally, it poses the basic question of whether governments should pursue macroeconomic goals with active or passive policies and notes that the issue is not new and not likely to see an early resolution.

Monetary and Fiscal Policies

Probably a majority of today's economists could live with a policy program which would employ discretionary stabilization policies to cope with private sector disturbances but would emphasize monetary policies as the fine-tuning device and would confine variations in the rate of money supply growth to a fairly narrow range. Fiscal policies would be used only occasionally in the activist sense of compensating for private sector disturbances, perhaps only in severe situations where the need for action is apparent and the prospects for quick legislative action promising. Changes in tax rates and levels of government spending would be targeted chiefly to longer-term objectives, such as filling general needs for public spending, reducing the natural rate of unemployment, and—most important for economic stability—eliminating the *fiscal drag* which develops over time as federal tax receipts increase in real terms with inflation and with growth in real income. (Federal tax receipts increase in real terms with inflation because individuals pay a higher percentage of their money incomes in federal income taxes as their money incomes rise.)

Of course, obtaining good price and employment results through activist monetary policies and a balanced full-employment government budget requires a correct assessment of the natural rate of unemployment, even if problems of execution are put aside. Underestimation of the natural rate of unemployment would result in too much inflation, with very little effect on the unemployment rate beyond the short term. Overestimation of the natural rate of unemployment would result in more unemployment than is necessary for achieving an acceptable inflation rate.

Fiscal Policies

Fiscal policies have a number of shortcomings which limit their role as activist stabilization policies. With government purchases, the categories of spending which actually lend themselves to countercyclical variation are fairly narrow. Defense expenditures and regular government civil service employment, two very large government purchasing categories, cannot be varied appreciably for such purposes, especially for restraint. Similarly, transfer payments cannot be reduced for cyclical restraint purposes, generally speaking.

Fiscal ease is limited by the crowding out effect on investment and other interest-sensitive expenditures. This effect conflicts with the growth goal and, since it reduces fiscal policy strength, means that very large increases in the federal deficit may be required to eliminate fairly modest deficiencies in aggregate demand. The implication for the deficit is an important political consideration, given the unpopularity of large federal deficits with the electorate.

Administrative Lag

Beyond these problems, fiscal policies are limited as a fine-tuning device by the administrative lag which afflicts them. *Administrative lag* is the lag between the forecast of the need for action and the signing into law of the changes in government tax and spending programs. It includes both the lag between the forecast by the president's advisers and the president's recommendation to Congress and the lags involved as the programs work their way through Congress. Depending on the time required for these steps and on the economic situation, the policies may not only be late in coming, they may be the opposite of what is needed when they finally take effect. Fiscal policies, like monetary policies, may be destabilizing rather than stabilizing because of lag problems.

The U.S. experience with the administrative lag for fiscal policies has been mixed and, on the whole, not very encouraging. As of 1979, there have been three prominent applications of general tax policies intended in part as activist fiscal policy actions. The first, a general tax cut enacted in February 1964, was recommended to Congress by President Kennedy in January 1963. The president's economic advisers had begun to urge the tax cut in 1961—the lag between forecast and enactment was almost three years.

The second, the 1968 tax surcharge, involved a similar administrative lag. President Johnson recommended the tax increase to Congress in January 1967. His economic advisers had advocated a tax increase in 1965, following the sharp increase in defense expenditures during the second half of that year in association with the military buildup in Vietnam. The lag from forecast to enactment was again three years.

The 1975 tax reduction case is more encouraging. That tax cut was first recommended to Congress in early 1975 and was passed in March of the same year. It is true, of course, that the forecast of the need for the tax cut had been made much earlier, within the Ford administration and elsewhere, so that considerable pressure for a tax cut had been present in Congress long before the president's recommendation was made.

It is possible that the administrative lag has become shorter with the precedents established by the two tax changes of the 1960s and that of 1975. In addition, in 1974 Congress instituted an important reform which may have shortened the administrative lag. The Budget and Impoundment Control Act of 1974 established the Congressional Budget Office, a joint staff for reviewing government expenditures and tax programs to assess their budget and economic stabilization impacts. It is possible that this office will evolve in such a way as to speed both the introduction of fiscal policy legislation into Congress and its passage through Congress.

One means of eliminating the legislative portion of administrative lag is for Congress to delegate discretionary authority for tax changes to the president. For example, Congress might empower the president to apply a surcharge of from plus to minus 10 percent to personal and corporate income taxes for purposes of economic stabilization, subject to a congressional veto. Congress—probably wisely—has not considered this idea seriously, however. What president could resist the temptation to schedule tax cuts with an eye as much to elections as to stabilization needs? Congress faces this temptation also, of course, but the responsibility is distributed among many individuals, and the minority party shares in both the deliberations and the credit.

Another approach is to accept the administrative lag constraint on fiscal policies but enhance the operation of automatic fiscal policies, providing *formula flexibility* to a number of categories of government expenditures and tax receipts. Under this approach, such things as revenue sharing payments to state and local government, public service employment, public works programs, and the number of weeks for which unemployment compensation payments could be received would be tied to the unemployment rate, rising during recessions and falling during high employment periods. Tax surcharges could be tied to the unemployment rate in a similar manner. Again, care would have to be taken to identify the natural rate of unemployment correctly. Otherwise, formula flexibility could destabilize the economy rather than stabilizing it.

Impact Lag

Fiscal policies involve an *impact lag* as well as an administrative lag. This is especially important for government construction purchases, where expenditures necessarily are spaced over time. It requires time to build up expenditure rates under newly authorized programs, and it may be difficult even to accelerate or decelerate expenditure rates appreciably for projects already under way. With public works programs which are funded by the federal government but proposed and administered by state and local governments, additional time is consumed in preparing proposals and making awards.

Impact lags are involved even with tax and transfer payment policies. It is true that effects on disposable income can begin with the next pay period for these policies, but impacts on expenditures may await impacts on consumers' conceptions of their "permanent" disposable incomes, and these impacts may build up rather slowly. Recall the view, noted in Chapter 6, that the 1968–69 tax surcharge had little effect because government authorities announced in advance that it was temporary; therefore, it did not greatly affect taxpayers' ideas of their permanent incomes. Again, this may be much less of a problem for increases in disposable income induced by tax reductions and increases in transfer payments, which may be treated as windfalls to be spent immediately on consumption.

Fiscal Drag and the Fiscal Dividend

The full-employment federal surplus tends to increase over time because of the effect of growth in real income and inflation on tax receipts. This tendency was noted earlier and defined as fiscal drag. Unless the economic situation calls for fiscal restraint, fiscal drag is a stabilization problem in itself. The growth in taxes inhibits consumption expenditures and complicates the problem of maintaining a full-employment aggregate demand. Of course, in the case of demand-pull inflation, the increase in the federal surplus it induces is in a sense a built-in stabilizer. But, in recent decades, inflation has tended to occur during recessions, when fiscal restraint is not needed. Moreover, even where inflation is occurring during full-employment situations, a problem arises: Since prices and money wages tend to be inflexible downward, the dampening effects of the inflation-induced tax increases remain in the system during subsequent recessions.

How should fiscal drag be eliminated? Should taxes be reduced, or should federal spending be increased?

Viewed from another perspective, fiscal drag is a fiscal dividend, available to be returned to the taxpayers through tax cuts or to be used to finance increases in federal spending. How should the dividend be allocated? Political conservatives usually favor using it chiefly for tax cuts, while nonconservatives recommend that it be used to finance increases in federal spending for such things as health programs or aid to urban areas.

Whatever use is made of the proceeds of fiscal drag, the tax cuts or spending increases which can eliminate it face the same administrative lag which afflicts fiscal policies in general. Fiscal drag has constituted a significant real disturbance in recent decades.

The recently created Congressional Budget Office referred to earlier may ultimately improve performance in this area. But it would be a major improvement if the federal tax system were modified so that appropriate tax cuts would take place automatically as inflation occurred. In effect, the federal tax system would be cost-of-living indexed. Individuals then would not move into higher marginal tax brackets with inflation, and tax receipts would not increase more than in proportion to inflation. The fiscal drag which occurs fairly predictably and regularly with growth in real income could be programmed away with regular increases in federal spending or periodic tax cuts, depending on how the fiscal dividend was to be allocated.

Monetary Policies

With monetary policies, the problem in fine-tuning applications is the impact lag rather than the administrative lag. Indeed, the administrative lag is very short with monetary policies. Once the need for action is determined, the course of open-market operations can be varied within a single day. The federal Open Market Committee meets once every three weeks in Washington, D.C., to issue its general directive for open-market operations, but policy is reviewed daily—even more frequently if necessary. There is no requirement for legislative or presidential action in the day-to-day conduct of monetary policies.

By contrast, the impact lag for monetary policies is long, uncertain, and probably variable. The impact lag here means the lag between effects on bank reserves and eventual full impacts on inflation rates and unemployment rates. Time is required for effects on costs and availabilities of bank credit and other loanable funds, for revisions in expenditure plans, for adjustments in expenditure flows, and for responses in output, employment, and inflation rates. It is this impact lag and the uncertainty as to the eventual strength of monetary policy impacts which give rise to the possibility of moving too strongly and ultimately destabilizing the economy instead of stabilizing it.

Immediate effects on inflation and employment rates are weak, even undetectable, but eventual effects are much stronger. Friedman suggests that major impacts occur six to fifteen months after the policy enactment. Simulations with the 1969 version of the Federal Reserve–MIT model presented monetary policy impacts as building to only a little more than half of peak values by the end of one year.

Some of the recent work in the area of rational expectations suggests that monetary policy impacts may build up more quickly than these estimates suggest. For example, to the extent that producers know from experience that applications of monetary ease in less than full employment situations ultimately lower interest rates and stimulate interest-sensitive expenditures, they may raise output and employment levels in anticipation of the expenditure increases, rather than waiting to adapt to the effect of the expenditure increases on their sales and inventories. Similarly, households may increase their consumption expenditures on the basis of the increases in income they expect when monetary ease is applied, knowing from experience that such applications ultimately increase income and employment levels.[1]

Monetary Policy Targets

For the administrators of discretionary monetary policies, the practical problem posed by the impact lag and the uncertainty as to the ultimate strength of monetary policies is the problem of selecting short- and intermediate-term target variables which relate usefully to ultimate impacts on inflation and unemployment rates. During the 1950s and 1960s, short-term interest rates were the primary targets for U.S. monetary policies, though other variables, such as the difference between excess reserves and borrowed reserves (an imperfect indicator of money market pressures), also were used.

Since 1970, the Federal Reserve has used both interest rate and money supply targets in conducting monetary policies. Indeed, since the mid-1970s, Congress has required the Federal Reserve to formulate ranges for intended money supply growth for the coming year and to report these targets to Congress on a quarterly basis.

The Federal Reserve indicated in 1976 that it was using the *federal*

[1] For the lag estimates of Friedman and of de Leeuw and Gramlich, see Milton Friedman, "The Role of Monetary Policy," *American Economic Review* 58 (March 1968): 16; and Frank de Leeuw and Edward M. Gramlich, "The Channels of Monetary Policy," *Federal Reserve Bulletin* 55 (June 1969): 489.

Rational expectations, in the extreme case where foresight is perfect and prices and money wages are flexible downward as well as upward, produce a situation in which monetary policies do not affect output, since output never leaves the full-employment level. See Thomas J. Sargent and Neil Wallace, "Rational Expectations and the Theory of Economic Policy," *Journal of Monetary Economics* 2 (April 1976): 169–183. Monetary policies would still affect the equilibriums for prices and money wages.

funds rate as the principal short-term target, managing it so as to foster growth in the money supply in accordance with intermediate-term and one-year money supply targets.[2] The federal funds rate is the interest rate banks pay when they borrow excess reserves from other banks. The Federal Reserve argued that the money supply itself could not be employed successfully as a day-to-day or even a weekly target, since good current data are not available for the money supply, although sample data, which are not highly accurate, are available for the preceding week.

Monetarists recommend that interest rate targets be dropped completely, even if stable money supply growth is not adopted as the monetary policy target. They argue that money supply targets are essential for avoiding the wide swings in the money supply which have been so troublesome in the past and that interest rate targets may interfere with achieving money supply targets. They would have the Federal Reserve simply increase member bank reserves plus cash by the amounts consistent with money supply targets. Member bank reserves plus cash are a much more serviceable short-term target than the actual money supply, from an operational point of view, since open-market operations affect member bank reserves promptly and dollar for dollar.

While the question of the relative merits of interest rate targets and money supply targets remains an open one, economists, neo-Keynesians as well as monetarists, have moved in the direction of recommending increased emphasis on money supply or monetary base (member bank reserves plus cash) targets. This may reflect an evolving belief (to put it in simplified *IS* and *LM* curve terms) that there is more uncertainty surrounding the *IS* curve than the *LM* curve. In general, the money supply target produces the superior result if the *LM* curve is more certain, while the interest rate target produces the superior result if the *IS* curve is more certain.

Figure 20–1 illustrates the point.[3] If, as in the upper portion of the figure, it is certain both that the *IS* curve is IS_1 and that money supply m_0' will produce *LM* curve LM_1, it makes no difference whether a money supply target or an interest rate target is chosen. The monetary authority can achieve full employment and price stability either by targeting m_0' or by

[2] Board of Governors of the Federal Reserve System, "The Strategy of Monetary Control," *Federal Reserve Bulletin* 62 (May 1976): 411–421. The article is adapted from a report by Alan R. Holmes and Peter D. Sternlight.

[3] This discussion is adapted from a paper by William Poole. See W. Poole, "Optimal Choice of Monetary Policy Instruments in a Simple Stochastic Macro Model," *Quarterly Journal of Economics* 84 (May 1970): 197–216.

Figure 20–1 **Monetary Policy Targets**

If the positions of both the *IS* and *LM* curves are known with certainty, it makes no difference whether the interest rate target or the money supply target is used. If the *IS* curve is certain and the *LM* curve uncertain, the interest rate target produces the better result. If it is the *LM* curve which is certain, the money supply target performs best.

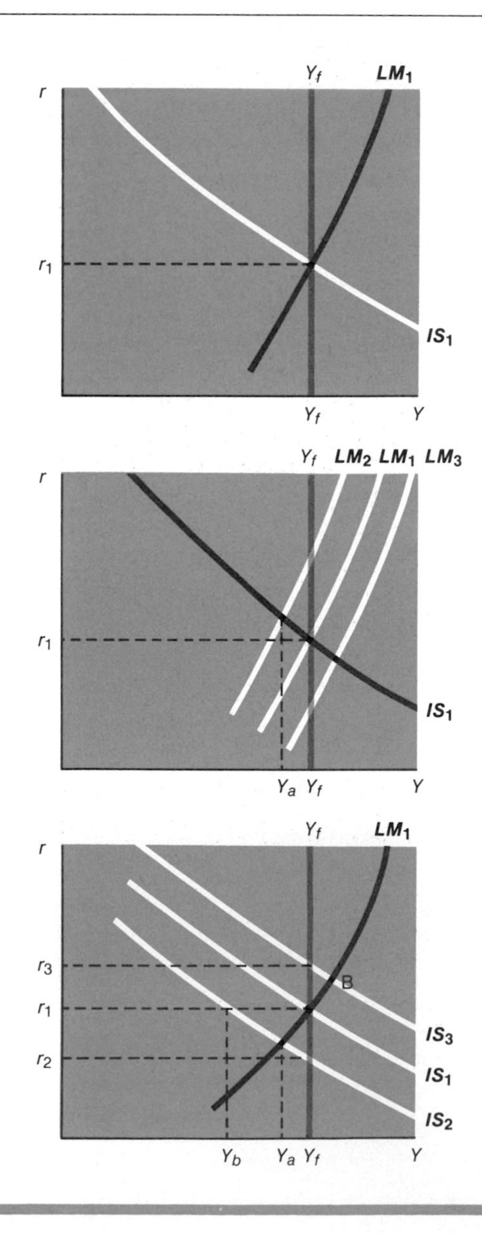

targeting r_1 and providing whatever m_0 is necessary for achieving r_1—which, of course, is m_0'.

Consider, however, the center portion of the figure. It is certain that the IS curve is IS_1, but m_0', while it most likely will produce LM_1, might produce LM_2 or LM_3. Therefore, the monetary authority would be better off targeting r_1, providing whatever m_0 is required for it, than targeting m_0'. Achieving r_1 will produce full employment and price stability with certainty, while m_0' may produce Y_a or an inflation sufficient to move the LM curve from LM_3 to LM_1.[4]

Finally, in the lower portion of the figure, the IS curve is most likely at IS_1 but might be at IS_2 or IS_3, whereas the LM curves given money supplies will produce are certain. In this case, the money supply target is superior to the interest rate target. For example, money supply m_0', which produces LM_1 with certainty, might produce an output as low as Y_a or inflation sufficient to close the expenditure gap indicated by Point B, but a target of r_1 might produce an output as low as Y_b or, if the IS curve is at IS_3, a permanent expenditure gap and inflation situation. In the latter case, the monetary authority would be perpetually trying to achieve an interest rate below the appropriate interest rate through money supply expansion.

The willingness of today's neo-Keynesians to apply money supply targets, or at least to consider money supply as well as interest rate targets, is consistent with the modern attitude that the money demand function is fairly stable and the LM curve therefore fairly predictable.

Monetary Policy Strength

While weakness in fiscal policies, and the associated crowding out effect, may be a factor discouraging their use, for fiscal ease at least, it is not clear that weakness in monetary policies is an important negative factor, barring the case Keynes postulated where monetary policies have no strength at all. If monetary policies are weak rather than strong, it means essentially that the Federal Reserve must change the money supply by more to remove a particular unemployment or inflation problem. They must buy or sell more U.S. securities in the open market. It is not clear that this is an important disadvantage. Indeed, for monetary ease, weakness means that the reduction in the U.S. debt outstanding with the private sector is larger, which may be an advantage if a small federal debt is a goal in itself. Monetary policy strength probably does not matter very much, unless

[4] In a growth context, the money supply target might produce chronic unemployment and deflation or chronic inflation by requiring that the money supply be increased too slowly or too rapidly to match demand to the expanding full-employment output.

strength is associated with the speed with which eventual impacts build up[5] or with the uncertainty surrounding them.[6]

Monetary and Fiscal Policies and the Balance of International Payments

Monetary and fiscal policies can be employed to balance international payments in situations where fixed foreign exchange rates are being maintained but imbalance has arisen because changes have occurred in underlying payments positions. It is best, however, to release monetary and fiscal policies from these responsibilities by allowing foreign exchange rate adjustments to balance international payments, since otherwise goals with respect to economic growth—and perhaps with respect to full employment, prices of domestic output, and free trade—will be compromised. If foreign exchange rate depreciation is required for balance, there are costs in that the terms on which domestic output is exchanged for foreign output may decline significantly, and import prices, and therefore consumer prices, will increase. But these are once and for all effects which end when the foreign exchange rate reaches the appropriate level, unless the international payments position is deteriorating chronically.

What if the currency depreciation is chronic? What if a factor such as continued expansion of domestic demand for oil products in the face of declining domestic oil production produces continuing currency depreciation and a continuing increase in import prices plus significant induced domestic cost-push inflation, so that price goals are compromised on a chronic basis?

One possibility is to place tax surcharges on oil imports or on oil products at the wholesale or retail level in order to reduce the quantity of oil products demanded domestically and thus diminish oil imports. Significant reductions in oil imports by this method may require very large increases in tax-inclusive prices of oil products to consumers, however, since the demand for oil and gasoline appears to be rather price inelastic. An alternative is to impose direct quantity quotas on oil imports and distribute oil products domestically by a rationing system.

While these methods are direct interferences with free trade, they are preferable to sacrificing full-employment and economic growth goals to balance international payments with monetary and fiscal policies in a

---

[5] Jack Vernon, "Money Demand Interest Elasticity and Monetary Policy Effectiveness," *Journal of Monetary Economics* 3 (April 1977): 179–190.

[6] William Brainard, "Uncertainty and the Effectiveness of Policy," *American Economic Review* 57 (May 1967): 411–425.

situation where the inflation effects of foreign exchange rate depreciation cannot be tolerated. Whatever the case, the monetary authority should not be inhibited from using the monetary policies appropriate to full-employment and economic growth goals because of the effect the policies would have on the balance of international payments.

Price and Wage Controls

Price and wage controls—and the broader concept of incomes policies, which place direct controls on profits and other forms of property income as well as on prices and wages—are additional policy options open to governments. They are inflation control devices, employed as supplements to monetary and fiscal policies. Most industrialized nations have imposed them at one time or another during the past several decades. They can be generally applied or restricted to producers and workers in key industries. They can be mandatory, voluntary, or something in between. The mandatory controls, which usually are imposed in situations regarded as emergencies, ordinarily begin as price and wage freezes and then evolve into more flexible systems in which government boards receive and act upon applications for price and wage adjustments.

Voluntary price and wage restraint programs sometimes involve little more than informal arrangements by which management and labor officials in key industries agree to keep government officials advised as to forthcoming price and wage decisions and to consult with government regarding them. Alternatively, they may involve formal voluntary guidelines announced by government and applicable to all areas of the economy. The guidelines usually specify that prices are to be held constant or restricted to small increases, while wage increases are to be restricted to the average increase in labor productivity in the economy. Voluntary programs often are referred to as *jawboning,* since in theory they involve persuasion rather than coercion.

Recently, there has been a good deal of interest in proposals which would control prices and wages through a system of tax penalties and rewards applied on the basis of price and wage performance. For example, credits against income taxes could be awarded where price and wage adjustments fall within specified levels, while firms exceeding the levels would pay tax penalties in proportion to the discrepancies involved.

In the United States, mandatory price and wage controls were imposed during both World Wars, during the Korean hostilities of the early 1950s, and in 1971–1973 by the Nixon administration during the later stages of the Vietnam conflict. Formal voluntary guidelines were imposed by the Kennedy and Johnson administrations during 1962–1968. President Carter imposed an informal voluntary guideline early in 1978 by asking that price and wage adjustments for 1978 be held below the average for the preceding two years. In October 1978, the Carter administration moved to a more formal and less voluntary system. An explicit voluntary guideline for wage and fringe benefit increases was set at 7 percent per year. And firms violating price or alternative profit guidelines were to be penalized, at the option of the government, by loss of government business.

Are Price and Wage Controls Needed?

Price and wage controls have substantial disadvantages. They are vulnerable to the philosophical criticism that they are government encroachments on the freedom of individuals to effect transactions at prices and wages agreed upon by mutual consent. Also, they are disadvantageous because they interfere with the price system in guiding production and rewards and therefore interfere with economic efficiency. A decision to use the controls must weigh these disadvantages against the need for controls.

Price and wage controls are not needed for demand-pull inflation, in ordinary circumstances, since monetary and fiscal policies can remove the excess demand and check the inflation. There are, however, two demand-pull situations in which the controls may be useful as temporary expedients.

The first is the situation where a substantial demand-pull based inflation already is under way. Price and wage controls might be employed on a short-term basis to check inflation while the lags which attend monetary and fiscal policy applications work themselves out. The problem with this use is that once the price and wage controls are in place the incentive to apply appropriate monetary and fiscal policies disappears, at least temporarily. As a result, the appropriate demand management policies may not be applied, so that an expenditure gap builds up underneath the price and wage ceilings and severe inflation reappears when the ceilings are dismantled.

The second situation is the wartime case where expenditures and output must be shifted rapidly from civilian to defense-related goods and services. If the required shift is a major one, as during World War II, monetary and fiscal policies alone probably will not be effective in containing inflationary pressures in either defense-related or civilian industries.

Production bottlenecks will defeat them in the defense-related area, while impact lags and anticipations of shortages will blunt their effectiveness on private sector expenditures.

The most persuasive case for price and wage controls occurs in the situation where labor groups with market power apply strong and chronic wage-push inflationary pressures before the economy reaches the natural rate of unemployment. That is the case posed by the wage-push trade-off hypothesis. There, monetary and fiscal policies can check the inflation only by provoking unacceptable levels of unemployment.

Fortunately, the United States does not seem to have experienced that type of inflationary problem—not through 1979, in any event. The inflation of the 1970s appears to have been mainly demand-pull, like those of the past, notwithstanding the higher unemployment rates of the period. It resulted chiefly from expansive demand management policies in the face of higher natural rates of unemployment. Of course, there were cost-push elements such as the sharp increases in the price of imported oil during 1973 and 1974 and the increases in prices of imported goods and services at large induced by the depreciation of the dollar in foreign exchange markets. But chronic wage-push inflation arising from labor union market power has not been a substantial factor in U.S. inflation experience.

Are Price and Wage Controls Effective?

Beyond the question of whether price and wage controls are needed, there is the question of whether they are effective. It is often argued that they are not effective in checking inflation, except on a short-term basis.

Voluntary programs have not been effective in the U.S. experience on either a long- or short-term basis. Moreover, they sometimes develop features which are even less compatible with U.S. traditions than are mandatory price and wage controls. Violations of guidelines occur, confrontations between public officials and labor and business leaders take place, egos become involved, and various forms of coercion may be applied. The threat to deny government business to offenders is a form of coercion, of course. Beyond that, government may threaten to sponsor unrelated regulatory or tax legislation or measures which would increase foreign competition as a penalty. It may threaten anti-trust investigations or even audits of tax returns of offending corporations and officials. Many U.S. citizens, on reflection, prefer mandatory price and wage controls to these devices.

Mandatory price and wage freezes have demonstrated themselves to be effective in curtailing inflation for periods of up to several months. Their advantage, in addition to this effectiveness in short-term applications, is that they are simple to apply and quick to act. This is the case, at any rate, if the president has been provided with standby authority to impose them in advance. Otherwise, a legislative lag is involved, and effectiveness is diluted by anticipatory price and wage increases which occur during the period of legislative deliberation.

Whatever the case for short-term applications, the view is widely held that mandatory price and wage controls cannot effectively check inflation for extended periods of time, except perhaps during "popular" wars such as World War I and World War II. The U.S. experience of 1971–1973 is cited as an example of the difficulties involved. It is argued that public support for mandatory price and wage controls declines over time and that democratic governments cannot maintain them as effective devices once public support has evaporated. They succumb to circumventions or exceptions or to dismantling, whichever comes first.

One of the difficulties is that the groups which have the most to gain from ending the controls, the labor and business groups with market power, also have great political power. Whereas ending the controls permits these groups to exercise market power, they are at a disadvantage under the controls—unless they can secure special treatment—because their price and wage actions are highly visible and easily monitored. Because of this, they cannot participate fully in circumventions—that is, black market prices and wages, job upgrading, quality reductions, and the like. Consequently, they employ political power or threats of strikes to secure either the end of controls or special treatment by price and wage boards. The program ends, or its effectiveness ends. Probably the program is eventually dismantled in any event, since special treatment evaporates support from the electorate at large.

This view appears too pessimistic, however. Probably it is true that price and wage controls cannot check demand-pull inflation for extended periods of time. Circumvention becomes a substantial problem as time passes, since groups which do not possess market power and whose price and wage actions are not highly visible are confronted with excess demand and therefore the opportunity for circumvention. But price and wage controls are not required for ordinary demand-pull inflation, since monetary and fiscal policies can check demand-pull inflation by removing excess demand.

Mandatory price and wage controls probably can be effective in the two demand-pull situations where they might be helpful and in the wage-push situation where they would be needed if such a situation were to arise on a chronic basis. The two demand-pull cases are short-term situations, and mandatory price and wage freezes are effective for brief periods. There is the problem, in the case where government is trying to "break the back" of an ongoing demand-pull inflation, that the incentive for pursuing appropriate monetary and fiscal policies is removed if the price and wage freeze is temporarily successful, so that the policies may not be pursued and excess demand still may be present when the controls become ineffective or are dismantled. But again, this problem is averted if the appropriate monetary and fiscal policies are applied.

Mandatory price and wage controls probably can be effective in checking cost-push inflation arising from the market power of labor unions or domestic producer groups (including domestic oil producers), provided that the policies are backed up with adequate monetary and fiscal policies so that demand-pull pressures do not complicate the problem. As noted above, the price and wage behavior of major groups with market power is highly visible and easily monitored. Business officials will not make illegal price and wage increases if severe fines or jail are the result. There are the problems of political pressure to secure special treatment or to end the system of controls and of strikes by labor, but they may not be great problems if monetary and fiscal policies rule out demand-pull pressures. Circumvention by other groups will not be serious in this case, and the controls will be easier to bear for groups with market power.

There is the problem of cost-push inflation from the international oil cartel and from increases in import prices resulting from dollar depreciation. Price controls will not be successful in these instances and should not be used. Also, if the government creates or accommodates sustained demand-pull inflation because of the political pressures it faces, price and wage controls will not be effective. Cost-of-living indexing, at least of the federal debt and of as many pension contracts as government can influence, may be the best solution in this case. Indexing does not check inflation, but it alleviates some of its burdens.

Macroeconomic Policy during the 1960s and 1970s

Table 20–1 is useful in tracing the record of macroeconomic policy during the 1960s and 1970s. The second column, which presents National Bureau of Economic Research reference dates for general business peaks and troughs, indicates that three business cycles occurred during the period. They are marked by the recessions of 1960, 1970, and late 1973 through early 1975 and the subsequent expansions. Columns 3 and 4 present unemployment and inflation rates for each year of the period.

Table 20–1

Price and Employment Performance and Policy Indicators, 1960–1978

Year	Peak or Trough	Unemployment Rate	%ΔP	%Δm_0 (Dec.)	Full-Employment Surplus
1960	Peak (Aug.)	5.5	1.6	0.6	12.8
1961	Trough (Feb.)	6.7	1.0	3.1	10.2
1962		5.5	1.1	1.5	7.8
1963		5.7	1.2	3.7	10.3
1964		5.2	1.3	4.6	3.3
1965		4.5	1.7	4.6	−1.5
1966		3.8	2.9	2.6	−5.3
1967		3.8	2.9	6.6	−14.1
1968		3.6	4.5	6.1	−9.6
1969	Peak (Dec.)	3.5	5.4	1.4	7.2
1970	Trough (Nov.)	4.9	5.9	5.1	2.0
1971		5.9	4.3	9.0	−8.5
1972		5.6	3.3	9.6	−16.7
1973	Peak (Nov.)	4.9	6.2	5.0	−6.7
1974		5.6	11.0	5.4	−3.0
1975	Trough (Mar.)	8.5	9.1	8.9	−31.0
1976		7.7	5.0	13.2	−26.9
1977		7.0	7.0	8.4	−34.6
1978		6.0	7.7	4.3	−22.8

The data for the M−1+ money supply begin with 1967. The figures for the percentage increase in the money supply for 1960–1967 relate to cash plus demand deposits only.

Sources: President's Council of Economic Advisers, *Economic Report of the President* (Washington, D.C.: Government Printing Office, 1979), pp. 214, 239, 251. Federal Reserve Bank of St. Louis, *Technical Notes for Estimates of the High-Employment Budget,* April 1979, pp. 8–9. The business cycle peak and trough dates are National Bureau of Economic Research reference dates, taken from U.S. Department of Commerce, Bureau of Economic Analysis, *Business Conditions Digest,* January 1979, p. 10.

They reflect the cyclical movements we would expect, for the most part, and also display an increase in unemployment rates for corresponding inflation rates for the 1970s as compared to the 1960s, an effect attributed here mainly to an increase in the natural rate of unemployment and the policy response to it.

The last two columns present indicators for monetary and fiscal policies. The percent increase in the money supply is used as the monetary indicator. A rise in the rate of money supply increase indicates a shift toward monetary ease; a fall indicates a shift toward monetary restraint. The dividing line for monetary ease and restraint probably should be placed at a 5 or 5.5 percent increase in the money supply.

The federal full-employment surplus is used as the fiscal indicator. A decrease indicates a shift toward fiscal ease and an increase a shift toward restraint. These fiscal shifts reflect both activist policies to cope with private sector disturbances and the sometimes unintentional shifts which occur as federal spending expands or as tax receipts change with changes in real income and inflation. There is no attempt here to designate the full-employment surplus which divides fiscal ease from fiscal restraint. Presumably, it is positive, since the tax multiplier is probably weaker than the government purchases multiplier.

Economic Expansion, 1961–1965: Keynesian Fiscal Policies Applied

The year 1960 is a useful beginning point in a survey of recent macroeconomic policy because it leads by one year the transition to the Kennedy administration. The Kennedy administration was the first to embrace, if hesitatingly at first, the Keynesian recommendation of moving the economy to full employment with fiscal policies, even if it meant unbalancing the government budget.

During 1961–1965, this policy worked very well. By 1964, the unemployment rate was below its 5.5 percent low point of the preceding business expansion, and the inflation rate remained below 2 percent. Of course, economic recovery from the recession of 1960 no doubt would have occurred even without the Kennedy-Johnson policies. The business trough assigned to February 1961 almost coincides with the Kennedy inauguration.

True to the Keynesian message, fiscal policies were the principal tool employed. The federal full-employment surplus fell sharply during 1961 and 1962, recovered slightly during 1963, and then declined again during 1964 and 1965. The 1961 and 1962 shifts toward fiscal ease resulted chiefly from increases in federal spending, though an investment tax credit was instituted in October 1962. The renewed decline during 1964 reflected the general income tax cut of that year. Monetary policy was easier during 1961–1965 than during 1960, but the rate of increase in the money supply remained below 5 percent. The emphasis was on fiscal ease.

Demand-Pull Inflation, 1966–1969

During the second half of 1965, with the economy already nearing full employment, defense expenditures began to increase very rapidly in conjunction with the U.S. military buildup in Vietnam. A full-employment federal deficit appeared in 1965 and increased in 1966 and 1967. There was no forecasting error insofar as fiscal policies were concerned. President Johnson's economic advisers urged him to recommend a tax increase to Congress. The president resisted this advice, however, delaying his recommendation for a tax surcharge until January 1967. A tax cut to stimulate the economy had been enacted in 1964. He felt that he would appear indecisive if he called for a tax increase in 1965 or in January 1966. Moreover, the president feared that a recommendation for a tax cut would be met in Congress with attempts to cut government expenditures instead, threatening his "war on poverty" programs.

Monetary ease was added to fiscal ease during 1967 and 1968. The money supply increased by 6.6 percent during 1967 and by 6.1 percent during 1968. These increases appear to have resulted chiefly from the desire of the Federal Reserve to prevent interest rates from rising during those years. It wished to avoid a repetition of the crisis which had occurred for savings institutions and mortgage and construction markets during 1966, when the money supply had increased by only 2.6 percent and interest rates had risen sharply, reducing the price-competitiveness of savings deposits. In 1967 and 1968, the Federal Reserve looked too much at interest rates as the target and not enough at the rate of increase in the money supply. In addition, the Federal Reserve apparently overestimated the restrictive effect on spending that the tax surcharge of 1968 would have (perhaps by neglecting the message of the permanent income hypothesis). As a result, it overestimated the increase in the money supply which was required.

The demand-pull phase of the 1961–1969 economic expansion ended with the application of the monetary and fiscal brakes in 1969. The full-employment federal surplus increased sharply, reflecting the effects of the extended tax surcharge and inflation on tax receipts and the leveling off of federal spending. The rate of money supply increase declined to 1.4 percent. The longest business expansion since the onset of the Great Depression of the 1930s came to an end.

The 1970s: Unemployment and Inflation

Both monetary and fiscal policies shifted toward ease during the recession of 1970 and the economic recovery of 1971 and 1972. However, when the inflation rate accelerated slightly during mid-1971, even though the unemployment rate had not declined from its 1970 recession level, the Nixon administration imposed a ninety-day freeze on prices and wages. Its purpose was to check inflation with the price and wage freeze while continuing to combat unemployment with monetary and fiscal ease. The freeze, known as Phase I, was followed by the more flexible Phases II and III, which extended to June 1973, when a second brief freeze was imposed. That was followed in August 1973 by a still more flexible system which ended effective controls. The price and wage control program was dismantled entirely in mid-1974.

The plan worked in the sense that the inflation rate subsided during the second half of 1971 and during 1972 under the lid imposed by price and wage controls, and in 1972 the unemployment rate finally declined. However, with the end of effective price and wage controls in mid-1973, the inflation rate began to accelerate, responding to the demand-pull inflationary pressures which had built up under the price and wage control lid by monetary and fiscal ease. Moreover, there were two complicating inflationary factors in 1973 and early 1974. One was the extremely poor grain harvests abroad during 1972, which produced a strong foreign demand for U.S. grain products in 1973. The second was the approximate tripling of prices of U.S. oil imports during late 1973 and early 1974, a cost-push inflationary factor administered by the newly effectual foreign oil producer cartel.

The resurgence of inflation was met by shifts toward monetary and fiscal restraint. The percentage increase in the money supply was much lower in 1973 and 1974 than in 1972, and the federal full-employment surplus was much larger (the deficit was smaller). The monetary shift was activist; the fiscal shift reflected mainly the effects of inflation on tax receipts. This convergence of factors—pent-up demand-pull inflationary pressures, cost-push inflationary pressures, and shifts toward monetary and fiscal restraint—produced, in the turn-around year 1974, an increase in the unemployment rate, even though prices rose at the highest rate since 1947. The unemployment rate increased further in 1975, while the inflation rate declined.

Fiscal policy shifted sharply to ease in 1975 with the general tax cut, and the same was true of monetary policies. The business trough occurred in March 1975, and, by 1976, both the unemployment rate and the inflation rate were showing an improved performance. Economic recovery continued through 1978. The unemployment rate declined below 7 percent, and even below 6 percent, on a monthly basis, but inflation again began to accelerate.

In retrospect, it seems clear that a better price and employment result would have occurred during 1974 and 1975 if monetary and fiscal policies had been less expansive during 1971 and 1972. Price and wage controls were a mistake in the sense that there was no real need for them, and monetary and fiscal policies would not have been so expansive had the controls not been in place. The shift toward monetary and fiscal restraint during 1973, just as the cost-push inflationary pressures from the increase in prices of oil imports appeared, was doubly unfortunate. Just as it would have been better to have been less expansive during 1971 and 1972, it would have been better to have eased monetary policy temporarily during late 1973 and early 1974 to accommodate the increase in oil prices, which, as cost-push inflationary pressures, could not have been contained by restrictive monetary and fiscal policies in any event.

Policy Performance during the 1960s and 1970s

Macroeconomic policy performance was not impressive during 1960 through 1978. The principal destabilizing influences in the U.S. economy during the period appear to have been the monetary and fiscal policies themselves. It is easy to believe that a balanced full-employment federal budget coupled with stable money supply growth (excepting a temporary rise in money supply growth to deal with the oil price increases of 1973 and 1974) would have produced a better result.

Still, that does not settle the issue against activist stabilization policies. Appropriate activist monetary and fiscal policies might have done better had they been followed. And private sector disturbances may be more severe in the future than they appear to have been during this period. Moreover, there is the problem of whether a reasonably balanced full-employment federal budget can be maintained with existing federal fiscal arrangements. Pending the emergence of better federal fiscal arrangements, activist monetary policies may be needed for offsetting fiscal disturbances, even putting other reasons for using them aside.

Passive or Active Government Policies?

One essential disagreement runs like a common thread through the major points of view on most macroeconomic policy issues. It concerns the extent to which governments should intervene in the economic activities of their citizens in an effort to increase the common good. In the United States and in similarly situated nations, where individual freedom is regarded as a goal in its own right, two questions are involved in most issues. First, is an active role for government more likely to improve upon or worsen the result a more passive stance by government would produce? Second, if there are gains from government intervention, are they great enough to justify encroaching upon the freedom of individuals to manage their economic affairs in their own interests?

Milton Friedman and other monetarists generally favor a passive stance by government, both because they feel that government intervention most often provides an inferior result and because they place a high value on individual freedom. They recommend stable money supply growth, a balanced full-employment government budget, and completely flexible foreign exchange rates. They would avoid general price and wage controls and would minimize all government regulation of domestic and foreign trade. They would rely on as competitive as possible a price and market system to provide for economic stability, economic growth, foreign trade, and other economic goals.

As a general rule, nonmonetarists favor a more active stance by government. They recommend activist monetary policies and sometimes activist fiscal policies as well. They are more receptive to price and wage controls, if the occasion seems to require them, and to management of foreign exchange markets, including even import quotas on oil as an extreme solution. They are prepared to see the government affect the aggregate saving and investment expenditure functions to bring about an economic growth objective and to influence growth through policies affecting technological advance and labor quality.

The issue of whether government should take an active or passive role in economic affairs predates the terms monetarists and neo-Keynesians, of course. No doubt it will survive them. Friedman's views reassert the laissez faire creed of the classical economics Keynes attacked. Classical economics, in turn, had supplanted the earlier *mercantilist* views of writers such as Thomas Mun (1571–1641), the Englishman, and practitioners such as Jean Baptiste Colbert (1619–1683), the French minister of finance from 1661 to 1683 under Louis XIV. The mercantilists had favored an activist role for government in economic activity. Government was to stimulate trade, and thereby the wealth and power of the nation. The precise points at issue change, but the common thread—the question of passive or active policies by government—remains.

Summary

1. The administrative lag is an important limitation with fiscal policies. It limits their usefulness as an activist stabilization policy device and makes even the more passive fiscal stance of balancing the full-employment federal budget difficult to accomplish. Other problems with

fiscal policies as an activist demand management tool include the crowding out effect, impact lags, and the fact that the greater portion of government purchases do not lend themselves well to cyclical variation.

2. The impact lag is a problem with monetary policies. This lag, together with uncertainty, gives rise to the target problem facing money managers and to the possibility that fine-tuning with monetary policies will destabilize the economy rather than stabilizing it. The absence of a significant administrative lag for monetary policies is their strong point as an activist stabilization policy device.

3. Price and wage controls probably are not very effective in containing demand-pull inflationary pressures for more than brief periods. However, they should not be needed for this job, since monetary and fiscal policies can do it.

4. Price and wage controls probably could be effective in checking chronic wage-push inflationary pressures of the type contemplated by the wage-push trade-off hypothesis if such pressures should become a problem in the United States. They might be needed for a serious problem of this kind, since monetary and fiscal policies provoke unacceptable unemployment when applied to check such pressures.

5. The debate over an active or passive role for government in economic affairs is a broad and enduring one. It exists apart from current labels and specific points at issue.

Concepts for Identification

administrative lag
impact lag
formula flexibility
fiscal drag
fiscal dividend
monetary policy targets
federal funds rate
jawboning
price and wage guidelines
mandatory price and wage controls
incomes policies
price and wage freeze

Questions and Problems for Review

1. Explain why it remains necessary for the government to correctly estimate the natural rate of unemployment even if it adopts a passive stabilization policy.

2. The federal government must employ discretionary fiscal policies to keep its full-employment budget balanced. Explain.

3. From the stabilization policy point of view, what is the advantage of cost-of-living indexing the federal tax system?

4. The fiscal dividend should be returned to the taxpayers in the form of tax cuts. The fiscal dividend should be used to increase federal spending. Discuss.

5. The Congressional Budget Office has potential for improving the performance of fiscal policies as activist stabilization policy devices. Explain.

6. What is formula flexibility? What is its significance for economic stability?

7. The interest rate is the better monetary policy target if the *IS* curve is more certain than the *LM* curve. The money supply is the better target if the *LM* curve is more certain. Explain.

8. The strength of a monetary policy (provided it has some strength) may not be related to its effectiveness. Explain.

9. Mandatory price and wage controls probably cannot check protracted demand-pull inflation, but may be able to check wage-push inflation. Evaluate this statement.

10. Evaluate macroeconomic policy performance in the United States during the 1960s and 1970s.

11. Monetarists generally prefer that government take a passive economic policy stance, while nonmonetarists usually recommend an activist stance. Describe passive and active stances as they relate to current economic problems.

References

Barro, R. J., and Fischer, Stanley. "Recent Developments in Monetary Theory." *Journal of Monetary Economics* 2 (April 1976): 133–167.

Board of Governors of the Federal Reserve System. "The Strategy of Monetary Control." *Federal Reserve Bulletin* 62 (May 1976): 411–421. (Adapted from a report by Alan R. Holmes and Peter D. Sternlight.)

Brainard, William. "Uncertainty and the Effectiveness of Policy." *American Economic Review* 57 (May 1967): 411–425.

De Leeuw, Frank, and Gramlich, Edward M. "The Channels of Monetary Policy." *Federal Reserve Bulletin* 55 (June 1969): 472–491.

Friedman, Milton. "The Role of Monetary Policy." *American Economic Review* 58 (March 1968): 1–17.

Lucas, R. E., Jr. "Expectations and the Neutrality of Money." *Journal of Economic Theory* 4 (April 1972): 103–124.

Poole, William. "Optimal Choice of Monetary Policy Instruments in a Simple Stochastic Macro Model." *Quarterly Journal of Economics* 84 (May 1970): 197–216.

President's Council of Economic Advisers. *Economic Report of the President.* Washington, D.C.: Government Printing Office, 1960–1979.

Sargent, Thomas J., and Wallace, Neil. "Rational Expectations and the Theory of Economic Policy." *Journal of Monetary Economics* 2 (April 1976): 169–183.

Smith, Warren L. "A Neo-Keynesian View of Monetary Policy." In *Readings in Money, National Income, and Stabilization Policy,"* edited by Warren L. Smith and R. L. Teigen. 3rd ed. Homewood, Ill.: Richard D. Irwin, 1974, pp. 349–360.

Vernon, Jack. "Money Demand Interest Elasticity and Monetary Policy Effectiveness." *Journal of Monetary Economics* 3 (April 1977): 179–190.

Glossary

accelerator effect (Chapter 17) An effect making investment expenditures a positive function of changes in aggregate output and real income. It arises from the production function relationship indicating the capital stock requirements for producing various levels of aggregate output.

adaptive expectations (Chapter 11) Expectations as to the values of economic variables for current and future periods formulated on the basis of the variables' past performance.

adjustment paths (Chapter 17) The paths economic variables follow when disturbed from equilibrium values.

administrative lag (Chapter 20) The time between when the need for a policy action is perceived by policy administrators (the president and his advisers, Congress, the Federal Reserve) and when the action is taken.

aggregate demand for output (Chapter 1) The sum of consumption expenditures, investment expenditures, government purchases of goods and services, and net exports of goods and services.

aggregate output market (Chapter 12) The market presenting demand and supply curves for aggregate output, with quantities demanded and supplied expressed as a function of price.

aggregate production function (Chapter 12) The function relating aggregate output to labor and capital inputs.

aggregate saving (Chapter 10) In the three-sector model (households, producers, and government), aggregate output and real income less the sum of consumption expenditures and government purchases of goods and services.

average propensity to consume (Chapter 5) Consumption expenditures divided by income (or by disposable income).

balance of international payments (Chapter 19) The supply of foreign exchange less the demand for foreign exchange (excluding official transactions in foreign exchange reserves and gold).

***BP* curve** (Chapter 19) The combinations of aggregate real income and the interest rate at which the demand and supply for foreign exchange are equal (excluding official transactions in foreign exchange reserves and gold).

Bretton Woods adjustable peg system (Chapter 19) A system in which official intervention with foreign exchange reserves and gold was to be used to maintain fixed foreign exchange rates in the face of temporary disturbances to balance of payments equilibrium but in which fundamental disturbances were to be met with foreign exchange rate adjustments.

broader Pigou effect (Chapter 16) The relationship making consumption expenditures a positive function of the real money supply plus real government debt.

budget study result (Chapter 5) Findings of statistical investigations which showed that the proportion of income consumed tends to diminish across the income distribution from lower to higher incomes at a point in time.

built-in fiscal policies (Chapter 6) The effect arising from the positive relationship between net taxes (taxes less transfer payments) and income which dampens the multiplier effect.

built-in money supply effects (Chapter 13) Interest rate effects on borrowed bank reserves, desired excess reserves, and perhaps time deposit liabilities which produce a positive relationship between the money supply and the interest rate.

business cycle (Chapter 1) The tendency toward recurrent periods of business expansion and recession evidenced in aggregate economic performance.

capital accumulation (Chapter 18) The increase over time in the capital stock produced by positive net investment expenditures.

capital consumption allowances (Chapter 3) The estimate of capital goods used up in production during a specified period.

capital stock (Chapter 12) The stock of producers' plants, equipment, and inventories plus residential housing.

change in business inventories (Chapter 3) The change (plus or minus) in business inventories of final and intermediate goods.

civilian labor force (Chapter 3) The sum of employed and officially unemployed workers, excluding members of the armed forces and employed workers under sixteen years of age.

classical economists (Chapter 15) David Ricardo (1772–1823), his predecessors, and those later economists who elaborated the basic Ricardian doctrines.

classical model (Chapter 15) The economic model which incorporates the views of the classical economists.

classical money demand function (Chapter 14) The theory proposed by the classical economists in which real money balances demanded bore a stable, proportionate relationship to total transactions and to aggregate income.

classical propositions (Chapter 15) The propositions, deriving from classical assumptions, that (1) full employment is assured and (2) money is neutral.

commercial banks (Chapter 8) The financial intermediaries which historically have been the major source of checking deposits and short-term business loans.

constant returns-to-scale (Chapter 12) The condition which exists when equal percentage increases in the inputs to a production process result in the same percentage increase in output.

consumer durable goods (Chapter 3) Consumer goods which have useful lives of one year or more.

consumer price index (Chapter 3) The price index reflecting prices of goods and services purchased by U.S. urban consumers. (Before January 1978, it reflected those purchased by urban wage earners and clerical workers only.)

consumption constant multiplier (Chapter 4) The change in aggregate output and real income divided by the change in the consumption constant provoking it. (The consumption constant is the a_0 in the equation $C = a_0 + bYd$.)

consumption expenditures (Chapter 3) Expenditures for final goods and services by consumers.

consumption function (Chapter 4) The function relating consumption expenditures to their determinants.

credit cards (Chapter 8) Cards involving a line of credit which permits the purchase of items on a delayed payment basis.

creditor (Chapter 2) A lender. The holder of a loan instrument or negotiable debt security acknowledging the debt of a borrower.

crowding out (Chapter 13) The check to the strength of fiscal ease applications which occurs because interest rates rise and diminish interest-sensitive expenditures.

currency depreciation (Chapter 19) A decrease in the value of a currency relative to the value of other currencies.

debtor (Chapter 2) A borrower. An issuer of a loan instrument or negotiable debt security.

demand deposits (Chapter 8) Deposits in commercial banks or thrift institutions against which checks can be drawn.

demand for money (Chapter 9) The desire to hold money.

desired excess reserves (Chapter 8) For commercial banks, desired reserves less required reserves.

diminishing marginal product of labor (Chapter 12) The diminishing increments in output that result when successive increments of labor input are added to a production process while other inputs are held constant.

diminishing returns-to-scale (Chapter 18) The condition which exists when increasing the inputs to a production process by the same percentage results in a smaller percentage increase in output.

discount rate (Chapter 8) The rate of interest member banks pay when they borrow reserves from the Federal Reserve banks (sometimes called the rediscount rate or the borrowing rate).

discretionary fiscal ease (Chapter 6) Increases in government purchase and transfer payment programs or reductions in tax programs applied to raise aggregate demand and contribute to employment objectives.

discretionary fiscal policies (Chapter 6) Adjustments in government purchase, tax, and transfer payment programs made to ease unemployment and inflation problems.

discretionary fiscal restraint (Chapter 6) Reductions in government purchase and transfer payment programs or increases in tax programs applied to contribute to price objectives by reducing expenditure gaps.

disposable personal income (Chapter 3) Personal income (which includes transfer payments to persons) less personal tax and nontax payments to government.

dynamic money supply disturbance (Chapter 11) A change in the rate at which the money supply is being changed each period.

economic growth (Chapter 18) The growth—either absolute or per capita—in aggregate output and real income.

economic growth rates (Chapter 18) The percent change in aggregate output and real income, either absolute or per capita, defined with respect to a unit of time.

economies of scale (Chapter 18) The condition which occurs when equal percentage increases in the inputs to a production process cause greater percentage increases in output.

equilibrium money supply (Chapter 8) The money supply which exists when actual excess reserves equal desired excess reserves.

equilibrium output and income (Chapter 4) A situation in which there is no tendency for aggregate output and real income to change.

excess money supply (Chapter 10) Real money balances less real money balances demanded.

excess reserves (Chapter 8) For commercial banks, reserves less required reserves.

expected inflation (Chapter 11) The percent increase in prices which is expected to occur over a specified period.

expenditure gap (Chapter 4) Aggregate output demanded at existing prices less full-employment output.

expenditure interest sensitivity (Chapter 14) The response of expenditures to changes in the interest rate.

federal deficit (Chapter 6) Federal transfer payments and purchases of goods and services less federal tax receipts.

federal funds rate (Chapter 20) The interest rate banks pay when they borrow excess reserves from one another.

Federal Reserve–MIT model (Chapter 7) A large econometric model originated under the joint sponsorship of the Board of Governors of the Federal Reserve System and economists at Massachusetts Institute of Technology during the late 1960s to describe the U.S. economy.

final goods and services (Chapter 3) Goods and services delivered to consumers, including the investment goods delivered to producers for consumption in production.

fiscal dividend (Chapter 20) The increase in government tax receipts which occurs automatically with growth in output and real income over time and with inflation.

fiscal drag (Chapter 20) The increase in the federal surplus which occurs if tax receipts, which grow automatically with growth in real income and inflation, grow over time relative to federal spending.

fiscal policies (Chapter 1) Changes in government purchases of goods and services, transfer payments, and taxes.

fixed factor proportions (Chapter 12) The condition which exists when the ratios the various inputs to a production process bear to one another are unchanging.

fixed foreign exchange rates (Chapter 19) The foreign exchange rates under which a nation operates when it commits itself to maintain its currency at a fixed value in relation to other currencies, except for making adjustments to accommodate fundamental changes in its international payments position.

flexible accelerator (Chapter 17) A mechanism which allows for qualifications to the rigid accelerator by including the blunting effect of excess capacity and the influence of changes in the relative prices of capital and labor on the optimum capital to output ratio. The flexible accelerator presents investment expenditures as closing only a portion of the gap between optimum and actual capital each period.

flexible foreign exchange rates (Chapter 19) The foreign exchange rates under which a nation operates when it does not intervene in the foreign exchange market with foreign exchange reserves and gold. It leaves exchange rates free to respond to the forces of demand and supply.

fluctuations in aggregate demand (Chapter 11) Changes in the amount of aggregate output demanded at the existing price level.

foreign exchange (Chapter 19) Foreign currencies.

foreign exchange market (Chapter 19) The market for foreign currencies. Physically, it pyramids upon the operations of large banks and specialized financial institutions in major international financial centers.

foreign exchange rate (Chapter 19) The price of a foreign currency in terms of the domestic currency.

formula flexibility (Chapter 20) The tying of tax, transfer payment, and government purchase programs to the unemployment rate, so that built-in fiscal policy effects will be stronger and lend greater automatic stability to the economy.

frictional unemployment (Chapter 2) Unemployment which occurs as workers move between jobs in the normal course of job separation and job search.

full-employment constraint on output (Chapter 4) The level of output produced when the unemployment rate equals the natural rate of unemployment.

full-employment government budget (Chapter 6) The budget which would occur if the economy were fully employed, given existing government purchase, tax, and transfer payment programs.

full-employment surplus (Chapter 6) The federal government surplus (tax receipts less government spending) which would occur if the economy were fully employed, given existing tax and spending programs.

gains from trade (Chapter 19) The increase in aggregate output and real income which results from international trade and specialization according to comparative advantage.

Golden Rule of Accumulation (Chapter 18) The rule holding that the optimum proportion of full-employment income to save is the proportion which maximizes consumption per unit of labor input at all points in time, once the long-term equilibrium growth path corresponding to it has been achieved.

government purchases multiplier (Chapter 6) The change in equilibrium aggregate output and real income divided by the change in government purchases provoking it.

government purchases of goods and services (Chapter 3) Government spending for items which reflect production of final goods and services. Government transfer payments are not included.

government saving (Chapter 10) Tax receipts less the sum of government purchases of goods and services and transfer payments (the same as the government surplus).

government surplus function (Chapter 6) Taxes less the sum of government purchases of goods and services and transfer payments expressed as a positive function of aggregate output and real income.

government transfer payments (Chapter 3) Government expenditures which are transfers of income rather than payments for productive activity occurring during the period in which they take place.

gross national product (Chapter 3) The aggregate national output for a specified period. Final goods and services produced by factors of production owned by domestic residents.

gross national product in constant dollars (Chapter 3) Gross national product with quantities valued in terms of prices of a specified base year.

gross national product in current dollars (Chapter 3) Gross national product with quantities valued in terms of prices of the year to which the measure relates.

gross private domestic investment (Chapter 3) Gross expenditures for business plant and equipment and residential housing plus the change in business inventories.

growth in full-employment output (Chapter 18) The growth in the level of output corresponding to an unemployment rate equal to the natural unemployment rate.

impact lag (Chapter 6) The period between the enacting of policies (open-market purchases, tax rates changes, and the like) and the impact of the actions on unemployment and inflation rates.

import surcharge (Chapter 19) A tax on imported goods and services. A tariff.

imputation (Chapter 3) Assigning a market value to production which does not actually pass through a market, so that its value can be included in the aggregate output estimate.

income elasticity of money demand (Chapter 9) The percentage change in real money balances demanded divided by the percentage change in real income provoking it. A measure of the sensitivity of real money balances demanded to changes in real income.

income-maintenance programs (Chapter 12) Programs which sustain income during periods of unemployment.

incomes policies (Chapter 13) An extension of the price and wage control concept which places ceilings on profits and other types of income.

income velocity of money supply circulation (Chapter 14) Gross national product in current dollars divided by the money supply.

indexing (Chapter 2) Tying income and wealth items to a cost-of-living index to protect them against purchasing power losses caused by inflation.

index number problem (Chapter 3) The upward bias created when back-year weights instead of current-period weights are used for weighting items as to importance in an aggregate price index. The upward bias results from consumers' tendencies to shift expenditures away from the items whose prices have increased the most.

indirect business taxes (Chapter 3) Taxes, such as sales and excise taxes, which are imposed on the value of transactions rather than directly on business and personal incomes and wealth.

inflation rate (Chapter 1) The percentage increase in prices during a specified period.

interest elasticity of money demand (Chapter 9) The percentage change in real money balances demanded divided by the percentage change in the interest rate which provokes it. A measure of the sensitivity of real money balances demanded to changes in the interest rate.

interest equalization tax (Chapter 19) A tax that was imposed during the 1960s and early 1970s on the interest and dividend income U.S. residents received from foreign securities. Its purpose was to improve the U.S. international payments balance by diminishing imports of such securities.

interest inelastic (Chapter 7) Not highly responsive to changes in interest rates. If a given percentage change in the interest rate provokes a smaller percentage change in an interest-sensitive item, the item is said to be interest inelastic.

intermediate goods (Chapter 3) Goods which have been produced or partially produced but have not yet been sold to business or consumer users.

investment demand schedule (Chapter 7) The schedule plotting aggregate investment expenditures desired against the interest rate, with the interest rate on the vertical axis.

investment expenditure function (Chapter 11) Aggregate investment expenditures desired expressed as a function of the interest rate and other determinants.

investment multiplier (Chapter 4) The change in equilibrium aggregate output and real income divided by the change in the investment expenditures constant which provokes it.

investment tax credit (Chapter 18) A credit against income taxes. A 10 percent investment tax credit permits firms or individuals to deduct 10 percent of any qualifying investment expenditures from income tax payments.

***IS* curve** (Chapter 10) A plotting of the combinations of r and Y at which $Y = E$ or, alternatively, $S = I$.

jawboning (Chapter 20) A form of negotiating voluntary price and wage controls in which government officials try to persuade firms and unions to keep price and wage increases within certain limits.

labor market (Chapter 12) The market presenting hours of labor services demanded and supplied plotted against the real wage.

laissez faire (Chapter 18) A doctrine opposing governmental interference in economic affairs beyond the minimum necessary for the maintenance of peace and property rights.

legislative lag (Chapter 6) The lag between the time when legislation calling for fiscal policy action is proposed to the U.S. Congress and the time when Congress passes the legislation.

life cycle theory (Chapter 5) The Ando-Modigliani-Brumberg theory that consumption spending depends on expected life cycle total resources rather than on the income of the current year only.

liquidity preference curve (Chapter 9) The curve presenting real money balances demanded as an inverse function of the interest rate, with the level of real income constant at a specified level.

liquidity trap (Chapter 9) The interest rate at which liquidity preference curves flatten out. The demand for real money balances becomes infinitely interest elastic.

***LM* curve** (Chapter 10) The curve plotting the combinations of r and Y at which real money balances demanded equal the real money supply for a given nominal money supply and price level.

long-term consumption function (Chapter 5) The function tracing the relationship between consumption expenditures and private disposable income as it emerges from points widely separated in time.

long-term growth path (Chapter 18) The path reflecting the long-term equilibrium level and growth rate for full-employment aggregate output and real income, on either an absolute, a per capita, or a per unit of labor input basis.

managed float system (Chapter 19) A system in which government intervenes to smooth out temporary fluctuations in foreign exchange rates but permits the rates to vary in response to fundamental changes in international payments positions.

mandatory price and wage controls (Chapter 20) A system of price and wage controls in which violations of government-imposed ceilings are unlawful.

marginal efficiency of investment (Chapter 7) The expected yield on an investment expenditure.

marginal product of labor (Chapter 12) The increase in aggregate output which occurs when a unit of labor services is added to the production process with other productive factors held constant.

marginal propensity to consume (Chapter 4) The coefficient of disposable income in the consumption expenditure function—$\Delta C/\Delta Yd$.

marginal propensity to invest from income (Chapter 17) The coefficient of real income in the investment expenditure function—$\Delta I/\Delta Y$.

market rate of interest (Chapter 11) A weighted average of the interest rates observed in the market for securities and savings deposits.

means of payment (Chapter 8) An asset which can be exchanged directly for goods, services, and other financial assets. A medium of exchange.

member bank reserves (Chapter 8) Reserve deposits at the Federal Reserve banks plus vault cash, for commercial banks which are members of the Federal Reserve System.

M-1 money supply (Chapter 8) Cash outside the Treasury, the Federal Reserve banks, and commercial banks plus demand deposits at commercial banks.

M-1+ money supply (Chapter 8) The M-1 money supply plus savings deposits at commercial banks, NOW accounts at commercial banks and thrift institutions, credit union share draft accounts, and demand deposits at thrift institutions.

monetarist propositions (Chapter 14) Ideas central to the monetarist position in economics. They include: (1) real disturbances have little effect on aggregate price and output equilibriums; (2) a fixed rate of money supply growth produces an acceptable price and output result in ordinary circumstances; and (3) fiscal policies have little effect on price and output equilibriums.

monetary dampener (Chapter 11) The effect of the money market in diminishing the decline in equilibrium output and real income which occurs when aggregate demand declines as a result of real disturbances.

monetary disturbances (Chapter 11) Changes in the money supply or shifts in the money demand function.

monetary policies (Chapter 1) Government policies which operate on the equilibrium money supply to achieve price, employment, or other macroeconomic goals.

monetary policy targets (Chapter 20) The short-term and intermediate-term targets (bank reserves, money supply, short-term interest rates, and the like) to which monetary policies are addressed.

monetary theory of interest (Chapter 15) A theory of the interest rate which holds that monetary disturbances can affect the equilibrium value for the real interest rate.

money (Chapter 1) Narrowly defined, cash outside the Treasury, the Federal Reserve banks, and commercial banks plus demand deposits at commercial banks. Broadly defined, those two items plus savings deposits at commercial banks and checking deposits in other financial institutions.

money demand function (Chapter 9) The function relating real money balances demanded to its determinants (the market interest rate and real income, in this book).

money demand interest sensitivity (Chapter 14) The responsiveness of real money balances demanded to changes in the interest rate.

money market (Chapter 7) The market in which the demand for real money balances is equated to the real money supply.

money supply multiplier (Chapter 8) The change in the equilibrium money supply divided by the change in bank reserves (or excess reserves) provoking it.

MPS model (Chapter 7) The large econometric model describing the U.S. economy jointly sponsored by the Massachusetts Institute of Technology, the University of Pennsylvania, and the Social Science Research Corporation. The evolved Federal Reserve–MIT model.

multiplier effect (Chapter 1) The effect arising from the relationship between consumption expenditures and disposable income which causes changes in autonomous expenditures to produce larger change in equilibrium output and real income (with the full-employment constraint on output and the dampening influence of the money market neglected).

national income (Chapter 3) Essentially, the income payments received by the private sector for sales of factor services used in production (not including retained earnings in the form of capital consumption allowances).

natural rate hypothesis (Chapter 13) The hypothesis which holds that the unemployment rate will not remain below its natural level in the long term regardless of the steady-state inflation rate produced by overly expansive demand management policies. It may move below its natural level in the short term, however, during the period in which expected inflation falls short of actual inflation.

natural rate of unemployment (Chapter 2) Pragmatically, the unemployment rate at which increases in aggregate demand begin to spill mostly into increases in prices rather than increases in output. More precisely, the unemployment rate occurring where the labor market is clearing and actual and expected inflation is the same.

natural real rate of interest (Chapter 15) The market rate of interest less the expected change in prices, for an economy which is in full-employment equilibrium and is correctly anticipating inflation.

natural unemployment (Chapter 4) Frictional, seasonal, and structural unemployment.

negative interest rate case (Chapter 14) The situation where the interest rate needed for a full-employment aggregate expenditure is negative.

neoclassical growth model (Chapter 18) A model used for conceptualizing the determinants of the level and growth rate of full-employment aggregate output.

net exports of goods and services (Chapter 3) Exports of goods and services (including factor services) to foreign residents less imports of goods and services (including factor services) from foreign residents.

net national product (Chapter 3) Gross national product less capital consumption allowances.

neutral money (Chapter 15) Something occurring when changes in the money supply leave the equilibrium values of the real variables of the economy unaffected.

neutral technological advance (Chapter 18) A technological advance which increases the marginal products of capital and labor by the same percentages.

nonbank public (Chapter 13) For the United States, everyone except the U.S. Treasury, the Federal Reserve, and commercial banks.

nonmember banks (Chapter 8) Commercial banks which are not members of the Federal Reserve System.

non-price terms of mortgage lending (Chapter 7) The terms on which mortgage loans are extended, excluding the mortgage interest rate. They include such things as down payment requirements, term to maturity, and maximum ratio of loan amount to borrower income permitted.

NOW accounts (Chapter 8) Negotiable order of withdrawal accounts. Savings deposits on which checks can be drawn directly. At present, their availability is confined to depository institutions in New England and New York State.

once and for all money supply increase (Chapter 11) The condition existing when the money supply is increased and remains fixed at the higher level.

open-market operations (Chapter 8) Purchases or sales of U.S. government securities in the open market by the Federal Reserve authorities.

optimum capital stock (Chapter 17) The stock of capital goods which maximizes profits.

oscillatory movement about equilibrium (Chapter 17) An adjustment path following a disturbance featuring a recurrent movement above and below the value yielding equilibrium.

past peak income (Chapter 5) The peak income achieved in the past. In

J. S. Duesenberry's consumption theory, past peak income sustains the average propensity to consume somewhat as the economy moves into recession.

period model (Chapter 17) A model tracing the paths of the variables it involves over successive time periods. A dynamic model.

permanent income (Chapter 5) The component of actual income regarded by spending units as reflecting their basic earning potential, which arises from their property net worth and personal attributes. It is the key concept in Milton Friedman's consumption theory.

perpetual bond (Chapter 9) A bond which has no maturity date. It yields a specified income payment in perpetuity.

personal consumption expenditures (Chapter 3) Expenditures for consumer durable and nondurable goods and for consumer services.

personal income (Chapter 3) The income of the personal sector before personal tax and nontax payments. It includes transfer payments and those components of national income not retained by the business sector or government.

Phillips curve (Chapter 13) A curve fitted to plottings of the percent increase in money wages (or prices) against the unemployment rate.

precautionary motive for holding money (Chapter 9) A desire for money balances as insurance against having to sell assets or borrow to cover shortages arising from unforeseen variations in payment and receipt streams.

present value method (Chapter 7) A method for predicting the profitability of an investment expenditure opportunity by computing its present value for comparison with the purchase price of the asset it involves.

price and money-wage flexibility (Chapter 14) The condition which exists when prices and money wages are free to respond to market forces.

price and wage freeze (Chapter 20) A version of mandatory price and wage controls which permits no increases in prices or wages.

price and wage guidelines (Chapter 20) A form of voluntary price and wage controls in which the government issues guidelines as to maximum price and wage increases and urges that they be followed. Sometimes they are combined with nonvoluntary systems, as when threats to withhold government contracts are used to secure compliance.

private saving (Chapter 10) Private disposable income less consumption expenditures (and less net exports of goods and services if the foreign sector is included).

producer cost-push inflation (Chapter 12) Inflation resulting from an application of market power by a producer monopoly.

proprietors' income (Chapter 3) Profits of unincorporated businesses.

public service employment programs (Chapter 1) Programs designed to add structurally unemployed workers directly to government employment.

quantity theory of money model (Chapter 14) A model that conceptualizes the forces influencing aggregate money expenditures in terms of the factors affecting the demand for money and the money supply.

rational expectations (Chapter 11) Expectations formulated on the basis of all available information. John Muth, in putting forward the rational expectations hypothesis, argued that the aggregate of rationally formulated expectations is essentially the same as the prediction of the relevant economic theory.

real disturbances (Chapter 11) Disturbances involving shifts in the investment and aggregate saving (including government saving) functions.

real government debt (Chapter 16) The market value of government securities outstanding divided by the price level.

real income (Chapter 2) Aggregate income in constant dollars.

real rate of interest (Chapter 11) The market rate of interest less the adjustment for purchasing power losses caused by inflation.

real theory of interest (Chapter 15) A theory in which shifts in the money supply or the money demand function leave the equilibrium interest rate unchanged.

real wage (Chapter 12) The money wage divided by the price level.

regular savings deposits at commercial banks (Chapter 8) Bank deposits which earn interest but do not have specified maturity dates.

relative income theory (Chapter 5) J. S. Duesenberry's theory that in the long term the proportion of income a household consumes depends on its income relative to the incomes of other households rather than on the absolute level of its income.

replacement capital goods (Chapter 17) Capital goods which merely replace those used up in production.

required reserves (Chapter 8) Reserve requirements times deposits outstanding.

reserve requirements (Chapter 8) Requirements stating the minimum percentage reserves can bear to deposits outstanding.

rigid accelerator mechanism (Chapter 17) The mechanism by which net investment expenditures are rigidly tied to changes in the level of output through capital accumulation requirements determined by a fixed capital to output ratio.

saving (Chapter 10) Income not consumed. For the purposes of the saving definition, government purchases (and net exports of goods and services, if the foreign sector is included) are treated as consumption.

saving and investment approach (Chapter 10) The approach which derives the *IS* curve by using the savings equals investment expenditures equilibrium condition.

saving ratio (Chapter 18) The ratio of aggregate saving to aggregate output and real income.

seasonal unemployment (Chapter 2) Unemployment which recurs at the same time each year because of seasonal factors.

secular stagnation (Chapter 5) A tendency toward a chronic shortfall of aggregate demand in the absence of government intervention to stimulate demand.

shortfall unemployment (Chapter 2) Unemployment which occurs because of a shortfall of aggregate demand.

short-term consumption function (Chapter 5) The function denoting the relationship between consumption expenditures and disposable income in the short term, as during a phase of the business cycle.

simple Pigou effect (Chapter 16) The relationship presenting consumption expenditures as a positive function of real money balances.

speculative motive for holding money (Chapter 9) Holding money rather than securities because of an expectation that interest rates will rise in the future and produce capital losses on securities.

steady-state equilibrium (Chapter 11) The equilibrium state of a period (or dynamic) model.

structural unemployment (Chapter 2) Unemployment which occurs even when there is no shortfall of aggregate demand because qualifications and requirements of job-seekers do not match requirements of jobs to be filled.

sum of series approach to multipliers (Chapter 4) The approach which expresses the eventual change in aggregate output and real income as the sum of the response to the initiating expenditure disturbance plus the responses to the induced effects on consumption expenditures which occurs in a series of rounds as output and income change.

tariffs (Chapter 19) Taxes imposed by government on goods and services imported from abroad.

tax constant multiplier (Chapter 6) The change in equilibrium aggregate output and real income divided by the change in the tax constant (Tx_0) provoking it.

tax function (Chapter 11) The function relating real government tax receipts to aggregate real income.

technological advance (Chapter 12) An improved manner of production, permitting a greater amount of output to be obtained for given factor inputs. It can arise from new techniques, machines, materials, or energy resources or from improvements in labor quality.

terms of trade (Chapter 19) The number of units of a specified mix of exports which must be given up for one unit of a specified mix of imports.

thrift institutions (Chapter 8) Savings and loan associations, mutual savings banks, and credit unions.

time deposits with specific maturity dates (Chapter 8) Deposits at commercial banks and thrift institutions on which the maturity date is specified at the time of deposit. Early redemption is penalized by a lower return or, in the case of negotiable certificates of deposit, by transactions costs.

time series result (Chapter 5) Results of studies that showed a tendency for the ratio of aggregate consumption expenditure to disposable income (the average propensity to consume) to remain constant, viewed at points widely separated in time.

trade-off hypothesis (Chapter 13) The hypothesis that the stabilization authorities face a trade-off between unemployment rate and inflation rate when using monetary and fiscal policies alone, a trade-off arising from wage-push pressures which become stronger as aggregate demand expands relative to full-employment output.

transactions motive for holding money (Chapter 9) The desire to hold money because it is useful in effecting transactions.

transfer payment multiplier (Chapter 6) The change in equilibrium aggregate output and real income divided by the change in the transfer payment constant which provokes it.

trial equilibrium for *Y* (Chapter 6) The equilibrium value for Y obtained under the assumption that output can adjust to any level of aggregate demand—that is, with the full-employment constraint on output ignored.

unemployment rate (Chapter 1) The percent of the labor force unemployed.

unstable equilibrium (Chapter 17) An equilibrium which is not restored when disturbed or which is achieved from the disequilibrium state.

wage-push inflation (Chapter 12) Inflation which occurs even without an expenditure gap because of wage bargains involving increases in money wages in excess of increases in labor productivity.

Index

A

D

E

F

G

H

I

N

Q

R

Y